Handbook of Public Relations

9th Edition

Chris Skinner

Llew von Essen

Gary Mersham

Sejamothopo Motau

OXFORD

UNIVERSITY PRESS

SOUTHERN AFRICA

UNIVERSITY PRESS

Southern Africa

Oxford University Press Southern Africa (Pty) Ltd
Vasco Boulevard, Goodwood, Cape Town, Republic of South Africa
P O Box 12119, N1 City, 7463, Cape Town, Republic of South Africa

Oxford University Press Southern Africa (Pty) Ltd is a subsidiary of
Oxford University Press, Great Clarendon Street, Oxford OX2 6DP.

The Press, a department of the University of Oxford, furthers the University's objective of
excellence in research, scholarship, and education by publishing worldwide in
Oxford New York
Auckland Cape Town Dar es Salaam Hong Kong Karachi
Kuala Lumpur Madrid Melbourne Mexico City Nairobi
New Delhi Shanghai Taipei Toronto

With offices in
Argentina Austria Brazil Chile Czech Republic France Greece
Guatemala Hungary Italy Japan Poland Portugal Singapore South Korea
Switzerland Turkey Ukraine Vietnam

Oxford is a registered trade mark of Oxford University Press
in the UK and in certain other countries

Published in South Africa
by Oxford University Press Southern Africa (Pty) Ltd, Cape Town

Handbook of Public Relations
Ninth edition
ISBN 978 019 5992908
© Oxford University Press Southern Africa (Pty) Ltd 2010

The moral rights of the author have been asserted
Database right Oxford University Press Southern Africa (Pty) Ltd (maker)

Previously published by Macmillan South Africa, Southern Book Publishers (Pty) Ltd and by
International Thomson Publishing Southern Africa (Pty) LTD (1 86864011 6)
First edition published 1982
Fifth edition published by Oxford University Press 1999
Sixth edition published 2001
Seventh edition published 2004
Eighth edition published 2007
Ninth edition published 2010

Commissioning Editor: Astrid Meyer
Editor: Nicola van Rhyn
Designer: Brigitte Rouillard
Cover designer: Sharna Samay
Cover image: iStockphoto
Set in 10pt minion on 12pt
Printed and bound by ABC Press, Cape Town

Contents

Foreword

Public relations is a growth industry, and it's estimated that some 3 million people worldwide practice public relations as their main professional activity. Fueling this growth, or because of it, the literature of public relations has also expanded in geometric proportions during the past 25 years.

The body of knowledge, primarily originating in the United States and then in Europe, is now being compiled by educators and practitioners in many nations such as China, Iran , Serbia, Russia, India, Chile, and even South Africa. One outstanding example is this new edition of the Handbook of Public Relations, which has continually developed and expanded since its first edition in 1982, almost 30 years ago. Indeed, this handbook retains its position as the leading South African textbook on public relations.

A handbook, by definition, is also a guidebook. And much like a tourist guidebook for a country, the *Handbook of Public Relations* is an excellent introduction to the field of public relations and its various components. A good guidebook is (1) comprehensive, (2) compiled by writers who have an intimate knowledge of the country, (3) offers practical advice in plain English, (4) gives readers 'what to do' lists in easy-to-read bullet form, and (5) provides up-to-date information. This guidebook follows the same rules.

First, this book is truly comprehensive. Its 32 chapters are virtually an inventory of public relations concepts and activities. Part one deals with the fundamental concepts of public relations, ranging from its scope and ethical precepts to the relationship of public relations to marketing and advertising. Part 2 shows how public relations personnel work with the print and electronic media. Part 3 is an extensive portrayal of various public relations techniques, including everything from house journals to trade fairs, plant open houses, and sponsorship of events. The focus of Part 4 is primarily on checklists for meeting protocol, business etiquette, and special events.

Second, the authors are experienced public relations professionals who are widely recognized for their expertise and have been among the leaders of the Public Relations Institute of Southern Africa (PRISA) for many years. In other words, they have an intimate knowledge of the 'territory' and how public relations is done in South Africa.

This valuable insight means that the book is highly relevant to students studying public relations in university and university of technology programmes around the nation. The handbook, unlike introductory books imported from other nations, focuses exclusively on South African examples and case studies. It also includes specific country information on such topics as broadcasting regulations, labour relations, South African mass media, the variety of multicultural audiences, and even the protocol for hosting a government official at a conference or a special event.

Third, this handbook is not the stereotypical 'textbook' filled with theoretical constructs, multiple compound sentences, and esoteric observations. It is written by experienced professionals who know the value of getting to the point and keeping it simple, which no doubt is appreciated by both students and working professionals. The authors wisely keep the chapters short and include a number of basic charts and tables.

The chart outlining the steps for planning a public relations programme, as well as the one about the basic components of the communication process, are particularly good. Each chapter also begins with a short box telling the reader what they should know after reading the chapter. Case studies describing actual South African campaigns and programmes, such as the Nelson Mandela Children's Fund, give readers a chance to see how the concepts in the chapter were applied in a 'real' situation. Other case studies give insights into such topics as using the Internet to improve media relations, the South African sports sponsorship market, and cultural influences in South African society.

Fourth, this book is not only valuable to students but also to working practitioners because it includes multiple checklists, boxed inserts, and key points in bulleted form. There are checklists for such activities as making effective presentations, organizing a conference or banquet, and even organizing the production schedule for a house publication. Boxed inserts include such topics as the PRISA code of ethics and 'Fifty Ways that Direct-Mail Works'.

Fifth, this 9th edition has been updated to include new information and case studies on a variety of topics. The audiovisual chapter, for example, has been completely revised to focus on the advent of what is now called 'new' media, which includes a variety of social networking sites that are now commonly used in all public relations campaigns. There is also increased focus on organizational web sites and digital distribution of media materials. There are also new case studies on South Africa's hosting of the World Cup, the African Centre for Disaster, and the Save the SABC campaign. Other valuable insights feature South Africa's Civil Society and the country's fight against HIV/Aids.

In sum, this handbook is an excellent introduction to the wonderful world of public relations and all of its facets. It provides an excellent framework for students just learning about the field, but it also should be on the shelf of every public relations practitioner as a basic reference book.

It has been an honor to write the foreword for this important contribution to the body of literature in public relations. I've known three of the authors – Chris Skinner, Llew von Essen, and Gary Mersham – for a number of years and have a high regard for their friendship and contributions to the advancement of the public relations profession. They, in part, have helped South Africa become the model for public relations practice throughout the African continent.

Dennis L. Wilcox, Ph.D., APR, Fellow PRSA (Public Relations Society of America)
Professor emeritus of Public Relations
San Jose State University, California

Dr. Wilcox is the primary author of the leading public relations textbook in the United States, Public Relations Strategies & Tactics, 9th edition, published by Pearson Education (Allyn & Bacon) which is widely used in many nations and has been translated into 10 languages. He is also the author of *Public Relations Writing and Media Techniques*, 6th edition, also published by Pearson. Wilcox has made frequent trips to South Africa over the past 25 years for holidays, university lectures, and PRISA presentations. He has also been a visiting professor at Rhodes University and a Fulbright senior lecturer at the University of Botswana. He can be contacted at dennis.wilcox@sjsu.edu or through www.facebook.com/dennis.wilcox.

Acknowledgements

We would like to make the following acknowledgements to individuals and organizations for this, the 9th edition.

The foreword was supplied by emeritus Professor Dennis Wilcox.

Chapter 1

The Code of Professional Standards for the Practice of Public Relations was supplied by the Institute for Public Relations and Communication Management (PRISA).

The Global Alliance for Public Relations and Communication Management Associations provided details of the Global Protocol on Ethics on Public Relations.

Chapter 2

The Global Alliance for Public Relations and Communication Management Associations information was taken from their website at www.globalalliancept.org.

PRISA provided the information on registration, qualifications, experience, and accreditation. Their website is www.prisa.co.za.

Chapter 3

Details were provided by PRISA's consultancy chapter, the PRCC.

Chapter 4

Material for this chapter was taken from Mersham et al. 2004. *Public Relations, Development and Social Investment: A Southern African Perspective*. Durban: JCS & Associates.

The case study was researched from material published in the Edelman Trust Barometer.

Chapter 5

The Kick Polio Out of Africa Campaign was provided by June Webber and the case study on Social Marketing was researched by Newsclip Monitoring Services.

Chapter 6

Jeremy Sampson, Chairman of Interbrand Sampson helped revise and update the material in this chapter.

Chapter 7

The eThekwini Water and Sanitation Department provided details of their Customer Services Charter and the Batho Pele Principles.

Chapter 8
The case study of South African cultural influences was based on material supplied by various sources, including embassies and trade offices in South Africa, and the Department of Foreign Affairs.

Chapter 9
Various sources were consulted including University and University of Technology departments of Communication and Business Science.

Chapter 10
PRISA, the Institute of People Management (IPM) plus a number of organizations were consulted for information on employee relations.

Chapter 11
The Public Relations programme drew on the experiences of local, American, and European academics. The Nelson Mandela Children's Fund was selected as the ideal case study to illustrate a successful working programme.

Chapter 12
The various editions South African Yearbook produced by the GCIS, was the source of the updated material on the print media.

Chapter 13
The South African Yearbook was also the source of the updated material on electronic media. The case study on Public Broadcasting in South Africa was provided by Kate Skinner and Professor Tawana Kupe.

Chapter 14
The case study on video assignments was researched by Professor Mersham, who drew on material provided by the Zululand Chamber of Business.

Chapter 15
Professor Gary Mersham researched and wrote the new chapter on Digital Communication.

Chapter 16
ITC, Toastmasters, and Rotary provided material for guidelines on public speaking.

Chapter 17
Material for this chapter was sourced both from the authors' personal experiences and selected training programmes.

Chapter 18
The new case study on CV writing was provided by Janene Lass.

Chapter 19
The Direct Marketing Association provided the guidelines for both the chapter and the letter.

Chapter 20
The professional bodies, the Chartered Accountants and the Chartered Institute of Secretaries provided guidelines for the research and presentation of the Annual Report.

Chapter 21
ICL and Creda Press provided the original material for this chapter.

Chapter 22
Various printing firms and individual designers helped with the preparation of this chapter.

Chapter 23
The Case study, Arrive Alive, was sourced from the web and Gautrain material was provided by eQuinox Communications.

Chapter 24
BMI Sports Research provided the figures for sports and arts sponsorships in South Africa.

Chapter 25
Various exhibition groups provided the background on exhibitions and trade fairs.

Chapter 26
Various hotel groups, including Southern Sun and the Peermont Group, provided details of their conference and gaming facilities. The case study on business tourism was researched from the Southern Africa Conference, Exhibition, and Events Guide.

Chapter 27
Umbogintwini Operations Services and Heartlands provided details of plant openings and open days.

Chapter 28
Design Unit and Interbrand Sampson were responsible for the guidelines on corporate image and identity and Proudly South African provided the case study. Particular mention must be made to Jeremy Sampson for all his professional input and additions to this chapter.

Chapter 29
Various editions of the Corporate Social Investment Handbook by Trialogue were consulted to provide the latest picture on CSI in South

Africa. These handbooks are the most authoritive source of material on CSR/CSI. The JSE provided the latest figures on the SRI Index.

Chapter 30

Our own Disaster Management Guide based on our book, *Disaster Management: a Guide to Issues Management and Crisis Communication*, provided the framework for this chapter.

The case study on the African Centre for Disaster Studies was provided by Professor Dewald van Niekerk.

Chapter 31

Material for this chapter was researched from the web, including the current details on the CCMA. Sally Falkow and Brad Kietzman provided the material on corporate and industrial theatre.

Chapter 32

This wide ranging review of our multicultural environment drew on the expertise of journalist and writer, Karen Lotter, for the review of religion and culture in South Africa, Colleen du Toit, Director of CAF Southern Africa for the comprehensive review of civil society in South Africa, and various studies on HIV/Aids pandemic in South Africa, published in journals and newspapers. Dr Renitha Rampersad kindly allowed us to use part of her study on Corporate Social Investment and HIV/Aids in South Africa for the case study.

The final section of the Handbook, devoted to protocol, business etiquette, and handling special events, drew on the collective experiences of the authors themselves, as well as the GCIS, the Department of Foreign Affairs, and research bodies at various universities and universities of technology.

Some 30 years have now elapsed since the first edition was published. Throughout that period, we have been conscious of the need to constantly update and revise our material so that it remains topical, relevant, as well as instructive. We hope that we have succeeded. A special thanks to the staff of the publishers Oxford University Press SA, for their wonderful support and encouragement in this special 30th year edition. We are most grateful for all their professional input and advice.

The authors

Chris Skinner, Llew von Essen, Gary Mersham, Sejamothopo Motau

The authors and publisher are grateful for permission that has been granted to use the relevant copyright material in this book. Every effort has been made to trace and acknowledge copyright holders; we apologise for any mistakes or omissions and would appreciate any correction of such errors.

Part I

Fundamentals of public relations

CHAPTER 1

The scope and ethics of public relations

When you have read this chapter, you should:

- be aware of the various definitions of public relations;
- be able to distinguish between public relations and advertising, marketing, sales promotion, propaganda, and publicity;
- understand the nature of public relations and be able to describe why public relations is regarded both as an art and a science, and why it should be a management function;
- be able to identify the different techniques of public relations;
- be able to identify the different functions of the public relations practitioner;
- be able to discuss the attributes of the public relations practitioner;
- know what characterizes ethical behaviour;
- know the Institute for Public Relations and Communication Management (PRISA) Code of Professional Standards and its application in a variety of contexts;
- be aware of the Global Alliance's Ethics Protocol.

Public relations in South Africa today is a sophisticated, multi-faceted discipline, able to help forge effective two-way communication between an organization and its various publics.

In commerce, industry, politics, the arts, education, religion, and charities, public relations plays an effective management role in its own right. South Africa has a first to its credit in being the first country to research and evolve a body of knowledge on public relations. Rapid strides continue to be made in the educational field to provide both theoretical and practical knowledge for those wishing to enter the public relations profession.

In this regard, the professional body called the Institute for Public Relations and Communication Management (PRISA) is making a major contribution at national, international, and tertiary level. It is now possible for students to achieve B.Tech. and M.Tech. degrees in public relations management, as well as to study for an MBA with a public relations specialization. Research is also being conducted at the Masters and Doctoral levels in a variety of PR specializations.

Definition of public relations

At the First World Assembly of Public Relations Associations held in Mexico City in December 1978, the following definition of the nature and purpose of public relations was unanimously adopted:

Public relations practice is the art and social science of analyzing trends, predicting their consequences, counselling organizations' leaders, and implementing a planned program of action which will serve both the organization and the public interest.

Later, two other official attempts were launched by the Public Relations Society of America (PRSA) in order to provide the basis for a consensus terminology. The latest attempt, by the Special Committee on Terminology in 1987, recommended the following two definitions, because they are regarded as establishing a perception of the role of public relations:

Public relations helps an organization and its publics adapt mutually to each other.

Public relations is an organization's efforts to win the co-operation of groups of people (Lesley 1987).

The International Public Relations Association (IPRA) states that public relations practice is the 'art and social science of analyzing trends, predicting their consequences, counselling the

leaders of organizations and implementing planned programmes of action which will serve both the organization and the public interest'.

The definition adopted by the Public Relations Institute of Southern Africa (PRISA) states that 'public relations is the management, through communication, of perceptions and strategic relationships between an organization and its internal and external stakeholders'.

Thus, whatever individuals and organizations may think their image is in the marketplace, the public's perceptions of them are all-important, whether based on fact or fiction. Public relations has a key role to play in developing understanding and support for a particular cause or event. Essentially it helps to define and explain relationships of mutual benefit between organizations and their key stakeholders, both among its own employees and with customers and clients with whom it does business. These must be managed, rather than be allowed to develop haphazardly as so often happens, so that a fair, balanced, and positive image can be created.

Public relations is often confused with advertising. Advertising may not be used by an organization, but every organization is involved in public relations. It embraces everyone and everything, whereas advertising is limited to special selling and buying tasks such as promoting goods and services, buying supplies, recruiting staff or announcing trading results.

Public relations has to do with the total communications of an organization: it is therefore more extensive and comprehensive than advertising. On occasions, public relations may use advertising, which is why it is neither a form of advertising nor a part of advertising.

In the commercial world, or private sector of the economy, public relations and advertising are associated with marketing. While marketing is only one function of business, public relations has to do with the financial and production functions, and can be applied to every part of the marketing mix, of which advertising is but one ingredient. Market education can make a vital public relations contribution, on which the success of advertising may well depend.

Public relations is also sometimes confused with sales promotions. This may be because sales promotion aims to bring the producer closer to the customer. Sales promotion is in fact a more personal form of marketing communication, consisting mainly of short-term schemes to launch products or to revise or increase sales.

Propaganda is yet another form of communication which is often wrongly regarded as public relations. The two could not be more different, if only because successful public relations must be credible, whereas propaganda is liable to invite suspicion or, at least, disagreement. For example, through information issued by government departments, propaganda would be aimed at keeping the government in power, whereas public relations would be aimed at getting its services understood and used properly.

Public relations is also confused with publicity. Publicity results from information being made known and it may be good or bad for the subject concerned. A pop star, for example, may gain good publicity from a concert or recording but bad publicity if accused of taking drugs. Behaviour has a great bearing on whether publicity is good or bad, and public relations is very much about the behaviour of individuals, organizations, products, and services in a wider context.

The nature of public relations

Basic assumptions

Public relations is based on the following propositions:

- In a modern democracy, every organization survives ultimately only by public consent.
- The consent of the public cannot exist in a communication vacuum (PRISA 1993).

Thus, fundamental to public relations is the establishment of mutual understanding between different parties, i.e. an organization on the one hand and special publics and/or the community at large on the other hand. Ideally, mutual understanding should form the basis of a sound relationship between the different parties, a relationship based on open, two-way communication which enables the organization to explain its policies and procedures, while enabling it to monitor feedback. Even more important is for this relationship – because of its accessible nature – to enable the organization to influence public opinion, judgment, and behaviour, with the obvious implication that the organization is dependent on the moral and financial support of its various publics in order to survive.

Characteristics of public relations

Viewed in the above manner, public relations exhibits the following characteristics:

- *It is dynamic.* The public relations process is one of continuous and constant change and adjustment in order to maintain old relationships and build new ones.
- *It is analytical.* It is a process of determining and analyzing a situation and the factors influencing it, as well as one of evaluating the progress of any remedial or other action.
- *It is planned.* Goals are set and priorities are determined in accordance with the problem or situation analysis and within the constraints of time and budget.
- *It implies action.* This means the execution of planned strategies and the implementation of alternative strategies in order to cope with the public's changing needs and demands. In this sense, public relations, in its purest and most effective form, should be proactive and not reactive.
- *It requires evaluation.* Performance is evaluated in terms of the achievement of goals.

5

- *It demands adjustment.* Public relations should be executed in a flexible manner in order to adjust to goals altered as a result of, for example, underachievement or the changing needs of the publics.

All of this can be summarized as follows:
Analyze societal opinions and trends, process these with regard to their possible effect on the organization, and plan and execute a course of action aimed at ensuring the organization's survival and success within the parameters of societal well-being and socially-responsible behaviour.

Public relations: an art and a science

Public relations is described as an art and a science. It is an art, because the selection and application of appropriate techniques require judgment from the practitioner, as well as being attuned to both the organization and its publics. It is also a science, because the identification of an organization's target publics and their needs and the evaluation of the impact of its actions, to name but two functions, call for the application of scientific principles.

Public relations: a management function

Public relations is also regarded as, and should of necessity be, a management function. This obviously refers to public relations practised at an advanced level by experienced practitioners. Execution of public relations at this level has the following beneficial results: a management position affords the public relations practitioner the opportunity of being sensitive to and coming into contact with both internal and external publics, whose collective views constitute public opinion. This enables the public relations practitioner to evaluate internal and external opinions, attitudes, and needs on an ongoing basis, to advise management regarding their possible effect, and to act as an instrument in bringing about policy changes and directing new courses of action. All of these actions are aimed at maintaining a harmonious and balanced relationship between the organization and its different target publics and, ultimately, between the organization and its environment.

In short, from the organization's business plan and subsequent marketing plan, the public relations practitioner devises the communication plan to support the corporate mission, policy, and goals. In order to become involved in strategic planning, the public relations practitioner should operate at the highest level of organizational management and have access to the most senior information and decision-making systems (PRISA 1993).

The various organograms of corporate management organization show the important position occupied by public relations:

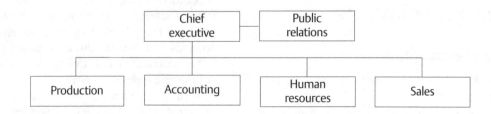

To operate effectively, however, the public relations manager needs to be positioned so that he or she is responsible to top management and serves all departments of the organization. Ideally, the public relations manager should have board director status, which is the case in most successful companies.

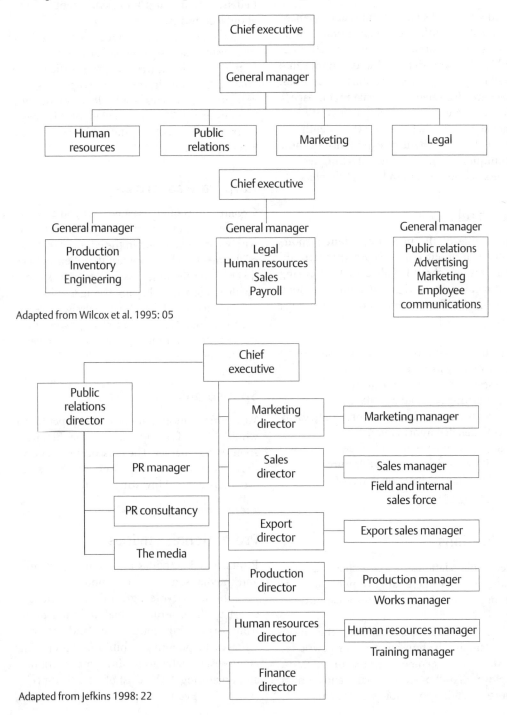

Adapted from Wilcox et al. 1995: 05

Adapted from Jefkins 1998: 22

Techniques of public relations

In order to establish harmonious and balanced relationships with the organization's target publics, the public relations practitioner should have knowledge of and training in a wide range of public relations techniques. These are illustrated in the diagram on page 9. Obviously, the level at which public relations is practised will determine the depth of knowledge and extent of experience in these techniques. Some of these techniques are discussed below and in individual chapters.

Media relations

This is one of the most important responsibilities of public relations practitioners and organizations should realize that practising good media relations is an ongoing task, not a last-minute effort employed only when publicity is required.

Steps to be taken in drawing up a successful media strategy include:
- researching the available media;
- identifying key media contacts;
- briefing these contacts and providing them with detailed information;
- arranging interviews and visits;
- writing special articles and features;
- encouraging debates on issues of importance.

Publications

After media relations, the research, design, and production of a whole range of publications is the next most important responsibility in public relations.

Of employee publications, the most important are the house journal or newsletter to staff, management letters or memos, employee handbooks, manuals, and annual reports, including an employee summary.

Corporate image

Corporate image is the net result of the interaction of all experiences, impressions, beliefs, feelings, and knowledge people have about a company.

In other words, everything a company does or does not do: its products and services, its letterheads, brochures, factories, offices and trucks, the way it treats its employees, its recruitment policies – all add to or detract from its image. The management of this image is therefore another vital public relations responsibility.

Corporate advertising

Organizations often use advertising in a public relations context when they are not satisfied with what is being said in the editorial sections of the media, when they feel that their publics do not understand issues or are simply apathetic, or when they are trying to add their voices to a cause. In the final analysis, however, organizations turn to advertising when they want control over message content, placement, and timing.

Sponsorship

Vast sums of money are now being spent by a whole host of companies in the lucrative sponsorship market. The bulk of it is spent on the broad sporting arena, although companies are increasingly investing in the arts and culture fields.

Promotional activities

Promotional activities are often high profile and media sensitive, and public relations practitioners devote a great deal of time and effort to them. Promotional activities range from organizing conferences and teleconferences to planning exhibitions, preparing audio-visual material and direct mail literature, and organizing a whole list of so-called special events. Each calls for specialized skills. These

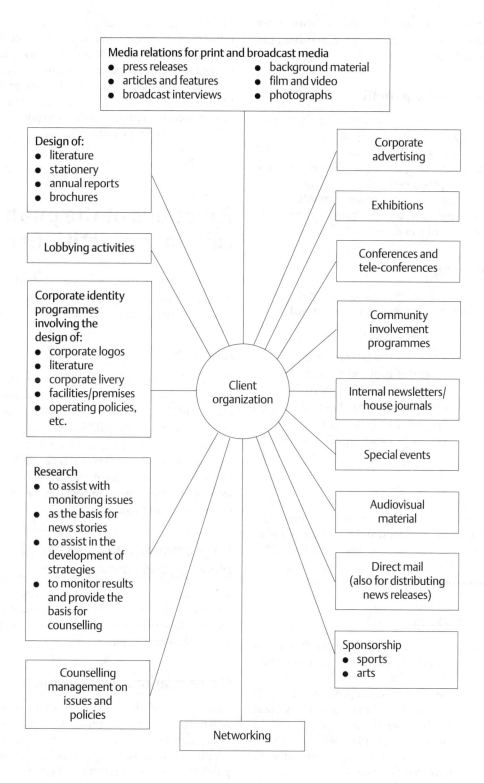

Media relations for print and broadcast media
- press releases
- articles and features
- broadcast interviews
- background material
- film and video
- photographs

Design of:
- literature
- stationery
- annual reports
- brochures

Lobbying activities

Corporate identity programmes involving the design of:
- corporate logos
- literature
- corporate livery
- facilities/premises
- operating policies, etc.

Research
- to assist with monitoring issues
- as the basis for news stories
- to assist in the development of strategies
- to monitor results and provide the basis for counselling

Counselling management on issues and policies

Client organization

Corporate advertising

Exhibitions

Conferences and tele-conferences

Community involvement programmes

Internal newsletters/ house journals

Special events

Audiovisual material

Direct mail (also for distributing news releases)

Sponsorship
- sports
- arts

Networking

activities often involve working with other professionals in the marketing, advertising, and design fields.

Issues management

Issues management can have a huge impact on a company's operations, policies and future direction, and thus needs very careful monitoring. It has been defined as 'the proactive process of anticipating, identifying, evaluating, and responding to public policy issues that affect organizations and their publics' (Cutlip et al. 1994: 16).

Lobbying

An even more specialized part of public relations is lobbying. It has been defined as:

the specialized part of public relations that builds and maintains relations with Government primarily for the purpose of influencing legislation and regulation (Cutlip et al. 1994: 17).

Lobbyists at all levels of government must understand legislative process, know how government functions, and be acquainted with individual law-makers and officials. This activity is becoming an increasingly important one for organizations.

Networking

In communicating with influential people in the various power structures to influence their behaviour, practitioners need to take into account the dynamic concept of networking. It is in community affairs specifically that networking becomes all-important. Networks are groups of people with different backgrounds who can tackle a problem from their different vantage points.

Identifying and developing networks of influential people is the starting point in community relations. Many networks are formed to meet a special objective or to solve a community problem. Public relations practitioners are often at the hub of these networks. One of their key responsibilities is to point out specific messages to influential people in a given area.

Functions of the public relations practitioner

Public relations practitioners are involved in a variety of work assignments or functions, which may include the following:

Research

Research involves gathering information about public opinion, trends, emerging issues, political climate, media coverage, concerns of consumer and environmental special-interest groups and so forth, and to plan programmes responsive to publics and problem situations. It also includes monitoring programme implementation and assessing programme impact to evaluate programme effectiveness.

Programming and counselling/ planning and advising

This involves determining needs, priorities, goals, publics, objectives, and categories. Essentially it means collaborating with management or clients in a problem-solving process.

Media relations and placement

This is one of the key functions in which practitioners may be engaged. It involves contacting news media, magazines, Sunday supplements, freelance writers, and trade publications with the intention of getting them

Core competencies of a PR practitioner

Time management

Press releases

Speeches

Technical specializations

Videos

Events

Publications

Internet communications

Media relations/Training

Skills/Tools (technical)

Negotiation

Reputation management

Facilitation/ Mediation

Marketing communications

Risk Analysis

Stakeholder Management (Managing relationships)

Annual reports

Issues management

Identifying opportunities/ Trends

Sponsorship

Community relations

Networking

Strategic planning

Corporate identity

Industry specializations (Body of knowledge)

Government relations

Investor relations

Internet communications

Exhibitions

Websites

Conferences

Source: Adapted and developed from the IPRA Wheel of Education, IPRA Gold Paper 4 with permission of the International Public Relations Association Ltd.

11

to publish or broadcast news and features about the organization. It may also involve responding to media requests for information or spokespersons. Finally, it may mean arranging for the production, booking, and placement or broadcasting of corporate advertisements used as part of a public relations programme.

Organizing

The public relations practitioner handles a variety of functions, ranging from organizing media conferences, conventions, and exhibitions to open-house days, anniversary celebrations, fundraising events, contests, awards programmes, and sponsorships.

Writing

The public relations practitioner should be adept at writing news releases, newsletters, correspondence, reports, booklets, texts, radio and television copy, film scripts, trade paper and magazine articles, corporate advertisements, product information, and technical material.

Editing

In addition to researching and writing special features, practitioners are involved in editing special publications, employee newsletters, shareholders' reports, and other communications directed at internal and external publics.

Production

Production is multi-faceted and very challenging. It involves creating communications using multimedia knowledge and skills, including art, photography, and design for brochures, booklets, reports, corporate advertisements, and occasional publications, recording and editing audio and video tapes, and preparing audiovisual presentations.

Speaking

The public relations practitioner either speaks him- or herself or arranges for others to address meetings. The process of gathering information enables organizations to plan programmes in response to their publics and problem situations, to monitor their effectiveness during implementation, and evaluate their overall impact.

Training

This involves working with executives and other organizational representatives to prepare them for dealing with the media and for making presentations and other public appearances. Practitioners could also assist with in-service staff development.

Management

Another very important duty is the management of the public relations function with regard to personnel, budget, and action programmes.

What to look for in a public relations practitioner

Such diversity of functions calls for a wide range of skills and experience.
- *Organizational ability and administrative talent.* There are no second chances in public relations, so any activity must be handled correctly the first time.
- *Communication proficiency (both written and spoken).* The ability to communicate in more than one language is a major advantage.
- *A lively, enquiring mind.* Public relations people are essentially problem-solvers. They look for new ways of doing both conventional and unconventional things.

- *Tenacity and adaptability.* The ability to work long and inconvenient hours is essential. The ability to work under pressure and to be flexible is important too.
- *Moral courage and integrity.* It is important for public relations people to stand up for what they believe is right. An independent spirit and moral integrity are essential.
- *Professionalism.* Ideally membership of the professional body PRISA should be given top priority.

Ethics of the public relations and communication practitioner

Ethics apply particularly to the way public relations and communication practitioners behave. Personal integrity is part of their professionalism. They are judged by the way they act. They give expert advice; they do not

PRISA – The Institute for Public Relations and Communication Management

Code of Ethics and Professional Standards for the Practice of Public Relations and Communication Management

We believe ethical practice is the most important obligation of PRISA members and we will strive at all times to enhance and protect the dignity of the profession.

PRISA subscribes to the same set of principles as contained in the Global Protocol on Ethics in Public Relations (see page 15).

Code of Ethics and Proffessional Standards

1. Definition

Public relations is the management, through communication, of perceptions and strategic relationships between an organization and its internal and external stakeholders.

2. Professional conduct

2.1 We shall acknowledge that there is an obligation to protect and enhance the profession.

2.2 We shall keep informed and educated about practices in the profession that ensure ethical conduct.

2.3 We shall actively pursue personal professional development.

2.4 We are committed to ethical practices, preservation of public trust, and the pursuit of communication excellence with powerful standards of performance, professionalism, and ethical conduct.

2.5 We shall accurately define what public

relations activities can and cannot accomplish. In the conduct of our professional activities, we shall respect the public interest and the dignity of the individual. It is our responsibility at all times to deal fairly and honestly with our clients or employers, past or present, with our colleagues, media communication, and with the public.

2.6 We shall conduct our professional lives in accordance with the public interest. We shall not conduct ourselves in any manner detrimental to the profession of public relations.

2.7 We have a positive duty to maintain integrity and accuracy, as well as generally accepted standards of good taste.

2.8 We shall not knowingly, intentionally or recklessly communicate false or misleading information. It is our obligation to use proper care to avoid doing so inadvertently.

2.9 We shall not guarantee the achievement of specified results beyond our direct control. We shall not negotiate nor agree terms with a prospective employer or client on the basis of payment only contingent upon specific future public relations achievements.

2.10 We shall, when acting for a client or employer who belongs to a profession, respect the code of ethics of that other profession and shall not knowingly be party to any breach of such a code.

2.11 We shall obey laws and public policies

governing our professional activities and will be sensitive to the spirit of all laws and regulations and, should any law or public policy be violated, for whatever reason, act promptly to correct the situation.

2.12 We shall give credit for unique expressions borrowed from others and identify the sources and purposes of all information disseminated to the public.

3. Conduct towards clients/employers

3.1 We shall safeguard the confidences of both present and former clients and employers. We shall not disclose or make use of information given or obtained in confidence from an employer or client, past or present, for personal gain or otherwise, or to the disadvantage or prejudice of such client or employer.

3.2 We shall not represent conflicting or competing interests without the express consent of those involved, given after full disclosure of the facts. We shall not place ourselves in a position where our interests are or may be in conflict with a duty to a client, without full disclosure of such interests to all involved.

3.3 We shall not be party to any activity which seeks to dissemble or mislead by promoting one disguised or undisclosed interest whilst appearing to further another. It is our duty to ensure that the actual interest of any organisation with which we may be professionally concerned is adequately declared.

3.4 In the course of our professional services to the employer or client we shall not accept payment either in cash or in kind in connection with these services from another source without the express consent of our employer or client.

4. Conduct towards colleagues

4.1 We shall not maliciously injure the professional reputation or practice of another individual engaged in the public relations profession.

4.2 We shall at all times uphold this Code, co-operate with colleagues in doing so and in enforcing decisions on any matter arising from this application.

4.3 Registered individuals who knowingly cause or permit another person or organization to act in a manner inconsistent with this Code or are party to such an action, shall be deemed to be in breach of it.

4.4 If we have reason to believe that another colleague has engaged in practices which may be in breach of this Code, or practices which may be unethical, unfair or illegal, it is our duty to advise the Institute promptly.

4.5 We shall not invite any employee of a client to consider alternative employment.

5. Conduct towards the business environment

5.1 We shall not recommend the use of any organization in which we have a financial interest, nor make use of its services on behalf of our clients or employers, without declaring our interest.

5.2 In performing professional services for a client or employer we shall not accept fees, commissions or any other consideration from anyone other than the client or employer in connection with those services, without the express consent of the client/employer, given after disclosure of the facts.

5.3 We shall sever relations, as soon as possible, with any organization or individual if such a relationship requires conduct contrary to this Code.

6. Conduct towards the channels of communication

6.1 We shall not engage in any practice which tends to corrupt the integrity of channels or media of communication.

6.2 We shall identify publicly the name of the client or employer on whose behalf any public communication is made.

7. Conduct towards the state

7.1 We respect the principles contained in the Constitution of the country in which we are resident.

7.2 We shall not offer or give any reward to any person holding public office, with intent to further our interests or those of our employer.

8. Conduct towards PRISA

8.1 We shall at all times respect the dignity and authority of PRISA.

8.2 We are bound to uphold the annual registration fee levied by PRISA, which fee is payable as determined by the PRISA Board.

9. Communication

9.1 PRISA encourages the widest possible communication about its Code.

9.2 The PRISA Code of Ethics and Professional Standards for the Practice of Public Relations and Communication Management is freely available to all. Permission is hereby granted to any individual or organisation wishing to copy and incorporate all or part of the PRISA Code into personal and corporate codes, with the understanding that appropriate credit be given to PRISA in any publication of such codes.

9.3 The Institute's magazine, *Communika*, publishes periodic articles dealing with ethical issues. At least one session at the annual conference is devoted to ethics. The national office of PRISA through its professional development activities encourages and supports efforts by PRISA student chapters, professional chapters and regions to conduct meetings and workshops devoted to the topic of ethics and the PRISA Code. New and renewing members of PRISA sign the following statement as part of their application: 'I have read, understand and subscribe to the PRISA Code of Ethics and Professional Standards for Public Relations and Communication Management.'

10. Enforcement

PRISA fosters compliance with its Code by engaging in global communication campaigns rather than through negative sanctions. However, in keeping with the 2.11 article of the PRISA Code, members of PRISA who are found guilty by the PRISA Disciplinary Committee or an appropriate governmental or judicial body of violating laws and public policies governing their professional activities may have their membership terminated by the PRISA board following procedures set forth in the Institute's bylaws.

bribe or corrupt. It follows, therefore, that public relations will not be successful unless it is trustworthy and a business will not succeed unless it is trusted.

Global Protocol on Ethics in Public Relations

After consulting with some 65 associations representing more than 150 000 public relations practitioners around the world, the following Global Protocol on Ethics in Public Relations has now been adopted.

Declaration of principles

We base our professional principles on the fundamental value and dignity of the individual. We believe in and support the free exercise of human rights, especially freedom of speech, freedom of assembly, and freedom of the media, which are essential to the practice of good public relations.

In serving the interest of clients and employers, we dedicate ourselves to the goals of better communication, understanding, and co-operation among diverse individuals, groups, and institutions of society. We also subscribe to and support equal opportunity of employment in the public relations profession and lifelong professional development.

We pledge to:
- conduct ourselves professionally, with integrity, truth, accuracy, fairness, and responsibility to our clients, our client publics, and to an informed society;

- improve our individual competence and advance the knowledge and proficiency of the profession through continuing education and research and where available, through the pursuit of professional accreditation;
- adhere to the principles of the Code of Professional Standards for the Practice of Public Relations.

Code of Professional Standards

Advocacy
We will serve our client and employer's interests by acting as responsible advocates and by providing a voice in the marketplace of ideas, facts, and viewpoints to aid informed public debate.

Honesty
We will adhere to the highest standards of accuracy and truth in advancing the interests of clients and employers.

Integrity
We will conduct our business with integrity and observe the principles and spirit of the Code in such a way that our personal reputation and that of our employer and the public relations profession in general is protected.

Expertise
We will encourage members to acquire and responsibly use specialized knowledge and experience to build understanding and client/employer credibility. Furthermore, we will actively promote and advance the profession through continued professional development, research, and education.

Loyalty
We will insist that members are faithful to those they represent, while honouring their obligations to serve the interests of society and support the right of free expression.

Code of Practice

We believe it is the duty of every association and every member within that association that is party to the Code of Professional Standards to:
- acknowledge that there is an obligation to protect and enhance the profession;
- keep informed and educated about practices in the profession that ensure ethical conduct;
- actively pursue personal professional development;
- accurately define what public relations activities can and cannot accomplish;
- counsel its individual members in proper ethical decision making in general, and on a case specific basis;
- require that individual members observe the ethical recommendations and behavioural requirements of the Code.

Advancing the Code

Although the Protocol is not mandatory, all national associations seeking membership of the Alliance are required to endorse the Protocol upon entry and to adjust their national codes to conform to Global Alliance standards within five years. PRISA has already modified its Code to comply with the new Protocol.

Conclusion

The adoption of a professional association's code of ethics does not automatically imply that all the practitioners will act in a moral and ethical manner. This is because bodies such as PRISA can enforce their codes of ethics only in respect of practitioners who are members. Codes of ethics are important, however, in that they reflect a concern and a willingness to raise ethical levels and serve as a yardstick of conduct.

Case study
Global Alliance for Public Relations and Communication Management (GA) and world trends

Among the many professional associations representing the PR industry internationally, the GA is the most representative and now includes some 65 national associations representing some 150 000 members.

One of its key requirements for membership is that all existing associations and those seeking accreditation must adapt their existing codes of ethics to a Global Ethics Protocol which was approved in Rome in 2003.

The GA is involved in a number of ongoing activities. These include:

- defining global standards in accreditation and curricula;
- analysing and tracking the regulatory climate in different parts of the world;
- representing the profession in the UN, the World Bank, and the EU;
- studying and comparing practices in various countries;
- organizing World Public Relations festivals;
- developing webinars and website.

For further particulars study their website at http://www.globalalliancepr.org

Some current trends in the PR industry

A global economy
The globalization of businesses has required companies to learn foreign cultures, business practices, and languages. The PR industry has been severley affected by the global financial downturn but its role continues to be of critical importance in a dramatic new world order.

The quality of the environment
People in many countries have come to believe that protecting the environment is important and that environmental issues influence their quality of life, so they take a personal interest in such issues as the greenhouse effect, global warming, acid rain, pollution, and toxic waste.

An increased management role for business
Impediments to sales success, such as environmental concerns, have convinced companies to include public relations in their strategic planning and policy formulation.

A new emphasis on issues management
Keeping abreast of public policy issues is a top priority for public relations in the current business environment. This requires experts skilled in problem analysis and conflict resolution. Managing the HIV/Aids pandemic is of particular concern in southern Africa and elsewhere on the African continent.

The proliferation of publics
In addition to traditional publics such as consumers and stakeholders, audiences are increasingly being fragmented into special interest groups. Public relations personnel now use micro-demographics (closely defining target audiences by age, sex, level of education, and the like) to reach multiple publics with tailored information.

The decline of the mass media
The fragmentation of publics has meant the decline of the mass media as a vehicle to reach audiences. The key terms now are 'niche programming' and 'narrow casting'. Technology provides many avenues for transmitting messages to specific audiences and public relations practitioners are becoming adept at tailoring messages to narrow, well-defined audiences.

The rapid spread of new media technologies
It is estimated that over 400 million people are using the Web. For this reason public relations practitioners are increasingly using electronic media as their principal means of communication. It is offering new challenges and opportunities on a huge scale.

International media relations

Press conferences and briefings by public relations professionals are now being transmitted by satellite. This has led to the decentralization of the public relations function, and the need to be multi-lingual and multi-cultural in the public relations field.

A greater emphasis on employee communication

The past decade has seen the severe downsizing of labour forces. This has been done to satisfy the demands of the global market place and company stakeholders, accompanied by large increases in the salaries of chief executives in the major corporations as well as various corruption scandals. This has weakened confidence in management as a whole. The management of some companies therefore, by using public relations, strives to restore or hold employee trust.

According to the Edelman Trust Barometer, which conducts a global survey of opinion leaders every year, in six of the 11 countries surveyed, 'a person like yourself or your peer' is seen as the most credible spokesperson about a company. This increased trust in peers has advanced steadily in the last three years, as has the popularity of peer to peer media. Friends, family, and colleagues rank as two of the three most credible sources of information about a company, just behind articles in business magazines. In contrast, CEOs continue to rank in the bottom half of credible spokespersons in all companies.

Education and training

Public relations became a serious academic discipline in the 1990s and a variety of PR courses are available at tertiary institutions across the globe. In a southern African context, universities, universities of technology, and selected colleges offer BA Communication degrees, national diplomas, BTech degrees in public relations, and the PRISA public relations diploma.

PRISA's preferred endorsed provider, ProVox (Pty) Ltd, offers a number of certificate courses for students who cannot afford to study full-time or who enter the profession having qualified in another field.

PRISA, the Institute of Public Relations and Communication Management, presents a comprehensive programme of continuing professional development (CPD) seminars, workshops, and conferences for its members. These events carry CPD points for all registered practitioners of PRISA.

Further reading

Cutlip, S.M., A.H. Center & G.M. Broom. 1994. *Effective Public Relations.* Englewood Cliffs, New Jersey: Prentice-Hall.

Jefkins, F. 1998. *Public Relations.* London: M & E Pitman Publishing.

Lesley, P. 1987. 'Report of the special committee on terminology', *International Public Relations Review.* 27(2): 5–9.

Lubbe, B.A. & G. Puth. 1994. *Public Relations in South Africa: A Management Reader.* Johannesburg: Heinemann.

Mersham, G.M. & J.C. Skinner. 1999. *New Insights into Public Relations and Communication.* Johannesburg: Heinemann.

PRISA. 1993. *Membership of the Code of Conduct.* Johannesburg: PRISA.

Seitel, F.P. 1995. *The Practice of Public Relations.* Englewood Cliffs, New Jersey: Prentice-Hall.

White, J. 1991. *How to Understand and Manage Public Relations.* London: Business Books.

White, 1991. *How to Understand and Manage Public Relations.* London: Business Books.

Wilcox, D.L., C.T. Cameron, P.H. Ault & W.K. Agee. 2003. *Public Relations Strategies and Tactics.* New York: Pearson Education.

Wilcox, D.L., C.T. Cameron, P.H. Ault & W.K. Agee. 2006. *Public Relations Strategies and Tactics.* New York: Pearson Education.

Please see the PRISA Library list at the end of the book for information of other local and international titles.

Chapter 2

The development of public relations

When you have read this chapter, you should:

- have an understanding of the origins of public relations;
- be aware of the impact of these origins on people's interpretation of the present place and purpose of public relations in society;
- be familiar with the main professional public relations bodies in the United States, Europe, and internationally;
- be familiar with the present structure of the professional public relations body in South Africa and its new registration system;
- be aware of the new marketing, advertising, and communication charter;
- know the aims of the Accreditation and Ethics Council of PRISA.

Published histories have usually tele-scoped and over-simplified a fascinating story by emphasizing novelty and a few colourful personalities. The evolution of the practice of public relations is a complex and dramatic story. The historical context of public relations is a vital part of today's practice
(Cutlip et al. 1994).

Early history

We are inclined to think of public relations as a 20th century phenomenon, but efforts to communicate with others and to deal with the force of opinion go back to antiquity. For example, in ancient Egypt the Pharaohs proclaimed their achievements through word-pictures on impressive monuments, and at certain times of the year, staged elaborate festival parades. While these actions mainly had a religious significance, they served, at the same time, to impress and entertain the people, and so win their support for the ruling class.

The leaders of Greece showed a thorough understanding of the value of word-of-mouth communication to persuade people to adopt a certain line of action. In their city-states political democracy was born and the male population fiercely debated matters of the day.

In the Roman Empire, with its slogan of '*Vox populi, vox dei*', this form of persuasion was continued by orators such as Cicero and Cato. The Romans went further, and some tyrants laid on free shows and parades to win support.

During early Christianity, St. Paul was one of the apostles to communicate successfully through the written word. However, it was only the invention of the printing press by Gutenberg and, later, the use of steam printing presses, that turned the written word into a medium for communicating news.

The 20th/21st century

Modern-day public relations, as we know it, originated in the United States, and the history of public relations in America has to a large extent determined its history in other countries.

While American politicians had been using press agents and various publicity methods for some time, at the turn of the century the great showman, PT Barnum, started doing the same. Not only did he buy advertising space, but he also knew how to exploit the news value of his attractions. Barnum started the trend, followed by many of the early film and press agents, of 'manufacturing news' and using stunts and gimmicks to get attention.

Public relations was later employed to defend powerful United States business interests against muck-raking journalism and government regulation. The emphasis was on 'telling our story' counter-attacks designed to influence public opinion and fend off changes in public policy that would affect the content of business.

For this purpose, more and more companies began hiring journalists in order to obtain positive publicity, and it is for this reason that public relations is regarded as having evolved from press agentry.

The concept of public relations as one-way persuasive communication continued to dominate as the United States entered World War I and created the Committee on Public Information. Headed by George Creel, the Committee was responsible for uniting public opinion behind the war effort through an extensive, nationwide propaganda campaign. During those early years, public relations was viewed as a publicity effort to influence others. Various types of communication, such as advertising, films, and exhibitions, were used

to such an extent that people eventually talked of 'the words that won the war'.

This concept of public relations as 'persuasive publicity' still lingers on, so that even present-day public relations practitioners find themselves dealing with managers and clients holding this concept of the public relations function.

Professional bodies

The United States

The Public Relations Society of America (PRSA) came into being in 1947 as a result of the merger of two other bodies. In 1964, the PRSA approved a voluntary accreditation scheme whereby it accredited all new members, who had to pass a series of written tests in order to become members of the association and use the designation APR (Accredited in Public Relations) after their name. This was the first initiative to control entrance to the practice and implement standards of conduct among practitioners.

The PRSA has a Code of Professional Standards for the Practice of Public Relations which was adopted in 1954. The Code is enforced by a grievance board and a judicial panel. The PRSA also publishes its own monthly magazine, *Public Relations Journal*, which is the oldest publication in the field and was started by a notable American public relations practitioner, Rex Harlow, in 1944.

Apart from the PRSA, there are a number of other professional bodies, the most notable being the Public Relations Student Society of America (PRSSA), established in 1970, and the International Association of Business Communicators (IABC), also founded in 1970. In addition, there are a number of specialized public relations associations, which include the National Association of Government Communicators, the National School Public Relations Association, the Academy of Hospital Public Relations, and Agricultural Communicators in Education.

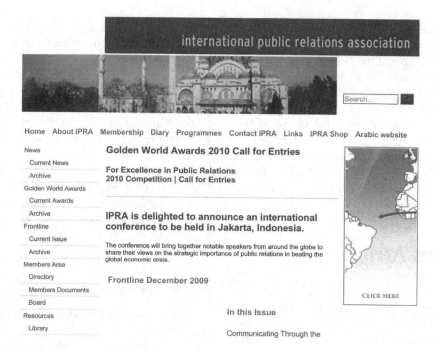

Source: http://www.ipra.org. Downloaded on 9 January 2010.

IPRA also publishes the *FrontLine*. Recently it accepted the new Code of Brussels as a guide for ethical behaviour for its members.

Europe and the international scene

The route taken by public relations in America created the trend for the post-war development of public relations in Europe. The period 1955 to 1980 is described as a 'remarkable period of transformation' in the history of European public relations. At its commencement, comparatively few pioneers were practising public relations and the profession was still heavily indebted to American know-how. By the 1980s, almost every country of modern Western Europe had an established public relations body.

The profession began organizing itself into associations at approximately the same time in most Western European countries – in the late 1940s and early 1950s. For example, the Institute of Public Relations (IPR) was established in England in 1948. In 1959, a regional confederation, Centre (now Confederation)

Européenne des Relations Publiques (CERP) was founded. This body established a European code of professional conduct, the Code of Athens, compiled by Lucien Matrat and named after the city where it was adopted in 1965. This is often referred to as the moral Magna Carta of public relations.

One of the most important international organizations in public relations is the International Public Relations Association (IPRA), which was founded in London in 1955. It is a worldwide professional and fraternal organization which furthers the continuing development of 'the highest possible standards of public relations ethics, practice and performance'. The IPRA Code of Conduct was accepted in Venice in 1961, and in 1965 IPRA accepted the Code of Athens, which was compiled by CERP and is based upon the principles of the United Nations Declaration of Human Rights. IPRA also publishes the *International Public Relations Review*.

Major international public relations federations, apart from CERP (based in Belgium) and IPRA (based in Geneva), include the African Public Relations Associations (APRA), registered in March 2008 in Nigeria; the Federation of Asian Public Relations Organizations (FAPRO) based in the Philippines; the Inter-American Federation of Public Relations Associations (FIARP) in Venezuela; and the Pan-Pacific Public Relations Federation (PPPRF) in Thailand (www.ipranet.org).

South Africa

Public relations in the true sense of the word came into being in South Africa after World War II. The first step toward the establishment of a public relations function was taken by the Government in 1937, when an Information Bureau was founded with the purpose of spreading official information.

The first public relations practitioner in South Africa was appointed by the South African Railways in 1943, while the first public relations consultancy opened in Johannesburg in 1948. Shortly thereafter, several large concerns created internal public relations departments.

PRISA – The Institute for Public Relations and Communication Management

PRISA was established as the Public Relations Institute of Southern Africa in Johannesburg in 1957 and today has more than 2 500 members. It is now recognized as one of the leading public relations professional bodies in the world.

PRISA's vision is the recognition of public relations professionals as role players of significance in South Africa and beyond. It hopes to achieve this by:

- fostering the dynamic and relevant professionalism of public relations practice in South Africa;
- establishing public relations as a strategic management function;
- maintaining professional ethics and standards among members of the Institute;
- providing dynamic, value-added services to members of the Institute.

PRISA runs ongoing professional development courses, seminars, and workshops in major centres around the country, as well as an annual conference addressing professional trends and issues.

PRISA registration

Two key principles – academic qualifications and experience – provide the basis for the registration system, and points (to a maximum of 100) are allocated as appropriate.

Currently all members, from affiliates to APRs, have voting rights. However, students belonging to the PRISA Students' Association do not have voting rights.

Academic qualifications

A predetermined number of points are allocated on the basis of the applicant's academic qualifications. Qualifications recognized range from any university degree or three-year diploma to PRISA's own approved short courses in public relations. Currently, much work is being done through SAQA, NQF, and SETA to improve the quality of public relations and communication training.

Experience

Points are allocated by the registration committee for tasks within the different functions. Within all functions there is also a maximum number of points to be accumulated through tasks. Proof of experience is required. Since some candidates have performed public relations tasks in other capacities over a number of

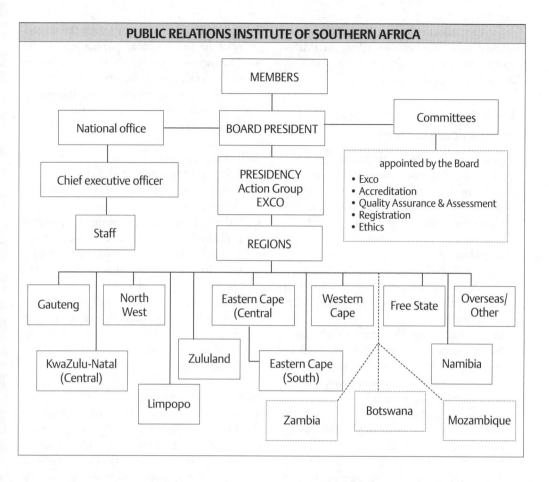

PUBLIC RELATIONS INSTITUTE OF SOUTHERN AFRICA

years, the sub-minimum of 20 points for experience should include at least three years of full-time public relations for a Public Relations Practitioner and more than five years for a Chartered Public Relations Practitioner. The registration committee, however, exercises discretion in considering weight and point allocations.

The levels of registration and minimum points required for each are as follows:

- Students/Learners — 5
- Affiliate (less than one year) — 10
- Associate (1–3 years) — 30
- Public Relations Practitioner (PRP) (3–6 years) — 50
- Chartered Public Relations Practitioner (CPRP) (6–10 years) — 60
- APR (Accredited in Public Relations) (more than 10 years). — 70

This is currently under review.

Accreditation

Accreditation is the professional designation awarded to public relations practitioners who possess those special qualifications that characterize a true professional. It is internationally recognized and is the highest level of the PRISA registration system which is based on academic qualification and experience.

Accreditation is consistent with PRISA's aim of professionalizing the public relations industry. It measures the scope and depth of candidates' knowledge as well as their professional orientation as a prerequisite for accreditation and ultimate professional recognition. Successful completion of the accreditation process results not only in the right to use 'APR' in business contracts, but also provides an increased sense of professional confidence and personal accomplishment.

Further information on the accreditation process can be obtained by visiting the PRISA website (www.prisa.co.za) or writing to P.O. Box 2825, Pinegowrie 2123.

Marketing, advertising, and communication charter

Members of the broader marketing, advertising, public relations, communication, and research industry as well as related sectors, recently drew up a charter which has the following values statement and commitment.

Values statement
'Of an industry which is global in its outlook and reach, and genuinely South African in its roots, we of the marketing and communication industry:
- acknowledge that like the rest of South African society, we have been plagued by the injustices of South Africa's racist past in terms of employee representivity, ownership, and decision making;
- recognize that the industry plays a critical role in the creation of wealth and the development of our economy;
- believe that transformation of the industry is essential for its long-term growth and upliftment of people who have historically been disadvantaged.'

In the spirit of the Constitution of South Africa, we believe that 'South Africa belongs to all who live in it, united in our diversity and committed to improve the quality of life of all citizens and the potential of each person.'

We hereby commit ourselves to the following values:

Inclusivity and diversity
- The sector reflects and shapes the norms of our society. As such it must be committed to reflecting the values and aspirations of all South Africans.
- This requires that the industry – in its ownership as well as in the traditions and cultures it draws upon – to reflect the diversity of the South African population.
- The industry is committed to sustainable skills development, which enables all our people to enjoy access to the knowledge base needed to shape their destinies within the industry.

Soul of the nation
- This industry works in the context of the unique transition – a transition described as a miracle.
- We shall use our strengths to promote pride in the South African brand.
- The industry can contribute to the transition by promoting understanding and appreciating our diverse cultures, traditions, histories, abilities, and disabilities. It can highlight prejudice where it exists by promoting tolerance of all human beings. In doing so, the sector can mirror the soul of the nation.

Respect and human dignity
- The industry works in a society where the poor, the illiterate, the disabled, women, and children suffer a myriad of intolerances. While working for their amelioration and empowerment, the industry shall ensure that the dignity of all human beings and in particular of those vulnerable groups is respected.
- The industry recognizes the difficulty of escaping the stereotyping of any group. Where this has to be resorted to, the industry shall take particular care not to stereotype or use humour in a manner to target groups mentioned above.

Business and people's needs
- We recognize that the consumer is at the core of our business, recognizing that the industry serves business in its endeavour to create wealth. We shall ensure that the requirement and sensitivities of the consumer are placed at the centre of all our creativity and planning. In doing so, we shall better serve the commercial needs of

business as well as the long-term aspirations of the South African nation.

- Furthermore, the industry shall be committed to abiding by the principles of good corporate governance and abide by the highest standards of ethical business practices.

Responsible creativity

- We are mindful that this is an industry that impacts on the views and aspirations of the entire population.
- This means that the industry must act sensitively while endeavouring to break the bounds of creative barriers. Such commitment will lay the basis for a self-regulation regime that can best serve all stakeholders.

This commitment must not place limits on the various freedoms enshrined in the Constitution and protected by the Bill of Rights, especially the freedom of expression.

Conclusion

Although modern public relations initially developed as a tool used in power struggles in America, its role in present-day society is vastly different. Because we are living in a complex society and are confronted by a knowledge explosion, which is fuelled by advancing technology, the role of public relations is changing. This is best reflected in the official statement on public relations by the Public Relations Society of America (PRSA), which reads as follows:

_____

Public relations helps our complex, pluralistic society to reach decisions and function more effectively by contributing to mutual understanding among groups and institutions. It serves to bring private and public policies into harmony.

_____

In short, as institutions have grown larger, they have been forced to refine their methods of communicating with their publics. This, therefore, is the role of public relations practitioners today – to interpret institutions to the publics they serve and to promote both the image and reputation of these institutions.

Further reading

Communika. Various editions including August 1992 and July 1993. Johannesburg: PRISA.

Cutlip, S.M., A.H. Center & G.M. Broom. 1994. _Effective Public Relations_. Englewood Cliffs, New Jersey: Prentice-Hall.

Derrimon, J. 1980. 'Europe – 25 Years of Progress', _IPRA Review_, 4(2): 35–6.

Grunig, J.E. & T. Hunt. 1984. _Managing Public Relations_. New York: Holt, Rinehart & Winston.

Lubbe, B.A. & G. Puth. 1994. _Public Relations in South Africa: A Management Reader_. Johannesburg: Heinemann.

Malan, J.P. & J.A. L'Estrange. 1977. _Public Relations Practice in South Africa_. Cape Town: Juta.

Newsom, D.A. & A. Scott. 1981. _This is Public Relations/The Relations of Public Relations_. California: Wadsworth.

Seitel, F.P. 1995. _The Practice of Public Relations_. Englewood Cliffs, New Jersey: Prentice-Hall.

Wilcox, D.L., P.H. Ault & W.K. Agee. 1995, 2003. _Public Relations: Strategies and Tactics_. New York: Harper & Row.

Also consult PRISA website (prisa.co.za) for the latest developments in the PR profession in southern Africa.

Chapter 3

The practice of public relations

When you have read this chapter, you should:

- be aware of the differences between line and staff management as they relate to public relations;
- be familiar with the two basic options regarding the execution of public relations;
- be able to discuss the advantages and disadvantages of each option;
- be aware of the areas of specialization in the public relations field.

An organization's public reputation derives in substantial part from its senior officials. As those with administrative responsibility and authority act and speak, so go the interpretations and echoes created by the public relations function. Thus, public relations is inescapably tied by nature and by necessity, to the management function (Cutlip et al. 1994: 59).

In this context, long-term success in an organization's public relations calls for:

- commitment and participation by management;
- competent public relations practitioners;
- centralized policy-making;
- communication (two-way) with both internal and external publics;
- co-ordination of all efforts towards defined goals and objectives.

Public relations is a staff function, one of several that advise and support senior management. Thus, practitioners need to understand the staff role.

The line-staff principle of management originated in the military, but has been extended to most organizations of the same size. In industry, for example, the product- and profit-producing functions – engineering, production and marketing – are line functions. Staff functions are those that advise and assist the executive – finance, legal, human resources, and public relations. These functions become more and more necessary as organizations increase in size and complexity.

The difference between line and staff management is important to remember. Line management determines the ground rules and sets the course. Public relations works within these rules and with others on matters that have an impact on the organization's relationships with others, inside and outside. In these matters, both line and staff managers must participate. Once all points of view have been aired and debated, the final decisions may result from consensus, or from choices made by line management. Final decisions are the province of senior line management.

However, since managing organizational relationships is an increasingly important function, many public relations practitioners have moved from staff support positions to line management. In this capacity, the public relations executive attends strategy meetings, where important corporate decisions are made, and helps to make those decisions.

The public relations industry, in serving the needs of different organizations and institutions, encompasses a number of different areas of specialization. Public relations practitioners could specialize in terms of one of the organization's target publics, for example relations with the media or with employees. They also specialize with regard to the types of institution they serve, such as practitioners, institutions, or non-profit organizations.

Whatever the type of organization on whose behalf it is executed, public relations is either practised on a corporate or a consultancy basis. Although there are a number of variations on these two approaches, in essence it means the following:

- an organization employs a public relations practitioner or has an internal public relations department with a number of public relations practitioners operating at different levels (for example, practitioner or manager) and specializing in different public relations functions (for example, publications or media);
- an organization retains a public relations consultant or consultancy to handle its public relations activities on a retainer or ad hoc basis.

It is not unusual for an organization to have an internal public relations practitioner or department, as well as to retain a consultant or consultancy.

Corporate public relations

The following aspects characterize public relations in the corporate sphere:

- most corporate practitioners fit into a well-established public relations department within the overall structure of the organization;
- in many manufacturing and marketing organizations, public relations falls under the marketing division;
- in service organizations, public relations may be split into product promotion and public affairs;
- the structure of in-house departments is fairly standard. In companies with a sophisticated approach to public relations, the practitioner is a member of the management team. These practitioners must understand the business or industry in which their companies operate;
- remuneration varies from industry to industry and even from company to company.

Advantages

Corporate practitioners have essentially four factors working in their favour:

- team membership;
- knowledge of the organization;
- cost-effectiveness to the organization;
- availability to other departments/associates.

Team membership is possibly the greatest advantage. The confidence, trust, and support of colleagues that go with it tend to overcome or to relegate to unimportance any antagonism towards the public relations function that might exist in a company. At the same time, the close connection between the function, the department, and the chief executive officer, provides first-team rather than marginal membership. The price of admission is confidentiality and loyalty.

Knowledge of the organization is another

important plus factor. Corporate practitioners know their organizations intimately – their history, policies, products, and services but, above all, the relationships between individuals and their functions. They can advize where needed, reconcile, and render services from within to induce attitudes and actions that will bring about harmonious relationships inside as well as outside.

The cost-effective aspect simply results from residence and integration in an organization. Full-time, permanent staff are typically more cost-effective than hiring outside counsel and services.

The availability of corporate practitioners has many facets: they are there when needed; they can execute a number of tasks at short notice; they can handle emergencies; and, most importantly, they can act as spokespersons for the organization. They therefore have acceptability and authority, both internally and externally.

Disadvantages

The factors working in favour of corporate practitioners can also work to their disadvantage. For example, availability and loyalty can result in loss of objectivity, especially with regard to internal conflict. There is the danger of being co-opted – becoming a yes-man or -woman. Such a situation can deteriorate into one of domination and subjectivity, resulting in a loss of respect for the person and the function by colleagues and employer. Practitioners walk a narrow line between rendering services that are valuable, helpful, and appreciated, and playing a subservient role that is easily replaced. The key is team play, while at the same time retaining one's individuality and objectivity.

Availability has another downside. Practitioners may find themselves in the role of stand-ins for top executives who make commitments and then find that they are unable to keep them. The corporate practitioner is seen as the second choice, but provided he or she has the authority to commit the organization to supporting a particular cause, this is often a good arrangement, since the chief executive is hard pressed to attend meetings.

Consulting public relations

The following aspects characterize public relations in this sphere:
- the size of a private practice is mostly determined by the number of clients involved;
- the people who handle a portfolio of clients are called account executives. They give advice to clients in shaping their public relations plans and execute them jointly;
- private practitioners usually base their working relationship with their clients on a contact report;
- the range of services offered by consultancies varies from the full-house services of larger consultancies to a fairly narrow range of specialist services such as promotions and media relations;
- costs and fees are determined on a project, hourly, or retainer basis;
- incidental costs are usually charged as extras.

Advantages

Public relations consultants rank their variety of talents and skills as their greatest advantage when compared with the internal corporate practitioner. Their objectivity, as relatively free agents untrammelled by the politics within an organization, ranks second. Their range of experience is third, the geographical scope of their operations is fourth, and the ability to reinforce and upgrade a client's internal staff, is fifth.

Depending on the size of the consultancy, clients can draw on the wide range of expertise of individual consultants, who collectively are exposed to a number of clients and different situations daily. Many consultants emphasize the flexibility of their staff and their operations as a prime advantage. Their large number of contacts and specialized knowledge provide immediate input to tackle clients' needs, whatever these may be – media relations, promotions, lobbying, social investment, industrial and community relations, and the environment.

Sometimes the consultant's reputation is a major advantage. Outside 'experts' can often introduce ideas that internal staffers have struggled unsuccessfully to place on the agenda. Knowing that the consultant's reputation and subsequent referrals are on the line helps ensure performance.

There is no doubt that the range of a successful consultant's services is wide. In a sense, a public relations firm is a repository of living case histories. Each project adds to its fund of knowledge. Experience and versatility of staff make this synergy possible. The consultant, therefore, approaches each case bolstered by familiarity with the type of situation and knowledge of the success or failure that attended previous encounters.

Disadvantages

With rare exceptions, the rendering of a consultancy service meets with some opposition, ranging from non-acceptance to antagonism. This is, at least in theory, the consultant's most serious handicap. Resistance to outsiders is a natural human trait.

Consultants, however, do not rank this problem as the major obstacle. They overwhelmingly cite questions of cost as the chief stumbling block with clients. They list 'threat to old guard and set ways' as the second most persistent handicap. Resistance to 'outside' advice comes in third, and fourth is unforeseen conflicts of personality or conviction.

Other problems include a lack of understanding of public relations by clients, clients' inertia when it comes to doing what consultants think ought to be done, and the unavailability of clients at times when consultants want decisions. This would suggest a problem of priorities.

Criticism of consultants by corporate practitioners includes their lack of real understanding of the organization and how it operates, their superficial grasp of an organization's corporate culture, and their lack of real commitment. For them it may be just another account. Consultants may also have divided loyalties, not on a professional basis, but with regard to

time and availability. Account executives may move on, so there could also be a loss of continuity between organization and consultancy, although this is not normally a problem.

Consultancy costs and selection criteria

The services of a consultancy firm may be obtained for a specific project or for a continuing service, reviewable and renewable at intervals.

Fees for continuing services are usually established in one of four ways:
- a monthly retainer (service fee);
- a retainer plus monthly billing for actual staff time on an hourly or per diem basis;
- a base fee, billed monthly, to which are added increments for services performed beyond those specified for the retainer;
- straight hourly charges.

Out-of-pocket expenses are generally billed at cost and are exclusive of the fee.

The variations in fees charged by different consultancies reflect to a large degree the cost of the staff used on the project, executive time and supervision, overhead costs, and a reasonable profit for doing the work. Unlike advertising agencies, which make their money from discounts on advertisements placed in the media on clients' behalf, plus production charges for creating these advertisements, public relations consultants charge their time in the same way as lawyers and accountants do. To get the best results, organizations are therefore advised to look for the following when selecting a consultant:
- experience in the fields with which the organization is concerned;
- professional background and competence;
- satisfactory reputation;
- current client list;
- required facilities (research or computer expert, etc.).

29

The PRCC and PRISM Awards

The Public Relations Consultants Chapter of PRISA – the PRCC – has been active since 1996 and is made up of a voluntary committee of consultants and other interested parties with a chairman and office bearers. The Chairman represents the interests of the PRCC on the PRISA Board and Executive Committee.

The PRCC is involved in several key initiatives as well as being represented on various industry bodies designed to enhance the profile of the industry and build capacity within Consultant members. Some of these initiatives and industry bodies include:

- organizing networking and professional development events;
- facilitate employment and training of disadvantaged public relations practitioners in established consultancies;
- lobbying and liaising with government;
- publishing standard client/consultancy contracts for members;
- representation on the Marketing, Advertising and Communication (MAC) Charter and as such was instrumental in developing the BBBEE standards;
- organizing and hosting the PRISA PRISM Awards, which are annual awards that recognize excellence in Public Relations and Communication Management.

The annual PRISA PRISM Awards are presented to public relations and communication professionals who have successfully incorporated strategy, creativity, and professionalism into public relations and communication programmes and strategies.

The 25 company categories and five individual categories for the PRISA PRISM Awards are aligned with international requirements and address a comprehensive scope of activities offered by public relations firms and communication departments. Categories include, but are not limited to: International Public Relations campaigns; NGO campaigns; Crisis Management; Media Relations; Corporate Communication; New Product or Service Launch; Consumer Public Relations for an Existing Product or Service; Social Media; Online Press Office; Public Relations on a Shoestring; Internal Communication; Public Sector; Environmental and Business-to-business.

The PRISA PRISM overall Gold Award is presented to the individual entry judged to have demonstrated the highest standards of competence and this award is automatically entered into the world acclaimed IPRA Golden World Awards for excellence in public relations.

Conclusion

The decision as to whether it is better for an organization to have its own staff, to use consultants exclusively, or to have a combination of the two, depends on the size of the organization and its needs.

The corporate public relations practitioner, working on his or her own, will be more of a generalist and use a wide range of techniques. Depending on the degree of specialization and size of operations, the corporate public relations practitioner might be involved in only one of the techniques of public relations, such as media relations or public affairs.

The best arrangement is a compact internal public relations department, working with outside consultants on specific assignments. This arrangement could provide outstanding results on a cost-effective basis.

Further reading

Beard, M. 1997. *Running a Public Relations Department.* London: Kogan Page.

Cutlip, S.M., A.H. Center & G.M. Broom. 1994. *Effective Public Relations.* Englewood Cliffs, New Jersey: Prentice-Hall.

Jefkins, F. 1998. *Public Relations.* London: M & E Pitman Publishing.

Lubbe, B.A. & G. Puth. 1994. *Public Relations in South Africa: A Management Reader.* Johannesburg: Heinemann.

Wilcox, D.L., P.H. Ault & W.K. Agee. 1995 and 2003. *Public Relations: Strategies and Tactics.* New York: Harper & Row.

Please consult the PRISA website (prisa.co.za).

Chapter 4

Public relations and research

When you have read this chapter, you should:

- be aware of the importance of research and the various objectives it should accomplish;
- be able to define public relations problems through research;
- be familiar with the various types of research;
- understand how to prepare a research brief and draw up a research proposal.

Why is research important?

Research is the key to the design and execution of a successful public relations programme. In the final instance, information and data must be gathered and facts compiled. It is also necessary to have a knowledge of target audiences. A public relations practitioner who understands his or her audiences – their attitudes, hopes, and fears – will be better able to formulate messages that appeal specifically to them. In addition, self-interest is a strong motivating force. If communication can be tailored to the self-interest of an audience, there is a much greater chance of reaching it.

Public relations research usually consists of investigating three aspects of the overall public relations procedure, namely:

- client or organization requiring the research;
- opportunity or problem to be addressed;
- audiences (publics) to be targeted.

Client or organizational research

Background data about the client or organization is an essential starting point for any public relations programme.

According to Mersham et al. (1995:118), client or organizational research involves the following five steps:

- being familiar with the nature of the client's business, whether for profit or non-profit;
- knowing the organization's precise mission, its management's goals, priorities, and problems;
- having a good working knowledge of the organization's personnel (total working force);

- having insight into the financial status of the organization;
- understanding the importance of corporate image and its impact on an organization.

Opportunity or problem research

The second aspect of public relations research consists of determining why the organization should conduct a particular public relations programme at a particular time.

Public relations programmes that arise out of opportunities are called proactive programmes. In the long run these are less expensive than reactive programmes, which may have to deal with crises within and outside organizations. There will always be crises and public relations practitioners must always be ready to deal with these.

Audience or publics research

The third aspect of research in the public relations process involves investigating the target audiences or publics of the public relations programme. This includes identifying the particular groups that should be targeted, determining appropriate research data that will be useful in communicating with these publics, and compiling and processing the data using appropriate research procedures.

Using research for planning, monitoring and evaluation

Research is critical at every stage of public relations work, from planning and setting objectives to prioritizing publics and evaluating the results for purposes of future planning and action. Research information is particularly useful at the initiation stage of the public relations effort (Newsom et al. 1993:95).

Planning

The main stages of the planning phase of research are issues forecasting, learning about publics, planning media use, and considering possible outcomes.

Issues forecasting is the research part of issues management and environmental scanning. In issues forecasting, an organization uses information collected to determine how it and its publics might react to a future event, trend, or controversy.

After the public relations practitioner has accumulated all the factors about a given issue or situation, he or she has to learn about the public involved. The two main tasks involved in exploring publics consist of:

- prioritizing publics by issues (identifying the major and minor publics of the organization involved);
- interpreting the behaviour of publics (how people look at certain situations and how they behave in them).

The public relations practitioner has to plan media use. Research indicating what media different publics use is widely available from a variety of sources. These include professional, trade, and academic journals as well as publications such as SARAD and the All Media and Product Survey (AMPS).

Finally, when public relations practitioners consider a public relations plan, they should closely examine possible outcomes. This is everything that can go right or wrong! Examining the possibilities of any plan often reveals that unexplored areas may exist. By researching the plan, problems may be identified and solved.

Monitoring

According to Newsom et al. (1993:99) it is important to arrange for feedback after a plan has been set in operation. Careful planning may have preceded a public relations programme but that does not ensure success.

Monitoring a public relations operation involves a specific check on results, as opposed to general monitoring of public opinion, which goes on in issue management. It can be as simple as checking a broadcast to make sure that advertising is running in the time slots purchased, or reading a magazine to confirm that an advertisement really does appear. On the other hand, it may be as complex as assessing whether consumers noticed a new package.

Final evaluation

The purpose of the final evaluation is to look at each objective to see whether and by how much it was achieved.

The public relations practitioner should check the effects of the public relations efforts on each public if possible. The following procedures (according to Newsom et al. 1993: 100) can therefore be adopted:

- compile the goal (objective) results and interpret their significance to the specific objective set, to the organization's overall objectives and to its mission;
- evaluate the impact of actions taken on the publics to see what their attitudes are now towards the organization (as well as its products, services, management, and so on);
- determine how the organization's overall objective and mission have been affected;
- measure the impact the programme has in three areas: financial responsibility, ethics, and social responsibility.

Types of research

Research can either be informal or formal. Both types are useful but both have limitations.

Informal research

This research is usually conducted without generally agreed-to rules and procedures that would enable someone else to replicate the same study. The results of this research can be used only for description and not for prediction (Newsom et al. 1993:106).

Some of the techniques used in informal research are unobtrusive measures, opinion and communication audits, and analysis of publicity broken down by audience, medium, message, and frequency.

Research methods

Methods	Characteristics
Individual question-naires	• Questionnaire is read to respondent and he or she answers it personally • Suitable for limited investigations • Takes time to complete and is therefore expensive
Group questionnaires	• Respondents meet in groups and complete questionnaire • If group co-operates, one of the cheapest methods of collecting data • May be difficult to find suitable group representing target market

Methods	Characteristics
Postal questionnaires	• Questionnaires are posted to group being investigated • Large numbers can be canvassed • Response, however, usually poor, with fewer than 20% replies • Postal costs can be prohibitive and survey can take a long time before an acceptable response is achieved
Telephone questionnaires	• Trained teleresearchers telephone respondents. Questionnaire is read and answers are indicated on answer sheet • Suitable for large investigations, regionally or nationally • Expensive, but can prove to be a method of collecting accurate data from specific camps
Competitions	• Contents are compiled in such a way that individuals who take the trouble to fill in the questionnaires stand a good chance of winning something • Depends on distribution to specific readers through newspapers and magazines • Advertising costs can be high and response may be no better than postal questionnaire
Focus groups	• Involves groups of between 10–15 representative of selected target market • Meets in a special venue for about two hours with a discussion leader focusing on a specific topic and answering certain prescribed questions • All discussion is recorded and responses analysed. However, focus groups are not always practicable and are time consuming
Individual interviews	• Key role players can be identified and in-depth discussion can be carried out on specific topics. Same agenda is used for all discussion • Can prove expensive and time consuming
Content analysis	• The nature and number of reports, newsflashes, and so on are determined according to specific categories • Able to quantify positive and negative reports in the mass media • Easy method of gathering information if media is available for evaluation
Informal discussions	• May be used initially to determine contents of a questionnaire or structured interview • Researcher can determine attitudes, level of knowledge, and behaviour patterns of proposed sample • Validity of results questionable
Observations	• Researcher is positioned so that he or she is able to observe the behaviour of target market • Method is quick, cheap but unfortunately has little credibility • Subjective and no feedback from audience

Formal research

This can be divided into two categories: qualitative and quantitative research. Qualitative research includes historical and legal research, in-depth interviews, focus groups, and panels. It is descriptive and informative but not measurable. Quantitative research can be done in the laboratory or in the field. It may include content analysis and survey analysis. Quantitative research results in a mathematical analysis because it produces measurable results.

The pros and cons of various techniques in informal and formal research are summarized in Mersham et al. (1995: 125–127).

The research brief

The research brief is drawn up by the research user or marketer. Its purpose is to communicate a clear description of the perceived problem (or the information required) to the researcher.

The researcher uses the brief as a basis for drafting the research proposal. The format for the research brief is discussed below.

Background

It is imperative that the problem is correctly identified and defined. This should be accompanied by any information that is pertinent to the company requesting the research, such as positioning, markets, and strategies.

Objectives of the research

This is the information the research user wants to obtain from the research.

Action standards

These are decisions that the research user will make based on the outcome of the results. For example, if more than 70 per cent of respondents prefer package X, the packaging will be revised to conform with this preference.

Target market

The nature and composition of the target market must be defined so that the researcher can define the universe (population).

Timing

The date by when the information is required and any other important deadlines should be included.

Budget

The money made available for the project should be determined by the importance of the marketing decision that will stem from the research results. An upper limit can be set to guide the researcher in his or her proposal.

Reporting requirements

The research user must state whether the report is required as a presentation, as a written report, or on computer disks.

The research proposal

The research proposal is drawn up by the researcher and is based on the research brief received from a prospective client. Once accepted by the client, the proposal serves as an agreement between researcher and client.

The format for the research proposal is discussed below.

Background

Important issues that provide an orientation for the research are dealt with in this section. The background sets the scene for the research proposal.

Problem definition (or information required)

The problem that gives rise to the research is stated. This may be the same as the problem stated in the research brief (once it is sanctioned by both client and researcher). The problem is usually stated in marketing terms. For example, the problem may be loss of market share or incomplete knowledge of buyer motives.

Research objectives

The objectives come out of the problem definition. The objectives are what the researcher wants to achieve from the research process. Many decisions made later on in the research proposal stem from these objectives. For example, the sampling technique, sample size, and the method of data collection all reflect the research objectives. In addition, the research objectives lay the foundation on which the questionnaire is designed.

Research design

The definition of universe (population) depends on the client's perception of the target market and must be clearly and specifically stated. For example, the target market may be all people between the ages of 18 and 25 inclusive, living in flats in Gauteng as at 1 October 2001.

Sampling design

This consists of three elements:
- *Sampling frame.* The sampling frame is a list of universe elements. It is only necessary to have such a list if you are drawing a probability sample.
- *Sampling techniques.* A probability sample is only necessary if the results of the research are to be projected onto the population. For example, one of the objectives may be to determine market share or to determine the demographic characteristics of the target market. A probability sample is preferred if the sample is easy to draw and the sampling frame is readily accessible. In this case, there

is little or no additional cost in drawing a probability sample. Non-probability sampling is typical in exploratory studies or in advertising research. The research objectives will indicate whether a non-probability sample is sufficient to do the job. The availability and cost of the sampling frame is another important consideration. The research budget may also limit the choice to a non-probability sample.
- *Sample size.* The size of the sample selected may be based on a number of considerations, including gut feel, industry standards, statistical calculation, and what can be afforded. The choice of sample size should be justified in accordance with one or more of these criteria.

Method of data collection

Data may be collected through observation, communication, and experimentation. A choice is made depending on the nature of the survey. If communication is selected, a further choice must be made whether to use personal interviews, telephone interviews, mail surveys, focus groups, or panels. Factors such as urgency, cost, flexibility, response rate, and research objectives influence the choice of data collection method.

Questionnaire design

The questionnaire is designed taking into account the method of data collection. For example, if mail survey is chosen as a method of data collection, then a covering letter must be drafted. The covering letter should include a return address, a deadline date, and possibly an incentive if appropriate.

The questions are drafted in such a way that the answers they elicit will enable the objectives of the research to be achieved. Types of questions include closed questions, open questions, and questions with answers on a given scale. Examples of each of these are shown on pages 37 to 39.

Instructions on how to answer the questionnaire should be provided and a classifica-

Types of questions

1. Closed questions

Name	Description	Example
Dichotomous	A question offering two answer choices	'In arranging this trip, did you personally phone SAA?'
Multiple choice	A question offering three or more choices	'With whom are you travelling on this flight?' No one () Children only () Spouse () Business associate(s)/friend(s)/relative(s) () Spouse and children () An organized tour group ()
Likert scale	A statement with which the respondent shows the amount of agreement/ disagreement	'Small airlines generally give better service than large ones.' Strongly disagree (1) () Disagree (2) () Neither agree or disagree (3) () Agree (4) () Strongly agree (5) ()
Semantic differential	A scale is inscribed between two bipolar words. The respondent selects the point that represents the direction and intensity of his or her feelings	SAA Large X _ _ _ _ _ _ _ _ _ Small Experienced _ _ _ _ _ _ _ _ X _ Inexperienced Modern _ _ _ _ X _ _ _ _ _ Old-fashioned
Importance scale	A scale that rates the importance of some attribute from 'not at all important' to 'extremely important'	'Airline food service to me is:' Extremely important (1) () Very important (2) () Somewhat important (3) () Not very important (4) () Not at all important (5) ()
Rating scale	A scale that rates some attribute from 'poor' to 'excellent'	'SAA's food service is:' Excellent (1) () Very good (2) () Good (3) () Fair (4) () Poor (5) ()

2. Open questions

Name	Description	Example
Completely unstructured	A question that respondents can answer in an almost unlimited number of ways	'What is your opinion of SAA?'
Word association	Words are presented, one at a time, and respondents mention the first word that comes to mind	'What is the first word that comes to mind when you hear the following?' Airline _____ SAA _____ Travel _____
Sentence completion	Incomplete sentences are presented, one at a time, and respondents complete the sentence	'When I choose an ariline, the most important consideration in my decision is:' _____
Story completion	An incomplete story is presented and respondents are asked to complete it	'I flew SAA a few days ago and noticed that the exterior and interior of the plane had very bright colours. This aroused in me the following thoughts and feelings.' Now complete the story
Picture completion	A picture of two characters is presented, with one making a statement. Respondents are asked to identify with the other and fill in the empty balloon	 WELL, HERE'S THE FOOD— Fill in the empty balloon
Thematic appercep-tion tests (TAT)	A picture is presented and respondents are asked to make up a story about what is happening or may happen in the picture	 Make up a story about what you see

3. Questions with answers on a given scale

Do you find that you get comfort and strength from religion, or not?

Yes ☐
No ☐
Don't know ☐

Do you take some moments of prayer, meditation, contemplation, or something similar?

Yes ☐
No ☐
Don't know ☐

Overall, how satisfied or dissatisfied are you with your home life?

Very dissatisfied								Very satisfied		Don't know
1	2	3	4	5	6	7	8	9	10	X

How important are each of the following to you personally? Give a score of 10 to something you consider absolutely all-important and a score of 1 to something not at all important.
One answer in each line

	Not important at all							All important			Don't know
1. A comfortable life	1	2	3	4	5	6	7	8	9	10	X
2. Fun and excitement in life	1	2	3	4	5	6	7	8	9	10	X
3. A sense of accomplishment	1	2	3	4	5	6	7	8	9	10	X
4. A secure family life	1	2	3	4	5	6	7	8	9	10	X
5. Being respected	1	2	3	4	5	6	7	8	9	10	X
6. Being prosperous	1	2	3	4	5	6	7	8	9	10	X
7. Salvation	1	2	3	4	5	6	7	8	9	10	X

Are you currently ...

1. Married ☐
2. Living as married ☐
3. Divorced ☐
4. Separated ☐
5. Widowed ☐
6. Single ☐

If someone said that individuals should have the chance to enjoy complete sexual freedom without being restricted, would you tend to agree or disagree?

1. Tend to agree ☐
2. Tend to disagree ☐
3. Neither/it depends ☐
4. Don't know ☐

tion section requesting relevant demographic details included.

If focus groups have been suggested as a means of data collection, then a moderator's outline (discussion guide) must be drawn up instead of a questionnaire. The moderator's outline should contain the following sections: introduction, warm-up, outline of questions for discussion, projective techniques, and close. Remember to provide a guideline on how much time to spend on each section. The discussion should move from general to specific.

Cost and timing

The cost of the research project should be displayed in a schedule format, with the costs of each process shown separately. This should relate back to previous sections. For example, the field costs are dependent on the size of the sample. The timetable should be displayed in schedule format in which the start and end dates are given for each step of the project.

Special needs

If there are any special needs for the research project, such as riot cover for field staff, then they should be listed here.

Resources of the firm

In this final section, the research house gives a presentation detailing its experience in the proposed market and may mention the name of the individual who will take charge of the research project.

Conclusion

The information gained through careful research can be used to guide planning, pre-test messages, evaluate results, and follow-up efforts. It is thus the first stage in the design and execution of a successful public relations programme.

Case study Edelman Trust Barometer

The need for Public Engagement
With the world experiencing its worst crisis in living memory, the 10th edition of the Edelman Trust Barometer reveals that 'nearly two in three informed publics – 62% of 25-to-64-year olds surveyed in 20 countries – say they trust corporations less now than they did a year ago (2008). When it comes to being distrusted, business is not alone. Globally, trust in business, media, and government is half empty; and trust in government scores even lower than trust in business'.

The overall lack of trust – particularly in business – is not unexpected, but the differences in trust across countries and economies are surprising. 'While globalization has muted lines between cultures and rendered many brands ubiquitous, there are clear disparities in trust between emerging markets and established economies'.

In no country is trust in a more dismal state than in the United States, where government, business, and the media are all distrusted by respondents (ages 25 to 64) to do what is right, even with a new administration elected to power. Europe has also witnessed a similar decline.

Emerging economies, however, indicated a much higher level of trust in business, as well as in specific industries, than did the United States and EU-member countries. What is clear from the survey is that the old order, in which business had the freedom to operate autonomously and without government restraint, is over.

Among the global sample of 25-to-64 year-olds in 20 countries, by a 3:1 margin, respondents say that government should intervene to regulate industry or nationalize companies to restore public trust.

In the major Western European economies of the UK, France, and Germany, three quarters of respondents say that government should step in to prevent future financial crises(73%,75% and 74% respectively).

In the United States, not even half (49%) say that the free market should be allowed to function independently.

Respondents also believe that business should step up to partner with government on global challenges. When asked what role business should play to help solve issues such as energy costs, the financial credit crisis, global warming, and access to affordable health care, two thirds of 25-to-64 year-olds around the world believe that businesses should partner with governments and other third parties to address global issues. Although NGOs are the most trusted institution globally (54% of 25-to-64 year-olds trust them to do what is right), they are not considered most responsible for solving these problems (global totals are below 6 % for each issue)

Trust in every type of news outlet including business magazines and stock or industry analysts reports, TV news coverage, and newspaper articles is now below 50%. Only 29% and 27% view information as credible when coming from a CEO or government official. In the United States, trust in information from a company's top leader now sits at a six year low at 17% among 25-to-64 year-olds. Outside experts remain the most trusted purveyors of information about a company, with 59% of 25-to-64 year-olds saying an academic or expert on a company's industry or issues would be extremely or very credible.

'Conventional wisdom suggests, and the data affirms, that trust does affect consumer spending, corporate reputation, and a company's ability to navigate the regulatory environment. Among our global audience of 25-to-64 year olds, being able to trust a company is one of the most important factors in determining a company's reputation. It ranks just below the quality of a company's products and its treatment of employees, on par with a company's financial future, and more important than job creation, giving back to the community, and innovation in products and services.'

Rebuilding Trust

These findings underscore the reality that if businesses are to regain trust, then they will need to adopt a strategy of Public Engagement, by means of a shift in policy and communications. The four pillars of Public Engagement are:

- *Private sector diplomacy*. Business has both the opportunity and the responsibility to become a primary actor in developing solutions to global problems. Business must, therefore, partner with governments and NGOs to address key policy issues and the world's most pressing problems, not merely the ones that impact on their bottom line. This is an opportunity for business to act as a private sector diplomat, recommending appropriate regulatory frameworks across borders. If companies fail to take the initiative to do so, they run the risk of having policies thrust on them.

- *Mutual social responsibility*. Companies must realign their business practices so they deliver dual objectives: benefit society and the bottom line. Companies must integrate into their products and services approaches to societal problems such as climate change, healthcare, and energy independence. Immediate stakeholders like employees and customers must be invited to participate in a company's social responsibility decisions and actions – and the public at large must be kept informed about the progress the company is making towards these goals.

- *Shared sacrifice*. CEOs must also demonstrate that they too feel the burden of the recession. At a time when workers are losing jobs and investors are seeing stock values plummet, voluntary executive pay cuts and forfeiting of bonuses send a powerful message that leaders are in tune with the realities facing employees. Leaders also must communicate with employees about the problems confronting the company and welcome their voices. This type of transparency and collaborative spirit will help engage employees in finding and embracing solutions.

- *Continuous conversation.* 60% of our respondents said they need to hear information about a company three to five times before they believe it. The CEO should set forth the company's position, but then it must be echoed by others – individuals who often sit outside the company- including industry experts, academics, and ordinary citizens. Companies will be well served by moving from a mindset of control to one of contribution. Mainstream media continues to be an important way to reach opinion formers, but it is not the only one. Companies should inform, with a real commitment to speed, the conversations among the new influencers – always under way on blogs, in discussion forums and bulletin boards. Every company can thus be a media company by creating easily accessed, substantive online content that can be improved by the public.

Conclusion

The report concludes by saying that an adherence to transparency is at the core of each of Public Engagement's pillars. 'Organizations must be forthright and honest in their actions and communications. When problems arise within companies, stakeholders need to see senior executives take a visible lead in acknowledging errors, correcting mistakes, and working with employees to avoid similar problems going forward. The essence of Public Engagement is the commitment of companies to say - and do as they say. In a time of utter distrust as we are experiencing today, business leaders must make the case for actions and then demonstrate their progress against those goals.'

It is widely believed that without trust, it will be difficult for business to rebuild the financial system or have the license to innovate – much less operate in today's climate.

For more information visit:
http/www.edelman.com/trust.

Further reading

Babbie, E. 1992. *Practice of Social Research.* 6th Edition. Belmont, California: Wadsworth.

Baskin, O. & C.E. Aronoff. 1992. *Public Relations: The Profession and the Practice.* Dubuque: WC Brown.

Crimp, M. 1990. *The Marketing Research Process.* 3rd edition. Englewood Cliffs, New Jersey: Prentice-Hall.

Emdry, C.W. & D.R. Cooper. 1991. *Business Research Methods.* 4th Edition. Homewood, Illinois: Irwin.

Hendrix, J.A. 1992. *Public Relations Cases.* 2nd Edition. Belmont, California: Wadsworth.

Holtzhauzen, D. 1993. 'Public Relations Research Techniques.' Unpublished position paper prepared at the request of PRISA, Johannesburg.

Jefkins, F. 1998. *Public Relations.* London: M & E Pitman Publishing.

Jefkins, F. & F. Ugboajah. 1986. *Communication in Industrializing Countries.* Hong Kong: Macmillan.

Lubbe, B.A. & G. Puth. 1994. *Public Relations in South Africa: A Management Reader.* Johannesburg: Heinemann.

Mersham, G.M., R.S. Rensburg & J.C. Skinner. 1995. *Public Relations, Development and Social Investment: A Southern African Perspective.* Pretoria: J.L. Van Schaik.

Newsom, D., A. Scott & J. Van Slyke Turk. 1993. *This is PR: The Realities of Public Relations.* 5th Edition: Belmont, California: Wadsworth.

Study Guide 1. Public Relations Research and Information. Unpublished notes. Port Elizabeth: Nelson Mandela Metropolitan University.

Wilcox, D.L., P.H. Ault & W.K. Agee. 1995. *Public Relations: Strategies and Tactics.* New York: Harper & Row.

Wilcox, D.L. & G. Cameron. 2008. *Public Relations: Strategies and Tactics.* 9th edition. Needham Heights, Massachusetts: Allyn & Bacon Publishers.

Wimmer, R.D. & J.R. Dominick. 1983. *Mass Media Research: An Introduction.* California: Belmont.

There are a number of associations and private companies involved in the field.

Chapter 5

Public relations and marketing

When you have read this chapter, you should:

- be informed of the role of public relations with regard to marketing;

- be able to identify the key facets of marketing;

- be aware of the different relationships between public relations and marketing;

- know practical ways in which public relations can assist the marketing effort;

- be aware of the impact of the Internet on public relations and marketing practices.

As communicators, marketers and public relations practitioners have a lot in common. Both deal with organizational relationships and employ similar processes, techniques, and strategies. The two functions, however, have to be separated by mission or goal. Public relations has the goal of attaining and maintaining accord with social groups on whom the organization depends in order to achieve its mission. Marketing has the goal of attracting and satisfying customers on a sustained basis in order to achieve an organization's economic objectives.

Every organization therefore needs both a marketing and a public relations function. They are equally essential to organizational survival and success.

In practice, marketing consists of a co-ordinated programme of research, product design, packaging, pricing, promotion, and distribution (often referred to as 'place'). The goal of marketing is to attract and satisfy customers (or clients) on a long-term basis in order to achieve an organization's economic objectives. Its fundamental responsibility is to build and maintain a market for an organization's product and services.

Basic to the marketing function is the creation of a 'product' for a particular market segment – basic in that it uses market research to identify consumer needs. Public relations helps to create a two-way communication with the consumer, and assists marketing in recognizing certain consumer needs. Public relations techniques are also used to explain the marketer's problems, to tell the story of product complexity and of market pressures, and above all, to show how the consumer benefits from product improvement, research, and keen competition.

Prime facets of marketing

Before discussing the role of public relations and marketing, it is essential to understand the six prime facets of marketing. These are:

- research;
- merchandising;
- advertising;
- sales promotion;
- selling;
- public relations.

Research

This vitally important ingredient is applied in both public relations and marketing. We have to research the following:

- *The market.* What is the size of the market? What proportion do we hold? What is the projected size at selected points in the future? What share of this future market are we going for? What is the competition like and what are they doing?
- *The consumer.* To whom am I trying to sell?
- *The product.* How does my product or service compare with the opposition, and do I need to improve? If so, how and where is this improvement needed?
- *The attitude.* How does the target market perceive us?

Merchandising

A short but reasonably accurate definition of merchandising is 'the presentation of the product to the best advantage'.

By the use of combinations of light, sound, pricing, effective packaging, design and colour, and the selection of a good brand name, a product can be made to stand out from the competition's – to your advantage.

Advertising

From a sales angle, a good advertisement, whether it be on radio, television, or in print,

should always seek to:

- attract attention;
- arouse curiosity;
- convey a message;
- instil in the target's mind a wish to own or use the product;
- encourage the target's buying reaction by convincing him or her that the commodity is good value for money.

Sales promotion

Promotion usually involves short-term projects designed to push or give impetus to the product or service for a planned period by generating interest or excitement. Examples are product launches, fashion shows, special deals or dates (Mother's Day, Christmas, etc.), or loss leaders (products offered at a discount to attract buyers). Public relations can play a supportive role if carefully used in this area. Selling is what it's really all about, though. (See also Chapter 23 on promotional activities.)

Selling

Selling can be summed up as the activity which brings to a culmination all of the other efforts already covered. By handling affairs in such a way as to effect the transfer of ownership, the sales force clinches the deal. (See Chapter 7 on public relations and selling.)

Public relations in the marketing mix

Where should public relations be positioned in the corporate structure? This is an important question because it intimately concerns the marketing and public relations relationship.

Simply stated, public relations is a management function and not a mere tool – today's complex society and the level of skills and creativity required elevate it above that.

The general rule is that when engaged on corporate work, the public relations specialist should answer directly to the top person in the organization and enjoy a lateral working relationship with other managers in, for example, marketing, human resources, finance, and production. However, when involved in purely marketing projects he or she must become part of the team headed by the expert – the marketing executive – in so far as this person co-ordinates the activities of production, advertising, sales, and public relations. The public relations person has the same right to voice opinions and make recommendations as colleagues on the team, and is an 'equal partner' in the venture.

It is an accepted fact that there are basically four major variables in the marketing mix: price, product, promotion, and place (see diagram below).

Used in its broadest sense, 'promotion' must be seen as only one of the variables, but an important link in communicating information between seller and buyer – influencing attitudes and behaviour.

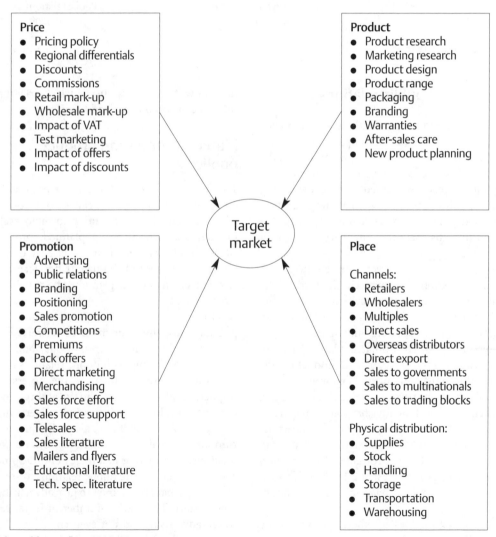

Price
- Pricing policy
- Regional differentials
- Discounts
- Commissions
- Retail mark-up
- Wholesale mark-up
- Impact of VAT
- Test marketing
- Impact of offers
- Impact of discounts

Product
- Product research
- Marketing research
- Product design
- Product range
- Packaging
- Branding
- Warranties
- After-sales care
- New product planning

Promotion
- Advertising
- Public relations
- Branding
- Positioning
- Sales promotion
- Competitions
- Premiums
- Pack offers
- Direct marketing
- Merchandising
- Sales force effort
- Sales force support
- Telesales
- Sales literature
- Mailers and flyers
- Educational literature
- Tech. spec. literature

Place

Channels:
- Retailers
- Wholesalers
- Multiples
- Direct sales
- Overseas distributors
- Direct export
- Sales to governments
- Sales to multinationals
- Sales to trading blocks

Physical distribution:
- Supplies
- Stock
- Handling
- Storage
- Transportation
- Warehousing

Target market

Adapted from Jefkins 1998: 10

Marketing Mix

Separate but equal functions

Equal, but overlapping

Marketing as dominant

Marketing and public relations as same function

Public relations as dominant

Source: Kotler: 1976

The role of public relations

Marketing and public relations are the major exterior functions of a company. Both functions start their analysis and planning from the point of view of satisfying one or more of the publics already identified. Before describing how public relations and marketing can best work together, we must identify the possible relationships between them (see diagram above).

For maximum effect, it is essential that public relations be involved right from the start in any campaign; indeed even in the absence of specific campaigns, constant liaison between public relations and marketing is a prerequisite for co-ordinated, planned activity in sustaining the company and product identity, positioning, and image. The input from the public relations person is valuable at all stages, whether it be of an advisory nature regarding public attitudes and so on, or expert recommendations and action relating to publicity back-up, literature production techniques, audiovisual possibilities, or related skills which professional public relations people should possess.

Having established where you should be positioned and what you can contribute, we

turn now to specifics. In which marketing spheres can you operate and how?

Market attitude and product publicity

This is probably one of the most noticeable areas where public relations can make a worthwhile and tangible contribution to the overall marketing effort. By using planned, professional public relations activity as part of an integrated approach formulated after accurate research, any marketing plan must be massively strengthened.

In some cases it may be wise to build up publicity to the launch with advertising (including direct mail, promotions, and so on), then combining with public relations in a co-ordinated exercise to make the necessary impact, and thereafter, maintaining the momentum. In other cases, an advertising tease campaign might be aided by planted rumours or small intriguing hints from public relations, culminating in a major effort. Some cases may even require public relations to soften up or prepare the market to give advertising a head start. There are a number of instances where advertising did not even enter into the picture until a very late stage, as we shall see in our study of the 'non-advertised position'. Whatever the circumstances, public relations has sufficient latitude and scope to supply effective results if skilfully used.

Consumerism is a growing power everywhere, and it can do a great deal of harm where misunderstanding exists. As far back as 1970, Dr Peter Drucker, well-known international writer on management themes, told the National Association of Manufacturers in the United States:

Consumerism means that the consumer looks upon the manufacturer as somebody who is interested, but who really doesn't know what the consumer's realities are.

He or she regards the manufacturer as somebody who has not made the effort to find out, who does not understand the world in which the consumer lives, and who expects the consumer to be able to make distinctions which the consumer is neither able nor willing to make.

As we have mentioned, the marketing person can use market research to help assess consumer attitudes, but this is really only part of the problem. Public relations, by creating two-way communication with the consumer, is often a far more effective aid in assisting marketing to appreciate and recognize consumer needs.

On the other hand, public relations techniques can be effectively used to put the company's side of the picture across: to explain marketers' problems, talk about product complexity, review market conditions and pressures, show how well companies are combating

these pressures, and above all, highlight how the consumer benefits from product improvement, research, and keen competition.

Then, too, business is already feeling the first twinges of discomfort from curbs placed on production as a result of pollution and environmental controls, and public relations can be a useful weapon in showing the other side of the coin.

Finally, legislative restrictions on certain types of product advertising have already become a feature of marketing overseas, although not in South Africa as yet, except in the case of tobacco. Public relations offers the only way of getting through in these cases.

Marketing communication

This is an area causing increasing concern to marketing people, who more than anyone else are conscious of the annual escalation in advertising costs. Today it costs more to reach the same target audience than it did yesterday, using the same media.

The impact and penetration of the paid sales message is an added worry. With the continual increase of commercial content in the mass media – the 'noise level' if you like – the consumer tends to 'tune out' of the traditional advertising message in sheer frustration.

Both of these situations can be alleviated by intelligent supplemental public relations work – getting the message across at low cost in a more subtle and credible way, using techniques such as third-party endorsement, editorial approval, or general market stimulation. The result will be an informed, well-disposed, and receptive consumer.

Extending the spread of the communications programme is another useful area for contribution by public relations. Advertising campaigns, in terms of the budgets available and because of rising costs, must concentrate on what research has shown to be the prime audience. Although this may comprise as little as 20 per cent of the consumer market, this segment may account for 80 per cent of the demand for the product by heavy usage.

Instead of regretfully ignoring the remaining 80 per cent of non-prime users, they can be reached by public relations techniques, which at the same time reinforce the prime target message.

Because public relations works with the complete and widely varied news and general media, it is not concerned with the spectre of waste circulation which haunts the advertising person.

Product launches

Product launches offer great possibilities for expanded coverage via public relations, whether the build-up is a slow 'leak' into the market, leading to greater things, or a launch function such as a promotional event or news conference. Back-up literature, photographs, and 'press kits' can all be prepared by the public relations practitioner, who also has the right media contacts to put together a guest list which will ensure maximum 'unpaid' penetration. His or her particular knowledge and skill are invaluable in liaison with radio and television personnel.

The ideal press kit or information pack should include the following:

- press releases written with either a technical (for trade media) or general slant;
- a selection of at least three good news photographs or possibly even artwork;
- a fact-sheet giving full details of the product and background information on how it was developed, by whom, over what period, why, when, its uses, differences it will make to the market, and similar information which may be relevant and interesting. (A fact-sheet enables the public relations person to present far more detailed information than the fundamental, hard-hitting facts already included in the press release.)

Public relations should also ensure that those media not invited receive a copy and material for publication, professionally prepared to achieve maximum effect.

Subtle pre-launch publicity might include 'softening up' the market or 'teasing' it to gen-erate the right climate at the launch, while planned follow-up activity maintains interest and exposure.

Areas to be explored for news potential might include features on personalities and the company; product development; unusual, unexpected, or exciting uses for the product; and new applications which open up novel and lucrative sales avenues. Export potential is another good slant, and of course anything which can result in a cut in production or living costs is always well received.

Sport sponsorship

Once a token gesture made by a marketing person to a chairperson obsessed with sport, sport sponsorship is now very much a weapon in the marketer's armoury.

That sponsorship is an invaluable form of relatively inexpensive publicity seems to be borne out by the very large number of sporting events currently sponsored by major firms: Standard Bank and MTN in cricket, ABSA, SAB and Vodacom in rugby, to name but a few.

The main point is that sport sponsorship works – particularly as visual impact on television can be combined with planned public relations follow-up to get maximum mileage. (Refer to Chapter 24 on sponsorships.)

Packaging, presentation, and product utility

In marketing 'packaged goods', advertising is the main communications tool, and the claims of a product on television, radio, and in the press continually remind the consumer of the benefits implicit in the package. Placement of that package in the supermarket, the attraction of its packaging, point-of-sale advertising, and promotion all contribute towards motivating the purchaser.

Sales promotion in the purest sense is not really a public relations concern. It tends to be one-way communication and does not concern itself with long-term effects. However, because it often involves the sympathetic attitude of the media, and frequently because sheer creativity in this sphere makes good news copy, public relations practitioners are often asked to assist in this type of programme.

Bearing in mind general management's concern for long-term results as well as product image, public relations should also keep a discreet watching brief to ensure that over-zealous promotional projects do not get out of hand.

In the packaging line, the public relations member of the marketing team (and remember, he or she should be involved at the very start of things) can make informed suggestions on the acceptability of the naming, colour, and design. For example, public relations practitioners have been known to contribute information on the choice of colours for Asian products, where colours have a social and religious significance. Because of their very practical streak, public relations specialists can often make very constructive suggestions on utility. A good example of this was the proposed packaging for an arthritic remedy, which featured a standard, round, screw-top lid. Following a recommendation by public relations specialists, it was found that a hexagonal lid was far more practical for a person crippled by the disease.

Customer education

Customer education by way of a public relations programme can do more than encourage correct use; it can also increase it. With certain commodities, the role of education is very important, so that the consumer is aware of the dangers of the product as well as the uses. This is the case with, for example, fertilizers, insecticides, medicines, detergents, and chemicals.

The non-advertised position

There are some areas where public relations can at least initially carry the entire marketing load and where it makes good strategic sense for it to do so. A classic example of this was the Witco Chemical launch of a new detergent, which took place in the United States.

The market was saturated with laundry detergent advertising (to the tune of around US $250 million a year), creating an intolerably high 'noise level'. It was obvious that it would be a prohibitively expensive exercise to launch an unknown brand and position it against numerous competitors through advertising, and so a public relations approach was decided on to introduce Active, the first non-advertised national brand of laundry detergent.

The non-advertised position became the news slant for an intensive public relations programme to reach consumers and consumer groups. Feature stories were flighted to women's food, living, and business pages in daily and weekly newspapers throughout New England, the selected launch area. An articulate economist was built up as the product's regional consumer spokesperson and appeared on radio and television talk shows, at speaking engagements for women's service, religious, fraternal, and consumer organizations, and on educational campuses. In-store promotions, where she met with and spoke to consumers, were also arranged.

The result? In the first three months, and at minimal expense, Active achieved 80 per cent supermarket distribution and more than 1,5 million consumers were reached through the media. With its product presence firmly established, advertising could again play its role with supplementary public relations activity to help retain the detergent's position.

Relations between dealers and distributors

Relations between dealers and distributors can frequently be enhanced by the use of public relations, and in many organizations this is recognized as an important public relations function. Dealer journals, visits, promotions, general co-operation, and publicity are all methods of motivating and achieving a happy commercial association and two-way communication with this valuable company 'public'. Where a dealer is selling a variety of essentially similar products, it is more often than not the company with whom he or she has the happiest relationship whose goods are given preference and recommendation.

Consumer complaints

Consumer complaints represent one of the reactive as opposed to innovative aspects of public relations activity. Elsewhere we discuss the creation, maintenance, and influencing of consumer attitudes, but unfortunately there comes a time for virtually every company when something goes wrong and a complaint is made. If it is fortunate, management can handle the issue and sort it out amicably before the issue bursts into print. But where the latter does occur, the public relations practitioner is the best person to intervene through media liaison and to put forward positive factors to improve the position.

This is an area where great tact and careful manoeuvring are called for, and one where a considerable amount of damage can result if the public relations person does not handle it properly. As a general rule, never have more than one spokesperson and take the time to look at the problem from every conceivable angle before replying. It should not be necessary to do more than mention reputation and integrity as two key words for personal conduct.

Employee attitude

In this vitally important area, the public relations person can profitably add his or her efforts to those of the marketing managers in motivating and guiding sales staff from the top to the bottom rungs of the rank structure. This can be done by encouragement, personal and product publicity in-house and externally, and by assisting in the provision of aids and well-compiled material for market promotion and training.

Positioning

By 'positioning' we do not merely mean the physical location of the product in the supermarket or its shelf position relative to the opposition's offering, but also its 'image' or identity relative to that of the competition. The latter aspect is very definitely a public relations responsibility as well as an advertising one.

What is positioning? You can demonstrate the basic principle by asking yourself a few questions: Who was the first person to fly solo across the North Atlantic? Charles Lindbergh, right? Now, can you name the second person? Not so easy, is it? What's the highest mountain in the world? Mount Everest of course. But the second highest?

The first person, the highest mountain, the best company: whichever occupies the position in the prospect's mind is usually very hard to dislodge. Toyota in cars, De Beers in diamonds and Coca-Cola in soft drinks. If a company or brand is not the first to occupy the position in the prospect's mind, it has a positioning problem.

Advertising executives are acutely conscious of this and direct considerable effort toward gaining the upper hand for 'their' product. Public relations practitioners should do the same, for they have a very significant role to play in dislodging the opposition or maintaining their company or product's position by sustained and innovative activity.

Always remember the old saying, 'You never get a second chance to make a first impression.'

Integrated marketing communication

The practice of integrated marketing communication is emerging as one of the most valuable tools companies can use to gain competitive advantage. Advertising, sales promotion, direct marketing, and public relations practitioners are finding common ground to meet the future challenges of selling to individual customers rather than markets.

The critical issues for most marketers is their ability to control the information consumers use to form and adjust their attitudes, especially as most consumers do not differentiate between the sources of information. A new source of information is the Internet.

Most marketers today face a parity marketplace in which the only true differentiating features are either logistics or communications. A company's marketing is, therefore, being increasingly defined by the customer's agenda. In such an environment, the emphasis will be placed more on developing good relationships between the marketer and the client, and less on the transaction itself.

A successful integrated marketing communication model requires:

- *Building a database of information on both customers and prospects.* What are their demographics, psychographics, and purchase history with you? Are they loyal users of your brand?

- *Formulating a contact management policy.* This will determine what will be communicated about the product or service and the conditions under which the communication will be delivered.

- *Developing a communications strategy.* This involves deciding how the message will be delivered, given the context (contact management) in which it will appear.

- *Setting marketing objectives.* These vary between brand-loyal customers and competitive users, but each can be measured and quantified.

- *Selecting the various techniques to achieve the established marketing and communication objectives.* These include direct marketing, advertising, sales promotion, public relations, and sponsorships.

The key to success in this integrated marketing communication planning approach is that all forms of communication are designed to achieve specific objectives. These objectives come from understanding how the marketer can contact the customer or prospect and interpreting the message to be communicated. All efforts are, therefore, devoted to satisfying customer needs or wants at a competitive price. Increasingly this will be provided through the touch of a button through digital technology and e- and t-commerce.

An integrated marketing communication checklist is provided on page 376.

Impact of the Internet

There is no doubt that the Internet is changing the face of public relations and marketing. Theoretically it sounds like a public relations and marketer's dream, as individuals and organizations can communicate directly with each other regardless of distance or time. Through multimedia, products and services can be marketed using full-colour graphics, sound, and video. Broadcasting and publishing will never be the same again.

The Internet has many faces and can be experienced in many different ways, depending on the purpose for which it is being used. Its three best-known faces are discussed below.

The World Wide Web (www)

The web allows individuals and organizations to display information, for all the world to see, in the form of text, photos, graphics, sound, animation, and even video. It is also a system for linking documents through 'hyperlinks'.

Electronic mail (e-mail)

E-mail enables subscribers to send letters, via the Internet, to anyone in the world who also has an e-mail address. Before the web, e-mail was the most powerful tool available to business on the Internet.

Newsgroups

Newsgroups are discussion forums conducted entirely by e-mail, but with contributions called 'postings' rather than messages or letters. Each message is 'posted' to the newsgroup in an on-line equivalent of a bulletin board. There are more than 20 000 newsgroups dedicated to specific interests, hobbies, and current affairs.

"KICK POLIO OUT OF AFRICA"
ROTARY MOVES BALL THROUGH 22 POLIO-AFFECTED COUNTRIES

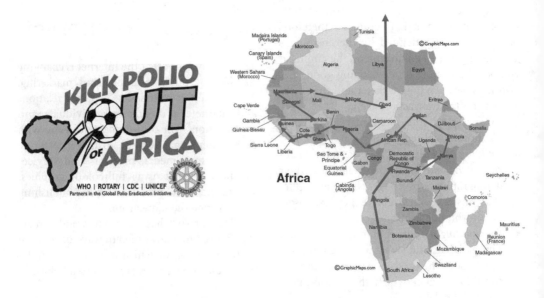

Source: http://www.southafrica.info/2010/fifa-090107.htm. Downloaded on 20 October 2009.

The role of the website in the marketing communication mix

While personal selling is usually the largest single item in the business-to-business marketing communication mix, broadcast advertising is typically the dominant method used to reach consumers. The website is something of a mix between personal selling (it can engage the visitors in a dialogue) and advertising (it can be designed to generate awareness, explain and demonstrate the product, and provide information – without interactive involvement). It can play a cost-effective role in the marketing communication mix, in the early stages of the process, by enabling need recognition, development of product specifications, and supplier search, but it can also be very potent as the buying process progresses toward evaluation and selection. The site can also be cost-effective in providing feedback on product or service performance. Thus, websites can typically be viewed as complementary to the direct selling activity by industrial marketers, and as supplementary to broadcast advertising by consumer marketers.

Recently, websites have been used to achieve the objectives of a number of marketing strategies:

- gaining access to previously unknown or inaccessible buying influences;
- projecting a favourable image;
- providing product information;
- fostering and encouraging consumer involvement with the product range;
- handling customer complaints, queries, and suggestions;
- serving as an electronic coupon device.

In summary, different organizations may have different marketing objectives for establishing and maintaining a web presence. One organization might wish to use the web as a means of introducing itself and its new products to a potentially wide international audience, to create corporate and product awareness, and to inform the market. On the other hand, if the web surfer knows of the firm and its products, then net dialogue can be used to propel this customer down to the lower phases in the buying progression. Another firm may be advertising and marketing well-known existing products, and its website objectives could be to solicit feedback from current customers as well as informing new customers, thus facilitating post-purchase evaluation.

Conclusion

Public relations invariably has a corporate responsibility embracing stakeholder relations, social involvement, and employee relations, among others. However, in a marketing environment, public relations should also aim to contribute to the sales and marketing objectives of the company.

Case study   Social marketing... the way of the future

What the experts predict.
Social marketing according to Dr James Canton, futurist, Chairman, and CEO of the Institute for Global Futures is an important new development that should not be ignored.

'How customers will buy into and business will sell will change. The convergence of TV, Internet, and wireless telephony across interactive, fast, real-time broadband networks is the click-stream. Every business must learn to understand the new click-stream customer, the online, multi-billion dollar buyer of fashion, games, stocks, media, health, information, and entertainment. This is a new customer who defies advertising, commercials, and traditional metrics.'

Social marketing can be broken down into two components: marketing on the web and mobile marketing. One should note that marketing on the web includes new Internet developments and trends. Hands-on interactivity with these tools unlock limitless marketing opportunities. Mobile marketing makes use of cellphone technology and the launch of mobile TV, sure to be popular during the 2010 FIFA World Cup, is set to unlock the mobile TV advertising market. While expensive bandwidth demands creative solutions, this is definitely an industry on the rise.

Dave Duarte of Creative Commons SA says social media marketing looks at ways to use technology to engage today's busy consumer on their terms. "Technologically speaking, there are two important components: Web and mobile marketing. Marketing on the web has recently been enhanced with the rise of blogs, social- networks, wikis and other web-based tools such as widgets, aggregators and search engines, which allow consumers to co-create brands and marketing. Mobile marketing technologies allow an even greater level of participation and personalisation, as well as the opportunity to engage with consumers in specific contexts. These technologies include SMS, WAP, mobile web games and GPS mashups, among other exciting new sites and tools. Perhaps even more important is the social and cultural shifts that have accompanied these developments.'

According to Gino Cosme, Founder and Chief Navigator of Cosmedia, having presence in the online environments that your target audience populates is priceless. 'The power of peer-to-peer referrals means word-of-mouth or viral marketing is one of the most effective advertising methods available to your brand. Social Media Marketing (SMM) focuses on creating opportunities for customers to associate themselves with your brand. It is also a proactive activity which monitors customers' dialogues – both good and bad- about your brand, through media monitoring and evaluation methodologies; which in turn leads to being proactive in engaging in the conversations that comprise social media marketing. Once you are in their space, SMM gives you the opportunity to discover your target market's feelings and experiences about your product, which again gives you competitive advantage.' This is evident if you examine ABSA's and FNB's Facebook pages, which allow customers to comment freely on the banks' walls and spark debate on any issue-good or bad.

Melissa Attree, social media consultant and online brand strategist says that if content is well-developed and positioned (content is king) then a brand's message will travel across different forms of social media, such as YouTube, Facebook, Twitter, blogs and the like. 'User-generated content makes up a very large percentage of the web, so if users start creating content for a brand, then the word-of-mouth perception may be higher'. Word-of-mouth and viral marketing form a key component of social media marketing campaigns.

Social media specialist Gino Cosme explains that an effective social or online marketing campaign must 'generate a lead; communicate an important message; improve reputation; cut down costs; and/or establish a relationship with current and potential customers, brand enthusiasts, and supporters.' Social media marketing takes this into account by engaging visitors with genuine, relevant two-way conversations and interactions related to their business. FoodCrEATions, the new baking community homepage sponsored by Stork, is a good example of this. The site offers users the opportunity to create profiles, blog about baking, and load their personal favourite (Stork) recipes on the page.

Universal McCann's latest global survey, titled 'When did we start trusting strangers?' looks at the increasing importance of social media, blogs and 'word of mouse' referrals from one complete stranger to another and emphasizes the fact that trustworthiness can be easily developed in cyberspace. Social marketing is thus becoming increasingly relevant and important. Based on a survey of 17 000 Internet users in 29 countries, the study examines the growth of consumer recommendations and the tools that drive it across the globe.

Universal McCann's MD, Nazeer Suliman, explains that in the past, mass media offered little in terms of audience interaction or recommendation. 'Readers' letters in newspapers and magazines or live radio phone-ins were as far as interaction and consumer influence went. Today, opinions and experiences are shared worldwide. Never before have we been exposed to so many opinions and recommendations from so many people- many of whom are strangers, without the aura of expertise or celebrity recognition.'

Mobile marketing

Mobile SMS marketing is a semi-new form of marketing, which uses the global communication medium of the cellular phone and SMS and MMS, to get your message across to an increased number of targeted consumers.

Marketing on a mobile phone has become increasingly popular since its launch in early 2000s. The Mobile Marketing Association says that mobile phones are now used for much more than just voice services, as mobile users also have access to data services such as text messaging, picture messaging and content downloads. Of key importance to marketers is that these channels carry both content and advertising.

According to Intoweb Marketing's e-traffic site, 'a number of big business companies are starting to recognize the advantages that this marketing medium can provide, such as immediacy and immense cost savings. Intoweb adds that the emergence of mobile marketing means that more customers can be reached than with traditional advertising methods, as they are targeted directly through their cell phones.'

There has been a definite surge in cellular phone technology in South Africa. Mobile marketing trends in the country now reach beyond SMS marketing to encompass marketing on WAP, MXit, Bluetooth, full multimedia Third Generation (3G) services, and mobile TV- which is sure to be popular during the 2010 FIFA World Cup. While expensive bandwidth demands creative solutions, this is definitely an industry that is on the rise.

According to Adam Clayton Powell III, vice-provost of the University of Southern California, speaking during his presentation on Technology for the Digital Citizen at Highway Africa in Grahamstown recently said: 'In addition to television and the personal computer, the most powerful future technology for the digital citizen is the mobile phone'. He adds that for the digital citizen using a mobile phone, keypad, and screen size can be an issue -- particularly when viewing advertising messages. Another challenge, especially in the third world, is the limited bandwidth available for the digital citizen to send and receive data, which has a large impact on the effectiveness of mobile marketing. This notwithstanding, Powell III concludes: 'The future is definitely one cellphone per child'.

Mobile marketing therefore, has a very important role to play in the future of marketing.

Research into this field has been conducted by Newsclip Media Monitoring to which full acknowledgement is made.

Further reading

Cohen, W.R. 1987. *Developing a Winning Marketing Plan*. Toronto: John Wiley.

DuBrey, W. 1991. *Profit from Effective Marketing*. Cape Town: Juta.

Duffy, N. & J. Cooper. 2003. *Passion Branding*. New Jersey: John Wiley and Sons.

Du Plessis, Jooste & Strydom. 2001. *Applied Strategic Marketing*. Johannesburg: Heineman.

Engel, J.F., M.R. Warshaw & T.C. Kinnear. 1994. *Promotional Strategy: Managing the Marketing Communications Process*. 8th Edition. Ontario: Irwin.

Internet guidelines. 1999. Bryanston: Association of Marketers.

Jefkins, F. 1998. *Public Relations*. London: M&E Pitman Publishing.

Koekemoer, L. (ed.) 1998. *Promotional Strategy*. Cape Town: Juta.

Koekermoer, L. (ed.) 2004. *Marketing Communications*. Cape Town: Juta.

Kotler, P. & G. Armstrong. 1991. *Principles of Marketing*. Englewood Cliffs, New Jersey: Prentice-Hall.

Kotler, P. 1976. *Marketing Management*. New York: Prentice-Hall.

Machado, R. & M. Cant. 2008. *Marketing Success Stories*. Cape Town: Oxford University Press.

Marx, S. & A. van der Walt. 1993. *Marketing Management*. Cape Town: Juta.

McCarthy, E.J. & W.D. Perrault. 1993. *Basic Marketing*. 10th edition. Boston: Irwin.

McDonald, M.H.B. 1989. *Marketing Plans: How to Prepare Them, How to Use Them*. London: Professional Publishing.

Rayport & Jaworski. 2001. *E-Commerce*. 1st edition. New York: McGraw-Hill.

Sanchez & Heene. 2004. *The New Strategic Management*. New Jersey: John Wiley and Sons.

Schultz, D.E., S.I. Tannenbaum & R.F. Lauterborn. 1996. *The New Marketing Paradigm*. Chicago, Illinois: Stanton, W.J.

Stone, Merlin, et al. 2003. *The Definitive Guide to Direct and Interactive Marketing*. London: Prentice-Hall.

Chapter 6

Public relations and advertising

When you have read this chapter, you should:

- know the basic requirements for good advertising;

- understand the structure, departments, and their functions of an advertising agency;

- be familiar with a simple, practical checklist for judging the qualities of any advertisement;

- be aware of how a creative strategy is developed;

- be familiar with some of the bodies serving the advertising industry.

Despite the vast sums spent on advertising – over R15 billion a year in South Africa – it is still regarded as the most economical means of communicating information from one source to a mass audience in the shortest space of time. Furthermore, without advertisements newspapers would cost up to 10 times their present price, television licences up to five times more, and magazines up to three times more.

Public relations and advertising are often confused in the public's mind, but they are essentially two different disciplines. Public rela-

tions establishes mutual understanding and good relationships with all the organization's target publics and is aimed at the long term.

Advertising, in its broadest sense, concentrates on one of the organization's target publics, namely its consumers, and is aimed at making them aware of its products and services, and persuading them to buy these products and services.

To be effective, good advertising has to meet certain basic requirements. It has to be developed according to clear objectives and with a precise strategy statement. It should also address itself to a well-defined group of potential users of a product or service in a language and style they understand. Distinct and easily recognizable differences between the product and its competition must be highlighted. Above all, the message must be clear and concise.

Advertising, however, is but one element in the marketing mix and on its own, cannot achieve the final objective of the marketing campaign, the sale itself. Its task is simply to inform, announce, influence, persuade, and educate. These very same tasks are also the responsibility of public relations. So, how do they work together? If a product is new, then it may require the services of public relations to achieve consumer acceptance. This was the case with a revolutionary form of damp-proofing

The advertising process

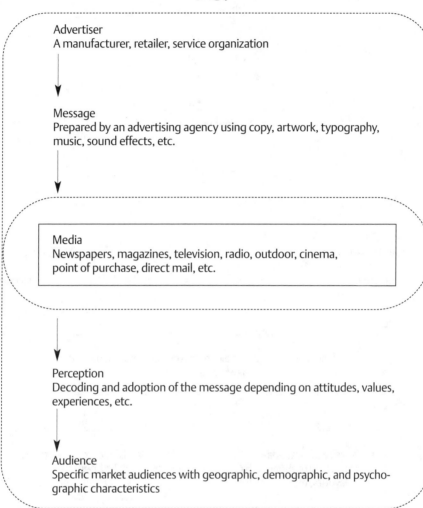

Advertiser
A manufacturer, retailer, service organization

Message
Prepared by an advertising agency using copy, artwork, typography, music, sound effects, etc.

Media
Newspapers, magazines, television, radio, outdoor, cinema, point of purchase, direct mail, etc.

Perception
Decoding and adoption of the message depending on attitudes, values, experiences, etc.

Audience
Specific market audiences with geographic, demographic, and psychographic characteristics

Advertiser's field of experience

Audience's field of experience

Adapted from Koekemoer. 1998: 56

system introduced in Britain by Rentokil. It required a massive public relations programme before it was advertised in order to prove by example and education that the system worked. In the same way, time share as a concept had to be explained to the South African public before extensive advertising of schemes was embarked upon. Another application of public relations is to achieve acceptability and a reputation for a company before the consumer will buy its products. This is all part of corporate identity and the need to establish the correct image. It is not necessary to know, however, that Surf is made by Unilever for the consumer to purchase

it. It is a product with its own reputation and is sufficiently inexpensive for its origin and pedigree not to be important.

On the other hand, it is necessary to know the stability of a bank or insurance company before investing in its product or to have assurances about the continuing service that will be given by an appliance company or motor manufacturer before one buys its products.

Advertising can assist public relations with corporate announcements, such as listing statements and special supplements, and with the research input and design of corporate advertisements.

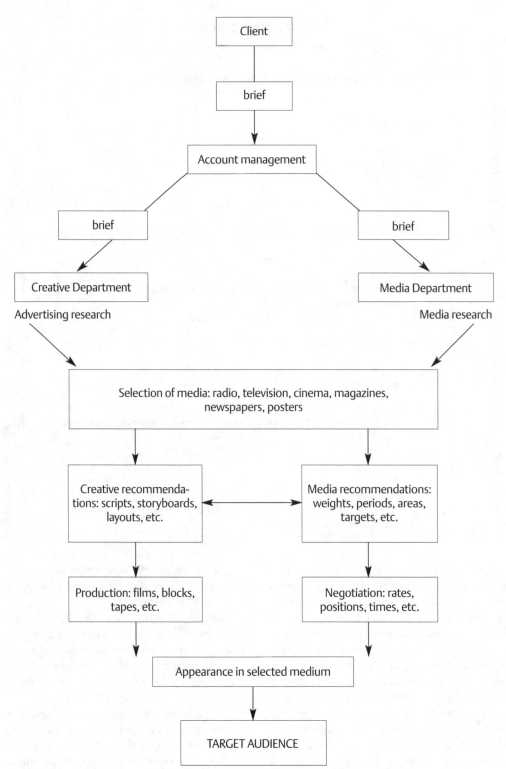

Adapted from Sinclair 1996: 37. *The South African Advertising Book: Make the Other Half Work too.*

The agency

An advertising agency has various specialist departments. The main ones are now discussed (see diagram on page 60).

Account management

The clients of an advertising agency are referred to in advertising jargon as 'accounts'. Agency people speak of 'the Volkswagen account', 'the Kleenex account', 'the IBM account', and so on. Responsibility for providing the appropriate service to a client is the responsibility of the account management team.

Each client of the agency has one or more account executives (depending on the size and complexity of the task and the level of expenditure). Other titles, such as account managers, are also sometimes used. These people are the point of contact between the client and the agency. It is their job to understand the client's business and advertising needs sufficiently to translate them into a brief to other agency staff. Usually the account executive (or his or her senior, the account director) is largely responsible for all campaign planning within the agency on the client's behalf. Normally this is done in close consultation with the client's own staff.

Creative department

The creative department contains the 'ideas people', who are able to express in words and pictures the essence of the benefits that have to be communicated to customers. They work to a brief from the account management staff. Copywriters produce the verbal elements and visualizers (the visual elements of the story), usually working side by side, and the basic idea of the advertisement comes from either or both of them.

Media department

Media executives analyse readership and viewing figures, compare costs of space and time, and recommend which media should be used for a particular advertising task. (Computer techniques are often used for the complex data-handling that may be necessary.) The job of these specialists is twofold: media planning and media buying. Once the plan is agreed, space and time must be bought (often some hard bargaining takes place) and media schedules are drawn up for everyone to work to. These show copy dates – the dates, often weeks ahead of publication, by when the publishers need material.

Production department

Designs for advertising campaigns emerge from the creative department in rough form – as copy and layout (typescript and a drawing or photograph) from which material will be printed, and as a storyboard (a series of 'stills', again with typescript) for television. Although these are spoken of as roughs (or visuals), they may look quite polished. Instead of using storyboards, television campaigns may be presented on videotape. Whatever method is chosen, the aim is to let everyone in the client's (advertiser's) company and in the agency see what the campaign will look like, without incurring the full cost of photography, finished illustrations, typesetting, models, actors, scenery, and props.

From these roughs the final product is developed. It is the task of the creative department to supervise the development and ensure that the final result is what was intended.

Planning and logistics are the responsibility of the production department. They order material, plan dates, chase suppliers, and generally ensure that jobs are completed in time to meet copy dates.

Sometimes there is also a traffic control department, to ensure the smooth passage of each campaign through all its stages, in order to meet the important copy dates when films, blocks, or artwork must reach the media.

Typical advertising agency organization chart

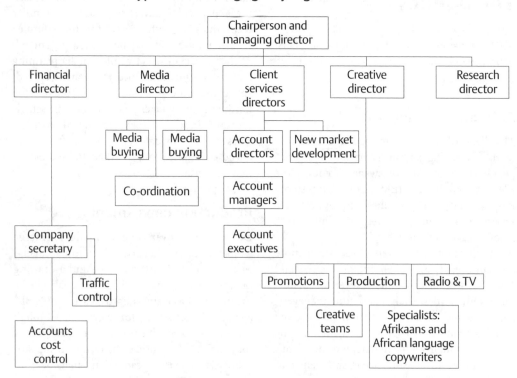

Other specialist departments

Each agency has a number of departments with special functions, in addition to departments such as accounting and human resources that are found in most companies. These departments vary from one agency to another, but may include marketing research, sales promotion, direct mail, exhibitions and display, and public relations. The exact mix depends on the agency's specialization and on the kind of client for whom it works. As profits become harder to maintain, there is a growing tendency for specialist departments to be hived off as separate trading units, or even separate companies, and made to stand on their own feet commercially.

Advertising agencies use the services of many other people and organizations: film production companies and photographers, model agencies, art studios, individual freelance writers and artists, blockmakers, printers, and so on. Advertisers too, deal directly with these people for some of their promotional material, even when they use an agency for most of the work.

How to judge a good advertisement

The most valuable commodity an advertising agency can offer its client is a good idea. This is because, while competent service can create happiness and a department store of facilities can give a feeling of security, only a good idea can bring riches, by drawing attention to the product itself and the advantages it offers. Above all else, a good idea is relevant to the product it promotes and meaningful to the consumer it addresses. Combining these two qualities is the essence of sound advertising practice.

Principles of good brand advertising

These principles reveal the characteristics of good brand advertising:

- *It is consumer orientated.* The benefits answer the needs of the consumer and the 'language' of the advertising makes it easy for consumers to see this. It is their language; it puts the case as the consumer sees it, not as a manufacturer or distributor sees it.
- *It concentrates on one selling idea.* It does not scatter its efforts or diffuse its impact. It establishes a penetrating, memorable reason for trial. (Note: 'Concentrates on' means that the advertisement draws attention to the selected basic consumer benefit. It does not mean that it is never right to make more than one claim in an advertisement.)
- *It concentrates on the most important and persuasive idea available.* It must be the true key to the consumer's mind. Research must establish whether the advertisement has this all-important quality.
- *It presents a unique and competitive idea.* It contains the promise of a unique benefit – of a unique quantity or quality of the benefit, at least.
- *It involves the consumer.* It gets attention and maintains it. It is personal. It appeals to the consumer's self-interest. It solves the consumer's problem. It uses the advertiser's knowledge that the consumer's motivation comes from both the heart and the head.
- *It is credible and sincere.* It is true. And it rings true – consumers feel that the advertiser is honest and knows what is being talked about. This principle does not rule out the use of exaggeration. 'Larger than life' expression of claims – provided that it does not mislead – is seen to be devoid of the intention to mislead, and is the best way of making claims clearly, forcefully, entertainingly, and persuasively.
- *It is simple, clear, and complete.* There is no possibility of misunderstanding. And it says all that the copy strategy calls for.
- *It clearly associates the selling idea with the brand name.* It clearly registers the brand name and links it with the selling idea.
- *It takes full advantage of the medium.* Certain selling ideas are better suited to one medium than another. Effective advertising uses the right medium for its purpose – and takes full advantage of its physical characteristics and the mood to which it predisposes consumers.
- *It makes the sale.* It establishes a strong wish to buy – so strong that a gentle reminder from displayed stock or a showcard in the shop will clinch the sale.

Brand awareness

Market research company, Ipsos Markinor, has been tracking consumer awareness of and confidence in brands since 1992. Until 2000, the findings related only to spontaneous awareness and levels of trust in a particular brand in several categories. In 2001, however, it incorporated a loyalty factor into the survey. These three scores have been combined to produce a Brand Relationship Score. The main categories are retailers and shops, fast food outlets, banks/financial institutions, cards, cellphones, food products, soft drinks, alcoholic beverages, cigarettes, over-the-counter medicines, vitamins, magazines, newspapers, and petrol, and from time to time, new categories are added.

South Africa's overall favourite brand

Coca-Cola is by far South Africa's favourite brand in both the metro and non-metro areas. There is big gap before SAB and Nike in second and third places, followed by Vodacom, Pick n Pay, Eskom, Nokia, MTN, Toyota, and BMW (2008 figures). Coca-Cola continues to be the leading brand in the build up to the Fifa 2010 World Cup in South Africa, as well as being the international brand leader.

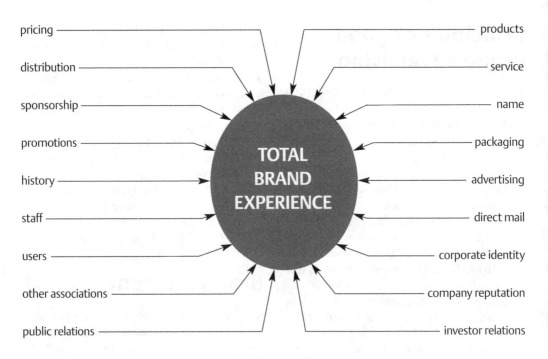

Source: Interbrand Sampson. 2010

Best Global Brands by value

	2008 Brand value million	Change in Brand value	2007 Brand value million
Coco Cola	$66,667	2%	$65,324
IBM	$59,301	3%	$57,090
Microsoft	$59,007	1%	$58,709
General Electric	$53,085	1%	$51,569
Nokia	$35,942	7%	$33,696
Toyota	$34,050	6%	$32,070
Intel	$31,261	1%	$30,954
McDonald's	$31,049	6%	$29,398
Disney	$29,251	0%	$29,210
Google	$25,590	43%	$17,837

Source: Interbrand. 2008

Company operating in South Africa that has done the most for community upliftment

As well as being South Africa's favourite brand, Coca-Cola is also seen as the company that has done the most for community upliftment. This is followed by Vodacom, SAB, Eskom, Pick n Pay, MTN, Telkom, ABSA, Sasol, Clover (2008 figures). Interesting how SAB, once it acknowledged that it was not simply a company owning brands, but a corporate brand in its own right, has propelled itself to the fore.

International brand identity

According to a survey by Business Week and Interbrand, Coca-Cola is still the world's most valuable brand at a staggering $67 000 million. It is followed by IBM, Microsoft, GE, Nokia, Toyota, Intel, McDonalds, Disney, and Google. The average age of these top ten most valuable brands is 74 years, despite the entry of Google at number 10, the fastest growing brand (born August 1998), and by far the youngest. The full list is available from *http://bwnt.businessweek.com/brand/2008*.

Creative strategy

Creative strategy is the key to the creative process and should serve as a 'road map' for all communications. This should be prepared by the marketing department in response to a brief and agreed to by the consultancy agency before creative work is commenced. The creative strategy document serves as the basis for creative development and as a check against presented work.

The following 10 points are to be considered when preparing a creative strategy:

Background

This section merely sets the scene. It provides a framework from which to view the strategy.

Brand values

This includes those associations (of which there could be a number) which come to mind about the brand or product, for example traditional, strong, locally manufactured, aromatic. It is a critically important area and central to creative thinking. Many brands are now global and need to be aligned internationally.

Target market

This is clearly an important area. It identifies at whom the message is directed, both demographically and psychographically.

Demographics refers to statistically based information. Psychographics is attitudinal information on the 'kind' of person for whom the message is intended. This should not be confused with the existing user profile.

Brand positioning

This area is the key to the whole strategy. It refers to how the product should be positioned in the minds of the identified target audience.

Brand promise

This refers to what the product or service offers the defined prospect and is often referred to as the consumer promise. It can be tangible or non-tangible, depending on the strategy, and should be simple and single-minded.

Reason why

This is the substance to verify position and promise. What are the consumer benefits? 'What's in it for me?'

Supporting evidence

Further detail may be included to support the promise made in response to the consumer's question of 'What's in it for me?' It is not mandatory but may spark off several creative thoughts. It is essentially a 'back-up' to the key message.

Executional considerations

These refer to suggested inputs for consideration by the creative team.

Creative requirements

These refer to the details identified by the agency for the application of concepts such as media specifications, number of advertisements required, etc.

Timing

Timing involves a critical path analysis outlining deadline dates. In addition, the following attitudes can be included:

- *Existing attitudes.* Designed to illustrate existing attitudes among the target market group prior to being exposed to the planned message.
- *Desired attitudes.* Having been exposed to the advertising message, the resultant communication should elicit this response.

The key to a successful strategy therefore lies in a close grasp and understanding of brand values, target market, brand positioning, and brand promise. The rest of the information is to add further perspective and aid the creative process. A good strategy should be kept as simple as possible with regard to the key areas mentioned above. Refer back to pages 35–40 for an example of an advertising research brief and proposal.

Advertising bodies

The advertising industry is served by various bodies, such as the Association of Advertising Agencies, the Advertising Standards Authority, the South African Advertising Research Foundation, and the South African Market Research Association.

The All Media and Products Survey (AMPS) is now firmly established as the definitive study covering adults, aged 16 years and over, throughout South Africa. It provides an ongoing, up-to-date picture of the economic well-being and development of South African adults and households. AMPS, together with the Radio Audience Measurement Survey (RAMS) and Television Audience Measurement Survey (TAMS), provides a common currency for the buying of cinema, outdoor, print, radio, and television advertising space and time.

The South African Advertising Research Foundation (SAARF) has established a Scenario Sub-Committee to review trends that could impact on the media scene during the next ten years. The results of the First SAARF media research project have been published in a report entitled 'Scenarios: anticipating stakeholders' needs' by the chairman of SAARF, Professor Clive Corder. It is available from SAARF at saarf@saarf.co.za together with a host of other key research reports.

Further reading

Arens, W.F. 2006. *Contemporary Advertising.* 10th edition. New York: McGraw-Hill.

De Beer, A.S. (ed.) 1998. *Mass Media Towards the Millenium: The South African Handbook of Mass Communication.* Pretoria: J.L. Van Schaik.

Koekemoer, L. 1991. *Profit from Effective Advertising.* Cape Town: Juta.

Koekemoer, L. 1998. *Marketing Communications.* Cape Town: Juta.

Mersham, G.M. & J.C. Skinner. 2001. *New Insights into Media and Communication.* Johannesburg: Heinemann.

Sinclair, R.W. 1996. *The South African Advertising Book: Make The Other Half Work Too.* Halfway House: International Thomson Publishing.

Wilmshurst, J. & A. Mackay. 1999. *The Fundamentals of Advertising.* Oxford: Butterworth-Heinemann.

The Encyclopaedia of Brands and Branding 2008. *Brands and Branding 2009.* 2nd edition. *The Economist*/Interbrand.

Brand Valuation (Interbrand) various contributing writers including J.D.R. Sampson.

Both *Financial Mail* and *Finweek* publish annual advertising surveys.

Chapter 7

Public relations and selling

When you have read this chapter, you should:

- be able to identify how public relations can assist the sales effort;
- understand how public relations, marketing, and sales interact;
- be aware of how public relations can contribute to better customer relations.

It is rare for management to consider public relations as a major aid to sales activity. It unfortunately tends to be one of the last 'marketing' tools to be brought into the sales strategy after an advertising programme has been worked out.

However, a new kind of teamwork is being created which involves the public relations executive as fully as any member of the marketing team. A salesperson who is motivated and believes in the product sells it far better than one who is not. The same applies to the trade. The introduction of a product has to involve more than just 'showing' it and presenting facts about the market. It has to be a total exercise in public relations and motivation. The diagram on page 66 shows the interaction between the salesperson and the customer.

Most people believe that the public relations practitioner's role in marketing simply involves thinking out clever and unusual ways of getting media coverage. Nothing could be further from the truth. Public relations has a distinct function which has to do with presenting a company and its products before a variety of experts whose opinions are considered authoritative and relatively objective by the public. This process, which can take place through the whole range of marketing activities, from the inception of the product idea to the first sales pitch, presents management with a new dimension of sales planning and development.

The different functions in the sales area – marketing, advertising, sales promotion, and public relations – are interrelated, and complement each other. It is difficult to decide where responsibility for the one begins and the other ends. But it is clear that through the co-ordination of the different functions more effective sales activities can be undertaken.

If marketing public relations is to be effective, certain set rules must be followed:

- The plan must have the full support of top management.
- Information must be available from all areas of the company.

Selling step by step

The customer		The salesperson

Attention ←——————→ Approach the customer so that you establish an awareness of what you are going to do and say.

Interest ←——————→ Ask questions to determine real needs and wants.

Creating confidence ←——————→ You have less than 60 seconds to convince the customer to continue to listen to you, because you have indicated that you can solve the problem.

Selling the product ←——————→ Show how its features have distinct customer benefits.

Creating the desire ←——————→ Review major benefits and additional benefits so that you create a realization that your product could solve the customer's problem.

Buying signals ←——————→ Watch for signals that the customer is deciding to buy.

Action ←——————→ Ask the customer to purchase your product, thereby creating a conviction that a good buying decision has been made.

- The programme must be well planned in advance and reported on regularly.
- There must be set objectives.
- There should be a commitment to continuing activity.
- Those responsible for the programme must keep the sales target constantly in sight.
- Most important of all, the programme must be properly merchandised, both to the salesperson and the consumer.

Consumer-orientated planning

Good consumer-orientated planning involves mentally placing yourself in your prospect's position and viewing the proposition as it would appear from his or her perspective. The four basic steps are attention, interest, desire, and action. They are commonly known as the AIDA principle. These four steps can be expanded in numerous ways, depending on experience, the type of product, and the specific industry. Careful advance planning according to the AIDA principle will greatly increase your chances of success.

Attention

It is important to gain the prospect's attention and interest so that he or she will willingly give the information that will enable you to determine his or her needs and wants. It is around these needs and wants that you will have to build the appeal of your product in terms of its benefits and value to the customer.

Interest

As in the previous step, it is important to hold the prospect's interest while he or she is being helped to discover and clarify his or her needs and wants, to admit them, and to indicate a willingness to consider your proposal as a solution.

Desire

At this stage the aim is to arouse the prospect's desire to enjoy the benefits that your product offers in fulfilling their needs or wants, and to secure their assurance that the benefits offered are of value to them. It is also the stage where you may have to handle questions or objections that the prospects might raise.

Action

This is the stage where the sale is closed, which means that action is taken to get the order.

Public relations and selling

Now, having set the scene, how can good public relations assist the selling effort?

Product knowledge

As we all know, this is a vital area. You must feel, dress, talk, and act the part of someone who knows his or her own business. You must have current, in-depth, detailed, and truthful knowledge of both the pros and cons of your product or service, market trends, etc. And you must provide detailed back-up information and advice if requested.

Prospecting

Selling, to be an art, must involve a genuine interest in the other person's needs. Otherwise it is only a subtle, civilized way of pointing a gun and forcing one into a temporary surrender.

We must know not only our product but also our client. This knowledge can be gleaned from many sources, depending on the area of concern. Friends, acquaintances, personal introductions, statistical data, financial reports, competitions, employers, and other commodity suppliers can be consulted and used to obtain additional personal information which will arm you to 'create a customer'.

Approach

It is said that the first ten words are more important than the next 10 thousand. Every salesperson's pledge should be: 'On my honour I pledge myself that I shall never present the body of my sales talk until I am sure I have the prospect's interest.'

Do not assume that your prospect is interested. Always take it for granted that he or she is not – until you have evidence to the contrary. One good piece of advice is to deliver every sales talk as if it were your last.

Establishing needs

It was the French writer Voltaire who said, 'Judge a man by his questions ... rather than by his answers.' A prospect's mind is like a parachute: it doesn't work unless it is open. It is vital for questions to be phrased on the what, where, when, to what extent, basis. The resulting answers will give a well-defined picture of the factors which may affect a decision.

Presentation

Let thy speech be short, comprehending much in few words (*Hamlet*, Shakespeare).

In any sales presentation it is important to strive for strength and not length, to talk 50 per cent less than your prospect, allowing you 50 per cent more time for thought. In order to structure a presentation:
- work out a list of the selling points;
- arrange these in logical order;
- select examples, statistics, and testimonials to support your case;
- speak the client's language;

- always remember: 'The salesperson who knows when to say nothing shows a fine command of language.'

Persuasion

Having established that the client can afford the product or service you are offering, you should persuade him or her of the need for this benefit by appealing to the emotions, not to the brain.

To make the prospect want what you are offering, first determine the buying motive. Then follow these three steps:
- point out the prospect's lack of, or want or need for, the article being sold;
- tell the prospect how the article will satisfy such want or need;
- paint a word picture of the satisfaction or gratification that will result from buying the article.

Using the right approach can prove to be a big advantage in accomplishing a successful sale.

Dealing with objections

It is important to treat objections not as invitations to argue but as requests for more information. To answer objections effectively, you must:
- know why prospects raise objections;
- know the various kinds of objection that may be raised, so that you have an answer for each one;
- know when to answer them;
- develop the right mental attitude towards both the objection and the objector.

Closing the sale

A good sales talk is a good procedure, but the signed order is the confirmation of success.

Throughout the whole presentation and negotiation the salesperson should:
- watch what the prospect does;
- note how the prospect looks;
- note what the prospect says.

If the prospect does something that indicates growing interest, it is a good sign. Better still, if something is done that indicates the prospect's mind has been made up and he or she wants whatever you are trying to sell, then the time has come to close the sale.

Follow-through

> We like a man to come right out and say what he thinks ... if we agree with him (Mark Twain).

The surest way of getting contracts is to make contacts. It is important to follow up any sales with personal contact. This establishes a channel for feedback. It also builds up sound product knowledge, proven performance, and excellent client relationships.

> Some men are failures not because they are stupid but because they are not sufficiently impassioned (Burt Struthers).

The most important ingredient of all the stages outlined above is enthusiasm. Remember the following rules to maintain enthusiasm:
- learn more about your product if you wish to become more enthusiastic about it;
- if you feel yourself losing your enthusiasm then work harder at it by making more calls;
- expose yourself to enthusiasm – it's contagious;
- be fit and glowing with health;
- act enthusiastically. The outward signs are fervour, intensity, animation, gestures, contact, and energy;
- always act as if it is impossible to fail.

Customer service

Today's customers have many choices of where to do business. Often, it is the way in which they are treated that determines whether they will come back. Since most organizations strive to produce quality products, it makes good sense for them to work hard at providing quality service as well.

Many companies have taken the trouble to prepare a mission statement. This not only spells out the purpose of the business but provides guidelines for sound business relationships. The following is an example of a statement on service excellence.

Service excellence

We are committed to taking exceptional care of our clients through unmatched service excellence in all our endeavours. We do this by:
- acting with honesty, integrity, professionalism, and responsibility at all times;
- ensuring that we stay close enough to our clients to anticipate and satisfy their needs and demands to the best of our ability;
- communicating accurately and openly, and placing a high premium on prompt, accurate, and effective response to all client queries;
- treating clients as an extension of our team so that our goals are achieved through mutual trust and interdependence;
- using our knowledge of our clients' business in order to provide proactive solutions to problems and opportunities for growth;
- never settling for second best in caring for our clients, but always striving zealously toward providing the kind of service excellence of which we can all be proud.

Keys to service excellence

The client has a right to excellent service. Why is this important? Because without customers, we would have no business!

What is good customer service?
- More than just smiling and saying, 'Have a nice day!'
- It is not always easy to define; but we know it when we don't get it.
- It is important to remember that the customer is the only person who is competent to judge whether or not good service has been received.

How do customers judge service? Customers judge the service they receive by comparing it with the service which they expect.

Factors or dimensions of service

- *Reliability*. The ability to perform the promised service dependably and accurately.
- *Tangibles*. The physical appearance of the employees, workplace, and communication materials.
- *Responsiveness*. The willingness of service staff to help customers and provide prompt service.
- *Confidence*. The knowledge and competence of staff and their ability to instil trust.

Research has shown that 'reliability' is rated most important, followed by 'people' factors, and then by 'tangibles'.

The client has a right to:

- recognition of his or her needs, preferences, and concerns;
- a prompt, courteous response;
- competent assistance;
- professional conduct;
- reliable, accurate information, and advice;
- adherence to promises;
- honest, intelligible communication;
- fair and ethical treatment;
- customer-friendly systems and procedures;
- effective complaint resolution.

How to achieve excellent customer service

Be reliable:
- Do the job right, and on time, first time and every time.
- Be prompt, and do not adopt the civil service approach of 'tomorrow is another day'.
- Pay attention to detail and know what you are talking about; if you don't know, say so. Then make a point of finding out.

Beware of what you promise:
- It pays to be honest and realistic when telling the customer what he or she is entitled to expect.
- Don't make rash claims or promises.
- Once you have made a promise, stick to it.

Remember the personal touch:
- The personal touch means more to customers than glossy brochures and smart offices.
- Remember to greet customers promptly, smile, mind your p's and q's, and call customers by name. It costs nothing.

Be alert and responsive to customer complaints:
- An already-unhappy customer will be harder to please.
- Never make the fatal mistake of failing your customer twice.

Build up customer goodwill:
- Customer goodwill will stand you in good stead if and when things do go wrong.

Never forget that customers are paramount:
- They are the sole judge of service quality.
- Their needs and expectations come first.
- If in doubt, ask them.

Show your appreciation:
- You are not doing them a favour by serving them.
- They are doing you a favour by patronizing your business.

Do small favours:
- big favours are expensive and are not expected, but small ones cost nothing and will be remembered.

Sell your organization:
- you chose to work there, after all!
- look the part and show your enthusiasm for your work.

Keep your cool:
- do not get drawn into unproductive arguments;
- focus on the problem, not the person.

Be a good example:
- do not follow the examples of others; set the example for others;
- if you are a manager, remember that your staff will treat your customers the way you treat them.

Conclusion

Selling is best regarded as helping people to see what they need and persuading them to get it. Persuasion by coercion or manipulation is bad for business in the long run because it is geared to the satisfaction of the seller. Only persuasion by enlightenment is permanently effective because it is geared to the satisfaction of the buyer. Excellent customer service is a prerequisite to enable successful selling on an ongoing basis.

Finally, selling should not be seen as a contest to be won. It is an information service to be rendered, and in selling, as in everything else, service must come before self-service.

Case study Customer Service Charter

Many companies today provide customers with a charter by which they can judge its services. This charter is essentially a document which helps people understand what a company does, what services they can expect, and how they can seek redress if something goes wrong. Its purpose is to improve access to public services and to promote provision of quality services. Above all, it helps staff to know what standards of service to deliver. Key features of a charter include:
- a statement of the standard of services users can expect
- arrangements for seeking redress should something go wrong
- brief information on the services provided and contact addresses.

The eThekwini Water and Sanitation Department is engaging in a vigorous communication drive to familiarize people with its customer services charter and other services provided by the department. The department has realised the importance of making the charter available to the Groupwise users (as fellow employees) as a medium for internal mass communication.

As part of its comprehensive strategy, the charter will be disseminated to the general public so that they too, will be properly informed of the department's commitment to delivering water and sanitation related services equitably, reliably, and professionally. This information has also been placed on the department's Intranet for easy access. Their service charter appears on the following page. It is based on Batho Pele principles.

Case study Batho Pele Principles

1. Consultation
You can tell us what you want from us. You will be asked for your views on existing public services and may also tell us what new basic services you would like. All levels of society will be consulted and your feelings will be conveyed to the city manager.

2. Service standards
Insist that our promises are kept. All units of the eThekwini municipality will be required to review and publish services. Standards may not be lowered! They will be monitored at least once a year and be raised progressively.

3. Access
One and all should get their fair share. Units of the eThekwini municipality will have to set targets for extending access to public servants and public services. They implement special programmes for improved service delivery to physically, socially and culturally disadvantaged persons.

4. Courtesy
One and all should get their fair share. All units will be set standards for the treatment of the public and incorporate these into their codes of conduct, values and training programmes. Staff performance will be irregularly monitored, and discourtesy will not be tolerated.

5. Information
You are entitled to full particulars. You will get full, accurate and up-to-date facts about services you are entitled to. Information should be provided at service points and in local media and languages. Contact numbers and names should appear in all departmental communications.

6. Openess and transparency
Administration must be an open book. You will get full, accurate and up to date facts about services you are entitled to. Information should be provided at service points and in local media and languages. Contact numbers and names should appear in all departmental communications

7. Redress
Your complaints must spark positive attention. Mechanism for recording any public dissatisfaction will be established and all staff will be trained to handle your complaints fast and efficiently. You will receive regular feedback on the outcomes.

8. Value for money
Your money should be employed wisely. You pay income, rates and other taxes to finance and administration of the council. You have the right to insist that your money should be used properly. Departments owe you proof that efficiency savings and improved service delivery are on the agenda.

Further reading

Blem, N. 2007. *Achieving Excellence in Selling.* Cape Town: Oxford University Press SA.

The Professional Salesmanship Association can also be approached for further reading.

Chapter 8

Public relations
and communication

When you have read this chapter, you should:

- understand the general aim of communication;

- be familiar with the different communication contexts;

- be able to identify and discuss briefly the different components in the communication process, using the model of Cutlip, Center, and Broom;

- be aware of and sensitive to barriers to effective communication;

- implement the seven Cs of communication;

- understand that public relations is in essence a process of communication.

Communication is central to the practice of public relations, with the general aim of establishing understanding but specifically to persuade, to inform, to influence attitudes, and to bring about action. The specific aims are related to the outcome of the communication.

Contemporary theory, however, regards communication not only as a dynamic process of exchanging meaningful messages, but as a transaction between participants during which a relationship develops between them. From this viewpoint 'communication is defined as a transactional process of exchanging messages and negotiating meaning to establish and maintain relationships' (Steinberg 1997: 13).

Communication settings

An identification of the aims of communication inevitably leads to a discussion of the different kinds of communication, or different communication settings. This is referred to as communication in different contexts.

Five broad categories may be discerned: two-person communication, small-group communication, public communication, organizational communication, and mass communication.

Two-person communication, also known as dyadic or interpersonal communication, is described as interaction between two persons. Because the communication between them is direct, both parties have an equal opportunity to communicate and to give feedback. The characteristics of this type of communication are that both parties are in close proximity;

both are able to send and receive messages; and the messages include both verbal and non-verbal stimuli. Very often, meaningful relationships are established.

The main criterion relating to small-group communication is that irrespective of the number of people involved (normally between three and 15), or the type of group, the people see themselves as belonging to, or being identified with, a group. All members are able to communicate among themselves on a face-to-face basis and create their own unique dynamics.

In contrast with two-person or small-group communication, public communication tends to occur within a more formal and structured setting. It takes place in public settings such as auditoriums or classrooms, as opposed to private places such as offices and boardrooms. It is planned in advance and individuals are given specific actions to perform. As a result, certain behavioural norms are projected and audiences only participate at the end of the address.

Organizational communication, which takes place vertically and horizontally through an organization, is concerned with the flow of messages within a network of interdependent relationships. It holds the organizational structure together by providing a basis for co-ordinating the relationships between individuals and reaching the organization's ultimate objectives.

Mass communication takes place through mass media such as newspapers, magazines, radio, film, and television. Generally a large number of people are involved in producing the message. Because of the way it is produced, there is little opportunity for direct feedback, but delayed feedback may occur. Mass communication has the following characteristics:

- its audience is relatively large, heterogeneous, and anonymous to the source;
- it is indirect, owing to the diverse nature of the receivers;
- communication is unilateral, as the roles of communicator and receiver are not interchangeable;
- it can be described as public;
- it is fleeting.

The communicator in mass communication makes use of a complex, corporate organization with a particular structure and accompanying costs in order to relay the message.

Another category of human communication is cross-cultural communication, which is defined as communication between members of different cultures, whether racial, ethnic, or socio-economic, or a combination of these. (A case study for discussion purposes is provided in this chapter.)

The public relations practitioner is involved in all of the identified communication contexts and should be aware of the opportunities afforded by them. He or she could, for example, advise the chief executive officer on public relations policy in a two-person context, explain the department's strategy to colleagues in a small-group context, deliver a speech on the organization in a public context, be responsible for healthy internal communication in the organizational context, or arrange a radio interview for the chief executive officer in the mass context. Naturally, any one of these situations could encompass the sphere of cross-cultural communication.

Components of the communication process

There are different models of communication and, depending on the particular model, the components of the communication process may vary slightly. Basically, the communication process comprises a triad: a communicator, a message, and a receiver. These three aspects, together with closely related factors such as code, medium, context, feedback, and interference, are the major components of the communication process. (See diagram on page 75.)

Components of the communication process

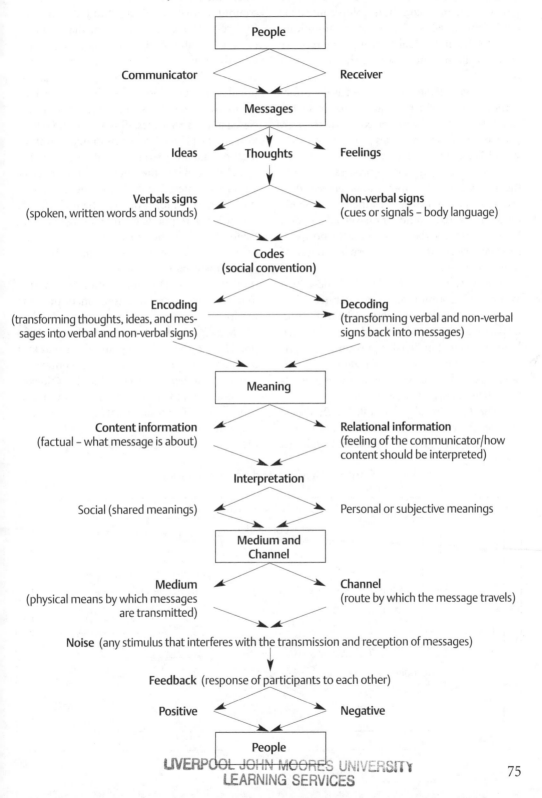

The communicator (sender or receiver, or source in the mass communication context) is the individual who attempts to communicate with another individual or group. The receiver refers to the person to whom the message is conveyed.

The message can be described as the information content which is transmitted in such a way as to be sensorily perceived by the receiver.

Communication codes (communicative stimuli) refer to all possible signs and symbols used in the communication process to convey the message in such a way as to be perceived by the receiver's senses. A distinction is made between verbal and non-verbal codes. Language is the verbal code, while the non-verbal code refers to all non-verbal aspects of human behaviour.

The many cues, signs or signals described as non-verbal stimuli have been defined within broad categories: proxemics (the utilization of personal space and physical environment), body movement or facial expressions, eye contact or visual interaction, vocalization or paralanguage, and chronemics or attitudes towards time, schedules, and appointments.

The term 'medium' is often used interchangeably with that of 'channel'. The simplest illustration of this is speaking on the telephone, where the telephone wires which transmit the communicative stimuli constitute the channel. In face-to-face communication, that is interpersonal, small-group, and public communication, the channels are the sensory organs, especially hearing, sight, and touch. In organizational communication, the channels include company newsletters and memorandums. Newspapers, magazines, film, radio, and television are the primary channels in mass communication and are referred to as the mass media.

On receiving the message, the receiver decodes or interprets it, that is, the message is translated into a form that can be understood. The receiver responds to the message or gives feedback and, in the process, conveys whether the message has been understood. Interference (noise, disturbance, or barriers) refers to anything that distorts the information transmitted to the receiver, causes a distraction, or prevents receipt.

Messages are not transmitted and interpreted in a vacuum. They are given within a complex, unique, and dynamic context in which a number of variables could influence the course and interpretation of the communication event. The components of this communication process are visually represented in the model below (Cutlip et al. 1994: 230).

Communication and process model

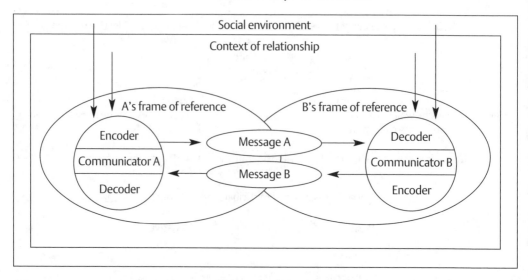

Public relations, in essence, is a process of communication. The public relations practitioner communicates on behalf of the organization (the constitutional communicator), with the organization's target audiences (the receivers), about the organization's policies, goals, and procedures (the message), by means of a speech, a newsletter, or publicity in the mass media (the channels or media), in situations involving either personal or indirect contact (the interpersonal, small-group, public, or mass communication context). The practitioner attempts to eliminate noise or barriers and is sensitive to feedback in order to establish whether the aim has been achieved, which is to establish mutual understanding between the organization and its target audiences.

As stated before, understanding is the key to effective communication. This has a number of implications: the communicator has to formulate the message clearly, unambiguously, and in accordance with the receiver's level of comprehension; the communicator must attempt to free the communication channel from interference or barriers; the receiver has to pay attention in order to receive the message; both parties have to be sensitive and react to non-verbal stimuli.

Barriers to communication

The process of communication may be hindered in three main respects: in the reception, understanding, or acceptance of the message.

The main barriers to reception include:
- certain needs, anxieties, and expectations of the listener;
- his or her attitudes and values;
- certain environmental stimuli.

The main barriers to understanding include:
- the sender's choice of language and jargon;
- the ability of the listener to concentrate completely on receiving the message;

- prejudices, the degree of open-mindedness of the listener, and the ability to consider factors that are disturbing to his or her ideas;
- the length of the communication process;
- the existing knowledge of the listener.

The main barriers to acceptance include:
- the attitudes and values of the listener;
- prejudices;
- any status clash between the sender and the listener;
- interpersonal emotional conflicts.

The seven Cs of communication

Cutlip et al. (1994) present seven useful guidelines for effective communication:
- *Credibility.* Communication starts with a climate of belief. This climate is built by performance on the part of the institution, reflecting an earnest desire to serve the receiver. The receiver must have confidence in the sender and a high regard for the source's competence on the subject.
- *Context.* A communication programme must square with the realities of its environment. Mechanical media are supplementary to the words and deeds that occur in daily living. The context must provide for participation and playback. It must confirm, not contradict, the message. Effective communication requires a supportive social environment, one largely set by the news media.
- *Content.* The message must have meaning for the receiver, and it must be compatible with his or her value system. It must be relevant to the receiver's situation. In general, people select those items of information that promise them the greatest rewards. The content determines the audience.
- *Clarity.* The message must be put in simple terms. Words must mean the same to the receiver as to the sender. Complex issues

Barriers to communication

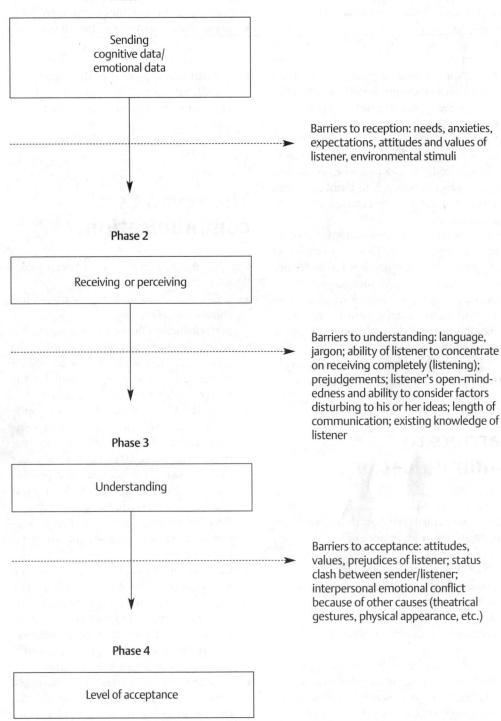

Phase 1

Sending
cognitive data/
emotional data

Barriers to reception: needs, anxieties,
expectations, attitudes and values of
listener, environmental stimuli

Phase 2

Receiving or perceiving

Barriers to understanding: language,
jargon; ability of listener to concentrate
on receiving completely (listening);
prejudgements; listener's open-mindedness and ability to consider factors
disturbing to his or her ideas; length of
communication; existing knowledge of
listener

Phase 3

Understanding

Barriers to acceptance: attitudes,
values, prejudices of listener; status
clash between sender/listener;
interpersonal emotional conflict
because of other causes (theatrical
gestures, physical appearance, etc.)

Phase 4

Level of acceptance

must be compressed into simple, clear themes, slogans, or stereotypes. The further a message has to travel, the simpler it must be. An institution must speak with one voice, not many voices.

- *Continuity and consistency.* Communication is a never-ending process. It requires repetition to achieve penetration. Repetition – with variation – contributes to both factual and attitudinal learning. The story must be consistent.
- *Channels.* Established channels of communication should be used – channels used and respected by the receiver. Creating new channels is difficult. Different channels have different effects and are effective in different stages of the diffusion process. Different channels are used for reaching different target audiences. People associate different values with the many channels of communication, and this, too, must be kept in mind.
- *Capability of the audience.* Communication must take into account the capability of the audience. Communication is most effective when it requires the least effort on the part of the recipient. This involves factors such as availability, habits, reading ability, and receivers' knowledge.

Avoiding cross-cultural misunderstanding

Cross-cultural misunderstanding can hamper successful communication and even prevent it from being achieved. There are essentially two ways of avoiding cross-cultural misunderstanding:

- by learning to speak the language of the other culture;
- by understanding the non-verbal communication or body language of the other culture.

The importance of language

If the success of the cross-cultural communicator is to be maximized, there is no substitute for an intimate knowledge of both the language and culture of those with whom business is conducted. In fact, because of the close relationship between language and culture, it is virtually impossible not to learn about one while studying the other.

With business becoming increasingly international, the role of language is becoming more important. Advertising campaigns, product marking and labelling, brochures, price lists, and business cards should be translated into the languages of each foreign market. Translations should be undertaken in the market concerned or at least by a native of that market, in order to avoid the numerous problems that can result from inaccurate translations.

Non-verbal communication

If language is important for sending and receiving messages, so too is non-verbal communication.

In cross-cultural interaction, both linguistic competence and a knowledge and understanding of non-verbal cues are needed in order to avoid misunderstandings. Although some non-verbal cues function in similar ways in many cultures, there are numerous differences in non-verbal patterns, and therefore non-verbal cues can be grouped into two main categories:

- *Non-verbal cues with different meanings in different cultures.* Hissing, for example, is used to indicate disapproval of a speaker in the United States, to ask for silence in certain Spanish-speaking countries, and to applaud in Lesotho.

Zone distances

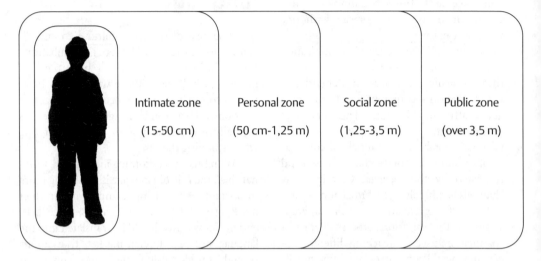

| Intimate zone | Personal zone | Social zone | Public zone |
| (15-50 cm) | (50 cm-1,25 m) | (1,25-3,5 m) | (over 3,5 m) |

- *Non-verbal cues with the same meaning in different cultures.* In most Western European countries and the United States, the non-verbal cue for signifying agreement is nodding the head up and down. However, in Malaysia, affirmation is indicated by thrusting the head forward sharply, and in Japan by bringing both hands to the chest and then gracefully moving them downwards with palms up.

Watch out for the man whose
stomach does not move when
he laughs (Chinese proverb).

The forms of non-verbal communication of significance in a multi-cultural environment are now discussed.

Body posture

In a cross-cultural environment, the various postures assumed and the meanings they convey can differ widely. For example, Western societies stand up to show respect, whereas in certain Polynesian and African cultures, people

sit down. A lack of knowledge of these customs can lead to considerable misunderstanding.

Hand gestures

The use of fingers, hands, and arms for the purpose of communicating varies considerably from one culture to another. Some cultures, such as those in Southern Europe and the Middle East, employ a wide variety of gestures frequently and with considerable force and purposefulness. Western Europeans tend to be much more conservative in their use of gestures, placing a higher value on verbal messages instead.

Facial expressions

Although certain facial expressions occur throughout the world, specific cultural norms may influence how, when, and why they are used. The face has the greatest potential of all parts of the body to communicate an emotional state. We speak of 'face-to-face' communication and the Japanese and other Eastern cultures speak of 'losing face' in certain unfortunate situations. Smiling is used to convey different messages in different cultures. In certain parts of Africa, for example, laughter and smiling are used to express surprise, wonder, and embarrassment, not amusement or happiness. In Japan, smiling can be both a sign of joy and a means of hiding displeasure, sorrow, or anger.

Eye contact

All cultures use eye contact as a very important mechanism for communicating non-verbally. People often use a direct gaze to attract another person's attention in situations where noise or gesticulation are inappropriate. Much of the meaning attached to gazing and gaze-avoidance is culturally determined. In Japan, rather than looking a person straight in the eye, you should focus your gaze somewhat lower, in the region of the Adam's apple.

In many parts of sub-Saharan Africa, direct eye contact must be avoided when addressing a person of higher status. So when we interact in an international business context with people from such cultures, we must realize that our insistence on maintaining a relatively high level of eye contact will probably be interpreted as threatening, disrespectful, haughty, or even insulting.

Personal space

How people use personal space in their interaction with others (refer again to the diagram on page 80) is another 'silent language' that must be understood if clear communication is to be achieved in an international business setting. What is an appropriate distance for one cultural group might appear to be 'crowding' to another or 'stand-offish' to a third. For example, North Americans choose a distance of approximately 50 cm for normal communication, with minor variations depending on gender and level of intimacy.

For certain cultural groups in South America and the Caribbean, the normal conversational distance is in the range of 35–40 cm, and for certain cultures in the Middle East, that distance is as small as 20–25 cm. South Americans, Asians, and Indians normally choose spatial distances that are midway between those preferred by Arabs and Northern Europeans.

The issue of personal space has important implications for the conduct of international business. The way in which different cultural groups use office space, for example, can lead to a breakdown in communication between business partners. Whereas many North Americans are accustomed to having a desk between themselves and business partners, South Americans see a desk as an unnecessary barrier. Unlike South Africans, who generally close their office doors only for private conferences, Germans are likely to keep their office doors closed all the time. To do otherwise is considered to be extremely unbusinesslike.

Touching (body contact)

Humans touch in a variety of ways and for a variety of purposes. Each culture has a well-defined system of meanings for different forms of touching and for touching various parts of the body. Each culture also defines who can touch whom, on which parts of the body, and under which circumstances.

Some are high-touch cultures and others are low-touch cultures. Mediterranean cultures, Arabs, Jews, and Eastern Europeans belong to high-touch cultures, whereas English, German, Northern European, and many Asian cultures are low-touch cultures.

Case study   Specific South African cultural influences

It should be noted that the following observations are of a general nature and are simply guidelines. There will be many exceptions depending on the education and background of the individual. The social context of the interaction will also play a role.

Greetings

In Western culture, it is reasonably common for a subordinate to greet a senior first. In traditional African cultures, the subordinate may wait until the senior person has acknowledged him or her before offering a greeting. The engagement of others through pleasantries and 'small talk' leads the way to further interaction and trust.

A brief, single grip is the norm for the handshake in Western culture. In African culture, the handshake incorporates a triple grip. In general, African cultures extend the period of hand contact beyond the first words of greeting and employ a less firm grip.

Eye contact

In Western culture, eye contact is normal and important for effective communication. African culture has different norms. For example, eye contact between junior and senior may be limited. Avoidance of eye contact is seen as a sign of respect.

Interaction

In African cultures, questioning of a superior may be frowned on.

The loudness of voice has different meanings. In African culture, a low, soft voice is respectful while a loud voice is normal when communicating with friends. In Western cultures, too soft a voice is 'annoying', too loud a mark of disrespect.

Agreement or disagreement

Western people are often confused by an African person's 'yes' or 'no' answer to a neg-ative question. The enquiry 'Don't you want me to work overtime?' might be answered by 'Yes', meaning 'I do not want you to work overtime.' For this reason, negative constructions in sentences should be avoided.

Conversation – the 'sounds of silence'

In Western culture there are seldom long periods of silence, except in churches and libraries. Verbal communication between South Africans with different home languages needs to allow for periods of silence. When one is communicating and thinking in a language other than one's own, one also needs time to formulate one's thoughts.

Seeking confirmation

People from Western cultures have a tendency to make a statement or ask a question, and then confirm the statement or answer for the African person he or she is communicating with. For example, a Western manager will say to an African employee: 'We have to deduct R30 for unemployment insurance, okay?' The African person, in an effort to be polite, may nod in the affirmative when in fact he or she may not agree. Similarly, Western people tend to add to their statements: 'Do you understand?' For example, 'This means that rationalization will have to take place. Do you understand?' The response may be yes, but again politeness or the fear of appearing ignorant may mask a lack of understanding.

Body language

The manner in which a person walks may be culture specific. For a black person an ululating or shuffling mode of walk may reflect the rhythm and steps of traditional dance.

Space

The distance between people when communicating (personal space) is culture specific. In Western culture, the more dominant and higher the status of the person, the larger the personal 'space bubble' which he or she finds acceptable when communicating with subordinates. This contrasts with African society, which immediately makes an individual of whatever status feel at home by means of close personal contact. In a social context at work, individuals are welcomed into the group – status may be temporarily 'frozen'.

Back-slapping

A common Western sign of appreciation or congratulation, a back slap, may be misinterpreted or seen as meaningless by some African people.

Smiling

In Western culture, smiling is almost entirely associated with humour, mirth or intimacy. In African cultures a smile may also indicate uneasiness, fear, misunderstanding, or helplessness.

Social events and invitations

In Western culture, it is polite to reply timeously to invitations of a social nature. In African society, anyone who feels that they have a right or interest in attending may do so, and bring along other friends or associates – whether or not he or she has replied or been invited.

Entrances and seating

Western culture assumes a forthright door-knocking technique to gain polite entry. In African culture it is polite to 'tap' very gently. In some cases the person will not respond to the first invitation to 'come in', but will wait for the second or third invitation.

African culture does not require that a person stand when a superior enters a room and it is not a requirement that one be invited to take a seat. On entering a room, an African person may sit immediately, without first being asked. It is considered polite to lower oneself below the height of the person one is addressing.

Women first versus men first

'Ladies first' is a traditional Western custom. According to tradition, the African male leads, to warn of danger and protect the woman.

Thanks

In Western culture it is expected that someone offers verbal thanks when presented, for example, with a gift. Among Zulu people, body language may fulfil this function. For example, in accepting or taking something that is given, both hands may be used, or one hand will receive the gift with the other hand touching the hand receiving the gift or item.

Time frames

Western culture is 'clock bound' – it views time as a valuable resource and expects punctuality. In African cultures, some people are less 'clock oriented'. Traditionally, work and leisure time are a seamless experience.

Community

'Ubuntuism' or communalism, has both traditional, and more recently political, components. Individualism, where it leads to one person seemingly enjoying benefits which do not apply to all members of a given community, may be rejected as unfair in African cultures.

Extended family system

Broader kinship ties than are experienced in the Western community may result in numerous requests by African employees for time off to attend funerals, weddings, and other functions. This is often seen as unnecessary and excessive by Western members of management, and even dishonest when reference to a 'once-removed' relative as a 'father', 'sister', or 'brother' is made. To illustrate, a person's paternal uncle is considered to have equal status as 'father' to the person concerned.

Conclusion

As important as language is to facilitating international communication within an international business setting, it is only the first step towards cross-cultural understanding. Of equal importance is the non-verbal dimension on which we all rely, but recognize only vaguely. However, verbal and non-verbal communications are inextricably linked. To learn just the spoken language and ignore non-verbal behaviour would be as inadequate a response to cross-cultural communication as doing just the opposite. Being able to read facial expressions, postures, hand gestures, eye contact, and space usage, among others, increases our sensitivity to the intricacies of cross-cultural communication so necessary for success in the international business arena. To really know another culture we must first learn its language and then we must be able to hear the silent messages and read the invisible words.

Further reading

Bell, S. & T. Marais. 1998. *Communication for Managers and Secretaries.* Halfway House: International Thomson Publishing.

Bittner, J.R. 1985. *Fundamentals of Communication.* Englewood Cliffs, New Jersey: Prentice-Hall.

Cutlip, S.M., A.H. Center & G.M. Broom. 1994. *Effective Public Relations.* Englewood Cliffs, New Jersey: Prentice-Hall.

Du Toit, D., H. Grobler & R. Schenk. 1998. *Person-centred Communication.* Halfway House: International Thomson Publishing.

Mersham, G.M. & J.C. Skinner. 1999. *New Insights into Public Relations and Communication.* Johannesburg: Heinemann.

Puth, G. 1994. *The Communicating Manager.* Pretoria: JL van Schaik.

Rensburg, R. & G. Angelopulo. 1996. *Effective Communication Campaigns.* Halfway House: International Thomson Publishing.

Steinberg, S. 1997. *Introduction to Communication.* Cape Town: Juta.

Tubbs, S.L. & S. Moss. 1980. *Human Communication.* New York: Random House.

Wilcox, D.L., P.M. Ault & W.K. Agee. 1995. *Public Relations: Strategies and Tactics.* New York: Harper & Row

Chapter 9

Effective listening

When you have read this chapter, you should:

- be familiar with the various obstacles to effective listening and understanding;
- be able to identify key factors to effective listening;
- be able to capitalize on thought speed.

For the manager, skill in speaking, listening, reading, and writing is vital. His or her environment and job are primarily involved with language and communication. The manager continually interacts with other people through conferences, meetings, interviews, telephone conversations, reports, letters, and so on. Senior and middle management typically devote 60 to 80 per cent of their total working hours to communicating, much of which directly involves the art of listening or the art of speaking.

Learning to listen

The obstacles to effective listening and understanding are many and varied. How we use our unoccupied thinking time (we think four times faster than we speak) is the difference that makes for effective listening. Misunderstandings occur when poor listening habits and their related mechanisms, which create problems in communication, occupy this special time differential. Attempts to improve our listening skills are largely concerned with eliminating these destructive mechanisms and replacing them with their counter-skills. In order to retain content and information, we must train our minds to actively concentrate on the message being given to us. One approach to improving listening skills in this area is through programmed instruction.

In one programmed listening course which has been done by thousands of sales and management people, participants listen to a series of taped statements. After each statement the trainees are asked to write a summary of the instruction or to give it orally. Immediately after their response, they compare it with a model answer to verify their learning or check how much they have missed. The initial statements are short and simple, but they become longer and increasingly complex as the programme progresses. The statements are sometimes technical, full of heavily accented anger or annoying sales pitches, to the accompaniment of clicking typewriters and

85

Listening skills	
Dos and Don'ts	
DO	**DON'T**
• Focus attention on the speaker	• Talk about yourself, be critical, or give advice
• Repeat things in your own words	
• Restate important thoughts and feelings	• Only say 'mm mm mm', 'ah hah', or parrot the speaker's words
• Reflect back so that the speakers can hear and understand themselves	
	• Ignore the facts or feelings
• Ask questions to make the subject clearer	• Pretend that you understand
• Show that you are listening with your voice, eyes, and body	• Assume you know it all
	• Be a passive listener
• Attempt to get more information via the speaker's body	• Fill every space with your talk
	• Fix, change, or improve what the speaker said
• Summarize facts and feelings	
• Stay neutral	• Take sides

ringing telephones. Sometimes the statements need to be rearranged for them to make sense.

The trainee has the opportunity to practise listening across a broad spectrum of communication, using the difference between speech speed and thought speed. The brain is kept working by focusing its attention on organizing material as the speaker proceeds, selecting main points and supporting reasons, summarizing the message with a key word or two, and receiving what has been said, or listening for what has not been said. After completing the programme, participants should be able to capture the critical content of conversational material and summarize spoken messages into meaningful and useful information.

A test that measures listening ability is given prior to taking the course and these results are then compared with those of a similar test administered at the end of the programme. A study of several hundred first-, second- and third-line supervisors showed that before training the average recall was only 25 per cent of what was said. At the end of the programme, the group average had increased to 90 per cent. A re-test of this same group one

year later showed an increase, however slight, rather than a decline.

Although we know that listening with understanding involves more than simply capturing words and holding information, it is still quite important to know what someone else has said. But words are not the only means we have for communicating. The illusion that communication has taken place because a speaker has said some words to a listener is common practice in mutual self-deception.

Guides to effective listening

Learning through listening is primarily an inside job – inside action on the part of the listener. What needs to be done is to replace some common, existing attitudes with others, as we have mentioned earlier.

The conviction seems to be growing that upper-level managers also need listening skills. As Dr Earl Planty, executive counsellor of

Johnson and Johnson, commented, 'By far the most effective method by which executives can tap ideas of subordinates is sympathetic listening in many day-to-day informal contacts within and outside the workplace. There is no system that will do the job in an easier manner. Nothing can equal an executive's willingness to hear.'

Studies of good and poor listeners, conducted over a period of time and in different situations, have led to the emergence of quite a number of guidelines to effective listening. Those interested in improving their own performance can use them to analyze their personal strengths and weaknesses. The guidelines to good listening include the following:

Use empathy in communication

The boundaries for understanding expand where empathy exists. In fact, the key to effective listening is empathy – the ability to see an idea or concept from another's point of view. One needs to be aware of the other person's background, values, and attitudes when listening to what is being said. It simply means putting yourself in someone else's shoes. Under these positive conditions, speakers usually relax their defence mechanisms, since they no longer find it necessary to argue with their listeners. Of course, empathy means understanding and does not necessarily involve agreement.

People are often afraid to understand what is being said in case they have to change their own way of thinking. If you have just agreed with a piece of information which conflicts with your attitudes and beliefs, a condition known as cognitive dissonance may arise. Cognitive dissonance is a system of non-fitting attitudes or beliefs that brings about psychological conflict. In trying to avoid this condition, you as a listener might refuse to try to understand information that is in conflict with what you already believe. In this case, you must have enough confidence in the logical consistency and validity of your own beliefs and attitudes, so that you can relax and try to under-stand new information. One has to realize that one does not necessarily have to agree with information just because one understands it.

Recognize your prejudices

One major barrier to good listening is prejudice. Because you dislike the way a man dresses, votes, or wears his hair, you tend to transfer your disapproval to what he is saying. But a man who wears loud clothes could be a brilliant supervisor or might be able to tell you a lot you do not know about the overseas market for your company's product. Ideally, your listening should be totally free of prejudice. Since this is practically impossible, do the next best thing by recognizing your prejudices and making a conscious effort to discount them.

Keep your mind open and beware of 'trigger' words

Related to the problem of prejudice is the problem of psychological deaf spots which impair our ability to perceive and understand. These deaf spots are a dwelling-place for many of our cherished notions, convictions, and complexes. A speaker may be able to invade one of these areas with merely one word or phrase. It is hard to believe in moments of cool detachment that just a word or phrase could cause such emotional disruption. Yet this often happens to poor listeners, and even sometimes to good listeners. Effective listeners try to identify and rationalize words or phrases that upset them emotionally. Often the emotional impact of these words can be decreased through discussing them freely and openly with friends or associates.

Find an area of interest

All studies point to the advantage of being interested in the topic under discussion. Bad listeners usually declare the subject boring after the first few sentences. Once this decision is made, it serves to rationalize any and all intentions. Good listeners follow different tactics: their first thought may be that the subject sounds dry, but a second one immediately follows, based on the realization that to get up and leave might prove a bit awkward. The final reflection is that, being trapped anyway, one might just as well use the situation to learn if anything is being said that can be put to use. Whenever we wish to listen efficiently we ought to ask ourselves, 'What's he or she saying that I can use? What worthwhile ideas does he or she have? Is he or she reporting any workable procedures?' Such questions lead us to screen what we are hearing in a continual effort to identify elements of personal value.

Resist distractions

Good listeners tend to adjust quickly to any kind of abnormal situation; poor listeners tend to react to bad conditions and in some instances even manage to create distractions themselves. We live in a noisy age. We are distracted not only by what we hear, but also by what we see. Poor listeners tend to be readily influenced by all manner of distraction, even in an intimate face-to-face situation.

A good listener instinctively fights distraction. Sometimes the fight is easily won by closing a door, turning off a radio, or moving closer to the person who is speaking. If the distractions cannot be overcome that easily, then it becomes a matter of concentration.

Learn to concentrate

Many people throw in the towel at the first sign that what someone else is saying will require some effort to understand. Others are the victims of persistent daydreaming. In each case the remedy is concentration. How can your powers of concentration be strengthened? By nipping in the bud the three attention-robbers most often responsible for careless listening. These are:

- *Fatigue.* Listening is not a passive affair; it requires real effort to absorb and understand what a speaker is saying, to constantly relate comments to known facts and logical

reasoning. Good listening takes a lot of energy. If you are tired or ill, you cannot possibly listen effectively.
- *Lack of incentive.* Frequently, the reason we do not listen is that we are not convinced that what we are about to hear is relevant to us. This lack of incentive was referred to earlier under the subheading 'Find an area of interest'. Take advantage of this selfish streak built into each of us by bringing a 'what's in it for me?' attitude to everything you hear. Then when something worthwhile is being said, you won't miss it.
- *Insufficient practice.* Like any skill, effective listening takes infinite practice. The more you do it, the better you become at it. By going out of your way to expose yourself to 'hard listening' by listening to interviews, discussions, and lectures on topics which are foreign to you, you will gain valuable practice in listening.

Be a critical listener

Everything you hear cannot, of course, be taken at face value. Just as you read the printed word with a critical eye, so you need to listen to the spoken word with a critical ear. As you listen, therefore, weigh up what the speaker is saying and the conclusions being drawn. What is the authority for the speaker's statements? Are certain facts being ignored? Are the examples one-sided? Are facts and theories lumped together? Is there over-generalization? Is the logic valid?

If you notice any weaknesses in the speaker's argument, bear them in mind when the time comes for agreeing or disagreeing with him or her.

Hold your fire

Over-stimulation is almost as bad as under-stimulation, and the two together constitute the twin evils of ineffective listening. The over-stimulated listener gets too excited, or excited too soon, by the speaker. Some of us are greatly addicted to this weakness. For us, a speaker can seldom talk for more than a few minutes without touching upon a pet bias or conviction. Occasionally, we are roused in support of the speaker's point; usually it is the reverse. In either case over-stimulation reflects the desire of the listener to enter immediately into the argument.

The aroused person usually becomes preoccupied with trying to do three things simultaneously: calculate what hurt is being done to his or her own pet ideas; plot an embarrassing question to ask the speaker; mentally enjoy all the discomfiture visualized for the speaker once the subsequent passages go unheard.

We must learn not to get excited about a speaker's point until we are certain that we thoroughly understand it. The secret is contained in the principle that we must always withhold our evaluation until our comprehension is complete.

Listen for ideas

Good listeners focus on central ideas; they tend to recognize the characteristic language in which central ideas are usually stated, and they are able to discriminate between fact and principle, idea and example, evidence and argument. Poor listeners are inclined to listen for the facts in every presentation.

To understand the fault, let us assume that a man is giving you instructions made up of facts A to Z. The man begins to talk. You hear fact A and think, 'I've got to remember it!' So you begin a memory exercise by repeating fact A. Meanwhile, the speaker is telling you fact B. Now you have two facts to memorize. You are so busy doing this that you miss fact C completely. And so it goes, up to fact Z. You catch a few facts, garble several others and miss the rest.

It is a significant fact that only about 25 per cent of persons listening to a formal talk are able to grasp the speaker's central idea. To develop this skill requires an ability to recognize conventional organizational patterns, transitional language, and the speaker's use of recapitulation. Fortunately, all these items can be readily mastered with a bit of effort.

Ask questions

Even if you believe that you have listened to someone, it's a good idea to double-check your understanding of what has been said. The best way to do this is to ask questions. There are basically two reasons for asking questions: clarification and amplification. In the case of clarification, the listener asks the speaker to repeat or rephrase remarks: 'What is your solution again?' 'Would you expand on your argument against increasing your quota?' In the case of amplification, the listener requests additional information: 'Would you recommend the same thing for the night shift?' 'Exactly when would this new policy go into effect?'

No speaker will object to an intelligent question, for such a query indicates interest on the part of the listener. But if your questions are obviously hostile or belittling, you risk insulting the speaker. Do that and he or she may never get to say the things that would profit you most. Politeness is the key word here. Be careful, too, of poorly timed questions. Unless the speaker is exceptionally experienced, an unexpected or abrupt question will throw him or her off the track and break a train of thought. It may possibly anticipate something the speaker is about to say. Or it may prevent others – if there are others – from listening. You owe it to the speaker, the rest of the audience, and yourself, to hold your questions until he or she has finished saying what is on his or her mind.

Make sure you understand

The most patient listeners in the world are probably psychiatrists and counsellors. It is a recognized part of their skill. Furthermore, not only must they listen to their patients and understand them, but they must also make sure at every stage that their patients realize that they are listening. Reflective questioning enables the good listener to confirm that he or she has correctly understood the speaker. If you are at all unsure that you have understood a speaker, briefly restate what you think was said, and ask, 'Is that what you mean?' If it is not, he or she will be only too glad to set you straight. If it is, you can compliment yourself on having really listened.

Although nature has wired us for sound, most of us transmit better than we receive. Yet most people have something worthwhile to say – if we would only really listen to them.

Be flexible

Research shows that the worst listeners think that taking notes and outlining are synonymous. They believe that there is but one way to take notes – by making an outline. Actually, no damage would be done if all talks followed some definite plan or scheme. Unfortunately, even where formal speeches are concerned, less than half are carefully organized. There are few things more frustrating than trying to outline a badly organized speech.

Note-taking may help or may become a distraction. Some people try to take down everything in shorthand. While studies are not clear on this point, there is some evidence to indicate that the volume of notes taken and their value to the taker are inversely related. In any case, the real issue is one of interpretation. Few of us have memories good enough to remember even the salient points we hear. If we can obtain brief, meaningful records for review at a later stage, we definitely improve our ability to learn and to remember. According to one survey, the best listeners apparently learned early in life that if they wanted to be efficient note-takers they had to have more than one system of taking notes. They equipped themselves with four or five systems, and learned to adjust their systems to the organizational pattern, or the absence of one, in each talk they heard. If we want to be good listeners, we must be flexible and adaptable note-takers.

Exercise your mind

Poor listeners are inexperienced in hearing difficult, expository material. Good listeners

apparently develop an appetite for listening to a variety of presentations difficult enough to challenge their mental capacities.

Perhaps the one word that best describes the bad listener is 'inexperienced'. Although a large percentage of the communication day is spent listening to something, he or she is inexperienced in hearing anything tough, technical, or expository. He or she has for years painstakingly sought light, recreational material. The problem created is deeply significant, because such a person is a poor producer – whether in the factory, office, or classroom. Inexperience is not easily or quickly overcome. However, knowledge of our own weakness may lead to repair. We never become too old to meet new challenges.

Capitalize on thought speed

Most people talk at a speed of about 125 words per minute. There is good evidence that if thought was measured in words per minute, most people could easily think at about four times that rate. It is difficult – almost painful – to try and slow down our thinking speed. Thus we normally have about 400 words of thinking time to spare during every minute a person talks to us.

What do we do with our excess thinking time while someone else is speaking? If we are poor listeners, we soon become impatient with the slow progress the speaker seems to be making. So our thoughts turn to something else for a moment, then dart back to the speaker. These brief side excursions of thought continue until our minds tarry too long on some enticing but irrelevant subject. Then when our thoughts return to the person talking, we find he or she is far ahead of us. Now it's harder to follow and increasingly easy to take off on side excursions. Finally, we give up; the person is still talking, but our minds are in another world.

Good listeners use thought speed to their advantage. They constantly apply their spare thinking time to what is being said. It is not difficult, once one has a definite pattern of thought to follow. To develop such a pattern we should do the following:

- *Try to anticipate what a person is going to talk about.* On the basis of what has already been said, ask yourself, 'What's he or she trying to get at? What point is he or she going to make?'
- *Mentally summarize what the person has been saying.* What point has already been made, if any?
- *Weigh the speaker's evidence by mentally questioning it.* As he or she presents facts, or illustrates with stories and statistics, continually ask yourself, 'Are they accurate? Do they come from an unprejudiced source? Am I getting the full picture, or am I only being told what proves the speaker's point?'
- *Listen between the lines.* The speaker doesn't always put everything that is important into words. The changing tones and volume of his or her voice may have a meaning. So may facial expressions, hand gestures, and body movements.

Not capitalizing on our thought speed is our single greatest handicap. The differential between thought speed and speech speed breeds false feelings of security and mental tangents. Yet through training in listening, the same differential can be readily converted into our greatest asset.

Conclusion

De Vito (1971) provides the following summary of effective listening:

- Find areas of interest to yourself in what the speaker is saying.
- Do not try to judge the delivery but concentrate your attention on the content of the speech.
- Do not be carried away by something that the speaker has said that arouses your ire or your enthusiasm, or on which you may wish to question him or her. Note what has been said, but listen further. The speaker may provide amplification or a correction.

Meanwhile you may miss important parts of the message.
- *Listen for ideas.* Do not try to remember facts. By trying too hard to store knowledge you may fail to grasp the message.
- *Be flexible.* Be prepared to go along with the speaker for a while, even if you fundamentally disagree with what is said. Hear him or her out. Be prepared to change your views if the arguments are sound.
- *Work at your listening.* Watch the speaker for special gestures that may indicate emphasis. Listen for special effects. Your attention will also help the speaker in his or her delivery.
- *Resist distractions.* External noise may divert your attention; try to keep your mind entirely on the speaker.
- *Exercise your mind.* Do not half-listen, hoping that the words will filter in automatically. Ask yourself what ideas are being put forward. Prepare for the next idea.
- *Keep your mind open.* Watch out for emotional reactions to words or ideas. Be objective in your responses while you are listening.
- *Remember that thought is nearly four times as fast as speech.* Capitalize on this speed.
- *While listening, ask yourself, 'What's he trying to say?'* Summarize. Question what the speaker says – but not emotionally. And listen between the lines.

Further reading

Adey, A.D. & M.G. Andrew. 1990. *Getting it Right: The Manager's Guide to Business Communication.* Cape Town: Juta.

De Vito, J.A. 1971. *Communication Concepts and Processes.* New York: Prentice-Hall.

Du Toit, P., M. Heese & M. Orr. 1995. *Practical Guide to Reading, Thinking and Writing Skills.* Halfway House: International Thomson Publishing.

Steinberg, S. 1997. *Introduction to Communication.* Cape Town: Juta.

Chapter 10

Employee communication

When you have read this chapter, you should:

- understand the background to communicating policies and practices;
- know employees' information rights;
- be familiar with the formal and informal communication networks;
- be able to contribute to a company's information programme;
- be familiar with various printed and graphic communications;
- be able to discuss the general principles of employee communication;
- be aware of research being conducted in the field of employee communication;
- understand the impact of the intranet on internal communication.

The first, Henry Ford maintained, that all workers wanted was a large pay packet and a job in which they did not have to think. How things have changed! Hard-earned experience, frequently measured in lost production, low productivity, discontent, low morale, high staff turnover, and confrontation between management and employees, has given a new importance to industrial relations.

The all-important human element in industry must not be underestimated. We cannot humanize society without humanizing work. Work for most people is first and foremost a source of income. But it also fulfils a social function.

The extent to which workers find a measure of satisfaction in their work and social contact with their fellow-workers in agreeable and healthy surroundings may determine, to a large extent, their attitudes and behaviour towards society. It also becomes a significant factor in their job performance.

Management cannot afford to ignore the aspirations, aptitudes, and preferences expressed by its employees. It has much to gain from a satisfied labour force, working at jobs to which they are best suited. The most successful management recognizes that it has a social as well as an economic function to perform. It can respond to this challenge by establishing a harmonious psychological climate within the company. An organization's total public relations is a product of the people who work for it.

A reputation as a good employer has to be earned, like goodwill towards the organization itself. The company is rewarded through having good internal public relations because employees are encouraged to make their contribution to the productivity and prosperity of the company.

Internal public relations is a broad field embracing near-neighbour activities like human resources, labour relations, and internal education and, in many respects, serves as a bridge between them.

The internal climate or atmosphere of an organization has a vital bearing on the individual employee's motivation. Experienced managers have found that they are not really able to motivate people but can merely create the right climate and provide the right tools for individuals to motivate themselves.

To create this climate, companies must look at the following three objectives with regard to employee communication:

- to help employees understand their job and their company;
- to help employees realize that their personal success is inseparable from the company's success;
- to help employees realize that their job is worth doing because their company's products are essential to society.

What are some of the ways we can use to achieve these objectives? First, an often unstated yet vital method of communication is direct personal contact between employee and supervisor. Second, commitment to change, to growth, or to virtually anything, can best be achieved by involvement. The better employees are informed about products, policies, and procedures, the better they will perform their tasks. Third, a spirit of teamwork, and a sense of participation in a common enterprise, can result in recognition of excellence and achievement by both the individual and the team. Finally, the climate should portray a certain amount of economic security. Employees need to know of the company's financial strength, its reputation among investors and clients. This knowledge will give them a general feeling of security regarding the welfare of their families.

Communicating policies and practices to employees

To ensure an understanding of its philosophy, policies, and practices, a corporation must maintain a two-way communication programme designed to inform employees and to give them a means of expressing their views about company affairs. Such a programme should provide employees with information about company practices in which they have a personal interest, such as employment, working conditions, fringe benefits, sales, new products, research and development, corporate finances, wage negotiations, plant expansion, remuneration, personnel, promotions, and other matters affecting their work and welfare.

The employee's right to information

There is a growing recognition throughout the world of the moral right of individual employees to receive financial and other information about the organization that employs them in a form they can understand. Britain has witnessed the introduction of legislation relating to the disclosure of information to employees and the publication of several documents advising government, management, and employees as to the financial and other information which ought to be disclosed. Australia has a National Employee Participation Steering Committee, which has published a report on the communication network.

The guide to employee surveys

	Attitude surveys	Communication audits	Awareness surveys	Readership surveys
	Also known as 'organizational climate' or 'environment' surveys, 'employee relations' or 'human relations' audits or surveys. Can measure feelings about a wide range of subjects, or zoom in on just one topic, e.g. benefits	Focus exclusively on what an organization (or any part of an organization) is doing to communicate with a given audience; may also include a review of all media being used	Assess employee knowledge and attitudes regarding specific issues; 'economic awareness' survey measures understanding of firm's business; 'health awareness' survey determines understanding of health insurance and how to contain health care costs	Simplest survey type; unlike communication audit, broadbased communication information
Some reasons why ...	• To assess employee understanding and/or acceptance of human resource policies and practices • To assess training needs • To measure morale and identify causes of employee discontent • To provide management with an objective overview of organizational characteristics • To check on supervisory effectiveness • To identify specific problems in individual demographic groups • To establish benchmarks • To measure progress against previously established benchmarks	• To find out how well a communication programme is working • To diagnose current or potential communication problems or missed opportunities • To evaluate a new communication policy or practice • To assess the relationship of communication to other organizational operations at corporate and local levels • To help develop communication budgets • To develop or restructure the communication function within an organization • To provide background or developing formal communication policies and plans	• To identify areas of special employee concern • To assess current levels of knowledge on a specific issue • To pinpoint gaps in knowledge • To gauge attitudes towards a specific issue as input for a possible communication programme • To evaluate the effectiveness of a current communication programme	• To find out if readers are receiving publications regularly • To evaluate the impact of content on readers • To assess readers' perceptions of the quality of publications • To get reactions or ideas about a possible new publication • To develop a list of topics that would interest readers • To establish benchmarks to ensure progress against previously established benchmarks • To provide background for developing an annual plan and budget for publications

	Attitude surveys	Communication audits	Awareness surveys	Readership surveys
Sometimes in the event of ...	• Major reorganization • Merger or acquisition • Business downturn (layoffs, cost-reduction programmes, plant shut-downs) • External events (unfavourable publicity, lawsuits) causing concern • Upcoming union negotiations	• Major reorganization • Merger or acquisition • New management team • Business downturn (layoffs, cost-reduction programmes, plant shut-downs) • External events (unfavourable publicity, lawsuits) causing concern • Upcoming union negotiations	• Issue spotlighted by current events • Knowledgeable spokesperson on issue needed by management • Policy shifts (organizational or national) affecting the firm • External events (unfavourable publicity, lawsuits) causing concern • Upcoming union negotiations	• Flagging interest in existing publications • Planned changes in publications • Development of publication budgets • Circulation of 'underground' publications
Some things to explore	• Physical working conditions • Basic job satisfaction • Personnel policies and practices • Pay and benefits • Working relationships with others • Attitudes towards management • Communication	• Management's communication philosophy • Are messages being sent and received? • How many messages are being received – accurately? favourably? uniformly? • Sources of information – real and preferred • Quality and effectiveness of current media	• Economic facts of the business • Productivity • The organization's role in a national or local issue/event • Pay and benefits • Personnel policies and practices	• Content • Readability • Distribution • Graphics • Frequency • Format
Some possible participants	• Senior executives, divisional managers, middle managers, professional employees, salaried employees, sales and field personnel, first-line supervisors, foremen, rank-and-file employees			• Anyone who received the publication(s); should be administered in such a way that non-readers also make inputs

PROCESS	INFORMAL	FORMAL
• Management to worker communication • Worker to management communication	• Effective supervision, house journals, newsletters, e-mail, mass social functions • Participative management, effective working groups	• Briefing groups, written circulars, notices, induction, disciplinary procedures, training, public address system • Works/liaison committees, consultative committees, grievance procedures

Formal and informal communication networks

Internal communication may be defined as all kinds of interaction that take place between members of one big or small organization. This type of communication may be looked at from different perspectives. It may be viewed in terms of whether it is formal or informal and it can also be seen as directed from the employer to workers or from workers to the employer.

Principles of employee communication

- Communication is a fundamental component of management. It should be viewed as a contributing partner with other key staff functions in influencing employee understanding of both business goals and public relations issues.
- Commitment by top management is essential, as is their participation in and support of the communication process at all levels of the organization. An overall company policy on organizational communication and definitive guidelines for managers and supervisors are also absolutely essential. Top management must be committed to open, honest communication.

- A communication strategy is essential. Communication must be a planned process, a strategy involving both communication professionals and key management people. Development of a strategic plan, including short and long-term goals, is necessary to put the management communication function professionally on a par with other management functions. Ideally, the plan should be revised each year.
- Managers are the key to success. They are the key conduits and catalysts for effective communication, and the system must recognize their need for information, training, and rewards for good communication performance. Top executives should set the example by being accessible, sharing important information, and encouraging the upward flow of information and ideas – even if negative. Above all they need to ensure that ideas and criticism are acted upon or transmitted to the right persons for appropriate action.
- Priority issues should form the content. These should be the core content of the management communication programme and should be discussed in an open and understandable manner through various channels of communication.
- Regular evaluation will ensure effectiveness. The communication process should undergo regular evaluation to prove its worth in terms of employee-management

relations as well as employee performance and awareness of key public issues. It is essential that the communication function be tested periodically to determine its effectiveness and to give direction for improvements.

Changing employee communication needs and expectations

Many professional organizations conduct surveys on a regular basis to monitor the effectiveness of their internal communications. Both local and international research reveal the following general trends:
- The majority of the workforce are concerned about a lack of information about their employing organization, including where the company is headed and the reasoning behind decisions.
- There is generally a failure to encourage a free exchange of information among employees and departments.
- There is little participatory management taking place within organizations.
- There is still a preponderance of top-down communications rather than bottom-up communications.
- The grapevine remains the single most influential tool in disseminating both personal information and company news of a sensitive nature.

With regard to the communication needs and expectations of employees, the surveys reveal:
- There is a preference for one-on-one communication in all key areas, including the conveyance of expectations for performances, rules, and regulations; strategies and goals; safety and productivity advice; and benefits information.
- Employees' preferred sources of organizational information are firstly their immedi-

ate supervisor, secondly small-group meetings, and thirdly senior executives.
- The forms of communication that need most improvement have been identified as those to and from top executives, those emanating from immediate supervisors, and orientation programmes.
- The information that is of particular interest to employees has been identified as organizational plans for the future, productivity improvements, and personnel policies and practices.

Media for internal communications

The source of information (communication technique or tool) selected will often depend on the subject matter that needs to be communicated to employees. Of the many communication techniques available, induction programmes and printed or graphic communication appear to be the more commonly used, either alone or in combination, to convey an important or complicated message.

The less sophisticated and educated the workforce, the less dependence there is on mediated communication, and the more dependence there is on interpersonal, small group, and public communication (mass meetings, forums, discussions, gatherings).

Forums

Usually, forums are group sessions comprising 10 to 25 employees and a senior manager, who acts as a facilitator or moderator. When more sensitive and controversial matters are at stake, it may be better to use a neutral facilitator brought in from outside the organization.

Forums are personal, open, and interactive – and they always have a specific topic and format identified ahead of time. They should be

Medium	Principal advantages
• Employee publications	• Treat subjects in depth; visually attractive
• Manual and booklets	• Flexible; complete in details
• Newsletters	• Easily prepared; low-cost coverage
• Posters	• Colourful; dramatic; attention-getting
• Notice boards/information racks	• Timely; strategically placed
• Exhibits and displays	• Highly flexible; attention-getting
• Closed-circuit television and teleconferencing	• Dramatic; attention-compelling; involves audience; good for training
• Motion pictures and videotapes	• Visual; realistic; good for demonstration of processes
• Grapevines	• Informal; timely
• Speeches and meetings	• Two-way communication; treats problem in depth
• Advisory groups	• Two-way communication; takes advantage of expertise
• Internet/intranet/extranet/web-based	• The technology of the future: allows one-to-one, one-to-many, formal and informal, multi-media, asynchronous and synchronous forms

Adapted from Engel et al. 1994: 467

carefully structured to encourage employee involvement and should not include lengthy one-way presentations. Employees should be encouraged to share their viewpoints, and extensive time for this must be structured into the sessions. The facilitator helps drive the discussion, engage participants, and get answers to questions that arise.

Forum participants can be given information and assignments ahead of time or after the fact. For example, employees who are invited to participate in the forum can be asked to interview colleagues about a topic, or act as chairpersons for smaller group discussions.

Forums enable and empower participants to have better comprehension of issues and to feel they are authentically part of the change process. Often, employees who are asked to be actively involved in the process actually become ambassadors of the topic at hand and communicate key messages to their colleagues. It is vitally important that forum participants see that their input is put to use in the organization. If it is not, credibility will be lost and future forums won't be taken seriously by employees.

A participative communication process also signals that the company is serious about the issues and about making sure employees are actively involved.

Furthermore, the straightforward forum process makes it easy for managers to get involved and to reach large numbers of employees. Since many employees say face-to-face communication is their preferred method of receiving information, forums are especially effective.

How do you conduct a forum? Here are some basic steps involved in the process that will help ensure your objectives are achieved:

- Get the support of the chief executive officer and enlist the help of senior managers. This demonstrates that the issue is important and gives employees the freedom to feel that time spent on the forum is fully sanctioned.
- Invite participants from all levels and locations within the organization. Employees at different locations (with different working cultures) may have a novel view of the topic.
- Develop a series of tools, such as invitation letters, a discussion guide, and feedback forms. Send them to local communicators, plant managers, or other colleagues who are helping you with the logistics.
- Help the moderators by giving them training ahead of time as well as providing them with tools (overheads, discussion guides, etc.). If an external moderator is used, brief them on the issues, possible points of dissension, and the organizational history and culture. Ask them to warm up the group by beginning with a topic that is not emotionally charged and then moving on to more difficult subjects.
- Conduct the first two or three forums as pilots and use them to iron out any kinks in the programme. Try to use senior managers who are known as good communicators, opinion leaders, or are trusted among employees.
- Compile results. Ask moderators or local communicators to collect notes, transcripts, and flip-chart points developed in the forums, as well as feedback forms, and send them back to you. Establish the key findings, trends, and recommendations of the groups. Make recommendations for change based on forum findings. In order for the forums to be successful, some action has to be taken.
- Communicate throughout the process. Use your other communication vehicles (such as newsletters and the intranet) to communicate about the forums before, during, and after they are held. Once the forums are finished, be sure to communicate the results and tell employees what steps will be taken.

While forums may not be the answer to every communication challenge, they are a powerful way to make complicated or emotional subjects more understandable, meaningful, and easier for employees to accept. The bottom line is that employees will feel more valued if they are involved and if you can demonstrate to them that their opinion matters.

Induction programmes

Induction programmes are run to introduce the new employee to the company. These are essentially a public relations responsibility, although sections of the programme, even its control, may well be handled by the human resources department. This dual responsibility and interdependence demand a close relationship between the two departments. Healthy staff relations are a prerequisite for good public relations.

Why induction?

In a survey into labour turnover undertaken in the Eastern Cape by the Nelson Mandela Metropol University, the following comment was made by the researchers:

In every case, separation interviews ... traced the cause of resignation to poor induction procedures. Typical comments were, 'Nobody seemed to know I was here,' and 'No one told me what to do.'

Induction can be fruitfully applied to all situations and in all groups. Hourly paid, salaried, and managerial employees share the same basic need for orientation into new work situations, although this need may differ with regard to context and emphasis for specific groups.

What is induction?

The aim of induction is to help the newcomer to adjust as quickly as possible to the new social and working environment in order to achieve maximum working efficiency in the shortest possible time.

Induction programmes may take a variety of forms, ranging from a tour of the organization or factory, a short induction course, or an open forum. Such programmes ensure a smooth transition for the new employee into the new working world.

Care should be exercised not to use the same induction programme for graduates and older entrants to industry. All programmes should be reassessed for effectiveness.

Printed and graphic communication

Employee publications (house journals, staff or employee newsletters, and reports to employees) have come of age in southern Africa.

An organization may publish various types of printed matter for use by employees. A distinction can be drawn between occasional publications (such as technical manuals, employee benefits handbooks, health and safety handbooks, and employee welcome brochures) and regular periodicals (such as the company newsletter, monthly managerial bulletins, quarterly sports and social club magazines, house journals, and financial reports to employees).

Employee publications should have three definite characteristics. They must be:

- informative;
- educational;
- entertaining.

Whether the publication belongs to a large or small organization, or just one of the branches in a group, the objectives for communicating with staff should be the following:

- to foster a feeling of unity;
- to keep employees informed of company activities;
- to enhance employee understanding of company operations, departments, and divisions;
- to discuss major policy changes, compensation policies, management changes, new activities, new products, and company benefits;
- to show the company's involvement in community affairs;
- to offer useful information, such as tax tips, preventive health measures, and financial advice;
- to improve productivity and instil a strong awareness and understanding of the importance of quality in all elements of the production process. This can be achieved by educating each employee about what productivity is and motivating employees by showing 'what's in it' for each one. After all, productivity and quality are the keys to job security, improved income, and expanded fringe benefits.

House journals or staff newsletters

The house journal or staff newsletter has become firmly established as a means of communication between an organization and its public. The British Association of Communicators in Business define house journals as follows:

... publications issued periodically, and not primarily for profit, by an industrial undertaking, a business house, or public service. The term covers not only all types of internal magazines, newspapers, bulletins, and news sheets for employees, but also external periodicals which are published primarily for shareholders, agents, dealers, distributors, retailers, or customers, in the interest of prestige, public relations, and sales promotion purposes.

It is apparent that there are three types of publication:

- *Internal:* Usually called a staff newsletter or staff journal, this publication is intended for the staff and created by the staff. It is usually published as a tabloid, although some companies prefer an A4 publication. The staff journal today is a management-staff publication which explains the organization to its members. It seeks to improve internal employee relationships with management and generally to strengthen the company spirit through shared information and achievements. Frequency is imperative and while a quarterly publication is acceptable, the more frequent the better – preferably monthly.
- *External:* This publication is usually made available to clients and has proved to be an effective means of communicating the company's products, people, and projects, as well as being a type of support to the marketing efforts. Frequency is not a critical factor but presentation is important.
- *Combination of internal/external:* Normally referred to as the house journal or house magazine, this publication is usually available to members of staff as well as those outside the organization, including clients, government, suppliers, shareholders, pensioners, and the press. It may even be distributed internationally. Published at least quarterly, the preferred format is a glossy A4, although some organizations use a

glossy tabloid and make considerable use of colour photography.

Annual staff reports

Few companies of any repute today neglect to produce a staff report on an annual basis, and, in some cases, more regularly.

This is a top-down strategic communications tool. Originally a staff report appeared as run-of-paper within the staff journal, but increasingly it is becoming a stand-alone high-end production, much like an environmental report, a social report, or even an annual report to shareholders.

The annual staff report should address those issues which have had the most impact on staff over the past financial year . It should outline the 'big three' issues:

- *Vision*: Where is the company going?
- *Mission*: How it is going to get there?
- *Values*: How does it conduct its business?

It should report on the state of the industry or sector in which the company does business. At the same time, it is necessary to contextualize the business: how it is doing within the local and international industry. This is a type of brief strengths-weaknesses-opportunities-threats (SWOT) analysis. The annual staff report contains information on specific divisions, as well as the financial position of the company over the past year.

What does the financial report contain? The staff report addresses the value added statement. The basic idea is to interpret this for employees in a simple and uncomplicated manner. This section of the report asks the following two questions:

- *Value added*: Where did the money come from over the past year?
- *Distribution of value added*: How was the money spent?

Value added is simply a matter of outlining turnover for the year under review and ideally giving some indication of annual turnover for at least three previous years. This will give employees some idea of the growth, or lack of it, of the company.

One should also show the divisional contributions to annual turnover and, again, this could also be shown over the past three years so that employees know whether their division's contribution has been growing or diminishing.

Distribution of value added would normally cover the following areas:
- staff (salaries and wages);
- shareholders (dividends) – detail as to the breakdown in shareholding;
- government (taxation);
- providers of finance (banks and other financial institutions);
- social investment;
- retained for reinvestment – where this retained income will be invested and within what time frame.

While the annual report to shareholders attempts to project the company's best image with the shareholders, investor community, media, customers, and suppliers, the staff report attempts to promote the company's image with staff and potential staff. It provides a perfect platform to promote staff benefits such as training schemes, scholarships and bursaries, pension/provident fund, medical aid, and staff housing, as well as community investment projects, sponsorships, and environmental policy. The general idea is to sell the company as a responsible employer and corporate citizen to the staff.

How should the staff report be packaged? There is one simple rule: use the KISS (keep it short and simple) principle. The staff report should be packaged so that it reaches people where they are in terms of literacy. Cartoons may be a good way forward, but beware of patronizing your readers.

Other forms of written and graphic communication

- *Management letters to employees.* Management letters discussing significant

company affairs can be distributed to employees by supervisors or mailed to the homes of workers. In the latter instance they are likely to be given more careful consideration by employees and their families. This kind of letter also includes anniversary-with-the-company and birthday cards to senior employees. Letters on the individual's performance, organizational changes, and explaining the remuneration and benefits programmes are further examples.

- *Bulletin boards (notice boards).* One of the least expensive, most neglected, and yet most effective medium of group communication with employees is the bulletin board. Properly located and supervised, bulletin boards command employee attention, are read by more people than would listen to public address broadcasts, and are given several viewings by individual employees. They should be located where they can be seen and read conveniently – in rest rooms, beside passenger elevators, and in the cafeteria. Material should be changed every week, and boards should be kept free of obsolete notices. In fact, there should be a distinct physical separation of official information (need to know) and informal information (nice to know).

- *Product exhibits.* Exhibits of raw materials, parts, and finished products impress employees with their own role in producing the product. Product exhibits include enlarged photographs of finished products, cross-sections or working models with charts and diagrams to describe important features, and promotional material. They show the organization's willingness to include the employee in all its strategies.

- *Employee handbooks and manuals.* Employee handbooks and manuals are used to inform employees of policies, procedures, hours, wages, benefits, and rules and regulations. They are an essential component of employee communication, but can easily become outdated 'dust collectors'.

- *Payroll-envelope inserts.* A convenient and inexpensive medium of employee communication is the payroll-envelope insert. It is also used to inform employees of wage changes, and pension and group insurance regulations.

- *Reading racks.* An inexpensive medium of communication with employees is the reading rack filled with booklets about corporate affairs; political, economic and social subjects; health, safety, hobbies, cooking, sport, and other matters of interest to employees. Racks are placed in plant locations where they are readily accessible to employees.

- *Suggestion schemes.* Through suggestions and safety schemes, employees can participate directly in company methods of operation by reducing costs, raising productivity levels, and reducing wastage, while at the same time benefiting financially and in prestige from their efforts.

Although suggestion schemes can be an excellent means of encouraging employee participation in the company, they have their weaknesses. When drafting rules for the scheme, it is essential to prohibit 'gripe' or complaints suggestions, although they are valid in human relations terms. The scheme should clearly state the type of suggestion required: ways to increase output, improve staff relations, cost savings, etc.

- *Audiovisuals, videos, and films.* Audiovisuals, videos, films, and slides can play an effective role in employee communication. These are used as part of the induction programme to inform new workers about company history, organization structure, products, and employee benefits. Annual report results on corporate finances, sales, earnings, and plant expansion are shown to employees and used to educate them with regard to economics, to explain the advantages of the free-enterprise system, to promote preventive health programmes, and to provide voter education, literacy, and numeracy training.

- *Internal television programmes.* Closed-circuit internal television broadcasts describing company progress and operations are used to communicate with employees in large corporations. On a monitor installed in each department, workers may see and hear the plant manager or managing director broadcast important plant news and business messages. Internal broadcasts, live or taped, may be re-broadcast in community television (where appropriate) and radio programmes.

- *Public address systems.* Public address systems in plants and offices are commonly used to transmit timely and important information quickly, without calling workers from their tasks. Broadcasts from top management are authoritative and impressive, and make a personal appeal through the voice of the speaker.

- *Document/computer conferencing.* All members that are involved in the conference, log in to their computers and into the Internet. The document or the issues to be discussed appears on the monitor of each computer. Participants read it, make changes and suggestions, while the change occurs on all monitors. They take turns doing the same thing until the final agreement or document is reached. The beauty of computer or document conferencing is that it saves both cost and time incurred in printing out the document and sending it to every member of the organization.

- *Audio conferencing.* A number of people will be linked via the telephone at one time on one line where they can all hear each other. The difference between this and teleconferencing is that individuals do not have to leave their home or office, while in teleconferencing they have to be in an office which has the right equipment.

- *Telephone and voicemail.* The voicemail service allows one to leave a message for a colleague when he or she is not available or unable to pick up the phone. The voicemail will state the time and the date on which the message was left as well as a reminder that there is a recorded message on the telephone.

- *Internet.* In a very short time, the Internet has become the ultimate tool in interactive communication in the corporate sector. The communication barriers of time and space have been obliterated through the use of on-line technology and with its multimedia capabilities, the World Wide Web has captured the imagination of computer users globally.

But even with the Internet, face-to-face interaction and company publications generally still seem to be the most effective and affordable media to reach and convey information to most employees. Specialized management publications, videotapes, paid radio and television, and satellite television are the media with the greatest potential for sharing information.

However, the media mix which will be optimal for a particular organization can be determined only by that specific organization itself. Each organization or location, therefore, should decide which mix of media would serve its own employee communication needs best.

Employee relations programmes

Other methods for improving employee relations which lead to better communication include:

- *Open days for employees and their families.* An open house for employees and their families provides opportunities for communication with workers. Management and foremen can tell and show workers about the nature and variety of products produced, the capital investment, new and improved machinery and facilities, and the significance of the individual's job in the overall company production.
- *Visits by senior executives to departments.* Visits by the chief executive and senior management executives to offices and plants, for informal talks with small groups

of workers, afford opportunities for good two-way communication.

- *Departmental (or intercompany) relations.* Interdepartmental (or intercompany) liaison is an important function of the public relations practitioner.

A barrier to improved internal communication is the departmental mind that says, 'Why does he or she want to know it? It's got nothing to do with him or her. This is a human resources department matter!' To put it bluntly, it is impossible to plan to meet likely problems without a high degree of interdepartmental co-operation, or for that matter, intercompany co-operation.

Social and sporting events can assist greatly towards improving interdepartmental relations.

- *Meetings of management and employees.* Management-employee meetings are a common medium of communication with workers. Meetings give management an opportunity to speak directly to the workers about new policies, products, methods, and internal problems. The programme usually includes panel discussions by executives, questions by employees, roundtable conferences, and films.
- *Service awards.* Management often tends to underestimate the value of recognizing an individual's long-time service with an organization. Recognition in some tangible form (e.g. ties, scarves, watches, pens, etc.) may be small, but will be appreciated by the recipient. Often there is also a financial award, but this must be realistic and in keeping with the economic climate. In addition, some form of publicity at a service function and inclusion in the company newsletter or house journal are useful.

Intranets

Intranets are having a major impact on internal communications. Memos, newsletters, guideline documents, internal phone books, training manuals, and product and competitor information can all be converted into HTML format and published, maintained, and updated on a company's intranet. This provides a far more cost-effective and time-saving method of running a business, as it helps employees find and access information more easily.

Office automation is the next area to move to the intranet, once companies have moved their paper-based internal publishing regimes to the web. After turning over phone lists and hefty manuals to intranets, it is now the turn of payroll and time cards, travel expense reporting, order forms, invoices, purchase order numbers, stock requisitions, and orders to be handled electronically and in real time. At present, most of these processes are done either manually or by unique computer application, all of which need to be learnt individually. With an intranet, users are able to access this information via a common interface – the browser – which also makes it far easier for them to learn.

By presenting information in the same way to every computer with an intranet, and as intranets develop to the next level, organizations will be able to pull all the computers, software, and databases that dot the corporate landscape into a single system that enables employees to find information wherever it resides, without actually having to re-programme or re-enter all the information into a single computer system.

In the long term, as the boundaries between the Internet and companies' internal networks are lowered, private corporate intranets will be linked to the public Internet with a security mission – protecting critical, confidential data from outside eyes. This will allow customers, business partners, and suppliers to participate in forum-style electronic conferencing with other users inside and outside of the organization's fire wall, as well as to view product and company information. Access needs to be flexibly controlled, depending on authorization – field representatives,

consultants, partners, home workers, and overseas or branch offices need access to different information than customers do. In the long term, therefore, intranets will expand the horizon of business and create new markets, customers, and business globally.

Further reading

Adams, C. (ed.) 1993. *Affirmative Action in a Democratic South Africa*. Cape Town: Juta.

Bovee, C.L. & J.V. Thill. 1992. *Business Communications Today*. 3rd edition. New York: McGraw-Hill.

Cutlip, S.M., A.H. Center & G.M. Broom. 1994. *Effective Public Relations*. 6th Edition. Englewood Cliffs, New Jersey: Prentice-Hall.

Davis, A. 1999. 'What have you done for me lately?' *Communika and Public Relations Tactics*. May. Johannesburg: PRISA.

Engel, J.F., M.R. Warshaw & T. Kinnear. 1994. *Promotional Strategy*. Chicago: Irwin.

Haywood, R. 1991. *All About Public Relations*. 2nd edition. New York: McGraw-Hill.

Lubbe, B.A. & G. Puth. 1994. *Public Relations in South Africa: A Management Reader*. Johannesburg: Heinemann.

Mersham, G.M., R. Rensburg & J.C. Skinner. 1995. *Public Relations, Development and Social Investment: A Southern African Perspective*. Pretoria: Van Schaik.

Mersham, G.M. & J.C. Skinner. 2001. *New Insights into Business and Organizational Communication*. Johannesburg: Heinemann.

Moore, M.F. 1977. *Public Relations: Principles, Cases and Problems*. Homewood, Illinois: Richard D Irwin.

Wilcox, D.L., P.H. Ault & W.K. Agee. 1989. *Public Relations: Strategies and Tactics*. New York: Harper & Row.

Wingrove, T. 1993. *Affirmative Action – A 'How To' Guide for Managers*. Johannesburg: Knowledge Resources.

Chapter 11

Planning a public relations programme

When you have read this chapter, you should:

- be able to discuss the four important reasons for planning;
- be able to identify the seven different steps in a public relations programme according to the PRISA approach;
- be informed as to what each of the different steps involves;
- be able to relate this process to an actual programme.

How to plan and measure the contribution of public relations to a company's overall image and success is a challenge being faced by all practitioners in the field.

According to Jefkins (1998:39) the four important reasons for planning are:

- to set targets for public relations operations against which results can be assessed;
- to estimate the working hours and other costs involved;
- to select priorities which will control the number and the timing of different operations in the programme;
- to decide the feasibility of carrying out the declared objectives according to the avail-

ability of: sufficient staff of the right calibre; physical equipment such as office machines, cameras, or vehicles, and adequate budget.

The public relations programme is thus the blueprint from which the public relations team operates and from which management judges its performance.

The traditional public relations programme consists of seven important elements:

- defining the situation (situation analysis);
- setting the objectives;
- determining the target audience;
- developing the message;
- activities – strategy and action plans (with timing and responsibilities);
- budget;
- review and evaluation.

Defining the situation

In looking at the public relations needs and opportunities of any company, it is first necessary to review the current situation before an overall plan can be developed.

What this means, is that public relations activities must be preceded by a proper analy-

Running a PR programme

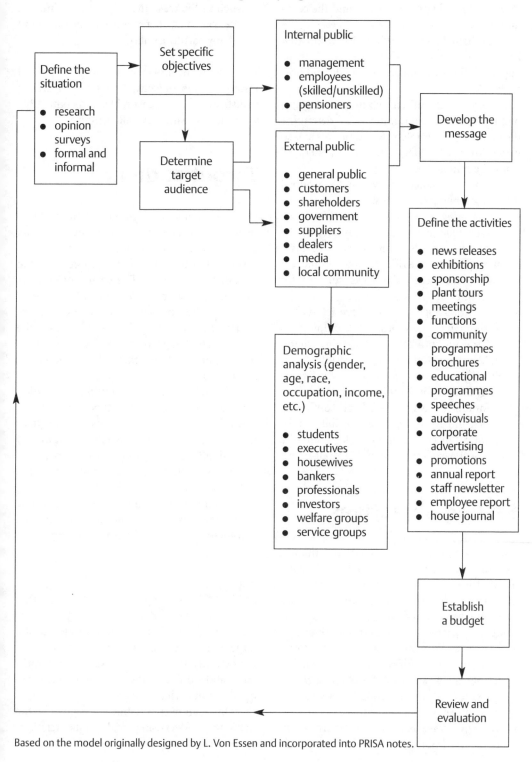

Based on the model originally designed by L. Von Essen and incorporated into PRISA notes.

sis of how an organization is perceived by its clients, shareholders, employees, and the community as a whole.

Abraham Lincoln said, 'If we could first know where we are and whither we are tending, we could better judge what to do and how to do it.'

Therefore, the initial step in formulating a public relations programme is to determine the nature of the problem. So numerous and so varied are the problems that to list them all would be impossible.

In most instances, they can be grouped into three general categories:

- *Overcoming a negative perception of an organization,* for example resistance by the public to a product on the basis of price and quality, or evidence that employees believe their company lacks concern for their interests.
- *Conducting a specific one-off project,* such as introducing a new product, conducting a fundraising project, or obtaining shareholders' approval for an acquisition.
- *Developing and expanding a continuing programme,* for example, maintaining a community's awareness of and confidence in a company's social responsibility programme, or convincing the electorate of a political party's interest in their well-being.

Setting objectives

What do you, the public relations practitioner, want to achieve, both quantitatively and qualitatively? It is essential to ensure that your objectives and evaluation criteria are compatible. There are two kinds of objectives, that is, informational objectives and motivational objectives:

- *Objectives that inform* are less ambitious, and are often typified by phrases such as 'create an awareness of ...', 'enhance the image of ...', 'educate consumers about ...' and 'inform the audience that ...'
- *Objectives that motivate* are more ambitious and impressive, but also more diffi-

cult to achieve and usually contain phrases such as 'increase the sales of ...', 'stimulate the trial of ...', 'increase attendance at ...' and 'change attitudes about ...'

You should aim to write the most precise and result-oriented objectives possible, which are realistic, credible, measurable, and compatible with the company's overall objectives.

Target audience

In nearly all instances, public relations objectives are achieved by influencing someone either to take action or not to take action; the action, of course, will have an effect on the industry's operations. The person or persons to be influenced become the target audience.

Again the temptation is to describe the target audience in non-specific terms, such as the government, the press, the buying community, the population, etc. Such descriptions are insufficient.

Ideally, the audience should be identified individually by name, but this is not always possible. The best alternative is an identification of the smallest possible grouping of individuals. This is important if massive, expensive communications programmes are to be avoided.

It is important that sufficient attention be paid to a company's internal public – its employees.

Message

The message is what is communicated to the target audience. For any given problem or opportunity, there may be several target audiences and a different message should be developed to suit each audience.

Often, an overall theme is designed by the marketing, advertising, and public relations team to convey the group's message.

There has been a further development in the evolution of the Standard Bank's Corporate Image and Identity programme. The new theme of 'Moving Forward' now more closely reflects the vision and mission of the Bank to be at the forefront of developments in the financial field particularly in the light of the dramatic changes in the banking world.

Of the other leading commercial banks, First National Bank (FNB) has developed its own personal campaign focussing on 'How can we help you?' (see www.fnb.co.za).

Absa Bank has focussed its attention on a wide ranging theme embracing 'Today, tomorrow, together' (see www.absabank.co.za).

Finally Nedbank for its part has focussed on 'Make things happen' for its customers and clients (see www.nedbank.co.za).

There are a whole host of other successful campaigns built around particular slogans. What is important is that the claims made are matched with excellence of product quality and service.

Activities

Public relations activities are the tools of communication. They transmit the appropriate message to the target audience.

These activities range from personal, individual contact to massive advertising or press relations programmes. They include plant tours, scientific symposia, public speaking engagements, authoritative briefs submitted to government agencies and committees, individual letters to persons or groups, media releases, press conferences, radio interviews, and house journals.

These activities are oral, written, and visual and they can be prepared for a highly educated audience or for illiterate people.

As in marketing, no single activity will carry the message and have it understood and acted upon by the target audience. Too often, it is assumed that a statement by an industry spokesperson is all that is needed for the

industry position to be accepted. More often than not, the message must be repeated over and over – many, many times in many, many different forms in order to have an impact on the audience. Very often the audience will not accept a message from the sender because of certain barriers. It may be that the sender first has to establish contact with the listener before anything communicated will be believed. The reputation of the communicator is an important factor in the acceptance of the message.

Development of public relations or public affairs activities should be assigned to professional communicators. The activities, however, must be related to the problem, the objective, the target audience, and the message, as previously described. Very often, public relations activities are developed first and then objectives are assigned to them. It is the responsibility of the policy-making body to scrutinize the proposed activities very carefully to ensure that they meet the objectives.

In developing activities, the resources of the industry should be made available and employed. The industry has many scientific, financial, and commercial experts who can make major contributions to the development of the industry position statement and to its communication to others.

Budgeting

Determining a budget for a public relations programme is always difficult. Two basic considerations in the preparation of a public relations budget are:
- the activities planned for a specific public relations programme;
- the costs involved in executing the activities included in the programme.

Before examining the costs likely to be incurred in these two areas, one must accept the concept of zero-based budgeting (ZBB).

This means identifying the 'key decision units'. These are defined as the lowest level at which a decision or series of similar decisions is taken in order to achieve the objective, or the minimum likely cost of achieving a particular objective.

The next step is for each decision unit to be identified as a 'cost centre'. The public relations practitioner usually has little control over cost centres, such as printing, photography, hiring of facilities, and catering. Activities involving these cost centres are therefore very susceptible to ZBB.

Cost of implementing the activities

The cost of implementing the projected public relations activities must include administrative costs and overheads.

Administrative costs include the salaries and fringe benefits of public relations practitioners, secretarial and clerical staff, motor vehicles, travel, entertainment, membership of professional associations, training, and seminars.

Administrative overheads include office space, office equipment, lighting, heating and air-conditioning, telephones, postage, insurance, taxes, and subscriptions to magazines and newspapers.

Having determined the total administrative costs and the proportion of administrative overheads, you are in a position to estimate the expenses likely to be incurred by each cost centre (in this instance the person) responsible for carrying out the activity or series of activities.

Example of corporate budget structure

Salaries and other employee costs	R
Salaries	X XXX,XX
Bonuses	X XXX,XX
National insurance	XXX,XX
Company pension contributions	X XXX,XX
Health insurance and other benefits	X XXX,XX
Company cars	X XXX,XX
Temporary staff	X XXX,XX
Training and professional development	X XXX,XX

Travel and personal expenses	R
Air travel	X XXX,XX
Other travel	X XXX,XX
Subsistence	X XXX,XX
Entertaining	X XXX,XX
Professional subscriptions	X XXX,XX
Telephones	X XXX,XX
Other	X XXX,XX

Office supplies, services and computing	R
Allocated overheads including rental	X XXX,XX
Equipment leases	X XXX,XX
Depreciation of capital equipment	X XXX,XX
Stationery and other office supplies	X XXX,XX
Computer supplies and services	X XXX,XX
Telephone and fax	X XXX,XX
Postage	X XXX,XX
Monitoring services	X XXX,XX
Distribution services	X XXX,XX

Financial communication programmes   R
Report and accounts and interim statements   X XXX,XX
Annual general meeting   X XXX,XX
Shareholder and broker meetings and visits   X XXX,XX
Financial results advertising   X XXX,XX
Financial communication consultancy   X XXX,XX

Government affairs programmes   R
Contact events and visits   X XXX,XX
Monitoring services   X XXX,XX
Government relations consultancy   X XXX,XX

Marketing communication programmes   R
(Shared with the marketing department)
Product literature   X XXX,XX
Product audiovisual   X XXX,XX
Product advertising   X XXX,XX
Exhibitions   X XXX,XX
Sales promotion   X XXX,XX
Product launches   X XXX,XX
Marketing communication consultancy   X XXX,XX

Internal communication programmes   R
(Shared with the human resources department)
Employee publications   X XXX,XX
E-mail and fax distribution services   X XXX,XX
Management and employee briefing conferences   X XXX,XX
Employee award schemes   X XXX,XX
Internal communication consultancy   X XXX,XX

Community relations programmes   R
Open days and other community events   X XXX,XX
Local sponsorship   X XXX,XX
Subscription and donations   X XXX,XX

Corporate activities   R
Corporate identity   X XXX,XX
Communication manuals   X XXX,XX
Group advertising (excluding product and service advertising)   X XXX,XX
Brochures and other literature   X XXX,XX
Display material   X XXX,XX
Promotional material   X XXX,XX
Audiovisual   X XXX,XX
Photography   X XXX,XX
Media relations   X XXX,XX
Periodical publications   X XXX,XX
Corporate events and hospitality   X XXX,XX
Exhibitions   X XXX,XX
Sponsorship   X XXX,XX
Opinion research   X XXX,XX
General public relations consultancy services   X XXX,XX

Adapted from Jefkins 1998:120

Evaluating results

There are essentially two kinds of results: qualitative and quantitative. Many results of public relations activity will be qualitative, that is, they will not be measured statistically. Instead, they will be measured by experience and self-evident qualities, for example, evidence that the job applicants are better educated, more proficient, or in some other way more suitable than in the past.

In contrast, quantitative results might show, for instance, a percentage increase in awareness, a reduced number of complaints, a larger number of job applicants, oversubscription of a share issue, or increased media exposure as a result of sports sponsorship.

No one measure can reflect the real effectiveness of a public relations programme, so most practitioners use a number of measurement tools and apply them singly or in combination, as appropriate. Formal research tools include opinions polls or surveys and the detailed analysis of press publicity and broadcast returns. Informal research tools include internal meetings to discuss the conduct of campaigns and their results, and complaints and criticism received by correspondence or by phone. The latter will need to be analysed on a regular basis and acted upon.

General feedback

In a survey undertaken in the United States, general feedback was the most popular measurement tool, despite the availability of more sophisticated procedures.

Press publicity

The primary reason for the evaluation of media exposure is validity – the determination of good media return on investment (different to monetary ROI). Other very obvious reasons are accountability, benchmarking for future activities and measurement of efficiencies.

Press publicity refers to publicity in all types of newspaper and magazine, across multiple media groups and media types. The traditional accounting method, and one that can be effectively measured, is counting the number of column centimetres achieved and converting them into rands (using advertising costs as the basis).

This quantitative form of measurement can be made more sophisticated by breaking down the information into the number of exposures to the target audience (in numbers of readers or circulation) in a designated market area. This involves a clear and thorough understanding of the target market and the tools available in the industry to provide the relevant data. Firstly, one would need to the circulation figures as determined by the ABC (Audit Bureau of Circulation) and the AMPS figures (All Media Product Survey) that are produced by the South African Advertising Research Foundation. The former provides a factual account of the number of copies in circulation, while the latter provides an indication of the number of people who may have read the publication. This is based on RPC (Readers Per Copy), which suggests that for every copy of a publication, X number of people could have read it, thereby expanding the target market.

The most commonly used tools to measure the rand value return is that of Advertising Value Equivalent (AVE). This method provides a unit of measure that determines the value of the editorial content that was received. AVE is determined in direct correlation to the advertising rates of each publication individually and the size of the article – i.e. no two publications will carry the same value for the same sized article.

In addition to the direct return in value, an often overlooked evaluation is that of 'sales leads' or enquiries that occur as a result of an editorial in a newspaper or trade magazine.

Broadcast returns

As with the press, time on radio or television is another measurement tool – especially if linked to the number of listeners or viewers. Similar to the AVE method discussed above, values for broadcast media are determined based on the unique 30-second ad cost on each station and each time slot individually. For example, 30 seconds of exposure at 06:15 on SABC2 will differ vastly from the same 30 seconds aired at 07:15. These values are determined by the station based on their known RAMS (Radio Audience Measurement Survey) or TAMS (Television Audience Measurement Survey) as provided by SAARF (South African Advertising Research Foundation) and are updated regularly. This means that a good understanding of the media landscape and constant updates are required.

Online returns

With the growth of digital media, the area of online media exposure is becoming more important. Monitoring and measurement companies make use of the ad rates on each individual website and calculate a cost per word based on the number of words that 'fit' into an ad block. That value is then multiplied by the number of words in the article and weighted on the number of page impressions. There is a complex algorithm that companies use to calculate the exact rand value.

Trended analysis

In the age of digital information, it is becoming increasingly important to provide trended data to clients. This data is usually based on a 10-week trend, so that an accurate assessment can be made that determines brand equity over the period. This trended data, while statistical, can be both quantitative and qualitative. For the former, simple units of measure are used – including AVE, circulation and clip count; while the latter will provide figures based on the favourability of the articles received. This information is critical for live assessment and brand positioning, allowing practitioners to view article favourability by journalist on a rolling cycle. It is not enough to measure share of voice, but also

the reputational elements of that share. For example. an increase in negative exposure will increase share of voice, but not favourability (and could even decrease market share).

Good management requires good measurement. It is becoming increasingly important, if not essential, to report back in the form of tangible and statistically-sound data sets as managerial accountability is on the rise.

Sales results

Although sales results are difficult to attribute to public relations, there is no doubt that a public relations programme integrated with the marketing and sales plan can have an impact on sales results.

This impact has been demonstrated effectively in the launching of a product where, because of a limited budget or an overcrowding of competitive products in the media (electronic or press), traditional promotion strategies such as advertising, sampling, direct mail, and sales promotions were not employed. Instead, a well-designed public relations programme was implemented with the specific objectives of achieving sales and market share.

Opinion polls and surveys

Studies have shown that companies that use a properly structured audit with clearly defined goals find this method extremely valuable. Unfortunately, it is too costly for 'everyday' public relations activity.

Subjective internal meetings

Discussions with sales, marketing, and general staff are an effective means of determining how successful a particular programme or part of a programme has been.

Complaints and criticism

Some companies or organizations, such as banks, Telkom, and Spoornet, are more prone to complaints or criticism than others. A programme aimed at negating the issues that tend to cause most of the problems is an obvious and simple yardstick, measurable by the mere reduction in complaints or criticism, or both.

Awards and prizes

Recognition in the form of awards or prizes in photographic, house journal, PRISM, or advertising competitions is another indication of how successful a particular public relations strategy has been.

Added to this could be awards for safety, fire protection, exports, or personnel achieve-

ments, all of which contribute to the image of the company.

Fewer government regulations

Public relations programmes designed to challenge certain government attitudes or to change or modify certain policies have proved effective.

Included in this area are lobbying and maintaining close contact with officials. These practices can be of immense help to management in achieving support in such areas as import permits and immigration.

Case study Nelson Mandela Children's Fund

The Nelson Mandela Children's Fund (NMCF) was established in 1994 by Chairman and Founder Mr Nelson Mandela. The NMCF's mandate is to address issues that affect children and youth, particularly those living in disadvantaged situations that places them in vulnerable circumstances. As an advocacy, development agency and a leading champion for the general well-being of children and youth, the NMCF operations are run in accordance within a strategic intent called *Sakha ikusasa* (Zulu expression which means building the future).

Precisely because our programmes do not claim to present the ultimate answer to universal development challenges facing the country, we have chosen key areas in which to make a demonstrable difference.

The Fund's focus does not for a moment suggest representing the totality of the plight that children and youth find themselves in. We humbly submit, that the problems are overwhelming and huge. However, we are expected to play our part in bringing relief in areas in which we can best practically deploy our resources with confidence, without suggestion that the choice we are making ranks higher or lower than those chosen by similar organizations that share our vision towards a child-centered society.

Once the NMCF has proven to be equal to the challenges facing children in its stipulated key areas of focus, so will the case to extend to further areas be stronger. The vision to change the way society treats its children and youth, and mission for a child-centered society is a lifetime undertaking of all concerned.

Vision
The Nelson Mandela Children's Fund strives to change the way society treats its children and youth.

Mission statement
In the pursuit of its vision and in order to ensure that the legacy of its founder, Nelson Mandela, is secured in perpetuity, the NMCF will:
- develop partnerships and initiate programmes which empower and improve the well-being of children and youth;
- promote the rights of children and youth through the influence of public policy and social awareness, and;
- sustain these initiatives through the development of a sound financial and knowledge support base.

Our values and principles

The NMCF's target beneficiaries are children and youth from birth to 22 years of age, and who come from impoverished backgrounds. To maximize the positive impact of our resources, the Fund works closely with fellow development organizations, government, the private sector, and other interested parties. The following values and principles guide the establishment of our partnerships to:

- define their ultimate goal as poverty eradication, and not just the amelioration of the difficult circumstances that the targeted beneficiaries find themselves in;
- embrace a holistic and integrated approach to the challenges confronting children as an integral part of families and communities;
- collaborate with implementing partners in the planning and implementation of projects and programmes;
- position their work within the national framework that aims to reduce hunger, prevent and eliminate abuse and end exploitation in order to bring about basic conditions that all children should enjoy;
- enhance the rights of children to reach their full potential;
- promote best practice, encourage professionalism, and be oriented toward achieving measurable results.

Our four key areas of operation

Wellbeing of a child	
Strategy:	The mandate of the well-being programme is to strengthen families and communities. Secondly the emphasis is to mitigate the impact of both HIV and Aids and Child abuse. The goal of the programme is to promote a rights-based, nurturing, caring, safe, and supportive environment for children and youth.
Objectives:	• improve policy environment for the promotion of children rights; • increase access to safety, care, and support for children exposed to abusive, traumatic, and difficult situations; • increase access to services for children and youth affected by HIV and Aids; • support the strengthening of household capacity to cope with conditions that create child vulnerability; • transform and strengthen Early Childhood Care and Development (ECCD) programmes and services in selected geographical areas through the development and dissemination of sustainable family and community-based ECCD models.
Activities:	• support organizations that prepare children for court and organizations that facilitate services to survivors of child abuse and their families; • support organizations that provide legal advice and assistance to communities; • support neighbourhood-based response to child abuse; • support and strengthen capacity of institutions involved in child protection; • advocacy campaigns; • research; • through sport, arts, culture, formal education and counselling, support organizations that facilitate the integration of refugee children into mainstream society; • support organizations that facilitate access to services for children and families affected by HIV and Aids; • support organizations that prepare children for formal schooling through Early Childhood Care and Development (ECCD).

	• support reintegration of children living on the street through the following steps: 1 street work and rehabilitation 2 facilitation of formal schooling and skills training 3 family tracing, visits, and preservation.

Leadership and excellence

Strategy:	The Leadership and Excellence Programme focus is to provide youth and children with opportunities that will enhance their leadership skills in the economic, sport, arts and culture, and community participation as volunteers and positive role models. It further showcases youth's talents and acknowledges their contribution in the rebuilding of communities.
Objectives:	• to increase access to information; • to promote the talents and self-esteem of youth; • to increase active participation in decision-making platforms by youth.
Activities:	• support and strengthen capacity building for institutions working with young people in sport, civic participation, arts and culture; • provide training through partners to youth to participate in decision-making; • provide support to young people through partners to advocate for their issues through media and public workshops and seminars; • to provide institutions that have programmes focused on the girl child to build their capacity, taking into account the condition of the boy child in some areas; • support organizations that develop models for building leaders, talent enhancement and showcasing through sports, arts and culture.

Skills development

Strategy	The Skills Development Programme focus is to provide youth with skills that create opportunities for them to engage in economic activities with confidence and appropriate skills.
Objectives	• to identify and address gaps in the current youth entrepreneurship models with a strong focus on increasing the options in rural areas, urban poor, and informal settlement areas; • strengthen institutional capacity to deliver of CBOs, NGOs, and partners that the NMCF works with; • to increase youths access to information and resources.
Activities	• support programmes that have existing models to identify gaps and develop models; • test existing models through implementation in different sites; • evaluate models; • support capacity building of institutions through training and hands-on experience; • through evaluation, support the impact of capacity training on partners.

Children and youth with disabilities

Strategy	The programme strives to ensure that children and youth living with disabilities are part of mainstream society. The overall goal is to improve the quality of life of children and youth with disabilities (CYWD).

Objectives	• increase access to existing government services for children and youth with disabilities; • children and youth with disabilities included in mainstream schools, as well as arts, culture, sports, leadership, and other activities; • improved and appropriate care services provided to children and youth with disabilities.
Activities	• support organizations that facilitate access to services for children and youth with disabilities; • advocacy campaigns; • support to organizations that facilitate access to mainstream schooling and participation of children and youth with disabilities in social activities; • support organizations that develop models for building leaders, talent enhancement and showcasing through sport, arts and culture; • through the assessment and stimulation of a child with special needs, support organizations that are aiming at improving the quality of life of children living with disabilities; • support and strengthen the capacity of institutions working with children and youth with disabilities.

Resource mobilization	
Strategy	To solicit and secure both restricted and unrestricted funds in order to build future sustainability and support current programmes.
Objectives	• manage transition from non-designated to comprehensive resource mobilization; • secure R12 million of non-designated funding per annum; • co-ordinate support from affiliates to be in line with our revised funding cycle business plan; • explore and support new affiliates; • explore, promote, and concretize public philanthropy fundraising opportunities; • support the NMCF Request for Proposals (RFP); • solicit new designated donors; • oversight and quality assurance of events; • staff development and mentorship plan.
Activities	• donor acquisition/solicitation; • negotiation of corporate partnership contracts; • supports efforts of international affiliates; • co-ordinate proposal writing for specific programme funding; • guide/monitor brand usage in corporate fundraising partnerships.

Crosscutting themes

NMCF has identified the following crosscutting themes that will be integrated into all projects and considered when assessing concepts for funding:

Gender

Emphasizes a deliberate effort to address the girl child, requiring projects to mainstream gender considerations, and to incorporate specific gender targeting strategies to address issues impacting girls. It is also an effort to consciously articulate, monitor, and assess the effects on the lives of girls.

Indigenous knowledge systems (IKS)

As part of formulating a strategy that ensures recognition of indigenous knowledge and best practices within the context of programmes, NMCF will consistently and consciously identify indigenous knowledge systems and responses at objective and project levels. NMCF will document and disseminate information on IKS to stakeholders for utilization and for further programming.

Access to information
This is important for empowering beneficiaries of development programmes, HIV and Aids and its impact on infected and affected children and youth.

Institutional transformation
Focuses on strengthening the influence of those institutions that have the greatest impact on children and youth – family, community, faith organizations, schools, and selected government institutions. This is based on the belief that children are best cared for within their families and communities.

Institutional development
Seeks to build and strengthen the internal capacity of implementing partners to perform service delivery.

Advocacy
The NMCF approach within each programme area is to ensure prioritization of crosscutting themes. For example, within the well-being programme area, NMCF will ensure that its interventions include and cater for the girl child; that children and youth affected or infected with HIV and Aids are included in skills development projects.

Beneficiaries
NMCF-supported projects in these programme areas will continue to target children and youth from the ages of 0 to 22 years (ultimate beneficiaries) who come from impoverished families and backgrounds. Support to these beneficiary groups will be provided as follows:

- **Ages 0 to 7 (pre-school):** Support will be provided both directly to the child/young person and indirectly to parents, communities and child or youth care homes.
- **Ages 7 to 18 (school age):** Support will be provided both directly and indirectly to parents, communities, child and youth care homes, and schools.
- **Ages 18 to 22 (out-of-school and unemployed):** Support will be provided both directly to the young person and to NGOs promoting improved conditions for out of school youth.

For more information, please visit our website at: *www.nelsonmandelachildrensfund.com* or *www.nmcf.co.za*

Further reading

Beard, M. 1997. *Running a Public Relations Department*. London: Kogan Page.

Cutlip, S.M., A.H. Center & G.M. Broom. 1994. *Effective Public Relations*. Englewood Cliffs, New Jersey: Prentice-Hall.

Gregory, A. 1996. *Planning and Managing a Public Relations Campaign*. London: Kogan Page.

Grunig, J.E. & T. Hunt. 1984. *Managing Public Relations*. New York: Holt Rinehart & Winston.

Jefkins, F. 1998. *Public Relations*. London: M & E Pitman Publishing.

Steyn, B. & E. Pull. 2000. *Corporate Communication Strategy*. Johannesburg: Heinemann.

White, J. & L. Mazur. 1996. *Strategic Communications Management – Making Public Relations Work*. London: Addison-Wesley.

White, J. 1991. *How to Understand and Manage Public Relations*. London: Business Books.

Wilcox, D.L., P.H. Ault & W.K. Agee. 1995 and 2003. *Public Relations: Strategies and Tactics*. New York: Harper & Row.

Part II

Public relations and the media

Chapter 12

The mass media: print media

When you have read this chapter, you should:

- be familiar with the structure and organization of the South African print media;
- be aware of some of the characteristics of the press;
- be aware of how newspapers and magazines are audited;
- be able to draw up a media release;
- understand the workings of the press;
- be able to prepare press kits;
- understand the various techniques used in creating news;
- be able to handle a variety of news situations.

South Africa has a highly complex media industry consisting of six local television stations, 23 radio stations, some 200 newspapers and 300 consumer magazines, together with over 500 trade, technical, and professional journals and directories.

Technical handling of the print media in South Africa rates among the best in the world and this is one reason why newspapers and magazines have held their own in a volatile information era, characterised by the vast development of various new forms of media-delivery platforms via the internet through modern ICT.

This must be viewed against the general trend in the developed world that saw dropping circulations and the cutting back on costs or closing down of newspapers.

Newspapers

Newspapers may be divided into different categories, according to circulation or according to frequency. Broadly speaking, however, one can distinguish between 'mass' newspapers and 'local' or 'speciality' newspapers. Mass newspapers are circulated nationally and are aimed at the public in general. Local and speciality newspapers are aimed at special publics and their circulation may be limited. With regard to circulation, newspapers may be classified as follows:

- *National*: e.g. *Sunday Times, Rapport, Sunday Independent, Sunday Sun,* and the weekly newspaper, *City Press.* A number of newspapers have introduced separate weekend editions of their daily newspapers, e.g. *Saturday Star, Saturday Dispatch,* and *Post Weekend.*

- *Regional*: e.g. *Daily News* and *Die Burger*.
- *Knock-and-drop*: Distributed free of charge mainly in the urban areas. More than 3,5 million such newspapers are distributed weekly.

There are currently 21 dailies and nine Sunday papers in South Africa. Almost 150 regional or country newspapers, most of which are weekly tabloids, serve particular towns or districts in the country.

Most South African newspapers and magazines are organised into several major publishing houses: Media24 (part of Naspers, the largest media group in Africa), the Irish-based Independent News and Media (Pty) Limited group, Caxton Publishers and Printers Limited group, and Avusa Limited (previously Johnnic Communications). Other important media players include M&G Media Limited; the Natal Witness Printing and Publishing Company (Pty) Limited: Primedia Publishing Limited; Ramsay, Son and Parker (Pty).

Globally competitive IT systems, especially among the large media houses, have helped to improve the overall technical quality of print media and have also positively affected distribution and circulation reach.

There is a range of general and specialized news websites which, in terms of the speed and breadth of their coverage, are on par with the best in the world.

Magazines

The trend to target certain niche markets with specialised publications is popular in the magazine industry but there is evidence to suggest that the overall reading population in South Africa is shrinking.

Magazines may be categorized according to whether they are mass magazines, speciality magazines, and technical periodicals.

Mass magazines are circulated nationally. Some appear weekly (*Huisgenoot, You, Drum*);

some appear fortnightly (*Fair Lady, Rooi Rose, Sarie*); others appear monthly (*Bona, Cosmopolitan, Femina*). Multichoice TV magazine (the M-Net television guide) circulates to almost 1,5 million viewers, making it the largest circulation magazine in South Africa.

Speciality magazines are usually addressed to a particular audience and provide for the interests of that group: women's magazines – *Women's Value, Your Family*; financial magazines – *Financial Mail, Finweek*; farmers' magazines – *Farmers' Weekly, Landbouweekblad*; entertainment magazines – *Scenario, Video Scene Magazine, Getaway, Razor* for men and *Glamour* for women.

Certain speciality and technical periodicals are addressed to the needs of a specific interest group, such as religious, literary, scientific, or medical. These include *Review, Communicare, Equid Novi*, and *Archimedes*.

As with newspapers, magazines may be categorized according to frequency: weekly, bi-weekly, monthly, quarterly, and half-yearly.

Within the advertising and public relations context, a distinction is made between trade, technical, and professional publications on the one hand and consumer magazines on the other.

The trade, technical, and professional press industry in South Africa plays an important role in the dissemination of specialist knowledge and information to specific audiences in a wide range of areas of activity and interest.

Online media

Creamer Media's industrial and political websites dominate this market producing three of the four fastest growing sites- Engineering News, Mining Weekly and Polity.

The most popular South African websites are:
- *News24*
- *MSN*
- *MWeb*

- *Webmail*
- *Hotmail*
- *Iol*
- *24.com*
- *Career Junction*
- *Supersport*
- *Yellow Pages.*

Media organizations

Several organizations and associations play an important role in the media field. Print Media South Africa (PMSA), formed in 1996, is an umbrella organization administering individual bodies, namely the Newspaper Association of South Africa, Magazine Publishers Association of South Africa, and the Association of Independent Publishers (AIP). PMSA represents some 700 newspaper and magazine titles in South Africa. Allied to PMSA but not a constituent member, is the ABC, responsible for auditing and verifying print media circulation figures.

The AIP was formed in September 2004 after the publishing groups withdrew from the Community Press Association (CPA). This move aims to give independent publishers an opportunity to transform the CPA into an association that would serve their own specific needs. The AIP represents the interests of more than 250 independent publishers in southern Africa

The South African National Editors' Forum (SANEF) was conceived at a meeting of the Black Editors' Forum, the Conference of Editors, and senior journalism educators and trainers in October 1996.

SANEF membership includes editors and senior journalists from the print, broadcast, and online (Internet) media, as well as journalism educators from all the major training institutions in South Africa. It is involved in training initiatives and in setting practical standards in journalism education.

SANEF has also facilitated the mobilization of the media in the Partnership Against Aids Campaign and in campaigns to end violence against women and children.

Against the backdrop of positive political developments on the African continent, SANEF has also spearheaded the formation of the All Africa's Editors' Conference.

Other organizations operating in the country include the Press Ombudsman, the Freedom of Expression Institute, the Audit Bureau of Circulations, the SA Chapter of the Media Institution of Southern African (MISA), Media Monitoring Africa (MMA), the Media Workers' Association of South Africa and the Foreign Correspondents' Association of South Africa.

News agencies

The South African Press Association (Sapa), which is a national news agency, is a co-operative, non-profit news-gathering organization operating in the interests of the public and its members. Sapa's foreign news is received from Reuters, Associated Press, and its representatives in London.

The main foreign news agencies operating in South Africa are Agence France Presse, Associated Press, Deutsche Presse Agentur, Reuters, and United Press International.

Network Radio Services (NRS), a specialist division of Sapa, was formed in June 1995. NRS provides a range of services, including advertising brokerage, to new radio stations. The brokerage service enables advertisers to get information about radio stations and group audience types across eight of the nine provinces and to book an entire radio campaign through one organization. NRS provides news and other services to 26 community stations and also offers training to affiliate stations in various fields, from management to news collection. It provides its affiliates with hourly news between 6:00 and 18:00 from Monday to Saturday, and six bulletins on a Sunday. It has the sole rights to redistribute news produced by Sapa, and has access to news produced by the newsrooms of Sapa's member newspapers.

Sapa has also formed a subsidiary company called link2media.co.za, an online media release database. www.link2media.co.za offers a free service through which the general public, media liaison officers, and journalists can easily track breaking media releases. A search facility allows a person to search for releases according to different categories. However, to have a media release placed on the database, a fee is charged.

The link2media database offers a direct link to the major newsrooms of the country. Media releases are distributed directly into the country's major newsrooms on the same network as Sapa's general editorial news, although the releases are clearly identified to editors as such. However, as is the case with all media releases, if the news is considered newsworthy some releases become the basis of soft and hard news reports and features.

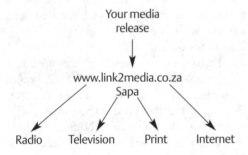

An advantage of using this service is that Sapa material is used extensively by many newsrooms. Generally, journalists perceive news from Sapa to be credible and relevant.

Characteristics of the press

According to Jefkins (1986), the advantages of the press as a public relations communication medium are the following:

- it can provide information in greater depth than can transient broadcasting media;
- it can be read anywhere, about the home or office, while travelling, walking out of doors, over a meal – at times and in places where electronic media may be inconvenient or unavailable. The press is a portable medium which can be taken almost anywhere;
- newspapers, and particularly magazines, often have an extended life because they are kept in binders or reference files;
- items can be cut out and retained, either personally or by libraries which maintain files on many subjects.

The press, however, also has certain disadvantages as a public relations communication medium, including the following:
- the time frame for printing a daily newspaper, a turnaround time sometimes as short as two to three hours, can lead to error;
- the rapid turnover of daily newspapers means that newspapers, particularly, have relatively short lives;
- sometimes false claims are made by publications of large circulation and readership figures. The Audit Bureau of Circulations, however, guarantees audited figures;
- there could be some bias or selectiveness in news reporting. Bias may derive from political, religious, ethnic, or simply proprietorial influence.

Auditing of the press

Newspapers and magazines of the major publishing groups belong to the Audit Bureau of Circulations of South Africa (ABC), which in turn is a member of the International Federation of Audit Bureau of Circulations. The major objectives of the ABC are:
- to secure accurate circulation figures and data relating to all member periodicals and media that sell advertising space;
- to set standard forms and methods for ascertaining the circulation figures of such media;

- to record such information and to circulate it to members of the bureau; and generally to establish a clearing house for information with regard to such media and to circulate it for the benefit of members of the ABC;
- to collect and distribute among its members information relating to all forms and methods of advertising.

The ABC figures are important in that they are used in the calculation of advertising rates and in the drawing up of advertising, public relations, and media strategies.

Press guidelines

Apart from understanding the *modus operandi* of the press, it is also important to contact the right section of the newspaper with news stories or press releases. The organizational chart below helps to identify the right contact.

The heart of all journalism is reporting. When you meet the press, the intended result is a story. Recognition of this journalistic fact of life should be the first step in the development of your media relations plan. Before sitting down with anyone from the press, ask yourself, 'What's the story?' When you consent to an interview, you consent to a story.

Never contact the editorial staff of a journal or newspaper to enquire whether the story you have sent is going to be used and never enquire as to why a particular story was not used. Whether a story is used or not is entirely up to the editor or chief sub-editor.

A story is often not used because of a lack of space. Hence you may encounter a situation where you have provided a paper with a good

Newsroom

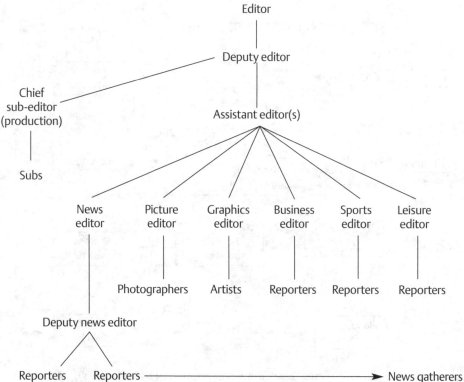

story with some solid news value which, in normal circumstances, would have been published – only to find that it had to make way for a more important story.

Deadlines are crucial to every newspaper. Just as you plan your activities, the press schedules deadlines that are critical to its performance. If you fail to meet the publication's deadline, the story will be developed without your input. In addition, disregarding an editor's deadline can jeopardize the rapport between your company and the publication. It can be construed as a 'no comment' or unwillingness to co-operate with the press.The diagram below shows the stages of production of a newspaper.

Each publication (or radio or television show) competes with other publications or shows. In dealing with a publication, you should know its competition and respect its rights to exclusive use of material.

Every editorial department within a newspaper has different wants and needs. Strive to learn what the needs of the editor are, so that you do not waste his or her time and jeopardize your own chances of future coverage.

Each editorial department reaches a well-defined audience, such as sports fans, women, business people, or taxpayers. Consider the audience in presenting information or in responding to enquiries from a publication.

No good publication shows any correlation whatsoever between advertising space purchased and editorial comment received. Always operate on the assumption that the newspaper is using your information because it is newsworthy. Do not try to use advertising revenue to influence an editor, and do not adopt the attitude that a publication has treated you badly with regard to editorial comment just because you do not advertise in it.

Reporters are individuals. Some are tougher to work with than others, but all of them have the same goal – to get the story. An interview will be a lot easier if you learn something about the personality of the reporter beforehand and plan to handle him or her accordingly.

Newspaper operations

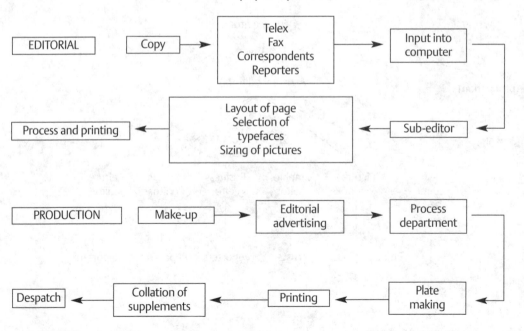

Other departments include: Advertising, Marketing, Subscriptions, Delivery (Sales).

Press kits

The contents of a press kit (also called a media kit) vary according to the occasion. Ideally a press kit should contain the relevant facts presented in the most concise way possible.

The usual press kit includes a basic press release. Where the subject matter is technical it is wise to provide information in layperson's language where appropriate.

Good visual material is essential. Brochures are cumbersome and not essential but good black-and-white prints depicting action, together with charts and graphs, if appropriate, are well received.

For special occasions, such as a factory opening, new product launches, and big promotional events, a comprehensive media package could include the following:

- a basic fact-sheet, detailing the event-making news and explaining its significance in strictly factual terms. It is crucial to include important dates, times, and relationships. Be sure that your name, address, and phone numbers where you can be reached for additional information appear on the sheet;
- a historical fact-sheet, giving the background of the event, and the individual or organization involved;
- a programme of events or schedule of activities, including detailed times. Give a script, where possible, for broadcast media;
- a straight news story, which should never be more than a page and a half of double-spaced typescript for print media and one or two short paragraphs for broadcast media. Give both print and broadcast versions to broadcast people. The print media need only the print version;
- a complete list of all participants, explaining their connection with the event;
- biographical background of principals, with the emphasis on current information about them, unless something in their background is specifically related to the event;

- visual material, consisting of 8 x 10 black-and-white glossy prints for newspapers and magazines, and 35 mm colour slides for television and publications using colour. Be sure that all visual material is of a good quality, is significant, and has been properly identified. If you mail kits, make sure photos are protected by cardboard;
- a longer, general news story, giving background information. It may be as long as three pages (double-spaced) for print media. Use only one full page (double-spaced) for broadcast media, which will run for about 60 seconds;
- two or three feature stories of varying length for print media. There will be no broadcast versions, but the features should be included in broadcast news kits for background information;
- a page of special, isolated facts that are of interest and can stand alone. These are often picked up for incorporation into copy written by the newspeople or are used as fillers;
- brochures about the event or organization. These publications serve as background material for newspeople.

The news release

The purpose of a news release is to provide news or information to the media that you would like to be published, and which is worthy of publication.

Your news will be competing with information from many other sources. Correct presentation of your news release is therefore essential for it to be noticed and used.

Contents of news releases

Be brief and factual, and separate technical data from the main news item. Always include the following:

- a title for a story (not a headline);
- the date, preferably in the style recommended in the *Oxford Dictionary for Writers and Editors*, for example 12 August 1995;

- a reference number, to make the release easily identifiable;
- the name and address of the organization issuing the release;
- the name, telephone number (both during working hours and after hours), and email address of a person from whom further information can be obtained.

Layout

Although most releases are now sent direct to media contacts by email, it is still important that the release is correctly set out.

The following are important points to bear in mind when issuing a news release:

- *Headings.* The news release should be clearly identifiable as such, to distinguish it from ordinary correspondence. Include a descriptive term such as 'News Release' or 'Press Release' boldly in the heading. Other descriptive phrases such as 'Press Information' are also acceptable. The heading should not be more than 60 to 75 mm deep.
- *Space between heading and title.* Leave a space of 40 mm between the heading and the title. This space is used by the news editor or copy taster to indicate how and where the story is to be used in the newspaper.
- *Title.* Type the title in capitals. Any second title, sidehead, or crosshead should be typed in upper and lower case.
- *Underlining.* Do not underline any part of the news release. (Underlining is a printer's mark meaning 'set in italics'.) Emphasis should be obtained by the relevance, content, and position of sideheads and crossheads.
- *Margins.* Leave a margin of at least 40 mm at either edge of the release for editing purposes. This allows the sub-editors to write instructions to compositors and make-up departments on the release.
- *Spacing.* Always use double spacing, with extra space between paragraphs.

- *Subheadings.* In a lengthy story, use subheadings. They help break up the story, and add to the visual appearance of the typewritten material.
- *Carry over copy.* Do not run over copy to the next page if it breaks up the sentence or paragraph.
- *Cues.* At the end of the article, type the word 'Ends'.
- *Continuation pages.* Number each page. Repeat the title at the top left of each continuation page.
- *Names of people.* Begin with first names. If not known, use initials. Include titles, such as Mr, Ms, Sir, Dr. Make sure you use correct abbreviations. Always use capital letters for proper names.
- *Full stops.* Full stops are not used in abbreviations consisting of capital letters, e.g. PRISA, USA. Full stops are retained in i.e. and e.g. Full stops are omitted in abbreviations ending with the last letter of the abbreviated word, e.g. Mr, Ms, Dr.
- *Quotation marks.* These should be restricted to quoted speech, not used for product names, ships' names, titles, or anything else.
- *Signs.* Do not use the % sign in a sentence. Spell out 'per cent'. Do not use the ampersand (&) in sentences, nor the abbreviation etc.
- *Figures.* Except in dates, times, prices, street numbers, weights and measures, and similar special uses of numbers, spell out from one to nine, then use figures until they become unwieldy. It is clearly better to write 10 thousand or 10 million than to use figures.

A useful tip is to ask the newspaper or magazine sub-editor with whom you may be dealing for a copy of the publication's house style. This is normally in the form of a booklet which can then be used for your own editing purposes.

Embargo

An embargo requests the recipient of a news release to withhold publication until a stated date and time. Embargoes should be avoided, if possible. Their use is a matter of convention, and they are not binding on the media. If an embargo is essential, then the reason for it should be made clear in the release. The word 'embargo', and the date and time for publication, should appear above the title of the release. The following is an example:

Embargo. This information is sent to you in advance for your convenience (give reason for embargo). It is not for publication, broadcast, or use on club tapes before (time, or when published internationally, GMT or BST) on (date).

Always keep the following in mind concerning embargoes:

- Never impose restrictions or conditions if they can be avoided.
- Use embargoes only to ensure equal opportunity for journalists with different deadlines or those working across time zones.
- Time embargoes are used to coincide with the event, announcement, launch, publication, completion of a speech, or in other circumstances, to suit the majority of the appropriate media. Keep the embargo period to a minimum consistent with its purpose.
- Never embargo any radio or television interview given prior to a press conference. The press publication time given in an embargo applies equally to broadcast time.
- Never break or vary an embargo to favour or suit the convenience of the few, or leak embargoed information through a third party.
- Strictly observe stock exchange rules in all matters relating to public companies.

Comply with the Company News Service requirements. Also take care to observe any other codes of practice which may apply to the use of embargoes.

- Do not give advance reportable information concerning an embargoed story unless it is similarly embargoed.
- Be precise about what is reportable, and what is not, in any background briefing.
- Remember copy deadlines when issuing a release. A morning release may appear in evening papers the same day, and 'kill' the story for the next morning's dailies. Weekly papers may have deadlines three days in advance of publication date.

Models for the construction of the news release

A variety of models are used in the construction of news releases, but the three most common are the five Ws and H, NIBSS, and SOLAADS.

Using any one of these as a framework, a media officer can write a successful news release.

The five Ws and H
- Who – Who is the story about?
- What – What happened?
- When – When did it happen?
- Where – Where did it happen?
- Why – Why did it happen?
- How – How something came about.

The SOLAADS seven point model
- Subject – What is the story about?
- Organization – What is the name of the organization?
- Location – What is the location of the organization?
- Advantages – What is new, special, or beneficial about the product or service?
- Applications – How or by whom can the product or service be used or enjoyed?
- Details – What are the specifications or details with regard to colour, price, size?
- Source – If this is different from location.

NIBSS
- New information
- Interesting facts
- Background
- Selling points
- Superfluities.

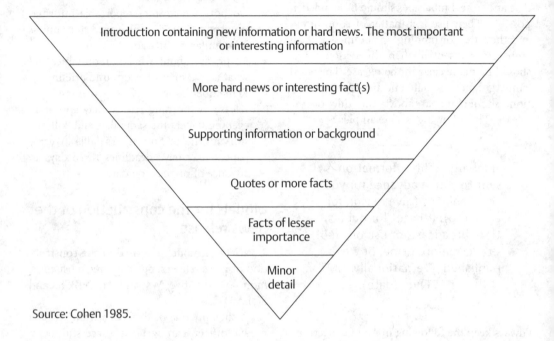

Introduction containing new information or hard news. The most important or interesting information

More hard news or interesting fact(s)

Supporting information or background

Quotes or more facts

Facts of lesser importance

Minor detail

Source: Cohen 1985.

How to create news for your company

Here are some possible ways of generating news and comment about your company.
- tie in with the news events of the day;
- arrange a trip;
- make an award;
- tie in with another publicity person;
- hold a contest;
- tie in with a newspaper or another medium on a mutual project;
- pass a resolution;
- appear before public bodies;
- conduct a poll or survey;
- issue a report;
- arrange an interview with a celebrity;
- take part in a controversy;
- stage a special event;
- write a letter;
- release a letter you have received;
- adapt national reports and surveys for local use;
- arrange for a testimonial;
- arrange for a speech to be made;
- make an analysis or prediction;
- form a committee and announce the names of its members;
- hold an election;
- announce an appointment;
- celebrate an anniversary;
- issue a summary of facts;
- start a debate;
- tie into a well-known week or day;
- honour an institution;
- organize a tour;
- inspect a project;
- issue praise;
- issue a protest;
- tie in with a holiday.

Dealing with the media during emergencies

In meeting the press at the scene of an emergency, several things should be remembered. Basic is the fact that the public is represented by the press and this medium has a recognized right to information that may vitally concern the community, employees, their friends and families, and the victims. It is also common knowledge that the best way to prevent the spread of false rumours and misinformation is through issuing factual information. Remember the following when dealing with the media:

- Speed in replying to a query is all-important. All newspeople have deadlines to meet.
- Keep cool. If a reporter gets snappy, chances are it's because he or she is under considerably more pressure at that moment than you are. Try to co-operate to the greatest extent possible.
- If you don't know the answer, attempt to get it for the reporter.
- Eliminate obstacles whenever possible. Most newspeople will agree that the more obstacles they find in their way, the harder they will work to ferret out the real story – from any source possible. They will almost always use something they have uncovered and you have no control over what that might be.
- Never ask to see a reporter's story. Time is usually a factor. If you feel the reporter may be misinformed, check back with him or her on the point to make sure.
- There is seldom a reason why you should not be quoted by name. As a member of management and one charged with public relations, you are speaking for the company.
- Never argue with a reporter about the value of a story.

- Any information that goes to one source in the emergency is fair game for all. Do not play favourites. Reporters listen to and read each other's copy anyway.
- Never flatly refuse to supply information. Always give a good reason why it is not available (for example, you want to be sure facts are correct, next of kin must be notified, trade secrets, the official investigation is not yet complete).
- Always know to whom you are talking. Get his or her name and phone number in case you need to contact the person later.
- Never give an answer that you feel might not stand up. It can embarrass you later.
- Never falsify, colour, or slant your answers. Reporters are trained to see a curved ball coming a mile away, and have fielded many of them before. If they think you are pitching one at them, they will remember it for a long time and tell colleagues and other members of the news media. It will also encourage them to independently investigate further.
- Be especially alert for photographers. You have no control over photographs taken off company property, but you have every right to control those taken within the plant. Consider the possibility of pool photos and films where it is impractical to have several photographers on the scene at once. Remember, photos can be as harmful as words.
- Be sure there is no time lag between the time you get information that can be put out and the time it is actually given to newspeople.
- Have safety, labour, and employee records available for your reference, if possible.
- Be quick to point out long safety records and any facts of heroism by employees.
- If damage must be estimated for the press immediately, confine your statement to a general description of what was destroyed.
- Always accentuate the positive. If your public relations is good, so are your chances for an even break.

Case study Using the Internet to improve your media relations

One of the most useful ways of communicating with the public is via the Internet, characterised by its immediacy and the extent of its reach. Many South African decision-makers and executives use it as a strategic news and information resource and it is increasingly used as the public face of organizations, for launching new products, announcing new policies, or simply setting the record straight.

More and more print-based publications have online versions and there are many new specialized industry-relevant publications that are exclusively electronic. It is essential, therefore, for public relations practitioners to have a good relationship with online publications, as well as with the more traditional media. Online technology has the ability to track and trace transactions and build portfolios of customers, enabling the practitioner to develop communication campaigns aimed specifically at the stakeholders of a public relations programme. But, in terms of public relations, the Internet is not a tool in isolation – it should form part of a holistic campaign to communicate with an organization's stakeholders, both internally, through its intranet, and externally, through a public web site. The Internet has an important place in the public relations practitioner's media plan and in the marketing mix (for a detailed explanation of the new digital media see 'New insights into communication media' by Mersham & Skinner, 2001).

Journalists increasingly regard company web pages as a vital source of information. Practitioners should therefore co-operate with their webmasters to ensure that their web sites are up to date at all times. Sites can also be designed to incorporate the latest media releases. It is the responsibility of the practitioner to see that these media advances are immediately added to the virtual press room.

In addition to providing access to valid information, a well-designed and fully functional website 'press room' can save a company money, provided the target markets have been conditioned to visit the site. Many companies have slashed the costs of distributing and printing paper-based product lists, media kits, and brochures in this way.

One result is fewer phone enquiries when information is available on the web. Public relations and marketing costs can be reduced by providing the most requested information – news releases, new product information, media kits, executive biographies, digitized photos, contact names and numbers, executive speeches, and regulatory filings – online, in one easy-to-access area.

For example, General Motors saved considerably when, after post-publication specification changes to one of its cars meant corrections to 100 different pages of its media kit, it simply updated its on-line version. The Ford motor company claims to have had over 900 photo downloads during the first year its site went live.

Although the South African market is much smaller, the same principles apply. The key to achieving a return on investment for 'cyber PR' is by encouraging journalists to use the site. For every media call, the standard reply should be: 'Have you been to the web site yet?' But the company should simultaneously ensure that the site is updated.

Web sites form only part of the digital communications associated with the Internet. E-mail opens up numerous possibilities for public relations practitioners as a means of communicating media releases and delivering media kits.

When using e-mail to communicate with the media, the following issues should be considered:

- The public relations practitioner needs to build a relationship of trust with his or her media contacts. E-mail, on its own, does not necessarily achieve this. Face-to-face interactions and, to a lesser extent, phone calls are more personal.

- It is dangerous to use e-mail as a form of junk mail. Mass mailings of a media release to journalists are not appreciated by them.
- Practitioners need to be aware of individual recipients' limitations. For example, not all journalists will access attachments because some journalists are more e-mail literate than others.
- Phone calls can be intrusive, especially if they are placed when a journalist is on a deadline, and faxes can be diverted or get lost, so e-mail is a good alternative in a pressured environment.
- E-mail also facilitates easier editing of material. It's easier to cut and paste information than it is to take notes and then formulate text, and it's easier than working from a fax or other hard copy.
- Time constraints on sourcing stories are growing and journalists have to rely more on organizations to supply them with the news of the day. E-mail is an effective medium to gather information.
- Neither the busy public relations professional nor the harassed journalist has the time for public relations lunches, breakfasts, or drinks every day. E-mail enables the public relations professional to manage relationships and stay in touch in a businesslike fashion, without spending too much time in extra meetings.
- E-mail can carry pictorial material that can be incorporated to illustrate stories. Expensive media kits with costly photographs are thereby avoided.
- The process prior to e-mailing material remains unchanged. The client and public relations practitioner still have to formulate input, the public relations practitioner still has to fine-tune this, have it approved, and only then pass it on to media contacts.

Further reading

Adams, T. & Clark, N. 2001. *The Internet: Effective Online Communication*. Orlando: Harcourt College Publishers.

Cohen, R. 1985. *Effective Press Releases*. Johannesburg: Ralph Cohen.

De Beer, A.S. (ed.) 1998. *Mass Media Towards the Millennium: The South African Handbook of Mass Communication*. Pretoria: JL van Schaik.

Jefkins, F. 1982. *Public Relations Made Simple*. London: Heinemann.

Jefkins, F. 1986. *Planned Press and Public Relations*. London: Blackie & Son.

Leahy, M. & P. Voice. 1991. *Media Book*. Johannesburg: Leahy.

Mersham, G.M. & J.C. Skinner. 2001. *New Insights into Media and Communication*. Johannesburg: Heinemann.

Nel, F. 2005. *Writing for the Media*. 3rd edition. Cape Town: Oxford University Press.

Skinner, J.C. & R. Cluver. 1990. *Advertising for Free: Winning Ways of Working with the Press, Radio and Television*. Durban.

South African Yearbook. 2003–2009. Pretoria: GCIS.

Chapter 13

The mass media: electronic media

When you have read this chapter, you should:

- be aware of the role of the various regulatory bodies and their impact on broadcasting in South Africa;
- be familiar with the new structure and organization of the South African electronic media;
- know the background to the radio and television services of the SABC and the independent stations;
- understand how public relations practitioners can use the broadcast media to good effect.

Policy and legislation

South Africa has an extremely diverse broadcast media catering for the unique demands of the local market. The convergence of technologies has led the Department of Communications to pass the Electronic Communications Act, 2005, followed by the Icasa Amendment Act of 2006 to regulate and control all broadcasting. Among other things, it aims to:

- contribute to democracy, nation-building, the provision of education, and strengthening the moral fibre of society;
- encourage ownership and control of broadcasting services by people from historically disadvantaged communities;
- ensure fair competition in the sector;
- provide for a three-tier system of public, commercial, and community broadcasting services;
- establish a strong and committed public broadcaster to service the needs of all South Africans.

The Broadcasting Act, 1999 (Act 4 of 1999) defined the objectives of the South African broadcasting system, the structure of the South African Broadcasting Corporation (SABC) at the time and the role of the various sectors in meeting those objectives.

It also guaranteed the independence of the SABC as a public broadcaster. Within the present Act, the SABC is being corporatised and restructured to better fulfil its mandate.

These include:
- broadcasting accurate and credible news and current affairs programmes;

- South African content programming in languages that reflect the country's cultural diversity;
- educational programming to advance life-long learning;
- programming targeted at children, women and people with disabilities.

The Act deals with the restructuring of the SABC to fit into the changing broadcasting environment and requires that the SABC Board establishes two management boards to focus on public and commercial services. Under the new dispensation, the public broadcasting wing will execute and meet its public-service mandate free from commercial interests. The commercial wing will be allowed to generate profit to be self sustainable.

In terms of the BDM, the SABC has been awarded five channels to allow for specialized services dedicated to the development needs of the country, in the areas of education, youth, health, and enterprise development.

During 2008 a local and digital content strategy was also developed in conjunction with other stakeholders such as the Department of Arts and Culture.

Regulatory authorities

In May 2000, the Independent Communications Authority Act was proclaimed, paving the way for the merger of the South African Telecommunications Regulatory Authority (Satra) and the IBA, and the establishment of the Independent Communications Authority of South Africa (Icasa).

The IBA was established on 31 March 1994 to promote the development of public, private, and community broadcasting services which are responsive to the needs of the public. The IBA's tasks included granting and amending broadcasting licences, making regulations, setting licence conditions, managing broadcasting licences, making regulations, managing broadcasting frequency spectrum, and monitoring the broadcasting industry as whole.

Icasa is currently looking at the issues of a signal distribution, convergence, a regulatory regime for multi-channel distribution services, and sections 49 and 50 of the IBA Act, 1993 (Act 153 of 1993) which deal with matters of control and cross ownership. Following these investigations, Icasa will determine the licence conditions, obligations, and tariff structure for a signal distribution. It is also investigating the level of foreign ownership. The level of ownership of private radio and television stations permitted for a foreigner is currently 20 per cent but Government would like to raise this in order to increase investment.

The Broadcasting Monitoring and Complaints Committee (BMCC) was established under sections 21 and 22 of the Independent Broadcasting Authority Act, 1993. It monitors broadcasting licensees for their compliance or adherence to the terms, conditions, and obligations of their broadcasting licences. The BMCC is an independent, self-regulatory body which serves as a voluntary watchdog to adjudicate complaints from the public about programmes flighted by association members subscribing to its code of conduct. It is also entitled to initiate its own investigation into suspected non-compliance by a broadcaster.

If a member of the public is concerned that a broadcaster is not observing its licence conditions, that person may lodge a complaint with Icasa and if a broadcaster is found guilty of contravening its licence conditions, the BMCC makes recommendations to Icasa about what should be done.

The BMCC is empowered by its members which, amongst others, include the SABC, M-Net, Radio 702, and Trinity Broadcasting Network. However, the Commission does not deal with X-rated material which, under criminal law, is prohibited for cinema, video, and broadcasting. Material that could be considered X-rated must be submitted to the Film and Publications Board prior to being shown. The mission of the National Association of

Broadcasters is to protect the interests of broadcasting as a whole, at the same time interfacing with Icasa on matters such as freedom of speech.

Radio in South Africa

The SABC is the country's public broadcaster that comprises 15 public broadcast service radio stations and three commercial radio stations, broadcasting in 11 languages, as well as an external radio service in four languages, that reaches an average daily adult audience of 19 million

For its internal coverage, Radio News uses about 13 editorial offices, a countrywide network of 2,300 correspondents, and more than 2000 news contacts.

World news is provided by its own bureaus, international news agencies and foreign correspondents.

Copy supplied to Radio News amounts to almost a million words a day, and is compiled around the clock into 300 news bulletins and 27 current affairs programmes broadcast daily on the SABC's radio services. There is a public broadcasting service radio station for each language group.

Channel Africa Network comprises four language services that reach millions of listeners throughout Africa. Broadcasts are in English, French, Kiswahili, Chinyanja, Silozi, and Portuguese. The shortwave broadcast covers south, east, central, and west Africa. The satellite broadcast covers the sub-Saharan region. The Internet broadcast is accessible worldwide.

Commercial radio stations

Icasa has granted licences to the following radio stations:
- Radio Algoa (ex-SABC);
- Classic FM (Greenfield);
- Kaya FM (Greenfield);
- YFM (Greenfield);
- High Veld Stereo (ex-SABC);
- Radio 702;
- Radio Jacaranda (ex-SABC);
- Radio Oranje (ex-SABC);
- East Coast Radio (ex-SABC);
- P4 (Greenfield);
- Cape Talk MW (Greenfield);
- Radio KFM (ex-SABC).

The SABC stations were sold to private owners to diversify radio ownership.

Community radio stations

Community radio stations have a huge potential for the support of cultural, and educational information exchange. They use indigenous languages, thus ensuring that people receive information in languages they understand. There are more than 90 community radio stations in South Africa.

Television in South Africa

SABC's national television network comprises three full-spectrum, free-to-air channels and one pay-TV channel, aimed at audiences in Africa. Combined, the free-to-air sound broadcasting stations broadcast in 11 languages and reach a daily adult audience of almost 20 million people via the terrestrial signal distribution network and a satellite signal.

South Africa has more than four million licensed television households and the largest television audience in Africa. Between 50 and 60 per cent of all programmes transmitted are produced in South Africa. Locally produced television programmes are augmented by programmes purchased abroad and by co-productions undertaken with other television programming organizations. Television news is fed by SABC news teams reporting from all parts of the country, using modern portable

A new vision for public broadcasting in South Africa

The SABC has for years been lurching from crisis to crisis to the extent that its editorial and programming credibility, financial viability, and institutional sustainability are now seriously questionable.

However, all is not lost! What is needed now is to get back to basics. First, we need a clear vision for the kind of broadcaster we want. Most people would agree that we want an editorially independent, accountable, publicly funded broadcaster that broadcasts robust, probing journalism reflecting a diversity of views, and a broadcaster that supports and promotes an independent production sector nurturing South African creativity.

Second, we need clear steps to get there starting with clarifying the roles of all the important players. One of the most controversial is the Minister's role. Currently (2009), as the SABC is a public company, the Minister plays a shareholder role and approves corporate plans, finances, and the appointments of the three senior executives. This is not appropriate for the governance and institutional arrangements appropriate for a public broadcaster. Principally his / her role is to create an enabling environment for the broadcasting sector; to draft policy and legislation, and to ensure sufficient finances are available.

The institutions that should have a direct oversight role over the SABC are the regulator, the Independent Communications Authority of South Africa (ICASA) and Parliament. The regulator's role is to ensure that the SABC adheres to all relevant broadcasting laws, particularly the SABC's Charter capturing the broadcaster's vision and mission. Further, the role is to ensure that the SABC adheres to its license conditions. Given these powers, ICASA should have called the SABC to account on the blacklisting saga and called the SABC board and management to account in terms of the Corporations' financial crisis.

Currently, Parliament drives the selection of the SABC board. This has become a problem given the serious political interference in the last process so an independent panel may seem to be the answer but possibilities for political interference and control by elite interests cannot be excluded here.

One possibility is to create a special parliamentary committee that is not dominated by the ruling party of the day. But whatever the decision, we need maximum public participation and transparency.

The Board should focus on strategic issues and monitor performance including financial performance and should not interfere in daily management.

Most importantly, the Board needs to ensure the appointment of a competent professional, independent, and publicly-minded management team. SABC management should then implement the strategic and financial plans and appoint respected, professional journalists, and commissioning editors.

Financial management and funding of an independent public broadcaster requires the Board and management to ensure proper adherence to financial controls. Broadcasting in all 11 national languages, developing local programming and providing information and entertainment to everyone is costly and cannot be met primarily through advertising, so public funding is also required. License fees are ideal as they protect the institution from political and commercial pressures. Whatever funding model is chosen, it must ensure that funds are secured and assured over the long term.

Minister General Siphiwe Nyanda (ret) has promised a policy and legislative review of the SABC's governing laws. It is the time for everyone to participate in the debate on the substantive issues so that we can get the public broadcaster that we want and deserve.

Kate Skinner is the Coordinator for "Save our SABC" Campaign and Professor Tawana Kupe is the Dean of the Faculty of Humanities at Wits University

electronic cameras and line-feed equipment via more than 220 television transmitters. Ad hoc satellite feeds are arranged from wherever news events occur. News bulletins are broadcast in all 11 official languages.

The SABC's terrestrial television channels devote roughly 18% and 20% of their airtime during prime time to news and news related programmes. NewsBreak 082 152, a news-by-telephone service, is one of the country's most popular audio news/information lines. The joint venture with Vodacom and Marketel gives the latest news in English and isiZulu with regular sports and weather updates.

M-Net

M-Net, South Africa's first private subscription television service, was launched in 1986. Today M-Net broadcasts its array of general entertainment and niche channels to more than 1,2 million subscribers in 50 countries across Africa and adjacent Indian Ocean islands.

M-Net's television channels are delivered to subscribers through analogue terrestrial and digital satellite distribution.

The main M-Net channel, which is available as a terrestrial and satellite service, offers movies, sport, children's programmes, international and local series, and local reality shows.

The second terrestrial channel, CSN (Community Service Network) offers sport as well as programming aimed at a variety of South African communities. M-Net is also well represented on the DSTV bouquet of satellite TV channels such as BBC and Sky News.

Promoting local film and television industries is a priority for M-Net and much has already been achieved in developing creative talent in Africa.

Satellite broadcasting

MultiChoice Africa (MCA) was formed in 1995 to manage the subscriber services of its sister company, M-Net. It became the first African company on the continent to offer digital satellite broadcasting.

Operations include subscriber-management services and digital satellite television platforms, broadcasting 55 video and 40 audio channels, 24 hours a day. Included are six data channels, which were the first interactive television offerings on the continent.

In 2008, MCA launched high definition television (HDTV) in the South Africa market, the first of its kind in Africa.

Free-to-air television

Launched in 1998, e.TV is South Africa's first private free-to-air television channel, which broadcasts a full spectrum programming service to close on 80% of South Africa's population. The station is owned by the BEE group, Hosken Consolidated Investments Limited, and Venfin Limited, and employs some 500 people.

Independent TV audience surveys confirm that eTV is the second largest channel in the country. The station's most popular programmes are wrestling, news, movies, and South African drama, with South African content comprising 45% of its daily programming. It was the first channel in South Africa to secure the rights to the Union of European Football Association's Champion League.

Signal distribution

Sentech was established in terms of the Sentech Act 1996 (Act 113 of 1996) as common carrier to provide broadcasting signal distribution for broadcasting licences. Over the medium term, Sentech will focus on the digitisation of its signal infrastructure and the roll out of the ICT infrastructure required for the 2010 World Cup.

The Sentech product line is split into five product portfolios namely
- signal distribution (regulated and unregulated);
- Very Small Aperture Terminal (Vsat);
- broadcast wireless (MyWireless and Biznet);

- international voice;
- value-adding network.

As part of its Apex projects, Government has started deploying Wireless Broadband to 500 Dinaledi schools and targeting clinics, hospitals, libraries, post offices, Thusong Service Centres and government centres in the same coverage areas. This will help not only in increasing uptake and use of ICTs but will also enhance inclusivity in building the information society.

Sentech is also partnering with various organisations to enhance e-services such as the Mindset Learning and Health projects; V-sat links to the Pre- Natal HIV Research Unit at Chris Hani Baragwanath Hospital; wireless platforms to over a hundred Home Affairs mobile units; as well as 78 community radio stations linked to the Government Communication and Information System (GCIS).

Broadband Infraco

In March 2007, government approved the establishment of a new SOE that will provide long –distance connectivity to the country's telecommunications market on a cost basis. Broadband Infraco, which became a stand alone SOE in January 2008, has succeeded in operationalizing and strengthening the national long-distance network and providing additional capacity. Infraco has increased its footprint by 30% and doubled its capacity.

Infraco has provisioned route-connectivity services and regional expansion sites. Additional fibre routes were added to close the long-distance ring and to provide redundant capacities. The Africa West-Coast Cable will be prioritised by government to meet 2010 objectives as well as other short- to medium- term strategic projects. Infraco brings together fibre-optic cable networks, originally built by state companies Eskom and Transnet. The move forms part of South Africa's attempts to bring down the cost of telecommunications and Internet connectivity in the country.

Public relations and the broadcasting media

The great variety of broadcasting services available in South Africa offers a unique opportunity for public relations practitioners to gain wide publicity for their companies in a most dramatic way. It is their job to familiarize themselves with the various programme services and slots available and to get to know radio and television staff.

Television

Television is the most persuasive and powerful medium of communication today, in terms of the number of people it can reach and the impact even a single appearance can have.

With the right technique, a television performer can achieve instant appeal. An unconvincing, erratic performance, on the other hand, can have an equally dramatic negative effect. Moreover, the audience might not only judge the performer but organization he or she represents too. Managers may be invited to take part in television interviews from time to time, so knowing how to handle interviews competently could be important for the public image and national reputation of the whole organization.

Viewers' judgments about a television performer can be significantly affected by a number of elements peculiar to the television interview. Many of these elements are under the control of the producer, but some can be deliberately manipulated or utilized by interviewees to enhance the quality of their performance and of the image they project.

Research by psychologists has revealed that viewers tend to judge speakers in two ways. Firstly, speakers are judged in terms of their degree of professionalism as indicated by apparent competence, expertise and mastery of the topic of discussion, poise, and control over nervousness. Secondly, they are judged in terms of personal qualities such as sincerity, modesty, and a pleasant manner. From a number of parallel but independent studies in several countries it has emerged that these attributes seem to represent the comprehensive set of criteria on which audiences base their opinions of interviewees.

It is therefore important for anyone who appears on television to accentuate those characteristics known to contribute to a lasting favourable impression with viewers.

Television techniques

Television interviews are pressure situations, unfamiliar to most people – this can jeopardize a solid performance in front of the cameras. Interviewees should never forget that mastery and poise are two essential ingredients of a favourable television image. Probably the main cause of nervousness before an interview is uncertainty and not knowing what to expect. Tension can be alleviated if the interviewee finds out in advance from the producer what he or she will be asked.

The first thing an interviewee needs to know is the purpose of the interview. This does not mean merely knowing what the topic of discussion is to be, but also specific details about the line of questioning. If the producer does not volunteer this information the interviewee should ask for it.

Getting the interview off to a confident start is all-important. There are two questions an interviewee should ask at this point. First, how will I be introduced? Second, what will the first question of the interview be?

Psychologists have found that a television performer who is introduced as having experience or expertise in the topic of discussion will usually be perceived as more reliable, more expert, and more poised than someone presented in more ambiguous terms or about whom little or no background information is given. It is, therefore, extremely important that the producer and interviewer get these details right.

It is a good idea for an interviewee, no matter how experienced a television performer, to find out from the producer or interviewer the exact form of the first question and to work out an answer beforehand. This can ensure an impressive start, which may set the tone for the whole interview.

A neat appearance is important, since it conveys much to viewers about the interviewee's status, personality, and attitude to the interview.

An interviewee who appears interested and attentive to questions tends to be more highly regarded by viewers, and this impression is conveyed largely through visual cues such as facial expression and direction of gaze. In particular, the interviewee should not glance around at the surroundings. It is important also not to worry about the position of the camera, and at no time should the interviewee look directly into it. As well as the visual image, vocal projection and verbal fluency are important. It is essential to put more vitality and authority into speaking on television than in ordinary conversation. An interviewee should sound as well as look serious – but without seeming to be anxious or tense.

Television interview skills can be learned and technique can be improved through proper training; there are a number of courses available in South Africa for business people. The interview is videotaped so that trainees can review their performance and become more aware of how they look and sound to observers.

As far as SABC TV is concerned, all television programmes fall into one of the following eight categories: magazine, sport, documentary, variety, children, drama, religious, and news. Within the framework of television programming, each of these categories constitutes a subdepartment which is headed by a programme organizer. If the public relations practitioner contacts the particular organizer, either by letter, fax, or telephone, he or she will elicit interest and might secure an interview for a client. But it should always be remembered that television seeks national news and does not exist to provide 'free' advertising for companies.

Radio

Although radio does not speak as powerfully as television, it is a more flexible medium, reaches a wider cross-section of the public throughout the day, and often provides the opportunity of talking directly to a specific target market.

The SABC's top actuality programmes AM Live and PM Live, for example, provide the business community with an outlet for good stories on products, personalities, and services. The Corporation does, however, have a specific policy code regulating decisions on business news. This lays down that programme material containing publicity for a commercial undertaking can be broadcast if the general news value exceeds the publicity value; if it is relevant to the contents of the news item; if withholding the name might cause confusion; or if emergency necessitates naming the company or product. In a nutshell, it means that the yardstick is factual news value, public interest, and clarity.

Radio techniques

Radio interviews are usually three minutes long, so brevity is essential. Longer, in-depth features, covering personalities and news events, are also presented.

Advance contact with the programme organizer or editor by letter, fax, or telephone will normally elicit interest and result in a visit to the studios. News reporters will often visit clients in their business environment.

Companies are well advised to draw up a communication strategy for handling bad news such as strikes or fires in a factory.

The most common and serious mistake public relations practitioners make is bringing the wrong person to the studio for an interview. The fact that someone is a successful businessperson does not necessarily mean that he or she is a good communicator. A professional public relations practitioner or someone of lesser rank who can communicate well would be preferable as the company's spokesperson.

Very few people are sufficiently bilingual to talk on television or radio in their 'second language'. The answer therefore is to use another employee to speak in his or her home language on the 'other' services.

Preparation well beforehand is essential. Studio time is strictly allocated and there is no time then for preparation or deliberation. Public relations practitioners are warned against suggesting the line of questioning that the radio interview should follow. However, handing a brief resumé of the problem to be discussed to the interviewer often prepares the ground for a constructive interview. Contact times and programme scheduling need to be carefully watched to ensure suitability. As with print media, the formula for success is to know the needs of the programme editor or producer, to develop the right personal contacts, and to produce the 'goods' as and when required.

Characteristics of electronic media

According to Jefkins (1982), radio has the following advantages as a public relations communication medium:

- radio is intimate and often provides companionship;
- it is flexible because of its many formats;
- it is portable thanks to the transistor and is thus accessible in many places;
- it has specialized stations with specialized publics;
- in South Africa, radio has long been an effective way of reaching people of different ethnic groups and languages;
- it is cost-effective. It is easier and more practical to produce a radio programme in several languages, or to broadcast locally in the appropriate language, than to publish vernacular newspapers which people may or may not be able to read.

Radio, however, also has the following disadvantages as a public relations communication medium:
● although the message may be repeated several times, it is often only a fleeting one;
● radio listeners tend to switch from one station to another and from one programme to another. Messages may therefore be missed;
● from a news perspective, radio messages tend to be brief and are therefore limited.

According to Jefkins, television has the following advantages as a public relations communication medium:
● the audiovisual impact provides realism, immediacy, and lasting impressions;
● programmes are watched in a variety of settings, which lend intimacy in the comfort of the home;
● it can provide instant feedback for the viewer, who can feel a strong like or dislike towards individuals being interviewed. Looking the part and being articulate are, therefore, essential;
● television can introduce new interests to viewers, which in turn stimulates back-up material;
● recent technological innovations allow recording and playback if equipment is available.

Television, however, has the following disadvantages as a public relations communication medium:
● it is a passive and sometimes anti-social medium. It has been criticized for destroying the reading habit in young people;
● television shooting is a time-consuming and expensive exercise, requiring many more technicians and equipment than radio. Many hours are spent on rehearsals and shooting to produce only a few minutes of screen time;
● editing of material can sometimes produce controversial juxtapositioning which was not apparent during the original shooting;
● facilities can be provided by organizations for television purposes without any due acknowledgement or publicity for the sponsor;
● messages cannot always be clearly and concisely targeted to a mass public, many of whom are not interested in what is being said.

Further reading

Bland, M., A. Theaket & D. Wragg. 1996. *Effective Media Relations: How to Get Results*. London: Kogan Page.

De Beer, A.S. (ed.) 1998. *Mass Media Towards the Millennium: The South African Handbook of Mass Communication*. Pretoria: J.L. van Schaik.

Jefkins, F. 1982. *Public Relations Made Simple*. London: Heinemann.

Jefkins, F. & D. Yadin. 1998. *Public Relations*. London: Pitman.

Mersham, G.M. & J.C. Skinner. 2001. *New Insights into Media and Communication*. Johannesburg: Heinemann.

Nel, F. 2005. *Writing for the Media*. 3rd edition. Cape Town: Oxford University Press.

SABC Annual Reports 2000–2009. Johannesburg: SABC.

South African Yearbook. 2003–2009. Pretoria: GCIS.

Monthly issues of SARAD, with updated circulation and contact lists, are an invaluable source of information on the media.

Chapter 14

Closed circuit television and video

When you have read this chapter, you should:

- be familiar with some of the main advantages of closed circuit television as a communication medium;

- be aware of the variety of possible uses for closed circuit television;

- understand some of the technological developments taking place in the industry.

No other medium of communication is potentially as powerful as television. Its intimate way of presenting ideas, information, and experiences, is unique. These qualities, coupled with flexibility and cost-effectiveness, have made this medium the most powerful communication tool for a wide variety of uses.

At present, education is probably the major user of closed circuit television and video. Although many companies in industry and commerce have made use of television for a number of technical tasks, such as security surveillance, monitoring the production process, and product development, where other forms of observation are impractical or provide inferior results, these applications do not exploit the potential of television as medium of communication between people.

Companies are already spending considerable time and money on improving organizational structures and developing communication channels. Memos, notice boards, house magazines, manuals, and committees are but a few of these channels. An increasing number of large companies are now adding video to the battery of communication media at their disposal.

Broadly speaking, there are three main ways in which television and video are used as an aid to management. These are:

- using video for external communication for public relations, marketing, and sales purposes;

- using video for internal communication throughout the organization;

- using video for internal staff training purposes both as a medium to present information and to give personal feedback to trainees.

Advantages of closed circuit television

Some of the main advantages of closed circuit television are worth highlighting:

- It is flexible (programmes can be tailored to any level of literacy and sophistication), economical (videotape can be erased or re-recorded any number of times), easily transported from one centre to another, and easily operated, even by an amateur.
- Because television is thought-provoking and demanding, it stimulates discussion and encourages participation.
- It allows the introduction of specialists at any stage of individual training pro-grammes, thus providing credibility and greater insight.
- Since the programme can be interrupted at any time, trainees can be given the oppor-tunity of copying out exercises or being involved in group discussions.
- It helps in marrying theory and practice, discussing individual case histories, and in drawing conclusions.
- It allows visits to actual situations and sites through the eyes of the camera.
- It maintains intimate contact between the presenter and every member of the class, thus communicating personal involvement and commitment.
- It is a very adaptable medium, allowing the introduction of multiple-choice techniques.
- The camera's ability to take close-ups makes it possible to magnify processes and techniques which would otherwise be diffi-cult to explain.
- There is no subject or skill which cannot be taught with television. If it can be demon-strated, television can demonstrate it.

Having said this, it is important to remember that television cannot perform miracles. Its main strength lies in its ability to involve the viewer to a larger degree than any other form of communication, by virtue of its stimulation of subconscious activity.

Uses of closed circuit television

Until recently, closed circuit television was most frequently applied to sales training and public speaking. Here, direct feedback on videotape was used to point out areas for improvement.

The variety of possible uses for closed cir-cuit television, however, has been expanding almost as fast as the technological develop-ment of videotape equipment.

Recruitment

One of the most obvious areas of application is in recruitment and selection interviews. By recording an interview on videotape and later playing the tape to a group of managers direct-ly concerned with the position for which the candidate is being considered, group decision-making can replace or confirm the decision made by the interviewer. It can also mitigate or eliminate many of the biasing factors involved in interviewing.

Management training

A second use of closed circuit television is management training. In the management training field, tape lectures with plenty of visu-al aids are used. Because the lecture is on tape, instructors are able to play back items that arise during discussions and to explore these in greater depth. On leadership courses, record-ings are made of teamwork exercises and these are then used for the final discussion. An essential feature of such exercises is the guided analysis of interaction behaviour which takes place during team activity. Much use is made of tele-recordings in order to show an individ-ual how his or her behaviour affects the rest of the group. Participants quickly begin to under-stand the dynamics of interpersonal relation-ships in group situations.

Closed circuit television is potentially a more valuable medium for many types of company presentation than ordinary film because good quality recordings can easily be made by companies themselves. Once used, tapes can be erased and used again and again. The tape does not have to be developed but can be used or edited immediately. There are also several other worthwhile uses.

The use of pre-recorded programmes

Professionally produced training programmes and packages can be used in company-owned closed circuit television systems. These programmes or packages are available from various sources. They are characterized by their flexibility – programmes are easily adapted to any 'in-company' training session.

Technical and industrial training

Many aspects of engineering, manufacturing, and craftsmanship can be taught effectively only if the apprentice or trainee actually sees the work being done. Closed circuit television brings the shop floor, workshop, assembly line, and expert into the classroom, eliminating time-consuming and costly visits to the factory. It allows for comments to be made and discussions to take place away from the bustle and often restricted space of these areas.

The expert is recorded on the videotape recorder, demonstrating how the job should be done. By playing back the videotape – which can be done as often as required – the lecturer is enabled to integrate theoretical lessons with examples of actual engineering practice. After familiarizing the student with all the necessary procedures in this way, the lecturer may then operate the machine while being watched on the television screen by colleagues and the instructor. By following this technique the actual training time spent on the factory floor can be reduced by as much as 60 per cent, which will have a tremendous cost-saving effect on the whole operation.

Sales training

Television allows groups of junior salespersons not only to observe experts giving sales talks, but also to sell their products to one another while the television camera and video recorder record the whole presentation. This is then replayed for discussion and evaluation. To save them the embarrassment of a group discussion, they can evaluate their presentations by themselves or with the sales manager, before the group discussion. Using closed circuit television in sales training reduces the time needed to train an effective salesperson considerably.

Training of older staff members

In this age of rapid and immense change, the older employee, who has been with the company for many years, often finds it difficult to keep abreast of new techniques and developments. The embarrassing situation of grouping people in senior positions with their younger colleagues for training sessions can be avoided by pre-recording training programmes, and then presenting them to selected groups of more senior staff. This will change a senior manager from being against a new project to being a motivator.

Service instructions

Manufacturers with widespread service organizations, such as car and computer manufacturers, can use video cassette recordings to demonstrate sales and service techniques, product developments, and maintenance procedures in all their main operational centres. If complicated service problems are experienced, recordings can be made of the malfunctioning piece of equipment and the tapes can be sent to overseas suppliers for their comments. They, in turn, can record the proper procedure for correcting the fault and return the tape, which can then be replayed on site while the equipment is being repaired.

Refresher courses

New products are continuously becoming available to professional people in virtually every field. Unparalleled scientific and industrial research results in the frequent development of new techniques. These facts are well known and doctors, architects, engineers, and many other professionals realize the need to go on refresher courses and devote an increasing amount of time to keeping abreast of innovations and developments. Fortunately, the vast potential of the video cassette recorder has been realized by all professional bodies and the industries serving them. Specialized video cassette programmes are being produced in their thousands. By using the highly skilled presentation techniques available to specialists working in conjunction with software producers, new knowledge can be communicated so that it is easily understood, convenient, and very economical to produce. Programmes can be replayed according to the needs of both the company and the individual. Provision can be made for individuals to learn a new job or technique at home while sticking to the 'old' one during the day.

Safety on the premises

There is no easier and safer way to train employees in safety procedures to be followed on the premises than by recording staged accidents that may result from failure to apply safety regulations and screening these at regular intervals. If an accident does occur and you can record and show it to all your staff, the awareness of safety will be even stronger.

Time and motion study

It is normally time consuming to conduct a time and motion study because operators have to repeat the same job over and over again. For the duration of the study, the operator and his or her machine are out of production, which means loss of revenue. By making a video recording of different people doing their jobs,

these recordings can be played back, at one's own convenience, as many times as one wishes. By means of the freeze-frame facility of the machine, particular motions can be evaluated and studied at leisure. This will reduce costs considerably and there will be a permanent visual record of the exercise which can be shown to the manager, or other senior members of staff, at a suitable time.

Public speaking

Speakers are not fully aware of how they come across when addressing an audience. They may judge their success from the reaction of the audience, or from past experience. Nevertheless, they cannot be certain whether they possess any irritating habits or idiosyncrasies. By video recording such an address, and later viewing it, a speaker may immediately identify problem areas and correct them. It may require more than one session to attain perfection.

A company director could well be asked to prepare for a televised interview. To step from the familiar world of the boardroom into the unrelenting environment of a television studio can be a frightening experience for any businessperson. To overcome this, it is a good idea to record a mock interview beforehand. During such a session, the director should be subjected to a rapid fire of probing questions, insults, or serious criticism, all of which should be countered conclusively and decisively. While reviewing the recording, mistakes will be identified that should be avoided during the actual interview. The director will also become accustomed to the studio lights, and more especially to the camera, which exploits any possible facial weakness. In addition, he or she will have to cope with make-up applied to hide pallor in the cheeks, or to disguise a jaw line. Nervousness is the bane of all novices, and to a hostile interviewer it presents an invitation for attack.

Being aware of these pitfalls beforehand will enable the director to counter them effectively. He or she will, therefore, appear at ease in front of the camera, be perceived by viewers as confident and dynamic, be assured of the subject, and be in full control of the situation.

Internal communication

If a company has a large number of plants or a network of national or international sales organizations, video cassette recordings are the best possible way to transmit visual information between people and places. Many large corporate organizations, such as BMW and Eskom, are using video newsletters to communicate important organizational changes, mergers, staff appointments, new product launches, and industrial relations matters to employees.

Induction training

Closed circuit television can be of great value in the induction sessions of new employees. Among other things, it can 'introduce' to the new employee, in person, the general manager or any other important employees of the company, who will normally not have time to attend each induction session. It can also introduce the new employee to the company organization and its products, the working conditions, past achievements of the company, and future goals and objectives. At each session, the presenter will be fresh and enthusiastic, which is not always the case in companies where induction programmes are a daily exercise. An induction training video will allow the session to go ahead even in the absence of senior personnel.

Corporate image

A new and exciting application of audiovisual material and videos is in the area of corporate image. A striking visual presentation of a company's diverse operations often sets the scene for a briefing of new employees, VIPs visiting head office, or for a marketing and sales presentation.

Depending on the facilities available, the ten-minute programme can be shown on a large screen using two or more projectors. Up to 48 projectors have been used for spectacular new product launch presentations at the Sun City Superbowl. The flexibility of this medium allows for the interchangeability of soundtracks in the language most familiar to the audience. On a much smaller scale, the original audiovisual material can be transferred to video and shown on a television monitor.

Public relations practitioners have a creative role to play in these productions. They can research and draft scripts together with professional scriptwriters, help select slides and music, and help with setting up locations for shoots.

Public relations

Closed circuit television and videos are increasingly being used for a variety of purposes in public relations. The case study which follows illustrates some of these purposes.

Case study Video assignments

The corporate video is a much-used tool of the practitioner but it is a relatively expensive exercise, costing anything from R50 000 upwards, depending on length and complexity. Its execution therefore requires careful planning. The first consideration is the target audience(s) and the objective(s) to be achieved. There is a tendency to try to make a video that serves more than one audience and more than one objective. The best advice is to try to avoid such an approach: define your objectives and audience clearly from the start, and keep them to a minimum. One objective and one clearly defined audience are better than two, which are better than three, and so on.

The second consideration is to always remember that video is a completely different medium to text and other kinds of visual media such as still photography and graphics. The words and structure that work well in the corporate report will more than likely be unsuitable for a video commentary.

The third consideration is length. Videos should be around 10 minutes long. They should not exceed 15 minutes because research has proven that attention declines rapidly after this period.

Planning the assignment

It is best to use a professional video producer with a good track record. Using amateurs usually turns out to be a false economy. Ask to see a 'show reel' of prospective production houses to get a feel for their style. Most production houses offer a full service including scriptwriting, but remember the scriptwriter will in most cases be starting from a position of complete ignorance. Therefore, at the first meeting, have ready an outline of what you want him or her to cover (aims, objectives, content). Create a two-column layout on a separate document. In the left-hand column, elaborate on each element of the outline in your own words which will form the starting point for the commentary. In the right-hand column, try to think of pictures and scenes that will best show what you are talking about.

At this point there may be an inclination to use lots of 'talking heads'. There may be pressure to include so and so just because, for example, they are in senior management and it is 'good PR' to do so. Be careful of such an approach. Use only talking heads in office situations where it is absolutely necessary and avoid them as far as possible. Where you include people in the organization, have them doing something while you interview them, or place them into contexts other than offices. For example, have the chief executive officer interviewed while he or she walks through the plant. Also, where possible, draft the actual

words you want them to say, or minimally the key phrases or concepts as a guideline.

After briefing the producer in this way, ask him or her to come back with a draft script that includes a storyboard. This script will contain a number of creative ideas that the producer has discussed with you, and should give you an idea of how he or she plans to execute the project. Make sure too that, where corporate colours, typefaces, or logos are used, they are correctly rendered. You can expect a number of script revisions.

Budgeting

Normally, there will be an amount payable upon acceptance of completed script. This is usually around 10 per cent of the total cost of the entire production. Production houses will budget costs by one of two principles: by the hour or by completed project. Whatever the case, ensure that you get a complete cost, even if it is using estimated hours. This should include the use of a professional voice for the 'voice-over' or commentary. Again, the temptation is to use someone who 'hasn't got a bad voice', but professionals will deliver a far superior product. A 10 per cent contingency fee for the entire project is usually included as standard practice.

Shooting usually begins after script approval. Script approval is an important stage, because the script is the 'architectural plan' for the whole project from which everyone works. Changes to the script after approval will in most cases attract an extra cost because they can impact significantly on the shooting and editing stages.

Quite often, the provider will request second payment upon completion of the shooting ('production') phase. This should not exceed half of the total cost, since the postproduction or editing stage is often more time-consuming than the actual video shooting stage, and requires more complex technology. Final payment is usually made only upon acceptance of the completed product.

Remember that you calculate any additional costs and budget accordingly. For example, you may require a number of copies to be made for distribution on video cassette or on CD. Or you may require a separate soundtrack in another language. This will incur translation costs and a fee for a second professional voice and studio time for the voice-over recording.

Organizing the shoot

The public relations practitioner is usually responsible for making sure that key people are available for the shoot according to the shooting schedule. It is tempting to think that, because a person may be required to appear in a particular sequence for only a few seconds, the demands on that person's time will be minimal during the actual shooting. This is hardly ever the case. More likely, he or she will have to be available for an hour or more. Time is required for setting up cameras, lights, and microphones, as well as for rehearsals. Time will have to be allocated for transport or movement from one location to another. Although most members of management and employees will be keen to be part of a video, they may baulk at the idea of having to leave their 'real work' for substantial periods. Warn them accordingly. Also, scheduled arrangements might have to change due to unforseen circumstances. Include contact telephone numbers of participants on the schedule and keep individuals up to date by confirming arrival times of the production team prior to arrival.

An example of part of a typical shooting schedule is shown below.

Time	Project	Contact
08:15	Meet at NGO Office Park	Thabo (Producer) 082554
08:30	Craft Action Body • Craft • Some words from the facilitator about ZCBF and how it has helped her and what she does to help rural crafters).	Khushu Dlamini 0839609229
09:30	Hydroponic Farm • Footage of crops • Footage of ladies working with crops	Peter Morrison 7973136
10:30	Edupark • Students milling around between buildings during their break-time (to show the activity at the Edupark during the day)	Maureen Pascoe 7973457
11:15	Afrox-Richtek Welding Centre • Training in progress • Close-ups of student welding	Charmaine Langley 7973191/0828760080
12:30	Lunch	
13:00	RBM Small Business Advice Centre • Manager talking about close co-operation between SBAC and BLC • Footage of some of the wall décor with someone using the 'Are you an entrepreneur' computer programme.	Peter Morrison 7973136
14:00	CASME Resource Centre • Staff member demonstrating kit to teacher	Dorothea Coppard 7973296/0828266809

Further reading

There are various specialized publications dealing with this subject. Consult either The Media Book or SARAD for further particulars.

Chapter 15

Digital communication

When you have read this chapter, you should:

- be familiar with the term digital communication and what it embraces;
- be able to review some of the key developments that are taking place in this field;
- examine how these new technologies can be applied to accomplish public relations objectives.

The advances and innovations in technology have had a huge impact on the practice of public relations in recent years. Digital devices of all kinds now enable practitioners to stay on top of the latest events in the external communication environment.

Impact of the Internet

There are many platforms, channels, and tools of importance to the practitioner that include Google, YouTube, Twitter, an array of social media sites (particularly Facebook), and a multitude of blogs. These should not be seen as separate entities but rather as part of the interconnecting mosaic of modern communications.

Google

The Internet and World Wide Web have become massive mirrors and repositories of human knowledge, thoughts, intentions, and actions. They are also the means used by millions of people to communicate every day. Web search engine, Google, is currently the most popular tool we have to find and aggregate information, monitor information exchange, and to communicate electronically through its services like Gmail, chat, and video chat. Google offers an impressive array of services spanning information retrieval, databases, distributed systems, human computer interaction, artificial intelligence, and data mining.

YouTube

YouTube is a video sharing website where users can upload and share videos about, amongst other things, demonstrations of commercial products and services. YouTube has turned video sharing into one of the most important parts of Internet culture. With over 100 million videos it has become the second largest search engine after Google.

Blogs

There are roughly 200 million blogs at the time of writing and thousands appearing online everyday and many of these discuss and evaluate products and services.

Twitter

Every Twitter user has their own little tiny 'blog' (microblog) that they can add messages to of up to 140 characters in length. They can also send these messages to other Twitter users and these messages will then appear on their recipient's microblog. Each of these messages is known as a tweet. Twitter is a form of 'microblogging' that allows individuals to post frequent tiny updates on what they are doing and thinking about. This is quite different from 'macro' blogging, because a blog post is usually much longer providing extended opinion pieces, stories, and detailed analysis. A key difference between tweets and SMS messaging is that tweeters can restrict delivery to those they choose or allow open access and that tweets are indexed in Google

As well as adding tweets to your miniblog and sending them to other people, you can "follow" and read other peoples Twitter blogs. When you "follow" someone, their tweets then start to appear on your Twitter page. In this way individuals can keep up to date with what friends, family, and business contacts are doing and their reactions and opinions. Twitter often provides a warning sign of what people are saying about your products and services before it turns into a significant issue. Existing customers and clients can follow your company to get inside news, information, and offers.

Facebook

Facebook is a popular social networking website that allows users to create profiles, upload photos and video, send messages and keep in touch with friends, family and colleagues. The site, includes features such as:

- marketplace – allows members to post, read and respond to classified ads;
- groups – allows members who have common interests to find each other and interact;
- events – allows members to publicize an event, invite guests, and track who plans to attend;
- pages – allows members to create and promote a public page built around a specific topic;
- presence technology – allows members to see which contacts are online and chat.

Within each member's personal profile, there are several key networking components. The most popular is the wall, which is essentially a virtual bulletin board. Messages left on a member's wall can be text, video or photos. Another popular component is the virtual photo album. Photos can be uploaded from the desktop or directly from a cellphone camera. Another popular profile component is the status updates, a microblogging feature that allows members to broadcast short Twitter-like announcements to their friends. All interactions are published in a newsfeed, which is distributed in real-time to the member's friends.

As Mersham, Theunissen & Peart (2009) suggest, social media are responsible for the biggest impact on public relations in recent years. The evolution of the Internet into Web 2.0 that lets people collaborate and share information online through social media in ways previously unavailable, means that the organization's approach to marketing, customer service, recruiting, and crucially public relations must change. But this rapid new development has left many organizations and public relations practitioners overwhelmed, wondering how they can best integrate these changes into their strategy.

In principle, the change is a simple one. The traditional one-way communication of the older mass media is re-invented as a multitude of interacting and overlapping "conversations" in the social media (Mersham et al., 2009:148).

For decades, practitioners have been talking at stakeholders but not with them, using mass communication. Communication became a limited version of the concept, focusing on the top-down, one-way, and controlled dissemination of messages (the "push and control" model). But in this era of the new social media, we are required to return to the basic idea of communication as dialogue where equality is key and where information cannot be locked down or controlled.

Conversation and shared interests

Mersham et al. (2009) suggest that social media can be likened to a conversation where public relations practitioners want to be part of the discussion or wish to engage consumers one-to-one. The conversation is alive and active with participants uploading, sharing and creating new content, and reflects real-life communication networks with friends, colleagues, and those who share their interests whether business or social. Mersham et al. (2009:148) use the metaphor of a massive cyberspace party already underway where groups of people are gathered, have existing networks of relationships, and are already talking. The "party floor" becomes a collective of multiple, virtual places around the world that exist at the same time –where information and knowledge is shared and ideas are formed. We can no more control the many discussions underway across the Internet than we can rudely command the floor at a large party.

Trust and credibility

According to Metz (2008), the popularity of social media reflects a growing lack of trust in traditional mass media and its ability to tell the truth. Smith (2008) suggests that social media is more trusted. It is therefore important for organizations to use social media to regain public trust.

In 2007, the Edelman Trust Barometer, commissioned by the global public relations firm of the same name, identified the trend towards growing faith in "people like me" – and that social media allow us to easily and quickly find these people, share opinions and learn about their experiences with products and services from what were previously "detached" organizations.

Finding and filtering

According to Holtz (2008), social media applications have a major advantage for communication practitioners who are skilled in their use. They make it easier to find and filter information, allowing users to cut through the clutter by searching for information already "tagged" (sorted and labelled) by like-minded people. Holtz (2008) also points out that social media allows for opportunities of self-expression. In that sense, it acts as an empowering tool and equalizer, eroding the value of controlling information. Honesty and transparency open the door to participation.

A new approach

To become part of this process a different way of thinking and a break with traditional communication practices is needed – particularly from organizations that are used to controlling and filtering information so that they can portray themselves in the best possible light. This highlights the need to spend more time in engaging with people on a more personal level online and in social network platforms as opposed to traditional print and broadcast media.

Top 20 most visited Internet sites in South Africa:

1. Google (google.co.za): Used mainly, but not exclusively, to search for South African-based sites.
2. Facebook (facebook.com): A social utility that connects people, to keep up with friends, upload photos, share links and videos.
3. Google (google.com): Enables users to search the web, Usenet, and images. Features include PageRank, caching and translation of results, and an option to find similar pages. The company's focus is developing search technology.
4. Yahoo! (yahoo.com): Personalized content and search options, chatrooms, free e-mail, clubs, and pager.
5. YouTube (youtube.com): Uploads, tags, and shares videos worldwide.
6. Wikipedia (wikipedia.org): An online collaborative encyclopaedia.
7. Blogger.com (blogger.com): Free, automated weblog publishing tool.
8. Twitter (twitter.com): Social networking and microblogging service utilizing instant messaging, SMS or a web interface.
9. Gumtree (gumtree.co.za): A free local classifieds site where advertisements can be posted for free.
10. Windows Live (live.com): A search engine from Microsoft.
11. News24 (news24.com): A 24-hour online news service situated in South Africa. It is the online arm of the South African newspaper group Naspers.
12. The Standard Bank of South Africa (standardbank.co.za): Internet banking site of one of South Africa's big four banks.
13. Absa Group Banks (absa.co.za): Another large South African bank offering Internet banking.
14. Microsoft Network (MSN) (msn.com): Dialup access and content provider.
15. Microsoft Corporation (microsoft.com): The main site for product information, support, and news.
16. WordPress.com (wordpress.com): Free blogs managed by the developers of the WordPress software. It includes custom design templates, integrated statistics, automatic spam protection, and other features.
17. Flickr (flickr.com): Picture galleries available with chat, groups, and photo ratings.
18. Independent Online (iol.co.za): South African, regional and world news, sport, business, motoring, classifieds, and RSS feeds from various wires services and the Independent group newspapers .
19. Amazon.com (amazon.com): Amazon.com seeks to be earth's most customer-centric company, where customers can find and discover anything they might want to buy online, and endeavours to offer its customers the lowest possible prices. Site has numerous personalization features and services, extensive customer and editorial product reviews.
20. Bid Or Buy (bidorbuy.co.za): Buy or sell everything from computers and travel to stamps, coins and collectibles.

Small, niche conversations in social media can create a long-lasting impact. Chris Anderson's "Long Tail" theory (2006) suggests that content and communication are becoming tightly focused among small groups rather than large mass audiences. A good example is how peer-to-peer free downloads forced the music industry to radically change its business model and go online. While the actual conversation might be among a relatively small group, social media makes it available to many others, now and in the future due to its digital "footprint" or "shadow". As Seth Godin put it, "Google never forgets" (Godin, 2009).

Several issues are raised when practitioners propose the idea of introducing social media into the existing communication strategy.

Foremost is the issue of control of information. Most organizations, particularly large and hierarchical organizations, are used to tightly controlling (or attempting to control) information flow to its stakeholders. Smaller organizations and those with organic or flatter structures may find it easier to adopt social media strategies.

The level of trust and support extended to employees – a matter of organizational culture – will determine the level of resistance experienced. A common argument of organizations with low levels of trust and support is that allowing employee blogging is like letting any "loose cannon" talk to the media. But the risk created by inadvertently posting something inappropriate may be less than one of an employee merely answering the phone and starting to chat to a friendly journalist on the hunt for a story. Also, blogs, wikis and podcasts have an advantage in that once posted, there is a record of comment, unlike an interview with a journalist where misquotes and misinterpretations are fairly common.

Providing training programmes for employees is important so that they understand their social media responsibilities and to ensure they are familiar with the organization's social media policy. This can further reduce potential risk.

Essentially we can think of engagement with social media as interaction based on total control of one-way messages (the traditional press release, the organization's web pages) through to partial control (credible media) and finally very little control (what individuals or organizations say about you via the digital media). As the organization relinquishes control, it invites others to engage. Through social media this process becomes transparent, which in turn fosters trust in and receptiveness of the organization's message leading to greater engagement and balanced two-way interaction.

Measurement of social media

Social media effects on brand and corporate reputation can be instantaneous and far-reaching, resulting in the growing need to monitor and measure this phenomenon.

As Mersham et al. (2009) argue, in public relations, being able to measure, track and compare the results, communication is a requirement in determining strategy and tactics. "Metrics" and "attributes" are two key concepts applied to measuring social media. These are analyzed to determine how they affect and are being affected by the actions of the organization, such as a marketing campaign (internal) or a crisis (external). The crucial question is: 'Which attributes should be measured'? Here we refer to the process of rating individual items: posts, comments, messages and articles – according to subject (topic), sentiment (feelings) and influence (readership).

Currently there are basically two approaches to the social media analysis process: computational methods and human analysis. Computing provides the speed and scalability of an automated process and the human analyst provides the subtlety and insight.

One end of the spectrum is fully automated analysis, and some organizations have invested significant time and capital in systems that automate content analysis. They use terms like "natural-language processing" to describe software that reads and scores social media. Automated processes are usually the basis of the so-called "client dashboards" that provide real-time updates.

On the other end of the spectrum is human analysis for those not convinced that computers can accurately interpret message content. Here human insight, subtlety and the ability to identify multiple, connotative meanings, sarcasm, and so on are critical.

In reality, human analysts benefit from the speed of computers, and automated processes benefit from human oversight. Thus, hybrid forms such as software-assisted human analysis and human-assisted software analysis are currently the most useful.

In conclusion, because of the Internet and new media, public relations will be increasingly about conversations rather than the traditional monologues of the past, public relations will have to adapt to the free exchange of opinions across groups and collectives that previously were merely recipients of communication messages. Mersham et al. (2009) suggest that customers will flow to companies with which they can have human interactions and move away from companies that persist in presenting unassailable, formal corporate faces to the world. Public relations "spin" and hyperbole will become more obvious, attracting wider condemnation and subject to repeated analysis. The alignment of marketing and corporate communications messages with the values and behaviours of organizational culture means increased emphasis on cause-related marketing and on corporate social responsibility. Public relations programmes will be held to high standards of authenticity by multiple stakeholder groups, rather than customers alone in a new era of community and business collaboration.

Sources

Anderson, C. 2006. *The Long Tail: Why the Future of Business is Selling Less of More.* New York: Hyperion Books.

Edelman Trust Barometer 2007. [Online]. Available: http://www.edelman.com/news/Show One.asp?ID=146. Last accessed 13 September 2008.

Godin, S. 2009. *Personal branding in the age of Google.* [Online] Available: http://sethgodin.typepad.com/seths_blog/2009/02/personal-branding-in-the-age-ofgoogle.html.Last accessed 2 March 2009.

Holtz, S. 2008. Bring your intranet into the 21st century. *Communication World.* January/February, 25(1), 14–18.

Locke, C., R. Levine, D. Searls, & D. Weinberger. 2001. *The Cluetrain Manifesto: The End of Business as Usual.* Cambridge, MA: Perseus Publishing.

Mersham, G.M., P. Petra Theunissen & J. Peart. 2009. *Public Relations and Communication Management: An Aotearoa/New Zealand Perspective.* Auckland: Pearson Education.

Metz, A. 2008. Social media is crucial for an agency. *PRWeek.* (US Ed.). 7 April, 11(14), 8.

Smith, S. 2008. Why employees are more trusted than the CEO. *Strategic Communication Management.* April/May, 11(3),7.

Wilcox, D.L., & G.T. Cameron. 2009. *Public Relations: Strategies and Tactics.* 9th edition. Boston: Allyn & Bacon.

Part III

The techniques of public relations

Chapter 16

Effective communication: the spoken word

When you have read this chapter, you should:
- be aware of the key factors that affect communication;
- be familiar with the various purposes of prepared speeches;
- be able to analyze audiences in order to prepare appropriate speeches;
- understand how to organize material for a speech;
- be familiar with the various phases of a speech;
- be aware of the points to look for and practise when presenting a speech.

The ability to express ideas in writing and in speaking heads the list of all the requirements for success ... In the very large organizations ... this ability to express oneself is perhaps the most important of all the skills someone can possess (Peter Drucker, international management consultant).

Speaking is a natural and integral part of daily life; fear of speaking is an unnatural, acquired behaviour. If we can come to see that all speaking, whether to one or one thousand, requires the same basic communication skills, we can begin to incorporate these qualities of effective interpersonal communication into our public speaking.

Key communication factors

Ten key communication factors that affect our communications are:
- our personality, the 'this is me' aspect of communication;
- how we look to others in our body, our expression, our posture, and how we sit, stand, and walk;
- the kind of eye contact we do or do not establish with others;
- the hand and facial gestures we use;
- our general appearance – dress, grooming, hair style, physical attitude;
- our use of language;
- our voice quality;

159

- the clarity with which we get our intended message across;
- the level of confidence we generate when we speak;
- the degree to which we participate and involve ourselves in public speaking situations.

Albert Mehrabian, in his book *Silent Messages*, points out that only 7 per cent of our impact comes from the words that we speak (the verbal component), whereas 38 per cent comes from our vocal qualities (the vocal component) and 55 per cent comes from how we look to others (the visual component).

Thus, the non-verbal aspects of our communication – voice and body – make up a decisive 93 per cent of our communication impact on others.

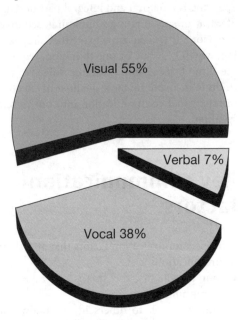

Purposes of communication

In examining individual-to-group communication we must be aware that the style, vocabulary, and tone of the speech may vary accord-

ing to its purpose. The various purposes may be summed up as follows:

- To interest or amuse. After-dinner speeches are typical of this category. Addresses to Rotarians by guest speakers, for example, are often planned to be very interesting, but not necessarily very informative.
- To inform or to teach. An academic lecture would fall in this category.
- To stimulate or impress. Speeches by marketing managers to stimulate salesmen into selling products fall in this category. Many political speeches are designed only to stimulate or impress – the information that they give is often inconsequential or coloured by the speaker's political bias.
- To motivate. This kind of speech is used to get an audience to act. Politicians try to motivate people to vote for them. Labour leaders try to get their audience to take industrial action.
- To coerce or persuade. Political speeches may fall in this category, especially if they are made to an audience whose views differ from those of the speaker.

Preparing to speak

With a clear understanding of the purpose of your speech, you may proceed to the first stage in its preparation, the analysis of your audience.

Analyzing the audience

Through analysis of the audience, you will be able to establish its group identity. You will be able to assess the way in which the audience may react to your message. Your message may be directed so that it has a personal appeal to the listeners. You will be able to avoid offending your audience through injudicious use of words or actions.

In analyzing your audience, the following questions will be very useful:

- Is the audience likely to be active? If they have just had a meal, they will probably not be active. If they have heard several other speeches before yours, they are also likely to be inactive. This will make your job harder.

- What are the practical limits placed on the purpose of the speech? For example, how much time is there? What knowledge of the subject does the audience have?
- What are the taboos and formal requirements of the audience? Will they be offended by allusions to politics or religion? Will a joke be taken in good faith?
- What other groups are relevant to the audience's response to this speech? If, for example, you are speaking to a Christian Women's Institute on economic theory, you have to bear in mind that they are not a body of women who meet for social reasons, and that they are going to be influenced by their religious beliefs in their reaction to what you say.
- What conventional beliefs and attitudes will apply? You ought to be particularly aware of the political, racial, and social attitudes and feelings of your audience.
- What do you expect the effect of your speech to be and when do you expect that effect to show itself? You may want your speech to rouse your audience to immediate action. You may merely want to rouse their minds at this stage with action to follow some time after. You must take the time factor and the effect that you expect to achieve into account when preparing your speech.

Audiences are made up of individuals who vary in their response to a stimulus. But, when individuals come together as an audience, they normally have some kind of common purpose. You should look for this common purpose and try to find out what the members of your audience have in common. You should determine whether these similarities are important enough for you to alter your intended message because of the effect it may have on your audience.

The nature of the audience will have certain influences on what you say and how you say it. These influences include the following:

- restraints on behaviour and vocabulary;
- constraints and requirements, for example, if you were to address a group of laypersons on a technical subject, you would be expected to define any technical terms that you used;
- criteria for selecting the message provided by audience characteristics, that is, a speech to a group of business people should contain business allusions and imagery;
- the opportunity to use special effects which will appeal to the audience identity, for example in talking on pollution to business people, you could give them examples of how they could win goodwill and markets through anti-pollution measures.

Organizing material

The material should be organized using the methods described below.

Brainstorming consists of jotting down points on the topic as you think of them or discover them in your research. You then read over the points that you have been jotting down, evaluate them, and organize them. Then you proceed to construct an outline for your speech along the lines indicated later. The drawback with the brainstorming approach is that it can give an unbalanced view if the material obtained is in itself unbalanced. There is also no in-built means of checking the balance.

Congeneric organization is essentially a method of finding a classification that is appropriate to the information available and the topic. There are many ways of classifying information.

In the systematic approach the original plan should be carefully examined and compared with the information available. The classification should then be based on the original outline, but modified to take account of the information available.

The analytical approach differs from the systematic congeneric approach described above in that the framework is fixed at the start of the research. This is sometimes desirable where the task is specified in detail. This approach should be used with caution as it may bias research and investigation, and lead to faulty conclusions.

With the chronological approach the results are reported in time sequence. This method is not often used, but can be very useful when the sequence of events is important, for example when investigating an accident or a disaster.

Good organization and presentation are most important, since the mind has a limited capacity to understand and interrelate unorganized information. The mind's recall of information that fits into a sound logical pattern is good and makes for effective communication.

Speech construction

A successful speech is arranged into three main sections: the opening or introduction; the body of the speech with three or four main points; and the conclusion or ending.

Introduction

It is vital that you get the attention of your audience from the very beginning of your presentation. You only have one chance at making a first impression. How can this be done?
- open with a striking quotation;
- relate an interesting human story;
- ask a question;
- start with shocking facts;
- arouse curiosity;
- use appropriate humour.

The introduction sets the stage and establishes the mood of your speech. It consists of approximately 10 per cent of your presentation.

Body

It is often easier to prepare the body of your speech before working on the introduction

and the conclusion. The body or middle part contains the factual information and should consist of three (sometimes four) main points and the subordinate support for each point. This makes up about 85 per cent of the presentation. Avoid choosing a subject which is too deep, too vast, or too complex. The subject should be of interest to the particular audience that is being addressed. Try if possible to select an unusual or original angle, subject, or point of view for your talk.

Conclusion

This final five per cent of your speech summarizes the main message. Your audience must be aware that you have come to the end of your speech without you necessarily saying it in so many words. Your conclusion may be signalled by:
- using an appropriate quotation;
- linking up with your opening;
- appealing for action;
- raising a laugh;
- paying the audience a sincere compliment.

However well structured a speech may be, remember it is the enthusiasm and conviction of the speaker that will impress. Warmth and sincerity are often rated higher than a speaker's technical proficiency. It is not so much what you have to say (although this is very important) but how you say it.

Introducing and thanking a speaker

Introductions and thank yous need to be brief, concise, and personal. To enable you to cover all the necessary information, answer the questions in the following formula:
- Why this subject?
- Why this subject for this audience?
- Why this subject for this audience at this time by this speaker?

Bear the following points in mind:

- Be brief, never more than two minutes unless it is a very formal occasion.
- Avoid stale and stilted phrases such as ' It is indeed a pleasure for me', 'This man needs no introduction' or ' We are gathered here tonight'.
- Avoid overstating the treat that awaits the audience. It may not happen.
- Avoid exaggerating your speaker's qualifications. Reading out a complete curriculum vitae is very boring and unnecessary. List only the most recent and relevant information.
- Avoid mentioning the speaker's name until you are ready to introduce him or her.
- Announce the speaker to the audience; do not turn around and face the seated speaker.
- Don't steal the spotlight. The hero of the function is the speaker, not you.
- Make sure that the lectern and in particular the microphone are the correct height for the speaker and that a glass of water is available.
- Make sure the overhead projector and video are ready for use at the touch of a button.
- Don't allow the speaker to go over his or her time. Indicate politely to the speaker that he or she should bring his or her talk to a successful conclusion.

In thanking a speaker remember these three simple points:

- What did you like about the speech or the person?
- What important message did you receive?
- Thank him or her.

It is not necessary to give a summary of what the speaker had to say or to go into any detail about the issues or points that were raised.

Presenting the speech

The presentation of a speech is complementary to its planning. Unless both are done properly, effective communication is unlikely to result.

Clarity

Present your speech in such a way that your meaning is absolutely clear to your audience. Avoid vague, confusing, or ambiguous statements and when necessary illustrate your meaning. Choose descriptive anecdotes, analogies, and word pictures. Define terms by using expressions such as 'By X I mean ...' and 'In other words ...' Make sure your illustrations are appropriate and that your audience is not left with the impression that your speech consisted of nothing but a series of anecdotes.

Articulation

Make sure the audience can hear you. A whisper, well used, is as effective as a shout. Raise and lower your pitch; avoid a monotonous tone. Speed up or slow down your speaking rate for emphasis and variety. Speak clearly; avoid mumbling and slurring. A pleasing voice, well used, adds to the impact of your message.

Emphasis

Speakers are not only heard, they are also seen, and their aim should be to enhance their speeches by their appearance, gestures, and animation (or the absence thereof). Animation involves facial expressions, body movements, and posture. Gestures should appear natural and should complement the spoken word.

Getting attention

Focus listeners' attention, so that they remember your points, by using memory-retention techniques. Some of these include:

- repeating a point, with deliberate emphasis;

- using a visual aid;
- using mnemonics;
- dramatization;
- using examples;
- choosing appealing words or phrases which will be remembered.

Maintaining interest

The following elements will help you keep your audience's attention:
- Vividness. Illustrate by means of word pictures or explanations.
- Humour. This can be used to emphasize a point. Avoid jokes that serve only to raise a laugh without adding to the purpose of your speech.
- Drama. Dramatize a facet of your speech, but avoid overacting.
- Personal appeal. Where appropriate, refer to your own experiences or to those of well-known personalities.
- Adjust the delivery of your message to the response. Within the limits of the structure of your message, and without deviating from the objective, your delivery should be flexible enough to allow you to make changes in pace, level, and detail to meet the needs of your audience as indicated by their response.

It is not difficult to tell when an audience is losing interest. You may have to slow down or speed up your speech to recapture their interest. Perhaps you are losing them because you are speaking in a monotonous voice. Put inflection into your voice. If they do not understand a point, you should have an example ready to serve as illustration. Repeat a point. Ask if there is anyone who has not understood. Be more positive – ask a question. If there is no adequate reply, explain the point again.

Addressing a large audience

In individual-to-group communication, when the audience is so big that visual and oral feedback is limited by distance and visibility, compensatory action must be taken to overcome these drawbacks.

The speaker should stand in a prominent place that is well illuminated, and sound amplification equipment should be available. The background should be such that it emphasizes but does not conflict with the speaker's message; at the same time it should not overshadow him or her or the message. The speaker should dress for the part to be played in the communication.

The speaker must take pains to ensure that, in the minds of the audience, there is no conflict between his or her personality, message, and method of presentation. Because of the concentration of attention on the speaker, he or she has the potential to evoke certain beliefs and attitudes from the audience and, in a sense, becomes 'larger than life'. The words emphasized and gestures used come to represent not only his or her own beliefs and attitudes, but those of the audience as well. Under these circumstances, the response of the audience, which can be gauged directly from murmurs, movement, applause, and occasional individual utterances, is interpreted by the speaker and voiced on their behalf.

To ensure success, the speaker must always be conscious of the reaction or response of the audience and adjust the level, pace, and if necessary, the form of the message to suit the audience. The substance of the message, however, must remain inviolate if the speaker is to preserve his or her integrity.

Pitfalls to be avoided by speakers

- Be honest with your audience. Don't misuse statistics.
- Remember that cold figures are quickly forgotten, while illustrations are remembered.
- Talk to the point. Don't get off the main line.
- Tell the truth. Don't misplace emphasis or tell a half-truth to create a false impression.
- Don't argue in a circle. Get straight to the point.
- Give proof when needed. Don't mistake assertion or contradiction for proof.
- Be concise. Don't use a dozen words to say what can be said in one or two.

Checklist for speakers

1. What is the date, time and place of the function?
2. What time am I expected to arrive?
3. Am I expected to bring a partner?
4. What is the dress - formal, semi-formal, or casual?
5. What form will the function take - sit-down dinner, buffet, cocktail?
6. What other speakers will there be?
7. How big is the audience likely to be?
8. How will the audience be seated - cinema style, at separate tables, at one big table?
9. What is the audience profile - men only, women only, men and women, sophisticated, informal, average age, language preference, composition?
10. Will I need a microphone, projector or screen, blackboard, flip chart, or any other visual aid?
11. How long am I required to speak?
12. Is there anyone I should thank, praise, congratulate, or propose a toast to?
13. Which VIPs are likely to be present? Am I sure I know the correct way to address them at the start of my speech?
14. What is there I need to know about the host or hosting organization?
15. Will a copy of my speech be required, for example by the local paper or the house journal?
16. Do I have to forward a photograph of myself, or my curriculum vitae (for inclusion, for instance, in a printed programme)?

Further reading

Both ITC (International Training in Communication) and Toastmasters offer a variety of books, pamphlets and courses for both the novice and experienced communicator.

Branford, J. 1993. *A Dictionary of South African English.* Cape Town: Oxford University Press.

Cohen, J.M. & M.J. Cohen. 1975. *The Penguin Dictionary of Quotations.* London: Penguin Books.

Davies, P. 1991. *Your Total Image: How to Communicate Success.* London: Piatkus.

Drummond, M. 1993. *Fearless and Flawless Public Speaking - with Power, Polish and Pizazz.* San Diego: Pfeiffer & Co.

Fowler, H.W. 1963. *A Dictionary of Modern English Usage.* Oxford: Oxford University Press.

Kagan, J. 1987. *Speak Easy: Playing the Grab Game.* Johannesburg: Heinemann.

Marais, F. 1988. *Master of Ceremonies: A Simple Guide to Public Speaking.* Johannesburg: Marais.

Sarnoff, D. 1988. *Never Be Nervous Again.* Bergville: Century Hutchinson.

Tack, A. 1986. *How to Overcome Nervous Tension and Speak Well in Public.* Johannesburg: Heinemann.

Chapter 17

Effective communication: the presentation of papers

When you have read this chapter, you should:
- be familiar with the golden rules of public speaking;
- be aware of how illustrations can complement an oral presentation;
- understand some of the simple guidelines in the preparation of visual material;
- be able to draw up a checklist for successful presentations.

Contrary to popular belief, the ability to speak in public is not an innate blessing restricted to a few fortunate people. No person is a 'born speaker'. Good speakers are made, and good speeches and presentations are always the result of hard, painstaking work and speakers' ability to learn from their own mistakes and those of others.

To speak well in public requires certain skills that must be learnt; to present a paper in public requires those same skills supplemented by others that are peculiar to presentations.

Every presentation has three aspects to it:
- the oral delivery;
- visual aids;
- the personal impression made by the speaker.

Each one is essential to the whole, but each can be dealt with separately. However, if a speaker 'fails to make the grade' in only one aspect, the whole presentation will be a failure.

The essential aim of all speakers is to communicate. If they are not heard, listened to, or understood, they will not communicate, and then they might just as well have saved themselves the trouble they have gone to, and not wasted their audience's time.

In conventional communication, any failure on the part of the speaker can often be counteracted by intelligent listening on the part of the audience. Yet public speakers must face the fact that the majority of audiences do not want to go to the trouble of listening intelligently. They want to be able to sit back and listen, and have everything presented to them in the way that will be easiest for them to comprehend.

The 'golden rules' of public speaking

If a presentation is considered as a whole, speakers must be guided by the golden rules of public speaking:

- they must be heard;
- they must be listened to;
- they must be understood.

Failure in any one aspect will nullify the best efforts in the other two.

Be heard

There is more to being heard than speaking in a loud voice, although that is essential. Speakers must speak deliberately and distinctly, and must enunciate well. A gabble of sound, especially if hurled at the audience like streams of machine-gun fire, will be neither heard nor understood, and as likely as not, it will not be listened to.

Right from the first word, speakers must be heard by everyone in the hall. In fact, the issue of audibility applies throughout the talk. Very often, speakers begin too softly and become audible only as they warm to their task. Or they drop their voices, to the extent that they become inaudible at the ends of sentences or paragraphs, sometimes even at the ends of words.

It has been observed that an absence of adequate light has a psychological effect on an audience. When speakers cannot be seen at all or can only be discerned vaguely, their voices seem to be softer. Speakers should therefore remember to raise their voices if the hall is darkened, as when slides are being shown.

Be listened to

All speakers are salespersons. They are selling their paper and the information and ideas in it. To achieve their goal, they must employ every device – every trick, if necessary – of the successful salesperson.

To start with, they must hold the attention of their audience throughout. Any salesperson who lets that attention wander will lose the sale. There are things speakers can do that will ensure success in this regard; equally, there are things they must not do.

On the one hand they must be orators: they must talk to the audience, addressing every member, and periodically should insert a sentence designed to shock them in some way. On the other hand they must not do anything that will distract them.

However, since the attention of some listeners may well wander in spite of attempts to hold their interest, speakers can ensure that they are at least brought back to the matter in hand. To do so, speakers should repeat essential points and key words, thus giving those listeners the opportunity to catch up again. If they cannot do that, they may well flounder for the remainder of the talk.

It is difficult to win back audiences once speakers have lost their interest and attention. It is therefore important to add variety and a touch of humour to maintain interest.

Be understood

Speakers may practise pitching their voices to reach the farthest corner of the hall, and practise some more until they are word (and action) perfect. But many speakers still fail completely to communicate, because they have forgotten one very important point: to communicate they must be understood.

Being understood entails a number of points, each of them essential. In the first place, speakers must talk slowly enough. As a general rule, the more esoteric or complicated the discourse, the slower one should speak. Of course, the type of audience has to be considered in relation to the content of the talk. A physicist speaking to an audience of erudite physicists on a subject they all know something about is in a different situation to a physicist speaking to an audience of, say, zoologists, on a subject about which they know nothing. In the first situation, provided he or she enunciates clearly, he or she can speak at normal speed; in the second situation, speech must be slower, with regular pauses to let points sink in.

There are two other important sides to being understood. In the first place, speakers must be explicit. They must not be woolly, their sentences must not seem confused (in common parlance, they must not 'waffle'). In the second place, sentences must not be over-loaded. A sentence should contain only one idea, and that idea must be expressed in the most concise yet most explicit way.

When speakers are practising or rehears-ing, they should try their presentation on a col-league who knows something about the sub-ject – but not too much about it. Such a col-league will be alert to possible errors because, not knowing too much about the subject, he or she will be trying hard to understand and to learn something from the speaker. On the other hand, a colleague who knows nothing about the topic will put his or her lack of understanding down to lack of knowledge. Yet again, those who know a lot will not realize that they are understanding the speaker in spite of, not because of, what is being said.

Rules for perfect presentations

There are a number of rules which a speaker needs to follow for a perfect presentation. These are discussed below.

Rehearse

Every aspect of a presentation must be pre-pared – practised – rehearsed. Speakers must be ready, completely ready, for their talk. Any self-respecting audience, having perhaps travelled a long way and given up valuable time to be pres-ent, demands (and deserves) nothing less.

The first step is preparation. It may be assumed that prospective speakers know what they want to talk about. They may have written a paper; then they are called on to present it. They must decide what they are going to say and how the talk will be illustrated. Having sketched a plan, they should expand it into a set of notes (reminders).

The next step is a private rehearsal. Speakers should run through the presentation, not mentally but aloud. Knowing how much

time has been allotted for the speech, they must time themselves. If the talk is too long or too short, the necessary adjustments must be made. They must continue to practise until they are satisfied with the presentation.

Then there must be a rehearsal in front of a friend or colleague, preferably in a large hall. The friend should sit at the back of the hall and be asked to comment on the performance. Speakers should bear in mind that, during the actual presentation, there will be a lot of back-ground noise emanating from the audience, and so their voices must be louder during the rehearsal than is necessary in the existing conditions.

Be at ease

Many speakers are nervous both before and during their talks. There is rarely a need to be nervous, and it should never be made obvious to the audience. Speakers who appear to be nervous (rather than those who are nervous but do not show it) tend to discomfort listen-ers. Instead of concentrating on what is being said, they become concerned about how it is being said and even wonder whether there will be a breakdown.

Speakers must not appear to be overawed. They should remember that they are in a posi-tion of superiority with regard to the audience; they are the teachers, the audience, the pupils. They should therefore be self-confident, and should show it.

There are three main causes of nervous-ness: speakers have not prepared their whole presentation, including the subject matter, as near to perfection as possible; they do not know their audience; they feel, or they are, vocally untrained. This again boils down to the fact that, apart from knowledge of the audi-ence and having self-confidence, thorough preparation of the talk is necessary.

Have a satisfactory introduction

First things first – the introduction is the first item on the agenda. We can assume that the chairperson will have introduced the speaker and that the audience will have been given, either by the chairperson or in the programme, the title of the paper. The speaker should address the chairperson (with a word of thanks in return for any words of praise or commendation) and the audience ('Gentlemen' or 'Ladies', depending on the composition of the audience, or 'Ladies and gentlemen', but never 'Lady and gentlemen', even if a head count was done beforehand). This point is important because the correct form immediately attracts the audience's attention. (Using an incorrect form may have the harmful effect of antagonizing the audience, which is something no speaker should ever do.) In fact, a good speaker will hold the audience's attention by making the first sentence very effective. This can be done by beginning with the conclusions, or the main conclusion, or the whole point of the paper summarized into as few words as possible; alternatively, a sentence designed to shock can be used.

The introduction conforms to the first part of a well-known piece of advice on public speaking: 'Tell them what it is you are going to tell them, then tell them what you want to tell them, and then tell them what it is you have told them.'

Talk, talk, talk

Reading from the text is considered a bad practice because, with most readers, it means that the audience is virtually excluded. There is none of the personal rapport between reader and audience that exists between speaker and audience. Also, very few people can read really well; most stumble over words, lose their place, and often enunciate in a sing-song fashion. As a result, the audience loses concentration and eventually 'tunes out'.

At some conferences, it is necessary for the full paper to be read because delegates do not get reprints. In those instances, a speaker should practise reading so that it sounds as if he or she were talking. This is not easy, and requires the text to be written not in the usual, rather formal style of technical writing, but so that it sounds like normal speech. Obviously, it requires a lot of practice 'to speak the written word', the more so because the speaker must know the text so well that only a glance at it every now and then is needed. Eye contact with the audience must be maintained at all times – not only with the audience as a whole, but with every single member.

The speaker must practise to the point where the speech can be 'said' from start to finish without a hitch, holding the attention of the audience. But over-practising is not at all desirable. An audience can very quickly judge when a presentation is being recited; the delivery is stilted or sing-song, and the speaker often assumes a glassy-eyed pose, gazing at a fixed point in the distance. Having made that judgment, the listeners, instead of concentrating on 'the what' of the talk, concentrate on 'the how'; instead of thinking about what information has been given and what could come next, they wonder when lines will be forgotten. Anyone who visits the theatre will know that only a few actors, those at the top, can make their lines sound like normal speech; the remainder are always 'acting'. Perhaps that type of delivery is acceptable on the theatre stage; it is not acceptable in the lecture hall, where the audience wishes to be informed, not to be entertained.

For this reason, speakers must be serious. Jokes and anecdotes are fine for after-dinner speeches, but they are out of place in the presentation of technical papers, because they distract the attention of the audience. If the joke is good, the listeners will roll around in mirth. Their guffaws will drown any attempt at carrying on with the talk, the listeners will probably discuss the punch line with one another, and then, when it is all over and quiet reigns once more, they will sit waiting for the next joke. A few of the slower recoverers may even continue chuckling to themselves. In other words, if the joke is good, concentration will be broken for quite a lengthy period. And if the joke is not good, why tell it?

Don't distract

The sole purpose of a presentation is for the speaker to communicate information to the audience. Any device that performs this task or aids in its performance is good and acceptable; anything that inhibits or prevents it should be avoided at all costs.

There used to be an adage, prevalent in Victorian times especially, that 'children should be seen and not heard'. The opposite holds to a large extent in public speaking: speakers should be heard and not seen. More specifically, they should be heard and not noticed. The speaker who draws attention to himself or herself is taking attention away from the communication process. Actions such as waving the arms about, walking around the rostrum, fiddling with objects like pencils, coins and papers, frequent drinking of water, smoking (absolutely forbidden in any acceptable presentation), and playing with a pointer are guaranteed to distract. The last really has a place to itself. Some lecturers insist on using a pointer to draw attention to certain aspects of their slides. In doing so, they move the pointer all over the screen, an action termed 'painting' (not pointing) and, if the pointer is illuminated, they forget to switch it off when not using it. In fact, in a properly prepared presentation, there should not be any need for a pointer. If the speaker cannot easily and unambiguously draw attention verbally to the points in the diagram to be emphasized, the slides should be prepared in such a way that attention is drawn automatically to them.

Another bad aspect of pointing is that it usually moves the speaker away from the lectern and his or her notes, and results in talking to the screen. Not only does any reasonable audience feel cheated at being left out of the proceedings (eye contact is completely lost), but the acoustics of many halls are such that any sound directed backwards, towards the screen, is not reflected to the audience and so is not heard.

Eye contact must be maintained throughout a presentation. Every member of the audience must feel drawn into the talk. A person who feels left out will let his or her attention wander.

Slides and other illustrative devices often prove more distracting than useful; so take care! The purpose of illustration is to elucidate and clarify points in a way that would otherwise take strings of words. Illustrations can also be used to summarize the spoken word, even to give force to it, and a very important use is to maintain the interest of the audience. Even the most monotonous of speakers can capture the audience's attention by providing visual appeal.

However, for visual aids (the common, all-embracing term for slides, overhead projector transparencies, and so on) to serve their purpose, they must be designed properly. If they are not, they will be distracting, and the audience's attention will be riveted to the screen instead of to the speaker's words.

Sell yourself

As has been pointed out above, all speakers must set out to sell their papers. Apart from holding the attention of their audience, there are other things that they must do.

Like any competent salesperson, they must be enthusiastic about their product. That enthusiasm must shine through every word and must be evident in the tone of voice. Audiences must be given the impression that, to speakers at least, papers, or the information in them, are the greatest things ever. Indifference or impassiveness on their part will lose them a 'sale'.

Speakers must appear to know their subject. Hesitation because of a lack of practice can well be construed by the audience to indicate imperfect knowledge of the subject.

The fact that presentations must be rehearsed until the speakers are completely fluent cannot be overemphasized. Not only does a lack of preparation give rise to distractions, it is guaranteed to switch the listeners off, since they regard it as an insult. After all, if they could take the trouble to attend, speakers could have taken the trouble to prepare.

Paradoxically, audiences prefer to be looked down on confidently, rather than to be faced by self-deprecating, apologetic, and seemingly inferior or submissive speakers. 'Looked down on' is not meant in the sense of despising, but rather in the sense of appearing superior, for that is what speakers should be, since they know something that their audience does not. Many successful salespeople have that superior air about them; without it they would not be successful. This sense of superiority underlies the prevention of nervousness; speakers need not even feel nervous, let alone show it. 'Looking down on' an audience means, in effect, talking down to the audience, using language that the listeners will understand. By doing that, speakers establish their position of authority and give the impression that they are worth listening to. But speakers must guard against overdoing this and appearing contemptuous or supercilious, or underrating their audience. Any one of these faults will switch an audience off.

Many of the points set out earlier are as much tricks of the salesperson's trade as they are essentials of good presentation. The most important ones are eye contact, oratory, and fluency.

Speak easy

In speaking, it is important for every word to be heard and understood. For this reason, speakers should not drop their voices at the end of words and sentences; they should speak distinctly and not slur words; they should pause occasionally when they want to make a special point. Another important aspect of oratory is that public speakers should vary their pitch constantly. A monotonous voice is most uninteresting and difficult to listen to, and so, without developing a sing-song delivery, speakers should vary not only their pitch, but also their volume, in other words, make their voices louder in some places, softer in others, though always loud enough to be heard with ease.

Finish, don't stop

'Tell them what it was you told them.' At the end of a lengthy discourse on an esoteric subject, especially if the speaker has ranged over a wide field, the audience may have lost track of the main argument. It is a speaker's duty to refresh their memories before concluding the talk. The main points must be summarized and a winding-up statement made, so that the audience is left in just the right frame of mind. The speaker will then have communicated to them just what he or she set out to do. In addition, they will at least have been warned that the talk will very soon be finished and that, as far as the speaker is concerned, they can soon go back to sleep!

Time, please, everyone

Usually speakers have set times in which to do their presentations and will know that time well in advance. One purpose of practising the talk is to time it. If the talk is too long, a decision must be made as to how much to cut out; if it is too short, some way must be found to extend it (without padding). Perhaps an extra slide or two, to bring out a point that might have been glossed over, will take the speaker up to the time limit.

No speakers should ever overrun their time; they would be in danger of being cut short by the chairperson, often at the crucial point in the argument.

To stop short is as bad as overrunning, because it leaves a gap in the proceedings that may not be easy to fill. The usual remedy adopted by chairpersons is to call upon the next speaker, with the result that people who time their arrival to listen to the later speaker could find themselves missing part of that talk.

Correct timing during rehearsals is essential. Speakers should not be so unrehearsed that they keep looking at their watches or a clock in the hall. Some lecterns have built-in, run-down clocks; if a speaker can surreptitiously set it and start it, it may be useful, but no clock is a substitute for properly rehearsed timing.

Many excuses may be offered for lost time: the wrong slide came up, the place in notes was lost, two pages were turned over by mistake, a page was dropped on the floor. Every one is inexcusable. With proper practice, none of these need happen. Any speaker who practises all the points outlined in these pages will be able to deliver a presentation without a single mishap.

Of course, no speaker can guard against events that are completely beyond his or her control, such as a breakdown of the projector, but any reasonable audience would excuse that. What any reasonable audience will certainly not excuse, is a speaker overrunning or underrunning because of lack of practice.

... worth a thousand words

Visual aids must not distract the audience in any way from listening to what the speaker has to tell them. The speaker must have sufficient visual aids: 'sufficient' meaning the right number of the right kind at the right time. *Illustrations must be complementary to the talk,* underlining what the speaker is saying or saving him or her a lot of words in illustrating a point. The speaker must prepare illustrations with that in mind.

When an illustration contains words that the audience must read, the speaker should on no account be saying something else while the audience is meant to be reading. The words on the slide should not be read out loud. When an illustration appears on the screen, the speaker should direct the audience's attention to it. When it is no longer required, it must be removed from sight, either by switching off the projector or, better, by inserting blank (opaque) slides whenever the screen is required to be dark.

Slides or overhead projector transparencies?

Both have a proper place in presentations, and they should not be confused. By the same token, they should not be mixed. If a talk calls for slides, only slides must be used; conversely, if it calls for the use of an overhead projector, only an overhead projector should be used.

Although overhead projector transparencies are much more versatile than slides, their use should be restricted to informal meetings – like seminars – where the speaker wants to develop a personal relationship with the audience. Overhead projector transparencies are totally out of place at more formal meetings such as symposia and conferences. Usually the formality built into such a meeting ensures that the speaker has no chance of becoming one with the audience, and he or she should not try to have it any other way.

Therefore, use overhead projector transparencies for the personal, instructive type of talk, and slides for the impersonal, often 'disembodied' lecture where the speaker should be heard and not noticed.

The preparation of slides

The most common mistake made when preparing slides is overloading them with information. What is acceptable as an illustration in a printed paper may not be acceptable on a screen. When it is remembered that illustrations must complement the talk and not distract from it, it can readily be seen that one should aim at having the minimum of information on a slide, and at presenting that information in the most accessible way.

No slide should try to illustrate more than one point. The prospective speaker who wants to make a slide out of a table of results is defeating the whole object. If a table is considered the best way of presenting data, it must be condensed as much as possible. It must certainly be condensed to present only one idea, and any other ideas to be illustrated from the same data must be made into other slides. The maximum number of words a slide should contain is 20; there should be no more than eight lines, and no line should contain more than 20 characters. A table should contain no more than 30 figures. This is the maximum number of figures; slides containing less will be better.

When the drawings for slides are being made, remember that there are restrictions with regard to the size of characters and the thickness of lines. Letters, which should be plain and unfussy, should be not less than 0,6 mm in height on the slide itself (that is 6 mm on an A4 drawing). A simple test for a finished slide is this: if the slide, when held at arm's length, can be read easily, the lettering will be large enough. Lines should be on the thick side, rather than too thin. A good criterion is that the thickness should be at least 0,8 mm on an A4 drawing. The same applies to lettering.

Another point about lettering is that it should be kept as near to horizontal as possible. For this reason, the legend of the vertical axis of a graph must not run parallel to the axis.

All slides should be prepared so that the larger dimension of the image area is horizontal. Many projectors and screens are set up so that the image fills the screen from top to bottom; a slide in which the larger dimension is vertical will lose about a third of its image. A second reason for this format is a psychological one: the eye takes more kindly to the horizontal format (wider than it is high), since reading across is easier and more useful than reading down.

Diagrams must be kept as simple as possible, with the minimum of detail; only the salient features should be shown. Photographing a diagram that has appeared in a paper is not the way to reproduce it as a slide. More often than not it needs to be redrawn and even redesigned.

Lettering should be kept to a minimum. For example, a flow chart in a paper can consist of connected blocks each containing a legend; for a slide, a pictorial representation of each block would be preferable. With colour photography, different colours can be used to distinguish different parts of a drawing or to highlight certain items. When only monochrome photography is available, the lines should be bold; different screens, which are available in press-down form, can be applied, but they must be used wisely and sparingly.

Once the slides have been prepared, they should be mounted in plastic or metal slide mountings – not in cardboard – and preferably between glass. Metal slide mountings and some modern plastic ones have glass; the older plastic type and cardboard ones do not.

Although it adds to the costs, glass serves two purposes. In the first place, glass protects the slides and keeps them clean. In the second place, some projectors with automatic focusing rely on the reflection of a light beam from the glass surface.

The preparation of overhead projector transparencies

It must be repeated that overhead projectors are completely out of place at formal conferences and symposia. This cannot be stressed too much. Their use should be confined to informal meetings, such as seminars and classroom or lecture hall presentations.

Transparencies can be prepared beforehand or during the lecture. Used in the latter way, they become the modern equivalent of the old blackboard, with the main advantage that the speaker's back is not turned on the audience. When creating transparencies during a lecture, the speaker must remember to draw and print boldly. This should be practised beforehand.

Of course, it may be asked, if one can practise beforehand, why can one not prepare the transparencies beforehand? This can be done quite simply and quickly by freehand drawing and lettering with special coloured pens. On the other hand, transparencies can be produced from professional drawings and even from photographs, and they can be built up into a story-telling sequence, so that the speaker, having exposed one, can easily flip another on top of it to show additional information, and yet another, and another.

For a normal projector, the image area of the transparency should not be bigger than 205 mm x 205 mm. Speakers should ascertain whether the projector they will use is larger or smaller than the normal size before designing their transparencies. For any transparency, however, the lettering should not be less than 6 mm high, and no line should be less than 0,8 mm thick.

Once the transparencies have been prepared, their edges should be bound with tape. (Paper masking tape can be used.) This makes them easier to handle, especially when picking them up from a pile. Those that are to be used as overlays should be taped together in such a way that the first one can be shown on its own and then, one by one, flipped over, so that they stay in focus. Even if the meeting is informal, the speaker must practise beforehand till the positioning of the transparencies on the projector is automatically correct. Too many speakers spend too much time looking at the screen and adjusting the position of every transparency.

If a drawing has to be shown more than once, a duplicate transparency must be provided. Nothing is worse for an audience than the sight of a speaker fumbling among a scattered pile of transparencies for the one wanted. The speaker should know beforehand that a duplicate is needed and there is no excuse for not having one. Of course, the situation is quite different during question time; nobody could know beforehand whether or not there would be a need to refer to one of the drawings. Every transparency should be numbered clearly on the binding tape, and a speaker should know the number of every one. If they are kept in a neat pile next to the projector, any one should be fairly quickly found.

The technique of using an overhead projector is simple. Firstly, it should be switched on when it is to be used and switched off only when all the transparencies have been shown. If there is an interval between two batches of transparencies, the lamp should be left on but the last transparency of the first batch must be removed from the projector. Secondly, the speaker must take care not to obscure the image; often the speaker's shoulder, unbeknown to him or her, comes between the projector and the screen. Once again, a speaker must practise so that he or she knows exactly where to stand in relation to the projector.

Checklist for successful presentations

Beforehand ...

- plan your presentation when your paper is written;
- decide what to say;
- decide what to illustrate and how;
- rehearse till you are word perfect;
- rehearse and amend till the timing is right;
- be sure your presentation will be explicit;
- find out about the type of audience;
- find out well beforehand when you will be speaking;
- familiarize yourself with the hall;
- familiarize yourself with the projection system;
- be sure you have sufficient visual aids;
- do not be nervous;
- remember, you are in command.

During the introduction ...

- address the chairperson and the audience;
- tell them what your talk will be about;
- be audible from the beginning;
- start off with a dynamic (shock) statement;
- don't handle the microphone;
- appear at ease (neither nervous nor overawed);
- talk, do not read;
- talk, don't recite;
- remember, you have an audience of people out there.

During the presentation ...

- be audible throughout, even to the farthest corner;
- talk, don't read and recite;
- look at every member of the audience; maintain eye contact;
- speak deliberately and enunciate well;
- speak 'down' to the audience;
- pause to give effect to important points;
- do not speak in a monotonous voice.

At the end ...

- keep your voice up, right to the end;
- finish right on time;
- keep the audience's interest right to the end;
- tell the audience what that was all about.
- indicate that you have finished by saying 'Thank you;
- feel satisfied and sorry that it is all over.

Case study Planning your presentation with the latest technology

Many speakers today give their presentation using computer technologies. Quite often this will mean constructing a presentation in a software programme such as Microsoft PowerPoint on a laptop computer, plugging the laptop into a data projector, and throwing the image onto a screen in much the same way as if one was using an older techno-logy such as an overhead projector. However, with all technologies attention to detail is very important.

PowerPoint presentations are so common these days that they have become somewhat mundane. This is because the programme offers a number of basic templates which allow one to decide on the way the screen is laid out, the positioning of text, background, anima-tions, and so on. Because most presentations are put together in a hurry against the inevitable deadline, there is a tendency to use the 'old faithful' approach and use the first template that pops up. Invest some time into the various options and customizations that the programme offers to give your presenta-tion a 'different look'.

Lighter text on darker backgrounds works better on data projectors than vice versa. However, if you are using PowerPoint to make overhead projector cells, the reverse is true.

Most computers (desktop and laptop) have a 'function key' that allows one to choose whether the image appears on the computer screen, or only on the large screen via the pro-jector, or on both. Check out your machine and set it up so that you have the image on your computer screen as well, which may be helpful when you do the presentation if space is cramped or you are in a position where you cannot see the entire image on the large screen. Also, there may be a time during the presentation when you want to find another image, screen, or application on your comput-er and do not necessarily want your audience to see you searching through the contents of your machine.

Work out the keyboard controls for mov-ing between images – sometimes using the mouse is awkward since it requires two actions, a 'point' and a 'click'. A keyboard con-trol requires just one tap.

Putting the presentation together and rehearsing it by running it through on your machine is only half the job. It is essential to check out the venue. Of course in sophisticated settings such as conference venues, most of the things that follow will be in place, but never take it for granted that they are.

First, check for the obvious things. Which is the right input into the data projector? There are usually two 'computer' inputs and two 'video' inputs.

Is there an electrical power supply socket close enough to enable you to plug in your data projector? Will you need an extension cord? If possible, you should run your laptop computer on mains since laptop batteries are famous for 'expiring' at the critical moment. If you are going to plug both into mains, you might need a double adapter to do so.

Does the facility have a proper screen for data projection? Ideally, a highly reflective screen, especially designed for data projection, should be employed, but 'ordinary' overhead projector screens and 'white boards' can be used. Even a section of wall can be used, as long as the section is not encumbered by light switches or pictures. If a section of wall is used, it should be white. Any other colour or shade will create a 'cast' and affect the rendition of the graphics and images in your presentation.

Try to run your presentation at the venue beforehand if this is possible. Check for lighting control. Data projectors do not work well in highly lit rooms and require dimming of house lights. Sunlight streaming into an office or boardroom will inevitably impact negatively on the quality of the presentation.

Check the position of the data projector vis-à-vis the projection image area. Although it is fitted with a zoom control there is an optimum functional distance. For example, if you are too close to the screen area, you may be confined to a very small image that lacks impact. On the other hand, too far back and the image strength and definition deteriorates. Check to see the focus setting you require for a particular zoom range. Too close to the screen and you will not be able to focus at all!

If you are a self-confessed technophobe and are used to leaving things technical to others, this does not usurp your responsibility to ensure that your system works the way you want it to. Liaise with the technical person who will set up the equipment for your presentation. Give him or her the detail on your computer and ascertain that cables and standards are common. For example, a simple thing such as the kind of power plug socket used varies from country to country, and it is sometimes best to buy a 'converter' similar to the kind used for electric shavers when travelling overseas.

Finally, avoid the temptation to think that one can substitute technological wizardry for good communication. Technology, however complex and advanced, remains simply an aid to communication and cannot replace its essential qualities of relevant content and human interaction. Make sure your presentation allows for time for people to interact with you, with the lights up, in a normal, face-to-face situation.

Further reading

Contact ITC (International Training in Communication) and Toastmasters for recommended reading.

Grossfeld, R. 1993. *A User-friendly Guide to Good English*. Cape Town: Juta.

Chapter 18

Business correspondence

When you have read this chapter, you should:

- be familiar with the hierarchy of communication levels;
- be aware of how to plan your correspondence;
- understand the importance of style in business correspondence;
- be able to set out a letter and memorandum correctly.

The letter is the most common form of written communication in business affairs. As with many other forms of communication, letter writing is a skill which must be practised actively, not a theory which can be read passively.

In Himstreet and Baty's *Hierarchy for Effective Communication Situations,* the letter falls into the third, or least effective, communication level.

Hierarchy of communication levels

Level One: The most effective communication occurs in a two-way, face-to-face situation where both verbal and non-verbal symbols and languages are apparent to both parties. Any inaccuracies can be resolved simply by observing the instructions accompanying messages or by questioning the other party. This ability of the receiver to react to the entire communication and to adjust his behaviour to it is called feedback.

Level Two: The second most effective communication occurs in the two-way but not face-to-face situation. Even though feedback is possible, as in a telephone call, non-verbal symbols are not apparent.

Level Three: The least effective

communication is the one-way communication, such as a letter, or a radio programme. At this level, neither immediate feedback nor the clear identification of accompanying non-verbal cues is possible (Himstreet and Baty 1963: 12).

Human relations in business communication

The absence of non-verbal cues and the lack of immediate feedback make the letter a 'cold' form of communication. In addition, it is going to be read by one or more people: people with likes, wants, opinions, sensitivities, and prejudices. So if you want your letter to meet its objectives, you have to consider the receiver very carefully.

The best way to do this is to imagine that you are in fact the receiver, for example, an irate customer who has complained about your business. People's egos are bound up with themselves, what they feel, want, and think. It is only after you have actively considered the other person that you can approach communication with the 'you' attitude.

Planning your correspondence

The rules concerning organization of information and composition apply as much to business correspondence as they do to other forms of communication. Therefore, drawing up a plan of what you are going to say, before you actually say it, is essential.

Audience analysis

The first item to establish is exactly who your reader will be. How much common background do you share? What are his or her wants and needs? Can you evaluate his or her level of education? Is his or her status above, below, or equal to yours? Once you have analyzed your audience, you may proceed to analyze the situation.

Situation analysis

Generally, letters can be divided into three broad categories:
- letters that inform and give positive information;
- letters that persuade;
- letters that give negative information.

Questions need to be answered in each of these categories:
- If you are conveying positive information: You should ask what information readers want and whether they will be pleased with what they are about to be told.
- If your purpose is to persuade: Will you have to overcome resistance because of the reader's probable unwillingness?
- If you are conveying negative information: Are you going to disappoint the reader? Are you going to refuse what has been asked for? Are you going to cause anger?

Only after you have established your objective in some detail should you think about how to achieve it.

Selecting a sequence of ideas

Numerous textbooks make a fetish of what they term 'persuasion plans'. First they determine the category into which a letter falls – sales, credit, adjustment, collection, gaining or retaining goodwill – and then they apply a highly refined formula, depending on the category. Greatly simplified, the plan can be outlined as follows:
- When you are giving good news or neutral information, give the important news first.

- When your information is going to be disappointing, give the justification before the actual news.
- When you want your persuasion to lead to action, put your reader's benefits first, followed by your own (the writer's) benefits, and conclude with the reader's benefits once again.

In all instances, the message should be designed from the reader's viewpoint, which is the antithesis of writer-centredness.

The problem with formulae like these is that they tend to categorize both writer and reader, and negate some of the value of analysing your reader.

In any plan it is important to come to the main point as soon as possible, certainly in the first paragraph. Business people, we are told, spend four hours a day in the office and a further hour at home reading correspondence, reports, journals, and magazines. It is thus unlikely that they will have patience with a letter which is filled with generalities and niceties, polite as these may be.

Style in business correspondence

Effective letter style is interesting, inconspicuous, and clear to read. You are interested in making your reader aware of what you have said, not how you have said it.

Choice of words

In conversation, you can adjust your choice of words so that they invite agreement or readily please the listener. You can explain in more detail when a frown appears on the receiver's face. You can make criticism more acceptable with a smile or an encouraging nod. Without these softening influences, written words can appear harsh, or tactless, and they are as permanent as your reader chooses them to be.

Of course, by choosing your words skilfully you can elect to appear curt, blunt, buoyant, convincing, or humble. Just make sure that the effect produced is the one you choose to produce and that it is closely tied to your objective.

Short, simple words – 'improve' instead of 'ameliorate', 'aware' instead of 'cognizant' – are more likely to be understood and will attract less attention to your style.

When you wish to stress favourable information, you should use concrete, accurate words, while less favourable information is more tactfully conveyed through general, abstract words.

Finally, try to choose the most economic alternative wherever possible: 'when' rather than 'during which time', 'during' rather than 'during the course of the'.

Emphasis

Through skilful arrangement of your material you can emphasize different parts of the content, or a specific idea. Emphasis in written communication can be achieved by:
- careful ordering of the main parts;
- repeating the main idea in the concluding paragraph;
- sentence structure which is simple and makes the idea clear.

Clarity

Once you have established who your reader is, it is important for you to use language that is appropriate to the situation and words that the reader will understand.

Sentences which are reasonably short and direct make it easier to assimilate information. Where relevant, itemization and tabulation add to the clarity of a letter.

Avoiding clichés

'With reference to your letter of the 6th inst.', 'We hope you will look into this at your earliest convenience', 'We are confident that ...', are all worn-out phrases. Since you have taken the trouble to write a letter rather than send a pro forma or circular, you should try to be original.

Conciseness

Neither you nor your reader can afford the time to write or read a rambling letter, so you should write as concisely as possible. Remember though that something which is too concise may be ambiguous to your reader, so the letter should be concise but complete.

Voice

The active voice is preferred because it introduces personal pronouns such as 'I', 'we', 'he', and 'they', which make your letter personal. It is also more positive. Consider: 'Various attempts have been made to attract him to our organization', and 'We have made various attempts to attract him to our organization'.

Tone

Tone can be a rather difficult concept to define. These are some views on the subject by various authors of textbooks on business communication.

Tone refers to the writer's attitude as perceived by the reader of the document. It can be viewed as either positive or negative, and if the message is to have maximum impact, tone should be positive (Vardaman and Vardaman 1973: 389).

Although we frequently refer to it, tone is an indefinable quality in business writing. Often an individual will say after reading a letter, 'The tone of Acme's letter was very friendly', or 'tactful', or 'impersonal'.

Interpretation of tone seems to depend on our reactions to the words used, the phrasing of the sentences, the order of the ideas. This interpretation and evaluation of the tone as 'friendly', 'formal', 'courteous', 'high-pressured', then becomes the characteristic we tend to apply to the company as a whole (Sigband 1982: 319-20).

Tone is important in letter writing. You cannot convey feelings, inflection, or smile, or make a gesture; you rely on the written word. The tone of your writing conveys your personality and that of your company. So if you sound pompous or discourteous or abrupt, that is how your company will be judged by your reader. It is impossible to discuss all the shades of tone in communication, positive or negative, helpful or indifferent, courteous or impertinent. It is important that you consider the reader's point of view (Shurter 1971: 79).

A good tone is achieved when there is an acceptable balance of personalities (writer versus reader), and a letter is courteous and sincere.

To recognize poor tone, you may find the following points useful:
- An acceptable balance of personalities is upset by undue humility, flattery, condescension, preaching, bragging.
- Courtesy is diminished by anger, accusations, unflattering implications, sarcasm, curtness, stereotyped language, poor presentation.
- Sincerity is harmed by effusiveness, exaggeration, undue familiarity.

Layout and format

Attractive layout of a letter makes your message more appealing, draws attention to the important parts of the message, and presents your meaning clearly.

Salutation and ending

The tone and degree of formality in your salutation and ending should be consistent. It is more appropriate to end with 'Yours faithfully', after a 'Dear Sir' opening than with 'Yours sincerely'. Likewise, a letter in which you mention the receiver's name, 'Dear Mr Brown' or 'Dear Bill', looks incongruous with the ending 'Yours faithfully'.

Note that a closing sentence, 'Hoping to hear from you', is not in fact a sentence, since it does not have a verb. Forms like this are the residue of an earlier (now archaic) format in which writers humbled themselves before readers:

> Hoping to hear from you at your earliest-convenience,
> I remain (*here is the verb*)
> Your obedient servant,
> Z. Smythe

Finally, a signature does in some measure commit the company legally. Therefore the rank of the person signing the letter should be stated.

Reference line

The reference line is the most useful pointer in a letter, since it tells the reader immediately what the letter is about and saves him or her from reading right through the letter if, in fact, it should have been addressed to someone else. It also helps filing clerks classify letters, and enables efficient secretaries to present their bosses with supporting documents relevant to the incoming letter.

Usually, the reference line is placed after the salutation and before the opening paragraph. The word 'Re' is no longer popular.

The reference line is of little use, however, if it merely conveys information without telling the reader more about that information. Compare:
Faulty forklift
    with
Forklift which has failed while under guarantee.

The memorandum

Strictly defined, a memorandum is a brief, handwritten reminder, the verbal counterpart of which is a telephone message. However, the memorandum format has become so popular that it is widely used to convey results of investigations and generally to provide information.

You might consider memoranda as letters that stay within the company. However, because of their print format, the need for addresses, salutations, complimentary endings, and irrelevant chit-chat is obviated. Generally speaking, a handwritten memorandum needs no signature, but a typewritten one benefits from some form of authentication such as the author's intitials.

In a memorandum you normally do not need to attract your reader's interest nor, if the memorandum reports an ongoing project, will you need to fill the reader in on details already known. Therefore, you should state your subject and purpose immediately. Do remember, however, that memoranda go from one person to another. Avoid being too cold and formal – use 'I' and 'you' frequently, particularly 'you'.

Case study The Curriculum Vitae

The important first step in a business career

First impressions are critical and in the recruitment process, the curriculum vitae or CV is a vital introduction of yourself to a potential employer. If it is not professional and suitably detailed, then you may not even be considered for an interview.

Here are some of the key elements you need to consider when drawing up your CV:

- Ensure that your CV is easy to read without the clutter of irrelevant information
- Always provide your prospective employer with an original copy of your CV, not a copy of a copy
- Never make corrections by hand on a CV, change the softcopy and reprint it
- The presentation of your CV is important. Make sure that it is neat and that pages are not torn or stained and that they are in the correct order
- It is unnecessary to include a cover page with the words "Curriculum Vitae followed by your name"
- It is important to make copies of your reference letters and certificates. Do not attach copies of your certifications to your CV as copies can be provided to the interviewer during the interview if requested
- Always check for spelling mistakes
- Always update your information on your CV with your most recent information
- Never exaggerate or lie on your CV.

If you have little work experience, include temporary jobs and non-paying/volunteer work. Omit this information when you have gained sufficient and relevant work experience.

Provide a detailed description of all your work experience particularly your current job. You will be judged on the relevant experience you have for the job that you are applying for.

Contents of the CV

With changes in legislation, it has become unnecessary to include certain information on your CV, especially if the information can be seen as discriminatory. The key information you need to provide includes the following:

- Name and surname
- Contact numbers
- Email address
- Home address/current location
- Nationality/ethnicity
- ID number
- Drivers licence and access to a vehicle
- Salary expectation
- Availability
- Spoken languages
- Your Secondary education
    - High school attended
    - Highest grades passed
    - Year completed
    - Subjects (Levels and Symbols can be included)
    - Leadership roles
    - Extramural activities

- Your Tertiary education
    - Institutions attended
    - Qualifications
    - Major subjects
    - Year completed

- Your employment details
    - Company name
    - Date employed: From – to
    - Job title
    - Duties
    - Reason for leaving

- Your References
    - Company name
    - Referee
    - Job title
    - Contact details.

The covering letter

The covering letter should be concise and to the point with details of the position for which you are applying. Should you be applying for a position via email it is very important to clearly state in the body of the email the position and reference number of the position for which you are applying. Remember to include a brief outline of the reasons you feel would make you a successful candidate.

Example of a Covering letter

Either

> *Name of person*
> *Company name*
> *Company address*
>
> Dear Sir/Madam
>
> I have recently completed my BSc Computer Science degree at the University of XXX where I gained valuable experience as a Software Developer
>
> I am currently looking for a permanent or contract position as a Java Software Developer and am able to start work immediately. My strengths include the ability to pay close attention to detail, a drive and passion for

the IT industry, and some background experience which I have already picked up by working as a volunteer in a local computer operation.

> Attached please find a copy of my CV. I can be contacted at 0825725308 or by email at jcsassociates @gmail.com. I look forward to hearing from you.
>
> Yours faithfully
> Your name

> **Or**

> Attached please find a copy of my CV for consideration for the post of Junior Software Developer, reference number JLPE 0000, as advertised on Career Junction
>
> I have recently completed my BSc Computer Science degree at the University of XXX where I gained valuable experience as a Software Developer.
>
> I look forward to your response
>
> Yours faithfully
>
> *Chris Skinner*
> *Telephone: 27319043045*
> *Cell: 0825725308*
> *Email: chris.skinner@telkomsa.net*

Email etiquette

Finally, here are some tips on e-mail etiquette.

1. Design and layout

   Incorporate your letterhead into the body of your e-mail, or at the very least use your company's logo. Use the same standard font (Times New Roman or Arial 10 point) for all e-mails. Above all, be consistent so that when an e-mail is received

   from you, it is automatically recognized as coming from your company.

2. Release your attachments

   Try to put the entirety of your messages and/or images in the body of your e-mail and avoid sending attachments. If you have to attach, ensure your attachments are scanned for viruses and as small as possible (under 1MB). If you need to send anything larger, check with the person beforehand that this is okay.

3. Salutations

If the person is not known personally to you address him/her as Mr/Ms and sign off with "Yours sincerely" or less formally, with "Regards". If the person is a friend or colleague, then the appropriate greeting "Dear Bob" and "Kind regards" can be used.

4. Slang

You should avoid using slang at all costs. You should write using good English.

5. Check spelling and grammar

With built in spelling, grammar, and punctuation checks on your computer, there are no excuses for mistakes.

6. Subject line

Always remember to include a subject line in your correspondence. It helps for reference purposes.

7. Capitals

Do not use capitals in the body of your email except where punctuation requires them.

8. Carbon copy

Only CC people who are directly involved in the subject of the e-mail. Ensure if you press "Reply to all" that the subject is really valid for all recipients.

9. Disclaimers

Your mail-sweeper should automatically scan your e-mails for viruses and add a virus-scan disclaimer, as well as a standard confidentiality disclaimer. Add it to you e-mail signature.

10. Use Auto-Reply

If you are going to be out of office for an extended period, use the "Auto-Reply" function. This will state the time frame you will be away and who to contact in case of emergencies.

Technology is supposed to make our lives easier and quicker, but courtesy must still be maintained!

Source: With acknowledgement to Personal and Finance: Johannesburg.

Public relations aspect

All business correspondence reflects the overall public relations image of the sender. Before you send out or evaluate an incoming letter you should check on the following:

- *Justification.* Why exactly are you sending or receiving this message?
- *Goodwill.* Are there elements in the message which will give the company a value beyond what it sells or offers?
- *Relevance.* Does the letter satisfy the needs of both the sender and the receiver (or the companies of the sender and the receiver)?
- *Accuracy.* Is the information correct?
- *Clarity.* Is the message unambiguous?
- *Presentation.* Does it reflect a good corporate image of the company?

Further reading

Adey, A.D. & M.G. Andrew. 1990. *Getting it Right: The Manager's Guide to Business Communications.* Cape Town: Juta.

Cleary, S. (ed.) 1999. *The Communication Hand- book.* Cape Town: Juta.

Fielding, M. 1997. *Effective Communication in Organizations.* Kenwyn: Juta.

Heubsh, J.D. 1995. *Communication Skills.* Pretoria: Kagiso.

Himstreet, W.G. & W.M. Baty. 1963. *Business Communications: Principles and Methods.* Belmont, California: Wadsworth.

Puth, G. 1994. *The Communicating Manager.* Pretoria: Van Schaik.

Shurter, R.L. 1971. *Written Communication in Business.* 3rd edition. New York: McGraw-Hill.

Sigband, N.B. 1982. *Communication for Management.* Glenview, Illinois: Scott Foresman.

Vardaman, E.T. & P.B. Vardaman. 1973. *Communication in Modern Organizations.* 3rd edition. New York: Wiley.

Chapter 19

Direct-mail marketing

When you have read this chapter, you should:

- be familiar with the basic guidelines for direct-mail marketing;
- be aware of the key elements and their importance in the direct-mail marketing process;
- understand some of the ways in which direct-mail marketing can be put to work.

Although this medium falls into the third, or least effective, communication category (see Chapter 18, page 177), the direct-mail method of marketing has grown into a multi-billion-rand-per-year industry in South Africa.

The recent surge in demand for direct-mail advertising has come about because it allows the marketer to measure the success of advertising. Direct mailing is also said to be a good back-up for radio, television, or print advertisements, creating a total campaign. It allows the marketer to conduct personal research.

The basic guidelines for those who wish to embark on direct-mail marketing are now discussed.

The right objective

Advertising which is done for a general reason only ('We must do some advertising – everyone does!') is likely to fail ... if only because, without any specific objective, there is no yardstick with which to measure its success.

Never advertise for the sake of advertising. In direct mailing you must be sure of your objective. Exactly what response do you want to elicit from the recipient of your mail?

- Do you want something bought by having an order card returned? (Mail order.)
- Do you want him or her to rush into your store? (Traffic builder.)
- Do you want a card returned requesting a salesman's visit? (Qualified sales lead.)
- Do you want to receive important, useful, or confidential information? (Market research.)
- Do you want a donation made? (Fund-raising.)

When your objective is clear, every element in your direct-mail package should be designed to lead the recipient towards the action you want taken.

The right mailing package

Most successful mailings contain at least these four elements:

- *Outer envelope.* It is often beneficial to print something on the envelope that will increase the chances of getting your reader sufficiently involved for him or her to open it and read the contents.
- *Letter.* This contains the offer, the selling copy. It tells the recipient why you have written, what you are offering, what the benefits are, and what action to take to get the benefits of the product or service advertised.
- *Illustrated enclosure.* This is the visual reinforcement of your message. It shows the product in detail and expands on the benefits of use and ownership. It illustrates the service and its value to the reader.
- *Reply elements.* This makes it easy for your recipient to take the action you urge. A business reply card is often used for this purpose. Where privacy is important, or for example money must be enclosed, a business reply envelope should be provided.

The right list

The most important ingredient in the success of any campaign is the mailing list. By way of example, a direct-mail campaign for babywear is more likely to succeed if it is directed at mothers. It is essential not to select people whom you suspect to be in your market, but only those you know to be in your market and who are therefore genuine prospects for your product or service.

To achieve this, you must know the current profile of your existing customers, for it is a fair assumption that your new customers will match the existing profile. The demographics you should know about your existing customer profile are:

- age;
- sex;
- marital status;
- language;
- type of dwelling (house or flat);
- where he or she lives (suburb/town/province);
- occupation;
- income group.

Add any psychographic information you can get hold of, for example interests and activities. (A subscriber to *Getaway* magazine is obviously a prime target for camera equipment and offers on travel.) With industrial 'people' (that is, companies) as your target, the same rules apply, except that you need to know things like type of industry, size of company, location, seasonal habits, and volume of purchases.

Once you know who your prospects are, you should try to obtain or rent mailing lists that match your customer profile as closely as possible. The closer the match, the more successful you will be with your mailings.

The right offer

This is the next most important ingredient in your mailing package. What is the benefit the prospect will derive from using or owning your product? What will be gained by taking the action you request? (Better health? ... money saved? ... greater prosperity? ... increased status? ... greater sexual power? etc.)

The right offer is important because it will get you better results. It can often mean the difference between success and failure. It can make a successful promotion dramatically more successful.

The more attractive you make your offer – to the right audience – the better your response will be. Your objective must be to come up with the most attractive offer you can afford.

Not all good offers are expensive. Consider this: in direct-mail advertising, you have both fixed and variable costs. Fixed costs are items like postage, list rental, printing, and production. Variable costs depend on the number of replies you receive (cost of fulfilment, sales calls, etc.). You can often improve your offer without increasing your fixed costs. Your variable costs will depend on how many more replies you get because of the gift offer.

For example, if a R10 free gift increases your replies from 10 to 20, you must give away R200 in gifts. The extra 10 replies cost you R200. Is it worth it? Usually the answer is an overwhelming yes ... but you must do your tests and sums very carefully.

The right copy

One of the biggest dangers in direct mailing is to underestimate the importance of copy. Nearly everyone believes they can write a direct-mail letter. 'After all,' they say, 'I write (business) letters every day of my life.'

And so they might. But these are not sales letters in the context of a direct-mail campaign.

Successful direct-mail copywriters usually serve an apprenticeship of many years before they succeed at writing good sales letters. These are the letters which grab the reader's attention from the very first glance. They involve readers and arouse their interest. They develop that interest into a strong desire for ownership of the product. They melt away recipients' (natural) inborn inertia. They get the desired action.

The ground rules for good copy are:
- always write from your reader's point of view, and in "you" terms ("We are pleased to announce ..." is nowhere near as effective as "You will be pleased to know ...");
- keep your sentences short;
- use as many one-syllable words as you can ("We furnish installation diagrams" is not as easily grasped as "You get full plans");
- use active words ("This car is designed to give good acceleration" is not as good as "This car accelerates ... fast!");

- write as long – or as short – a letter as will do the job. Short letters are not invariably better. In many cases they are worse because they do not do a complete job in the attention-interest-desire-action chain. If the reader is in your target market, and the letter copy is brisk, relevant, and interesting, three or four pages will often work better than single-page letters. Tests have proved this over and over again. "The more you tell, the more you sell," says David Ogilvy, advertising guru. He's right. Try it, and see the difference.

The right graphics

This covers the visual treatment you must give each individual item in your mailing package. How you 'dress' it up – your choice of graphics, of colour, of style – is important. How will it look? How will it feel? What mood will it create?

Empathy and self-identification must be your watchwords. How does your prospect expect your direct-mail correspondence to look? If you are a bank, then a sober, conservative image is probably right. But if you are a discount store, then a bright, breezy, colourful, snappy appearance will be more in keeping with the nature of your business. If you are selling cosmetics, then a "high-class", prestigious appearance will do you more good than a wishy-washy print job on cheap paper.

Your mailing package – every part of it – must look right and feel right to the reader. The right graphics communicate the right feeling; they encourage readership and involvement.

The right test

No one can tell you exactly how successful your direct-mail package is going to be. The only sure way to success is to run tests. Only when you have carefully tested your mailing package can you predict, with reasonable certainty, the probable results when your total mailing list is sent out.

And remember, only the direct-mail medium permits you to test a small percentage of your market. Moreover, you can run tests at a modest cost. You need not spend several thousand rands on space advertising before you can judge whether your promotion will be successful or not. When you use direct-mail marketing you can mail to 10 per cent of a representative cross-section of your mailing list to find out how well your campaign is likely to work.

Unless you have a large budget and a large market, do not test the effect of small differences. Test completely different packages. Remember big differences in the package will yield big differences in response; small differences will yield small and sometimes insignificant differences in response.

The most sensible practice is to test continuously. Let us say you have a package which is successful – call this Package A. Now try to develop another, Package B, which hopefully will surpass Package A. When you find it does, Package B now becomes your control. And now you must develop a new package – or a significant improvement – to try and beat Package B. If it does, then Package C becomes your control. And so on.

The right analysis

The unique benefit of direct-mail advertising is that you can (quite easily) measure its effectiveness. In virtually no other advertising medium can you say that for an expenditure of X rand, you got back Y amount of business.

Be careful to analyze the right things. For example, nearly everyone asks 'What is a normal percentage response?' There is no such thing. Some firms get 0,5 per cent response ... and others get 50 per cent or more. All are

happy and continue to use direct-mail marketing because it is not the percentage response which matters. What matters is only 'How much did you profit from the mailing?'

So do your arithmetic right through to the end. By all means count the percentage replies. But follow through and record how many of those replies were converted into sales, and even more important, what net profit was generated.

Even more important than making a sale is making a customer. One thing you must be aware of is the importance and value of a customer. What is a new customer worth to you? For example, let us say your cost per new customer (achieved by direct-mail advertising) is R25. What is the annual worth of a customer? In gross profit? And how long does the average new customer stay with you?

The right frequency

Most users of direct-mail marketing make one big mistake: they mail to their prospects only once. They reason that if the prospects do not reply, they are not interested. Presumably this means now and in the future.

These users could not be more wrong! You can often squeeze extra profits out of a continuous mailing programme.

Why is this? Well, out of every 100 prospects to whom you mail, let us say three reply 'Yes' to your offer, and three definitely say 'No' (in their minds, that is). That leaves 94 who are uncommitted. Now, out of those 94 there are plenty who almost said 'Yes', but for one reason or another, did not do anything. Perhaps your direct mail was put to one side for further study, and then forgotten about, or perhaps your original package did not contain the right 'trigger' for that particular person. A further mailing, with different treatment, different emphasis, may contain the 'trigger' that will motivate him or her to act.

Direct Marketing Association of South Africa

The Direct Marketing Association of South Africa (DMA) aims to protect both the industry and consumers from unethical or ignorant practitioners and lobby against adverse legislation from government and other regulatory bodies. Key to DMA's activities is the promotion and expansion of direct marketing within the country. While remaining a separate entity, the DMASA is however, globally aligned with links with 46 countries giving it access to global insights, trends, and best practices in the field.

Over and above its role as protector, the DMA also sets out to promote best practice and raise the standard of direct marketing through the origination and regular updating of DM Codes of Practice and best practice guidelines. Further to this, the DMA's Assegai Awards have been developed to benchmark and continuously raise the bar with respect to the creative effectiveness, strategic and ROI aspects of direct campaigns, projects, and business.

Other initiatives include tariff negotiations with primary industry suppliers on behalf of its members, lobbying on Data Privacy issues, database protection, and anti-spam. The DMA is also committed to providing members access to formalised education, networking forums offering the latest information and informed legal opinion.

The DMA has a number of portfolios covering the following activities-:

- equity transformation – ensuring the creation, management, and adherence to a direct marketing BEE Charter (aligned with other marketing charters)
- financial portfolio – ensuring good governance, rigorous budgeting, and management of the DMA
- legislative/ Lobbying / Legal PR portfolio – split into two portfolios, here the association ensures that it is vigorous in the area of lobbying with Government, constructing of best practice submissions around bills and providing informed legal opinion to its members
- member benefit portfolio – this portfolio seeks to build a broad range of relevant benefits on an ongoing basis as well as providing tactical member opportunities that provide exceptional value
- education portfolio –within this portfolio, a selection of short-, medium-, and long-term courses have been developed. In- and out-sourced training is made available and special educational events are arranged
- marketing portfolio – this portfolio focuses on maintaining good communication with markets, ensuring awareness of the DMA and its critical role, and provides relevant and valuable content to a selection of media
- database portfolio – let us 'practice what we preach'. This critical aspect of the DMA provides various 'channel to market'
- allied industry representation portfolio – there are numerous bodies and associations within the full gambit of marketing, representing everything from research to PR, and media to advertising. The DMA encourages collaboration and inter-dependence with other bodies to ensure that the marketing profession in South Africa 'speaks with one voice'.

Bringing benefit to the DM industry
Tel: 0861 362 362 (DMA DMA)
www.dmasa.org

Also, people's circumstances change. Last month when you wrote inviting your prospect to test-drive a new car, he or she did nothing. But since then there may have been a promotion in the company, or a rise in salary, or he or she has become more conscious of the dilapidated appearance of the present car. Result? When your invitation arrives this month there may well be a favourable response, and a new customer obtained.

Finally, know how much a new customer is worth to you. If every new customer gives you a substantial net profit for the year ahead – let's say R2 000 – and each direct-mail package costs R20, it makes sense to send several mailings to your prospect to gain his or her custom.

The right priority

It is a truism of direct mail, as it is of commerce, that optimization of sales must start with existing customers. After all, your existing customers need your product or service. They already have a working relationship with you. They trust you. It makes the best of good sense to concentrate your promotional efforts on your existing customers as reflected by your current accounts. You can only use the direct-mail medium to do this.

For example, a bank should campaign among existing current account holders to promote the full range of bank services; a departmental store should mail to its current charge account customers to promote special sales, other departments, and so on.

Past customers come next on the list of priorities. Direct-mail campaigns should be designed to reactivate them as current customers.

And finally, you must continue to seek new customers. As recommended earlier, once you have identified the profile of your existing customers, you must choose a list of potential customers who share the same basic characteristics. The closer you match this profile, the more successful your mailing will be.

Fifty ways that direct-mail works

The Direct Mail Association of the United States has provided a list of 50 ways that directmail can be put to work. They are:

1. Building morale of employees. A bulletin or house magazine published regularly, carrying announcements of company policy, stimulating ambition, encouraging thrift, promoting safety and efficiency, will make for greater loyalty among employees.
2. Securing data from employees. Letters and questionnaires occasionally directed at employees help cement a common interest in the organization and bring back practical ideas and much useful data.
3. Stimulating sales staff to greater efforts. Interesting sales magazines, bulletins or letters, carrying success stories and sound ideas that have made sales. help in unifying a scattered selling organization, in speeding up sales, and in making better sales staff.

4. Paving the way for sales staff. Forceful and intelligent direct mail, persistent and continuous, will create a field of prospective buyers who are alive and ready to buy.
5. Securing enquiries for sales staff. Direct mail can bring back actual enquiries from interested prospective customers ... qualified prospects your staff can call on and sell to.
6. Teaching sales staff 'how to sell'. A sales manual, or a series of messages, will help educate and stimulate sales staff to close more and bigger sales.
7. Selling to shareholders and others interested in your company. Enclosures with dividend cheques, in pay envelopes, and other direct messages, will encourage shareholders and employees to make greater use of company products and services, and to suggest their use to others.

8. Keeping contact with customers between calls by sales staff. Messages to customers between visits by sales staff will help secure for your firm the maximum amount of business from each customer.

9. Further selling to prospective customers after a demonstration or salesperson's call. Direct mail emphasizing the superiority of your product or service will help clinch sales and make it difficult for competition to gain a foothold.

10. Acknowledging orders or payments. Mailing an interesting letter, folder, or mailing card is a simple gesture that will cement a closer friendship between you and your customers.

11. Welcoming new customers. A letter welcoming new customers can go a long way towards keeping them sold on your company, products, and services.

12. Collecting accounts. A series of diplomatic collection letters will bring and keep accounts up to date, leave the recipients in a friendly frame of mind, and hold them as customers.

13. Securing new dealers. Direct mail offers many concerns unlimited possibilities for lining up and selling to new dealers.

14. Securing direct orders. Many organizations have built extremely profitable business through orders secured only with the help of direct mail. Many concerns not presently selling by direct mail can and should do so.

15. Building up weak territories. Direct mail will provide intensified local sales stimulation wherever you may wish to apply it.

16. Winning back inactive customers. A series of direct-mail messages to 'lost' customers often revives a large number of them.

17. Developing sales in territories not covered by sales staff. Communities which are inaccessible because of distance, bad transportation schedules, or poor roads, offer the alert organization vast possibilities to increase its sales by direct mail.

18. Developing sales among specified groups. With direct mail you can direct your selling messages specifically to those to whom you wish to sell, in the language they will understand, and in a form that will stimulate action.

19. Following up enquiries received from direct advertising or other forms of advertising. A series of messages outlining the 'reasons why' your product or service should be bought, will help you cash in on enquiries whose initial interest was aroused by other media: publications, radio, television, etc.

20. Driving home sales arguments. Several mailings, each planned to stress one or more selling points, will progressively educate your prospective customer on the many reasons why your product or service should be bought ... and from you.

21. Selling other items in line. Mailing pieces, package inserts, or 'hand-out' folders will educate your customers on products and services other than those they are buying.

22. Getting the product prescribed or specified. Professional people, such as physicians and dentists, will prescribe a product for their patients if they are correctly educated on its merits and what it will accomplish. Likewise, consumers and dealers will ask for a product by name if they are thoroughly familiar with it. Direct advertising can be profitably used for this purpose.

23. Selling to a new type of buyer. Perhaps there are new outlets through which your product or service might be sold. Direct mail is a powerful tool in the development of new sales channels.

24. Bringing the buyer to the showroom. Invitations through letter or printed announcements will bring prospective customers to your showroom or factory.

25. Helping the present dealer sell more. Assisting your dealer with direct mail and 'point-of-purchase' help will sell your product or service faster and step up turnover. The right kind of dealer help will win his or her hearty co-operation.

26. Merchandising your plans to the dealer. Direct mail can forcefully present and explain your merchandising plans to the dealer ... and show him or her how to put your promotion ideas and material to work as sales builders.

27. Educating dealers on the superiority of your product or service. Memories are short when it comes to remembering the other fellow's product or service and its superior attributes, especially when you keep telling your dealers the benefits and advantages of your own.

28. Educating retail clerks in the selling of a product. Clerks are the neck of the retail selling bottle. If they believe in a company and a product, their influence is a powerful aid to sales. If indifferent, they lose their sales-making effectiveness. Direct mail that is friendly, understanding, helpful, and stimulating, will enlist their co-operation and up the sales curve.

29. Securing information from dealers or dealers' clerks. Letters, printed messages, a bulletin, or a house magazine will bring back helpful information from the individuals who sell your product or your service ... information you can pass along to other dealers or sales clerks to help them sell more.

30. Referring enquiries from consumer advertising to local dealers. The manufacturer can use direct mail to refer an enquirer to the local dealer for prompt attention. At the same time, the dealer can be alerted with the details of the prospect's enquiry.

31. Increasing consumption of a product among present users. Package inserts, booklets, etc. can be used to educate customers on the full use of the products they buy, especially new benefits and advantages.

32. Bringing customers into a store to buy. This applies to retailers. Personal, friendly, cordial, and interesting direct-mail messages, telling about the merchandise you have, and creating the desire to own that merchandise, will bring back past customers, stimulate present patrons, and lure new people to your store.

33. Opening new charge accounts. This also applies to retailers. There are many people in every community who pay their accounts promptly and do the bulk of their buying where they have accounts. A careful compilation of such a list and a well-planned direct-mail programme inviting them to open charge accounts will bring new customers to your store.

34. Capitalizing on special events. Direct mail helps retailers to capitalize on such events as marriages, births, graduations, promotions, etc. Likewise, letters can be sent to select lists featuring private sales. Other lists and formats can cover general sales.

35. Creating a need or a demand for a product. Direct mail, consistently used, will stimulate the demand for your product or service, and will remind the customer to ask for it by name.

36. Building goodwill. The possibilities of building goodwill and solidifying friendships through direct advertising are unlimited. It is the little handshake through the mail that cements business relationships and holds your customers. Certain 'reminder' forms can also help build goodwill.

37. Capitalizing on other advertising. Direct advertising is the salesmate of all other media. As the 'workhorse' among advertising and promotion mediums, it helps sponsors capitalize on their investment in all visual and audio advertising – especially when initial interest can be given a lift and converted into action and sales.

38. As a 'leader' or 'hook' in other forms of advertising. Publication space, and radio and television commercials are often too limited to tell enough of the story about a product or service to make a sale. Direct mail provides the 'leader' or 'hook' – in the form of booklets, folders, catalogues, instruction manuals – that other mediums of advertising can feature, to stimulate action as well as to satisfy the enquirer with a full story of the product and service.

39. Breaking down resistance to a product or service. Direct mail helps to overcome resistance in the minds of prospective customers.

40. Stimulating interest in forthcoming events. A special 'week' or 'day' devoted to the greater use of a product, an anniversary, a new line launched by a dealer, special 'openings', and scores of other happenings can all be promoted by direct mail to produce sales.

41. Distribution of samples. There are thousands of logical prospects who could be converted into users of your product if you proved its merits to them. Direct mail can help you to do this by letting prospects convince themselves by actually testing your product ... provided it lends itself to sampling by mail.

42. Announcing a new product, new policy, or new addition. There is no quicker way to make announcements to specific individuals or groups, to create interest and stimulate sales, than through the personal, action-producing medium – direct mail.

43. Announcing a new address or change in telephone number. When these important changes are made, a letter or printed announcement sent through the mail has a personal appeal that will register your message better than any other form of advertising.

44. Keeping a concern or product 'in mind'. Direct advertising includes many forms of 'reminder' advertising – blotters, calendars, novelties. Regular mailings help keep you in the minds of customers and prospects.

45. Research for new ideas and suggestions. Direct-advertising research is a powerful force in building sales. Direct mail can be used to find market facts, cut sales fumbling, and chart direct, profitable trails to sales. It furnishes all the important tools for sales research, to discover what, where, how and to whom to sell ... and at what price.

46. Correcting present mailing lists. Householders have an average annual change of 22 per cent, merchants of 23 per cent, agents of 29 per cent, and advertising people of 37 per cent. Keeping a mailing list up to date is most important. Direct mail can be employed to keep your list accurate, by occasionally asking your customer if his or her name and address are correct ... or whether there are others in the organization you should be reaching.

47. Securing names for lists. Direct mail can help you build mailing lists by securing names of customers and prospects from many sources: directly from distributors, sales staff, clerks, shareholders, employees; from people who have access to the names of individuals in specific groups; from recommendations of customers and friends; from special mail surveys, questionnaires, etc.

48. Protecting patents or special processes. Shouting forth the ownership of such patents or processes by direct advertising can leave no question in the mind of your customer – present or prospective – as to who owns the product or process. At the same time it gives you greater protection from possible infringers.

49. Raising funds. Direct advertising affords an effective, economical method of raising funds for worthy causes.

50. Don't forget the telephone. It can produce outstanding response in combination with any of the 49 uses listed above.

Further reading

Jones, S.K. 1991. *Creative Strategy in Direct Marketing*. Lincolnwood, Illinois: NTC Business Books.

Katzenstein, H. & W.S. Sachs. 1992. *Direct Marketing*. 2nd edition. London: Macmillan.

Koekemoer, L. (ed.) 2003. *Marketing Communications*. Cape Town: Juta.

Contact should also be made with the Direct Marketing Association of South Africa (DMASA) whose details are mentioned in this chapter.

Chapter 20

Annual reports and special publications

When you have read this chapter, you should:
- be familiar with the modern purpose of annual financial statements;
- be aware of the key elements of successful annual financial statements;
- be able to formulate a design brief for annual financial statements;
- be aware of the public relations opportunities presented by annual financial statements;
- be familiar with other publications allied to these statements.

Most organizations, whether business concerns or non-profit organizations, are required to make periodic reports of some kind – to shareholders, lenders of money, members, sponsors, subscribers – normally on an annual basis.

Alert managements and public relations practitioners have come to realize the value of these reports as public relations tools – if expanded beyond the barest minimum in terms of information disclosed.

An increasing number of companies, with or without stock exchange listings, as well as welfare bodies, youth movements, and non-governmental organizations, are now using their annual financial statements to inform publics, other than those directly involved, about their affairs. Greater disclosure on a wide range of subjects means that the annual financial statements have become the single most important document produced during the course of a year.

Since these statements are of such obvious public relations importance, it follows that an organization's public relations practitioners should be intimately involved in their planning, preparation, presentation, production, and distribution.

The annual report

The annual report is the most important document that a company publishes every year. Not only is it a statutory document, but it is also a marketing tool pitched at a wide variety of audiences. It is a company's calling card. It is important therefore, to make it informative, relevant, credible, and exciting by incorporating the answers to the following questions: What is our corporate personality? What is our reputation? What are our strengths? (Is the company relevant in its sphere of activities in the marketplace today? What are its growth areas?) What are our weaknesses? What steps have we taken to increase earnings? What external factors have impacted on us? (What local or international influences came to bear on the company's fortunes during the past year?) How have we performed as a business? How have we performed in the community? What were our greatest accomplishments during the year? What problems did we encounter and what steps are we taking to solve them? (Were trading conditions against us? Did retrenchments take place? If so, what is the company going to do to minimize the process during the coming year?)

It is important to remember that it is the financial community that is the main target audience for the annual report. It will be judged therefore, on the relevance of the information provided, its financial integrity and what it reveals of the company's prospects and vision for the future.

The target publics

These can be defined as shareholders, the financial community (bankers, analysts, stockbrokers, investment funds), business media, employees, suppliers, trading partners, distributors and dealers, major customers, government, legislators, and community leaders. Some even consider the general public as a target audience, but this is questionable, except in a general sense through media advertising.

Key elements of a successful report

In addition to the statutory financial information, an effective annual report should contain the following supplementary information:

- corporate profile;
- financial highlights;
- corporate goals;
- group structure;
- profile of directors and management;
- chairperson's report;
- divisions, sectors, and associates;
- financial summary;
- analysis of shareholders;
- value added statement;
- director's report, income statement, balance sheet, source of application;
- notice of annual general meeting;
- shareholders' diary;
- exceptional items.

Corporate profile

This should provide a succinct summary in one or two paragraphs of the business in which the group is engaged. It should distinguish between major and minor activities.

Financial highlights

Data required include:

- from the income statement: turnover, pre-tax income, earnings and dividends per share, and dividend cover;
- from the balance sheet: net assets and net asset value per share;
- in the form of ratios: the debt equity ratio, interest cover, and return on equity.

The ratios are important and should appear in this bird's-eye view of the company. In the case of ratios, it is useful to give the five-year compound growth rate or the average alongside each figure. This will put the current year's figures in perspective.

Corporate goals

Increasingly, the inclusion of corporate goals is becoming standard practice in the United States. Corporate goals are sometimes combined with the corporate profile. The statement generally outlines both the short- and long-term corporate goals and targets at which management is aiming.

Suggested items for inclusion in this section are the long-term growth targets (preferably in real terms), the company's objectives in relation to its industry, and policy regarding financial structure. These can be outlined in general policy terms, but the specific quantitative goals must be given. Then, to avoid a pie-in-the-sky impression, the statement must comment on how and when management expects to achieve the long-term targets. The actual performance against these predetermined goals needs to be disclosed and commented on. This could form part of the chairperson's statement or be in the corporate goals sector.

Charts can be most effective in highlighting key goals and measuring achievements against these.

Group structure

There is nothing better than a schematic representation of the group structure to create understanding of the various components and their interrelationships. This is essential in any group with diverse interests.

It may sometimes be necessary to present divisions instead of companies, particularly where sector reporting is also done along divisional lines. However, where this is done, company interrelationships need to be indicated, especially in the case of listed companies.

Profile of directors and management

Today analysts pay a lot more attention to who the directors of a company are, and to the management and management structure of a business. This is another consequence of the ever-increasing proportions of company capital acquired by institutions.

The report should distinguish between executive and non-executive directors. Photographs are important. The affiliations of non-executive directors need to be spelt out.

For the executive directors, even more detail is needed. How they fit into the overall group structure is very valuable and can be indicated on the chart of company interrelationships – where appropriate.

To assess the stability and depth of management, divisional management structures should be outlined. The title and responsibility, qualifications, age, and period of service of each manager need to be given. Major management changes must, of course, be dealt with in some detail.

Chairperson's report

This should be a brief but highly pertinent overview of the year's achievements, commenting on items of significance to the group as a whole rather than on divisional detail. It must be objective and provide a candid assessment of problems, but should address key issues only.

It should include factors which either impeded or assisted growth in the past year. It should highlight changes in strategy or policy objectives, major management changes, new products (if significant), and research and development activity. It should also mention acquisitions and disposals and how these fit in with group expansion programmes.

In addition, it is necessary to include a definitive statement on the short-term outlook with a clear and unambiguous forecast – even if it has to be fairly heavily qualified.

When a forecast has to be changed, either up or down, this should be done as soon as possible – either in the interim statement or by means of a special announcement. This softens the blow as far as shareholders (and the press) are concerned and enhances management credibility.

Group financing, and the impact of capital expenditure plans on this, should also be dealt with in this report. It is important to provide a longer-term perspective, particularly when current trading is volatile and uncertain.

Review of divisions, sectors and associates

Unlike the chairperson's report, this review examines the operations of individual sectors in some detail and must address the key issues which materially affected the financial results over the past year. Steps taken to counter adverse developments need to be mentioned. A reconciliation of divisional growth and operating results with the group figures shown in the income statement is necessary.

An analysis of assets, sales, pre-tax profits, and especially attributable profits from major divisions (after tax and minority interests) is highly desirable to enable a better assessment of past performance and future prospects of the group. The inclusion of other divisional facts such as the number of employees, factory locations, distribution outlets, market share, industry production, and capacity ratios are all highly appreciated.

The pressures faced by the company and the measures taken to counter these should be detailed. For example, mention should be made of:

- technological change or government regulation;
- in the operational area, whether margins were cut to maintain market share (and whether this proved successful or not)
- what success was achieved with cost-cutting programmes (give concrete figures);
- what rationalizations were effected (factory closures, joint-projection strategies);
- individual divisions' operating details such as market share, geographic representation, competitive conditions, export sales and profits, capacity utilization, capital expenditure planned, what this will add to capacity, new products or ventures and when these are likely to become profitable, etc.

Photographs of the products of each division are very effective in putting the nature of business across.

Financial summary

A financial history with figures for at least six years is required. (Figures for six years are required to calculate five-year trends.) A ten-year trend is even more useful, as it allows analysts to examine the trends and evaluate performance through up and down economic cycles. Effective graphs are essential for the rapid assimilation of key trends.

The purpose of the review is to offer a quick appreciation of recent financial and operating results.

The financial summary is the ideal place to provide ratios which are far more important in terms of their trend than they are in isolation. Items in financial trends should include the following:

Income items:
- turnover;
- pre-interest profit;
- pre-tax profit;
- earnings per share (percentage change and compound growth);
- dividend per share (percentage change and compound growth);
- dividend cover.

Balance sheet:
- total assets;
- shareholders' net assets;
- net asset value per share (percentage change and compound growth);
- number of shares in issue.

Ratios:
- return on shareholders' funds;
- interest-bearing debt to shareholders' funds;
- interest and preference dividend cover;
- pre-interest margin.

Other:
- number of employees.

Analysis of shareholders

The split between the size of holding and the type of shareholder assists in determining the nature of the following a company enjoys and, presumably therefore, in giving some idea of the float of shares available. What is generally omitted from these analyses, however, is perhaps the most pertinent point of all – the annual volume of shares traded. This puts the other data in perspective.

Value added statement

Despite its name, this is generally of little or no value to analysts, but is no doubt useful from the point of view of employee or trade union relations. By taking all costs except interest paid, depreciation, and employees' salaries off group sales to establish value added, you can be sure that employee benefits will appear as a large portion of the value added.

Director's report, income statement, balance sheet, source of application

These aspects are, in general, covered by legislation and the statement of Generally Accepted Accounting Practice (GAAP). Given the extraordinarily long lead time in producing GAAP statements, it is obvious that company managements should try to provide information ahead of the issue of local GAAP statements.

Notice of annual general meeting

This is a statutory requirement and, given the almost total lack of interest of shareholders in this annual event, it should appropriately be tucked away at the back of the report rather than use valuable space at the front.

Shareholders' diary

Another small but very necessary reference point for the user of financial statements is the shareholders' diary.

Exceptional items

In certain industries there are items requiring special emphasis which would not be the case in other industries. Where this is applicable, the key factors should be identified and reported on.

Design requirements

For the design and production of annual reports, the following points are worth considering:

- *Visual appeal.* Attractive cover, design, graphics, artwork and typography.
- *Good, readable text.* Clear, concise, understandable language.
- *Length.* It should be long enough to interpret the year's developments and to touch on subjects central to the long-term success of the operations (market share, environmental projects, competition, employees, etc.).
- *Credibility.* All statements must be credible and justifiable.
- *Realism.* It is important to avoid too formal a look, except in financial sections.
- *Pictures and graphs.* Use these to interpret key statements.
- *Planning.* Plan, in writing and with critical dates, the entire production programme from conceptualization (three months before the financial year end) right through to the annual general meeting. Dispatch as soon as possible, within three months of the financial year end. A sample production schedule is shown on page 199.
- *Paper.* Use good quality paper to enhance your message.
- *Photographs.* Full colour is the norm. Photographs must tell a story.
- *Illustrations.* Use charts, graphs, maps. Keep them simple.
- *Cost control.* Set a realistic budget. Get quotations from reputable printers and minimize changes to proofs as far as possible.
- *Review.* After publication, review the report critically and seek outside opinions as to the impact of the document. Did it achieve its objectives? How were other reports received? What scope is there for improvement?

Production schedule for annual report

Activity	February	March	April	May	June	July	August
Initial briefing session with agency on design requirements	■						
Agency provides design concepts and mock-up		■					
Approval of design by executive team		■					
Contact individual departments for input			■	■			
Edit material supplied				■			
Provide updated data on organization structure, map, projects, and addresses				■			
Prepare executive director's review				■	■		
Prepare chairperson's review				■	■		
Assist with auditor's review					■		
Submission of drafts to management for approval					■		
Proceed to typesetting			■		■		
Preparation of artwork			■		■		
Selection of photographs				■	■		
Proofing of galleys from printer					■	■	
Checking of final draft/layout						■	
Submission to audit committee for approval					■		
Proceed to final make-up					■		
Checking of chromalins					■	■	
Give final approval for printing						■	
Report produced by printers						■	
First copies delivered						■	
Bulk copies delivered						■	■
Copies sent individually addressed to VIP list							■
Senior staff provided with their own copies							■
Delivery of abridged version of report for staff distribution							■

Public relations opportunities

Apart from the financial figures, which will tell their own story, the annual financial statements have immense public relations potential. The document represents a large investment in communication, and among other things it can raise the value of shares, credit ratings, employee morale, customer and supplier confidence, and give the company a 'personality' and a reputation for integrity. In presenting the company review it is important to identify as far as possible the following positive aspects of the company:

- a good financial record and high integrity;
- past levels or earnings in excess of the market;
- past growth of earnings in excess of the market;
- future profit opportunities – do not hide substantial capital requirements, as these indicate high profit growth;
- consistent dividend policy;
- consistent debt ratios;
- high growth potential of the South African market;
- qualities, experience, and achievements of management;
- price reductions in relation to the inflation rate;
- meeting the need for natural resources;
- expenditure on anti-pollution measures, combating public nuisance, etc.;
- money spent on donations, bursaries, education, and training;
- growth in exports;
- extent of import replacement with locally manufactured goods;
- corporate goals and social consciousness;
- policy on wages and pensions;
- development of employee skills;
- successful, top-notch, alert employees and managers;
- non-financial achievements – new products and processes, safety records, etc.;

- employment record – length of service, few dismissals, growth in earnings;
- highlight quality products and excellent service;
- care about long-standing customer and supplier relationships;
- attitude towards product shortage – fair allocation of limited resources to selected customers;
- express attitude to profit-making by suppliers and in-group trading;
- response to decentralization policy;
- taxes paid on profits, employee earnings, and as sales tax and import duties;
- co-operation with government bodies;
- flexibility and capability to adapt to change;
- geographical spread and coverage.

Certain negative aspects should be treated with circumspection, including:

- the need for high profits and high retained earnings;
- political problems – continued violence, internal unrest;
- lay-offs;
- strike action;
- unprofitable areas.

Special publications

Other publications allied to the annual report include the interim report, preliminary report, and statistical reports.

Interim (or half-year) report

This is stipulated in the Companies Act and indicates how a company is performing after six months' trading. Few companies put much effort into the content or visual appeal of interim reports.

Preliminary (or consolidated) report

This report is usually audited and reflects corporate performance for the financial year. The minimum facts are disclosed pending publication of the annual report.

Statistical reports

Analysts are interested in the text of the annual report, but even more interested in statistics and facts. In the United States, it is relatively commonplace to find companies preparing special statistical reports for analysts. It is not difficult for analysts to extract from a report the ratios and data they require, but if you do it for them it will create a very positive impression.

Employee annual reports

The recent acknowledgement of employees' right to be 'in the know' about the organization for which they work is nowhere more clearly demonstrated than in the increasing popularity of employee annual reports. In most organizations, the employee annual report has evolved from the practice of simply giving employees copies of the annual report to shareholders. Although this is better than no effort at communication, it is nevertheless an excellent example of mismatching medium and audience.

The basis of the employee annual report, like the corporate annual report, is financial. However, the kind of financial information that interests employees and their families differs significantly from that appearing in the shareholders' report. Employees do not merely want financial charts and pages of figures. They want an interpretation of the figures in terms of their probable impact on their jobs. The ideal employee annual report should contain the following:

- a review by the chief executive of the firm's goals, prospects for reaching them, problems, achievements, and failures;
- a summary of the year's major events;

- a discussion of employment in the organization with special reference to job security;
- a discussion of trends, both in the firm and in the industry;
- a projection of operating results;
- a graphic analysis of expenditure with an accompanying narrative explanation. The emphasis should be on expenditure that often confuses employees, such as borrowing money; payments to stockholders and depreciation; the hows and whys of material costs; compensations and benefits; machinery and equipment costs; interest payments; taxes; and retained earnings;
- an analysis of income, which is generally easier for most people to understand than a mere statement of income and an explanation of profits;
- comments on the contributions of various divisions to the total financial picture of the organization;
- an easily understood explanation of financial jargon;
- if possible, a parallel between 'economics' familiar to employees (for example, budgets, wages) and the 'economics' of the firm;
- a tie-in, if possible, with relevant external social, political, and general economic issues;
- employee education and training programmes as expenditure;
- the company community involvement programme;
- photographs of employees in the workplace.

There are many ways to present the information. One way is to build the report around a theme. Another technique is to give a 'diary' of the year's significant events.

One of the most popular approaches to an employee annual report is the photo story. The report is for and about employees, so what better way to illustrate it and tell the year's story than through photographs of employees?

Annual reports naturally lend themselves to comparisons – either a long-range (five- or ten-year) historical analysis or a comparison between this year and previous ones. There are many kinds of information that can be compared: employment rates, company growth, diversification, and benefits.

No matter what material is included or how it is presented, the essential element is candour. This means that top management must be committed to an honest presentation of the facts. An organization that ignores or skirts sensitive issues is asking for trouble. Employees eventually learn about them and it is better for the organization to give the information than for employees to hear about these issues through the grapevine and the mass media.

Because of the effort that goes into producing an annual report for employees, it's worth a little more planning and effort to gain added impact at the time of distribution. Regular employee publications, special publications for supervisors and managers, and bulletin boards should all be used to stimulate interest in the forthcoming annual report. Employee meetings at the time of distribution are also an excellent way to derive maximum benefit from the report.

Further reading

Bowman, P. (ed.) 1989. *Handbook of Financial Public Relations*. Oxford: Heinemann (published on behalf of the CAM foundation).
The JSE Securities Exchange provides a range of useful publications.
Schuitema, J. 1998. *Econosense: Understanding Your Economic Environment*. Halfway House: International Thomson Publishing.

Chapter 21

House journals (in-house newsletters/ magazines)

When you have read this chapter, you should:

- be aware of the five different types of house journal;

- be familiar with the guidelines that underpin a successful working relationship between editorial staff of a house journal and management;

- understand some of the special considerations concerning the publishing, editing, production, and distribution of house journals;

- be able to plan for the successful launch of a house journal;

- be familiar with general guidelines for researching, writing, editing, and producing house journals.

The house journal, sometimes referred to as in-house newsletters and magazines, is one of the oldest forms of public relations, the Americans having pioneered this medium way back in the 1850s. House journals have been given a variety of names, such as house organs, employee newspapers, and company newspapers. They are private publications and over the years they have tended to change from pulpits for management to more candid forms of management-employee relations.

Types of house journal

House journals may be internal journals for staff or external journals for outside publics. There are five types of house journal:

- the sales bulletin, which is a regular communication, perhaps weekly, between a sales manager and sales staff in the field. Marketing departments issue similar communications;

- the newsletter, which is a digest of news for busy readers;

- the magazine, which contains feature articles and pictures, and may be published monthly or quarterly;

- the tabloid newspaper, which resembles a popular newspaper and contains mostly news items, short articles, and illustrations, and may be published weekly, fortnightly, monthly, or bi-monthly;

- the wall newspaper, which is a useful form of staff communication if staff are contained in one location, such as a factory, department store, or hospital.

These are general descriptions and very large organizations may have all five types of publications, addressed to different types of reader. Tabloids are generally addressed to the majority of workers, whereas the newsletter may be for executives and the magazine for more serious readers.

'10 commandments' for publication of journals

Norman Woodhouse, of the British Association of Industrial Editors, suggested the following guidelines, or '10 commandments', to help management get its communication right.

1. The policies of the board must be fully understood by all management staff and by the unions.
2. These policies must be clearly explained to the people employed in the enterprise. Here the internal publication has an important place among the many skills and techniques of effective communication.
3. The editor must be at the heart of the communication network. He or she must be kept informed of management problems and decisions, and have access to the entire management team.
4. The editor's task must be clearly defined and he or she must be directly responsible to top management, preferably to the chairman or managing director.
5. The editor, his or her staff, and their publication need to be professional and as well equipped as any other part of the enterprise.
6. The publication must be regular and on time.
7. The publication must be credible to its readers.

8. It should cover the full range of their interests, as employees, as trade union members, as family men and women, and as citizens.
9. It should promote two-way communication.
10. The overriding aim must be to inform, educate, and interest readers in an entertaining way.

Techniques for publication of journals

There are special considerations concerning the publishing, editing, production and distribution of house journals. They are:

- *The readers.* This is a vital area and the sponsor and editor of a house journal should be absolutely clear about who the readers of the publication are. It is difficult for a journal to be all things to all people, hence the need for separate publications to cater for the different interests of different people. This is not always appreciated and too many journals attempt to appeal to too wide a readership.
- *Frequency.* For reasons of cost, it may be decided to publish a journal only infrequently, but there should not be too large a gap between issues, otherwise the sense of regularity and continuity will be lost. Readers should look forward to the next issue, and it should appear on a regular date or day, such as the first of the month. Frequency can be determined on a cost basis (which is influenced by the number of pages and whether there is only black-and-white or colour printing). Frequency may also be determined by the need to publish news as soon as possible. Another cost factor that will have a bearing on frequency could be the number of copies required to reach all readers.
- *Title.* Just as the naming of a company or the branding of a product is a form of com-

munication which creates distinctiveness and character, so the title of a house journal establishes the image of the publication. If it is a newspaper, it may be a good idea to incorporate a typical newspaper name, like 'Times', 'Express' or 'Mail', into the title. If it is a magazine, a typical name such as 'Review' may be used.

- *Free issue or cover price.* Some people argue that a company journal should be issued free of charge; others say a journal will be valued more highly if there is a cover price. In South Africa, house journals are issued free but some of the biggest circulation house journals in the United Kingdom, such as *Coal and Rail News*, are sold like commercial newspapers.

- *Distribution.* There is no point in going to a lot of trouble to produce a house journal, only to let it suffer from ineffective distribution. If an organization has many branches or locations and bulk supplies are sent to each address, there should be systematic distribution to individual readers. If employees are merely expected to pick up copies from a central point they may not bother and copies will be wasted. Similarly, if copies are handed out at the work bench, they may be discarded on the floor. Although individual distribution may be costly – in terms of wrappers, envelopes, and postage, and keeping the mailing list up to date – the best method is to post copies to home addresses. Employees (and their families) can then read the journal at their leisure.

- *Advertisements.* The inclusion of advertisements can help to make a journal look more attractive and may be of value to readers. Three types of advertisement may be included: those inserted by the organization about its new products and services or, perhaps, vacancies; outside commercial advertisements if the circulation is attractive; and readers' 'sales and wants' advertisements. The latter can be a reader service which adds to reader interest.

- *Contributors.* There should be a planned supply of editorial material. The editor should plan future articles in consultation with contributors, while correspondents can be appointed to collect news and submit regular reports. The development of an active and enthusiastic correspondent network is of vital importance. So, too, is the taking of photographs of newsworthy events. This should not be left to an amateur.

- *Production.* This is a key area for house journals and calls for a combination of writing, print design, and print buying skills. It is sound policy to review the achievements of a house journal every year. This should include an analysis of the contents and design of the publication, as well as calling for three quotes for printing the house jounal. Do not select a printer on price alone as quality, service, and delivery are equally important.

New developments are house journals on video cassette which can be shown, whenever convenient, on video cassette recorders located throughout the organization. The SABC, for example, uses this technique to communicate important policy decisions and news to staff on a weekly basis. A number of banks also communicate in this way with their branch staff.

Other organizations have introduced an electronic newspaper. Information is edited, pages are stored in the computer, and viewers at numerous locations can call up pages on a television receiver. The editor collects or receives information and new 'pages' are produced daily.

Launching a new publication

Before any publication can be launched, a great deal of research has to be undertaken. First, the objectives of the publication have to be determined, as well as the target market and the available budget. Having decided on these aspects, a number of additional factors have to be finalized. These include:

- the title;
- the format and volume of the publication;
- the typeface;
- the type of paper to be used;
- the number and width of columns;
- the language;
- the frequency of publication;
- whether the publication will be a newspaper or a magazine.

Magazines versus newspapers and newsletters

When producing a corporate publication, one is often faced with having to make a choice between a magazine and a newspaper. Theoretically, a newspaper is cheaper to produce than a magazine, but this depends on the frequency of the publication. Should an organization issue a newspaper on a fortnightly basis, the cost of publishing it will soon be on a par with the cost of publishing a quarterly magazine. Irrespective of the choice, a winning publication is always one which is read rather than displayed. Remember that magazines, newspapers, and newsletters all have a place in the organization. So, what should it be?

To a large extent, this decision will be determined by the frequency of the publication. Newspapers and newsletters always contain short, newsworthy reports which should be read immediately, since this type of news soon becomes dated. No one wants to read history. Such a publication should appear at least once a month, but preferably on a weekly or fortnightly basis. Per edition, newspapers are cheaper to produce because cheaper paper is used and colour photographs are not essential. The number of pages in a newspaper is flexible, with one exception: it must consist of a minimum of four pages.

Magazines, on the other hand, have a less formal character, are composed of lengthier articles including photographs and visual material, and can be published less regularly,

perhaps monthly or quarterly. A second aspect to consider is the number of pages of the magazine. While a newspaper consisting of only a few pages is quite acceptable, a magazine consisting of fewer than 20 pages looks 'skimpy'.

An advantage of a magazine is that it allows for creativity, imaginative design, and colour. Appearance is not all-important, though, since the main aim of the publication is to ensure that it gets read. Its visual impact is a secondary consideration. However, if the corporate objective of a magazine is to promote the image of the company, then a glossy, full-colour magazine will be the natural choice. If the primary objective is to disseminate information, a newspaper is a far better choice.

Criteria for a successful publication

Title

Ideally the title of a publication should:

- be unique;
- be simple and consist of a single word of six to twelve characters;
- have a bearing on the organization;
- indicate its connection with the publication;
- have the same meaning or spelling in different languages;
- allow for good graphic design.

Should a title comply with four of the above aspects, then it merits consideration.

Mast-head design

Once the title has been decided upon, arrangements must be made for the design of either a mast-head, in the case of a newspaper, or for a cover, in the case of a magazine. It is essential to commission a professional graphic designer for this purpose and to brief him or her on the corporate colours which must be carried through in the design. Although the initial costs attached to this professional service are high, the end result is well worth the expense. A poorly designed mast-head or cover reflects adversely on the quality of the publication and creates a bad impression.

In the case of magazines, it is essential to have a striking, full-colour photograph, which has particular reference to an article in the publication, on the cover of each edition. Alternatively, sketches or drawings may be used, providing, of course, that these allow for variation and reflect organizational activities.

Language

The language of the publication must receive considerable attention. Where an organization's internal staff all speak the same language, for example English, the internal as well as external publications can be printed in that language. But this is the exception. If the internal public speaks one language and external public another, then the publications cannot be printed in only one language, but must reflect a 50/50 split. In the event of one internal language, and various languages for the external public, it must be determined which language is spoken by the majority of the external public and then to print in two languages: one for the internal public and the other for the external public. The language split should still be 50/50.

Format

Various factors must be considered in this regard:
- a magazine is usually an A4 format or size;
- A4 is the most popular format since it is easy to handle, fits easily into a standard envelope, and allows for creative design;
- newspapers and newsletters vary between A5 and A3 (tabloid);
- avoid an A5 format since it is small, hardly allows for photographs, and limits imaginative design;

- A3 (tabloid) format can be very effective since its large pages allow for imaginative design and good use of photographs. The disadvantage, however, is that it does not fit into an A4 envelope and must also be folded to fit into most mailboxes. Should one wish to increase the number of pages, this can easily be done by adding an extra four pages. However, significantly more material will be needed since an A3 page is double the size of an A4 page.

Grid

Once the format has been finalized, one must determine the number of columns per page as well as their width. This, in turn, has an effect on the 'feel' of the publication. The fewer the columns, the wider they will be. Wide columns are advantageous since they allow for relaxed reading. They are particularly suitable for magazines. Narrow columns, on the other hand, are better suited to newspapers or newsletters.

The same grid must be followed throughout the publication, but it can be broken to allow for impact or to draw attention.

It is important, however, to avoid having text run right across the page or to have only two columns per page, since such a wide page or column is difficult to read. Although two columns are sometimes used for annual reports, three columns are easier to read and a popular choice for magazines. Four columns provide for variation and for placing photographs and are therefore best suited to newspapers. Some tabloid publications have as many as seven columns, but these are very narrow.

Ensure that adequate gutters (white margins) are left at the top and sides of each page. A wider gutter must be left at the bottom of the page than at the top. A wider gutter is also called for along the inside of two facing pages.

Before deciding on the column width of your publication, bear in mind the typeface, length of lines, and the spacing between the lines, since these aspects should all be in harmony with one another.

Narrow columns are characterized by shorter lines, a smaller typeface, and lines which are closer to one another. Wider columns allow for longer lines, a bigger typeface, and bigger leading (space between lines). An ideal column width makes provision for approximately eight words. Six words or less force the eye to jump and twelve words cause the eye to move further across the page than is comfortable.

Typeface

The typeface (font) is an important aspect of any publication. An unsuitable typeface will have a negative effect on the publication's communication objectives. The typeface used for the body text of any publication must, therefore, be chosen very carefully. Legibility is a priority and the typeface must not attract attention, but rather lead the eye to the information or content. Italics, decorative typefaces, and the 'curly' type used for Christmas messages, for example, are difficult to read and must be avoided.

Justification

Text can be set evenly (flush/justified) or unevenly (ragged) at the right-hand side of the page. When text is justified (set flush), both the left and the right edges will be neatly aligned, but the spacing between words will not be exactly the same in each line. Unjustified text is even on the left edge, but the right edge will be ragged. Word spacing is the same in every line. Unjustified text has the advantage that there are fewer word breaks at the end of lines to distract the reader. Unjustified text is more suited to an informal, creative design. For these reasons, the format of all corporate correspondence must be considered when a decision is made in this regard.

Frequency

Most publications should appear as often as possible. Newspapers or newsletters will appear more often because of their newsworthy content, while magazines, being of a more casual nature, can appear less frequently. Most newspapers or newsletters appear on a fortnightly or monthly basis, while magazines are published either monthly or quarterly. Irrespective of the frequency, a publication must never be late – stick to the publication dates so that readers know when to expect the next edition.

With acknowledgement to T.R. Ferreira and I. Staude. *Write Angles: The ABC for House Journals.*

Promoting a new house journal

Once it has been decided to produce a company house magazine, how does one get going? And, how do you get that much-needed enthusiasm required from staff, at all levels of the organization, to get the first edition off the ground?

Do you just 'print and be damned'? Wait for the response after it has gone out? What about the fact that the magazine, although necessary from, say, management's point of view, might not be felt to be necessary by workers?

These questions were asked by International Computers Limited (ICL) before the launch of what was seen by corporate management as a very necessary tool in aiding company communication, both downward and upward.

What became evident was that all staff should be able to provide input for the magazine and that the publication would, therefore, be heavily dependent on material from correspondents. How to motivate correspondents to supply material regularly required further investigation.

ICL promotions consultant, Jack Liebenberg, came up with a mini-campaign for internal use by the company:

- A dummy of the front page of the proposed publication – aptly named *Input* – was pro-

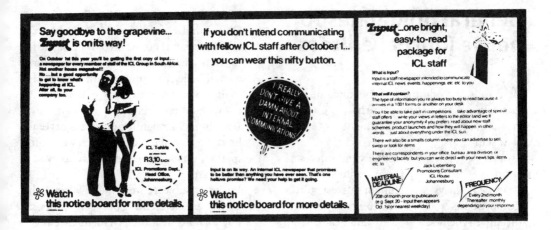

duced, featuring the reasons for publishing the magazine, the aims of the publication in terms of better communication and so on, the type of material that would be featured, how the material would be collected (through correspondents), and how correspondents would be rewarded.

- The dummy was printed with the feature article headline dropped out. Each headline was then overprinted by means of the repro-pull process to contain the names of 50 people chosen at random by a computer from a cross-section of the company's more than 1 300 staff located in 20 offices around South Africa, Namibia, and Swaziland. Each of the 50 people chosen would then receive a dummy copy of the front page of *Input* with the main feature article addressed to him or her, 'Jean Smith we need your input.' A reply section on the back of the dummy gave staff the opportunity to reply and provide comments on what they thought the publication should contain and what it should look like. The replies provided a wide range of comments and opinions canvassed from this cross-section.

Once these comments and opinions had been carefully studied, all who had provided input were advised as to how their material had been of assistance in starting the publication.

A further mailing announced the names of correspondents in branch offices and indicated the type of material that would be required and how they were to go about collecting it.

- A teaser campaign comprising two posters was then initiated and sent out at two-week intervals, telling staff that *Input* was on its way ... but little else. A third poster explained the objectives of the publication, its frequency, deadlines, and types of article that would be featured.

The poster campaign featured on notice boards in all the company's offices and succeeded in building up the right amount of enthusiasm and expectancy for the publication when it eventually appeared. The third poster generated an enormous amount of material via correspondents or directly to the editor.

The first copy of *Input* (produced on a ten-day deadline, which included writing, rewriting, layout, printing, and mailing) arrived on the desks of all company staff before the deadline. The campaign which had preceded publication proved successful in getting just the right amount of enthusiasm required for a new publication. It also provided a vital link in getting reaction and support from the outset and proved that while management thought the newspaper was necessary, staff really wanted it.

General guidelines for house journal editors

Here are some examples of the kinds of story that have a place in house journals:

Promotions	Retirements
New staff	Transfers
Awards	Hobbies and interests
Sport	Exam results
Unusual holidays	Human interest stories
Competitions	Conferences
Incentive schemes	Safety and health schemes
Social events	Community involvement
Clients' or associates' activities	Company performance
Product development and research	New products and processes
Company reorganizations	Company achievements
Sales records	Financial planning
Health care	Aids education

- Remember, your readers want news and facts. Find out what the news is and get all the facts – 100 per cent right.
- Give dates and locations of events, and where relevant, why they took place and who organized them.
- Identify sources of information fully, unless they have good reason to object, for example 'Durban branch manager John Brown confirmed ...' If you cannot identify a source, then use phrases like an eyewitness, a spectator, an employee, an innocent bystander, or any other descriptive label.
- Give complete information. The editor can take out what is not wanted. If he or she has to come back to you that's time and money wasted. Relegate unimportant information to the bottom of your story so that it can be cut without rewriting.
- Use simple, straightforward language and be concise, while giving all relevant information, unless the editor has asked you to 'pad out'.
- Put your subject into context where other events are relevant. 'Following proposals put forward at a management meeting in October, the human resources department has revised ...' is preferable to: 'The personnel department has revised ...'
- Use quotes – they lend strength and credibility to your story. For example: 'Profits in the engineering divizion have risen by a spectacular 35 per cent over the past 12 months. "It's been a great year," said divisional manager John Gerber.' (Get the name and title right.)
- Check the spelling of names (people and places) carefully, especially of people, including their first names.
- Get business or other titles right. Check with the person concerned wherever possible, or with the human resources department. Do not rely on hearsay.

Humour

- Have fun with light subjects, but keep your touch gentle. Do not try so hard to be funny that you end up hurting people's feelings.
- Never make fun of a person's work.

Style

- Do not use long sentences with many commas dividing up complex information. Rather break up the passage into two or more shorter sentences. Keep paragraphs relatively short. Start a new paragraph when there is a change in perspective or angle in the story, or to introduce a new idea.
- Watch singulars and plurals. Group nouns such as herd, flock, crowd, company, association, etc. are always singular, for example: 'Volkswagen is expected to introduce a new model in December' and 'The dairy herd is in the paddock.'
- Capital letters should not be used for business titles, only for proper names. Therefore: 'managing director', 'chairperson', 'branch manager', 'foreman'. Also, '... that is a group of public relations consultants', but 'Premier Public Relations Consultants (Pty) Ltd'. Also 'the agricultural industry' and 'the southern hemisphere' – yes, 'the prime minister' too. And note – 'South Africa is a republic' but 'the Republic of South Africa'. In the second case Republic is part of a proper name. In the first, republic is just a description.
- Examine your publication to see whether first names or initials with the titles Mr, Mrs, Ms are used. Follow the house style for the publication when writing your stories.
- Be consistent. If you spell 'mechanize' with 'z', go on spelling it like that.
- Remember to write figures correctly. One hundred thousand is written 100 000 (note space but no punctuation). One thousand is written 1 000. The decimal point is marked by a comma, thus: 6,7. Square metres should be written out or abbreviated as 'm^2'.
- Check whether your magazine uses % or per cent, and follow style.
- Resist the temptation to invent composite nouns like 'servicebay'. In English, the general rule is to separate nouns from other words that qualify them. Once you get on the slippery slope, where do you stop? Try

this: 'She lives in the whitehouse and he lives in the greenhouse'. Note the misunderstandings that arises over both their abodes. When a noun and adjective are joined together in English they can have a totally different meaning. Thus, 'greenhouse' means a specialized horticultural structure, not a green house. That may be obvious, but there are other, less obvious, traps into which you could fall.
- Language is a precision tool. You are a craftsperson. So, rather than tinker, learn to use correct language with skill and imagination to produce good work.

Punctuation

While we cannot go into all the many rules that govern punctuation, here are a few guidelines to help you avoid the most common errors. Study your magazine's style on the use of quotation marks and other punctuation marks, as well as the placing of full stops (inside or outside brackets). When commas are used to isolate included clauses, position them so as to separate the included clause, not before the word 'and'.

Wrong: He was captain of the team, and besides that, a fine batsman.

Right: He was captain of the team and, besides that, a fine batsman.

The rule is as follows: if all the words between the two commas are taken out, the sentence should still read fluently. If it doesn't, the commas are in the wrong place. Check the above sentences.

Avoid the use of exclamation marks, except in the case of quoted exclamations, for example '"Damn!" he yelled.' Your use of words, not exclamation marks, should give force to your sentences.

Captions

- Do not write patently false captions, for example 'Engineering director Allan Bates discusses a point with marketing manager Chris van der Walt', when it is obvious that they are just posing for a picture. Just knock out 'discusses a point' and you will regain credibility.

- Do not write, 'A view of the factory from West Street.' Just say 'The factory from West Street.' Everybody knows it is a view.
- Do not write, 'Joyce Brent looks happy at the Christmas party.' She either does or doesn't. Think of something else to say about her that adds to what the picture already says. Apply this rule generally. Pictures speak for themselves in many ways and your captions should add to their message, not just repeat it.
- Never write, 'A house in Doornfontein.' The Doornfontein bit is fine. Telling your readers this is a picture of a house is downright insulting. You could write, 'Many buildings in Doornfontein date back to the 1920s', thus providing additional information. This is a general rule. If you have a picture of a ship, don't tell readers it is a ship. The same goes for tractors, bottles of whisky, and all other universally recognized things. But if you have a picture of a complex and mysterious contraption, tell them what it is. If you don't know either – find out.
- Do not be afraid to put in a picture without a caption, if it doesn't need one, but write 'no caption' on the back to put the editor's and the printer's minds at rest.

Interviews

- Develop a relaxed style. If you are tense, your subject will find it hard to relax and will not communicate easily.
- When your subject is talking – listen. Do not interrupt with questions that raise other issues. You will miss opportunities if you do.
- Make a list of the questions you want answered before you begin the interview. A good starting point for a news item is: 'Who – what – when – where – how – why' (not necessarily in that order). Try to build up background information before the interview.
- Do not expect to have everything buttoned up in your mind beforehand. What the subject says during the interview will open up new avenues. Do not let these opportunities slip by.
- Subjects often wander off the point. Do not let this worry you. Let things ride a while, then steer them back gently if necessary.
- Remember to get the correct spelling of full names and titles. Write them down in block capitals to avoid confusion when you later type your article.
- Remember to get dates and venues correct.
- Try to relate to your subject – sense his or her mood or feeling about things; be receptive to enthusiasm. If you can do this, your

writing will gain variety and colour. If you do not, it will always be you communicating – in the same tone of voice, so to speak.

- Put yourself in your subject's shoes. Try to imagine how you would feel if you had done or seen this 'thing'. This helps you draw out excitement, pride, enthusiasm, horror – whatever.
- Ask searching, even cheeky, questions. But do not ask them arrogantly – do it with a grin.
- If you are not sure of certain aspects of your story, check them with the subject before sending the story off.
- Do not fawn when you are interviewing the boss or your department head; come out straight with the questions if you want a good story.
- Do not exaggerate wildly, lie or gush over very ordinary happenings – report them straight. Cultivate a balanced enthusiasm for people and the things they do.
- Never use your position as a correspondent to show favouritism or to further a purpose of your own. You are in a position of trust.
- 'Whitewash jobs' should be written, and signed, by the person who wants to paint something white. 'Whitewash jobs' should actually never appear in house magazines because if they do, then it's goodbye to credibility and goodbye to the company's investment in the magazine. Readers are not fools.

Preparing copy

- Always type your stories in double spacing, so that they can be 'subbed' without the need for microscopic writing.
- Identify your copy with a key word or 'slug' at the top right-hand corner. A story about a new chemical development, for example, might carry the slug 'chemical'. The first page would be 'chemical – 1', the second page 'chemical – 2', etc. Put 'more' at the bottom right if the story continues. Put 'ends' at the bottom of the last page. If the headline is on a separate sheet slug it 'chemical head'. Use the same slug on all pictures and captions, e.g. 'chemical – pic 1, chemical – pic 2', etc. Number the captions to tie up with the pictures: 'chemical – caption pic 1', etc.
- Put a circle around anything you do not want typeset, such as an explanatory note to the editor (which should be in pencil) or the words 'more' and 'ends' and the identifying slug.

This identification is essential to avoid confusion during editing and the complex printing process. How would you like your chemical story to end up with a picture of Mother Goose? Or a caption that reads, 'Lovely Brenda was fairest of them all at the Pick-a-Popsie competition.'

Photographs

This is not intended as a treatise on what is a very complex subject. We are just giving a few tips on common pitfalls.

- Try to avoid taking pictures of staring 'dummies'. Go for shots of people in their work (or play) environment, not necessarily looking at the camera, but at what they are doing, where this is relevant.
- Take action shots where you can. Remember that these need fast shutter speeds (1/250 or faster) and therefore the light must be good. Lack of sharpness is usually the result of a shutter speed that is too low, a wobbly hand, or both. You can compensate for 'camera shake' by using a higher shutter speed, but remember this will force you to use a wider aperture – thus reducing the depth of focus.
- If you want just about everything in focus (stationary subjects), use minimum aperture (which will force a lower shutter speed) and a tripod. Then use a remote cable release to trigger the camera or, failing that, use the delayed-action release fitted on most modern single lens reflex cameras. (These remarks apply to available light photography, not flash photography.) If the light is very good and you can use minimum aperture and a high shutter speed, then you won't need to go to these lengths to eliminate shake.
- Look at backgrounds – the camera will. You do not want a telegraph pole growing out of your subject's head. (Pictures are 'flat', not three-dimensional, so this unfortunate effect is emphasized in a photographic print. By contrast, your eyes do give a three-dimensional view, so you can be fooled.)
- If you photograph dark-skinned people against a bright background, they will be underexposed. Bright, glaring backgrounds are never beneficial except for special effects.

If you photograph a fair-skinned profile against a light background, it will disappear; a dark-skinned profile will disappear against a dark background. Neutral, medium-tone backgrounds are best – a bit lighter for dark subjects in profile and vice versa. Backgrounds with vertical or horizontal lines (or any other prominent pattern of lines) are bad. Backgrounds with sharp differences in light and shade are also bad.

- Take your exposure reading on the subject, not the background. Approach the subject to do this.
- Do not try to squeeze too many people into a picture. None of them will be recognizable.
- Not all subjects are potential beauty contest winners. If some look better in profile, give them a break. If they have three teeth missing, do not ask them to smile.
- Try to get people looking into the picture (the picture, not the camera) rather than out of it.
- If you get a lousy picture and can't retake, don't use it. It will detract from your magazine.
- Use professionals for tricky work, unless you really are an expert.
- The camera does lie, as you will discover.

With acknowledgement to *Scriber Guider* by Creda Press.

Working with a photographer

Always brief the photographer properly. If you are not taking the picture yourself, give the photographer as much information as possible about the story. If you cannot accompany him or her to the shoot, give a written brief as to what you require. If assignment cards are used, fill in the names of the important subjects and suggestions for types of poses. Consider whether you need vertical or horizontal photos to suit the page design. It is sensible to get photographs shot in both formats. Also, do you need overall panoramic shots or close-ups? Do not forget to include directions to the shoot – not just an address. Also give a telephone number in case the photographer gets lost or has a problem.

Go with the photographer, or meet him or her there, if possible. Working as a team will usually improve a story because you will be seeing the action from another point of view. Usually, the photographer will question you about the story and this, in turn, will often help you to clarify the story in your own mind. Organize the setting up of the shot. It is not the photographer's duty to gather props or prepare the venue in advance.

Be imaginative. If you are obliged to take yet another photograph of a cheque-giving ceremony, consider taking the photograph from a different angle or watching the recipient's face for a reaction. Avoid boring pictures of posed handshakes – grip-and-grin shots – and other visual clichés. Look for examples from local and international news magazines and photography books.

Do not interfere with the photographer. If you have suggestions, be tactful. Remember photographers have professional pride and are not writer's lackeys. If it is a complex shot, investigate it beforehand. It will pay off in the long run.

Experienced house journal and newspaper editors usually choose photographs from contact sheets or proof sheets (strips of negatives laid side by side and printed on a single sheet of photographic paper). This allows them to see all the work the photographer has done. Always ask the photographer to print the full frame of the photographs and do the cropping yourself. Often photographers crop out just the extra millimetre or two you need to make the photo fit snugly into your design.

Doing your own photography

Developing your own skills is important. As a corporate journalist, more often than not you will end up being your own photographer. Your success will depend not only on your technical know-how and artistic flair; to a larger degree it will be determined by your ability to relate to and manage people. Bear the following in mind:

- The key to good subject rapport is patience and professionalism.
- Be on time every time.
- Dress properly for the occasion. If you are doing a dirty industrial shoot, jeans and a T-shirt may be fine, but they are not the right attire for photographing your board of directors or a black-tie gala affair. Always take your dress cue from the subject(s). Dress so that they will feel comfortable with you as a guest.
- When working with people, always stay in control. If you have planned your picture in advance this is relatively easy to achieve. Introduce yourself politely but firmly. Explain to your subjects what you are trying to achieve and why, and then arrange them. If you are with a difficult or moody client, point out that you are trying to capture an image that will make him or her appear acceptable and professional to the specific target audience. You can only succeed if he or she co-operates.
- Be aware of other people's personal space. If you encroach on this without asking permission and explaining why, you are likely to end up with an extremely tense subject. Make sure that you involve everybody present when working with a group. It takes only one bored individual to ruin an otherwise excellent shot.

With acknowledgement to F Nel. *Writing for the Media.*

Further reading

Ferreira, T.R. & I. Staude. 1991. *Write Angles: The ABC for House Journals.* Johannesburg: Write Minds.
Nel, F. 1998. *Writing for the Media.* Cape Town: Oxford University Press.
Sutton, T. 1986. *Creative Newspaper Design: A Manual for Editors and Designers of Corporate Publications.* Johannesburg: Review Press.

Chapter 22

Background to printing and publishing

Since most public relations practitioners are involved in the design and production of a wide range of company publications, a few guidelines on working with printers are worth outlining.

Printing establishments

There are more than 1 200 registered printing companies in South Africa and in excess of 130 in the graphics and reproduction industry. It is important to choose a good printer and then to go to some pains to develop a close and honest relationship.

Before any printing is put in hand, it is common sense to obtain comparative estimates. These can vary surprisingly for the same job. Printing establishments differ considerably in the type and size of machines they use. Also, fluctuations in workload may make one establishment more eager than another to take on new work. It is well worth shopping around.

Before a printer can give an estimate, the following information is required from you, the client:
- the method of printing (letterpress, litho, gravure, web-offset);
- size and number of pages;
- paper quality;
- sizes of type;
- proportion of display and heading material;

- illustrations and photographs. Are bleeds involved? (A rough dummy showing the presentation of a typical page or pages should accompany the request for a quote.);
- quantity and run-on price (example: 5 000 copies and per 500 additional);
- frequency of publication and dates of issues;
- how many colours on how many pages;
- binding (saddle-stitched, drawn-on covers, or loose pages as in a newspaper);
- where and how the job is to be delivered;
- any insertions in the publication;
- wrappers, envelopes, addressing, dispatching;
- preparation of illustrations (are blocks or plates to be included in the estimate or quoted for as an extra?);
- proposed schedule for supplying copy and make-up.

You are likely to get a competitive quotation if the printer can be given an undertaking for continuous production over six months or a year on a variety of jobs. Other tips include the following:

- Visit the printing works yourself to familiarize yourself with printing operations.
- Remember, there are three main factors to be considered in obtaining printing services: cost, service, and quality of the finished job.
- Try and find a printer whose standards are high but whose prices are reasonable.
- Ask a printer for a time schedule on your job. In order to stick to it you must provide copy on time and pass page proofs without undue delay.
- A well-conceived publication can fail in its objective if it is poorly printed and contains typographical errors. It is therefore always false economy to seek the lowest printing price at all costs.

Finally, get some sort of reference about your printer. When the representative calls with the quotation for your job he or she will probably bring along examples of work done by the company. These will be the best examples produced under ideal conditions and will not necessarily be representative of what is being put out most of the time. One way to check consistency is to take a look at several editions of a magazine produced by the printer to see the usual quality of work. The most obvious suggestion is still the best, however – speak to a few people who are using the printer or repro shop, find out what its strong points are, whether they have any reservations about it, and ask to see examples of work done for them.

Always invite at least three tenders for printing a new house journal. For normal 'jobbing' you must know your printer and trust it to charge a fair price. An ideal arrangement is to use a number of printers, choosing the most suitable for each particular job.

There should be no condoning bad printing. Inspect advance copies of the publication. If there are any serious errors they should be corrected before the job is issued, even if this involves reprinting.

The greatest expense in printing is when one changes one's mind at the print stage. Once proofs have been submitted it can cost a lot of money to accommodate second thoughts. This point should be emphasized at every opportunity. Ask printers to justify charges for authors' corrections.

One of the main gripes that printers have is that all too often customers don't really know what they want. A vague and casual briefing often results in a botched-up job requiring a re-run. This involves overtime that was never budgeted for – a shameful waste of time and money – and a great deal of ill feeling as everyone tries to shift the blame. Therefore it is vital to know exactly what you want, but do not be too rigid or too afraid to ask the printer's advice.

Printing processes

Various printing processes are used in the industry.

- *Silk-screen*. This process is used for short runs or for work in which particular effects are sought. The inks used are more durable

Letterpress   **Lithography**   **Photogravure**

than those used in other processes. It may be used on many different surfaces. It is also used to reproduce colour photographs, although it has marked limitations in this regard. Silk-screen is likely to be used when producing short runs of showcards and window bills, outdoor signs, and short runs of hoarding posters.

- *Photogravure*. This process is expensive and is confined mainly to the printing of magazines and long packaging runs. It is unlikely to be used on a day-to-day basis. A new development which is at present in its initial stages

looks as if it may allow gravure to become more competitive on fairly short runs.

- *Letterpress*. This process, though common until quite recently, is being replaced by lithography. Letterpress is often used where changes may be made to the printed item. It is still widely used for printing stationery, leaflets, brochures, booklets, etc. The process gives excellent colour reproduction.
- *Lithography*. The lithographic process is almost universally used today. The process can be used on a wide range of papers, with the cartridge-type finishes particularly suit-

The anatomy of a print litho job, from disk to delivery

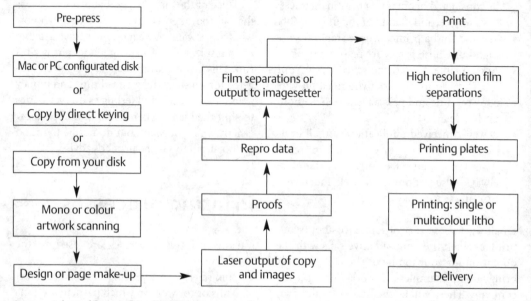

Source: Adapted from Jefkins. 1998: 162.

able and glossy papers probably the least suitable. The process is widely used for economic reasons where the design calls for large areas of tone printing. It is also useful for office forms, particularly those that are ruled or lined because of the ease, compared with other processes, of reproducing the form. This is done by merely photographing artwork and making a plate.

The qualities of good design

A good design should be simple yet attractive, giving the illusion of movement in the direction the eye normally moves. If colour is used it should be introduced subtly and sparingly, and not simply for its own sake.

Each publication should have its own recognizable identity. In addition, articles in the publication should always follow the same sequence: readers' letters, sports, features for women, and so on. These should always be in the same place, to help the reader find them quickly.

Unity in design is foremost in a designer's mind. It will not be achieved if:
- eye movement is directed off the page;
- each element has so much contrast that it stands out sharply and distinctly on its own;
- the elements are not in harmony with each other;
- gutters of white space divide the page up into distinct segments.

Designers should use methods that are economical and save time for themselves and the printer.

The design should have balance, which is achieved by the careful placing of items of relative weight of colour (that is, black, white, and grey) on either side of a vertical or horizontal line bisecting the page. A disorganized page is very difficult to read. At the same time, a sense of proportion should be achieved, guided by the relative importance of the various articles.

There are hundreds of different types of layout. However, all follow certain rules:
- *Vertical layout.* This is the simplest (and oldest) form of layout, where the text runs in single columns and the headlines are the width of one column. Following this style, the headlines should always be set on the left to avoid clashing with those adjacent.
- *Horizontal layout.* This is also a very simple layout in which the text is squared up under multi-column headlines to create horizontal units. The page is then made up of a series of these units lying horizontally, one on top of the other.
- *Frame layout.* Here the first and last columns are in solid text, which creates a frame around the rest of the text. This is not such a good style since a frame is already created by the margins.
- *Circus layout.* With this style, there are many stories on the page with no emphasis on any particular one of them. There are also many headlines of equal importance.
- *Symmetrical layout.* This layout has equal text on both sides of an imaginary line or central article. The main article should be set one third of the distance from the top of the page (this would be the optical centre of the page, not the actual centre). It is very difficult to achieve perfect symmetry without cutting or lengthening text (and this ruins the fluency of copy). This style looks neat and orderly, but is often dull and lifeless.
- *Asymmetrical layout.* This is similar to a symmetrical layout, but the balance is imperfect. It is therefore far more interesting visually. It is achieved by balancing a picture on one side with a picture of a different size on the other, or with a headline or a block of text.

Contrast is an important factor in design. Every item on the page must have sufficient contrast to its surroundings to be legible. For example, if the type is too light on a tinted background, it is very difficult to read. Headlines should not run into each other; this can be avoided by using different typefaces and leaving ample space between them. Captions should be close to the photographs and they should be in a distinctly different typeface to the body copy (for example in bold type or italics).

Copy on the whole has a grey tone and its positioning provides contrast to photographs and headlines. Headlines and subheadings are black and this also provides contrast. If contrast is not used correctly, it destroys the balance of the page. There are various factors regarding contrast to remember:

- typeface and size;
- rules and frames;
- half-tones;
- line work including reverse blocks and tints;
- white space.

Margins create a natural frame around a page, giving it unity. Areas of white space should be placed near the margins, rather than in the centre of the page. This technique creates an uneven look without sacrificing the unity of the page. The use of white space is integral to the layout and should not be considered as blank space which needs to be 'filled in'.

Layout devices

The purpose of a good layout is to attract the reader's eye and entice him or her to continue reading. Certain layout devices help achieve this.

Mast-head

The mast-head of a publication should always be positioned consistently for easy identification. It should never be moved down the page to give prominence to another article.

Lead-in devices

The layout can have a central area of interest to attract the reader. A good photograph dominating the page or double-page spread is an excellent lead-in device. *Time* often uses this type of layout. It is simple yet effective. A large photograph dominates the page, the caption appears below the photograph, followed by a headline and then the text.

Captions should preferably appear below the photograph, or on the bottom left or right of the picture. The reason for this is that the eye will look at the picture and then automatically look below it for the caption. Positioning the caption anywhere else will confuse the reader.

Other lead-in devices that can be used are line drawings, headlines, and colour.

Headlines

Headlines are a very important layout device. They should always have enough white space around them to make them legible, and should not appear crowded. They should be set in a typesize large enough to distinguish them from the rest of the copy. They can be positioned either flush left or centred, but whichever method is used should be consistent throughout the publication. The importance of an article on the page is often indicated by the size, weight, and length of the headline. The length of the headline should be in relation to the importance of the article, that is, the longest article should have the biggest headline. Headlines need not necessarily be in capitals; they can be as effective in upper and lower case.

Subheadings in a bold or bigger type than the body copy (usually one or two points bigger) should be used to break up large sections of copy. They, too, can be either centred or set flush left, but again, whichever method is chosen, should be used consistently throughout the publication.

Colour

Colour is an important element in printed communication. It can be used effectively in a number of ways:

- to highlight critical portions of a black-and-white illustration or to emphasize portions of the text;
- to create the mood of an article, feature or abstract illustration, for example by using tinted blocks or screens;

- to differentiate between editorial comment and the contents of the publication;
- to add interest to mast-heads or subheadings;
- to make diagrams, charts, or formulae easier to understand;
- to pinpoint key locations on maps by using arrows or wedges in the copy.

It is a good idea to obtain a Pantone Matching System (PMS) colour chart from your printer. This chart consists of hundreds of different shades of colours, each with its own code number. Colour swatches can be detached from the chart and attached to the copy or section to be printed in the desired colour. Using a colour chart enables you to be very specific in your choice of colour and is a far safer means of specifying colour than using broad terms such as 'dark blue' or 'pale green'.

Keep in mind that weak colours such as pale yellow do not have enough contrast on a white background to be clearly legible.

Type may be superimposed on tinted blocks. This is only effective if the type is bold and the tint very light.

If colour is to be used for a headline, it should be a strong colour. Long, sensational headlines (such as 'Humankind's first landing on the moon') are more effective in black than in colour. Using one word in colour in a black headline can be striking. Headlines can also be placed in blocks of colour or reversed out (for example, white type on a black or red block).

The use of colour drastically increases printing costs. However, if the publication carries colour advertisements, colour will automatically be available on certain pages. For instance, if the publication is printed in 16-page sections (that is, eight pages are printed in one process), colour will be available on pages 1, 4, 5, 8, 9, 12, 13, and 16 at minimal extra cost, if any, if these pages carry a colour advertisement. The same will apply to pages 2, 3, 6, 7, 10, 11, 14, and 15.

Margins

Margins play an important role in page layout. A margin creates a frame around the page, which gives it unity. Readers are conditioned to read from left to right until they reach a white space (a fence). The eye then returns to the left again. If copy or headlines run into the margin, the fence becomes broken or inadequate and readability is reduced. Therefore, never allow copy or headlines to run into margins.

Columns must be separated from each other either by rules or by white space. If white space is used, it must not be too wide, because this will cause the page to look fragmented. Column dividers should not be wider than 1–1,5 picas.

Margins can vary in width, but they should be wider than column dividers. The four margins on a page are usually not of equal width. The optical centre of a page is higher than the actual centre. Therefore, the bottom margin should be wider than the top to give the illusion that the page is correctly centred. If the publication is bound, the two centre margins of a double-page spread will be narrower because they are joined to the spine. This must be kept in mind when deciding on margin widths. Page numbers may be considered as:

- part of the margins;
- part of the copy if they are placed next to the identification logo of the publication.

Photographs

Photographs are very useful to bring colour and contrast to the page. Photographs which run off the page are said to bleed. Bleeding can be very effective for the following reasons:

- it can add variety to a page;
- it gives a sense of magnitude to striking photographs (especially full-page ones) because it creates the impression that the photograph goes on forever.

Bleeding will result in slightly more expensive printing costs. If a photograph is not very clear, a tint can be placed over it to improve the quality.

Headlines may be superimposed on photographs, but ensure that the type is bold enough to provide adequate contrast. Text can also be placed over photographs, but take great care because it can be very difficult to read. Text that is printed over photographs should preferably be put in blocks.

Portraits should always face inwards – never off the page.

Rules

Rules can box small areas of type which would otherwise not be noticeable. They also provide guidelines for the eye to follow, break up large sections of text, help fill up white spaces, separate one article from another, and give unity to the page.

Line drawings and cartoons

Line drawings are useful to help break copy. Never superimpose text on a line drawing because it will be virtually impossible to read.

Cartoons can be used to liven up a page and to fill in spaces.

Blocks of text

Blocks of text should always run horizontally across the page, never vertically down it, because then the reader would have to turn the page to read it. Some time ago, it was considered clever to put blocks of type in fancy shapes. For instance, if the article was about films, the shape of the text was in the form of an unwinding roll of film. Today this is considered to be poor design (as well as unnecessarily time-consuming).

Logos

Logos can be used to identify particular sections within a publication. For example, in *The Star* the 'Star Classified', 'Tonight', 'Woman' and the 'Property Star' are all labelled with their own logos. The positioning of these logos should always be consistent.

Tear-out sections

Tear-out sections, which are intended to be pulled out and kept for future reference by the reader, should be positioned in the centre or on a separate sheet. They can also be tinted for easy identification.

Left-hand page

The left-hand page should have a stronger design than the right, because the eye reads from left to right. Many advertisers will insist that their advertisement appear on the left-hand page since this is the page the reader looks at first. The eye sees the upper left-hand corner of the page first, so this should be the strongest section of the page.

Typography

Typography is very important. There are more than 300 different typefaces from which to choose. The typeface, the type size, and linear spacing or leading (space between lines) must all be considered carefully when doing a layout.

A line of text should not contain more than 10 to 12 words for comfortable reading. If, after choosing the type size, this is not achieved, the type size or the width of the columns must be changed. Type should not be so small that it causes eyestrain, so any type size smaller than 10-point should not be used for body copy.

Type is either roman (upright letters) or italic (slanting). Roman faces may be classified as follows:

- **Oldstyle typefaces** are often used where large masses of text are printed, for example books and newspapers. In oldstyle type there is not much difference in the thickness of the upstrokes and downstrokes of the letters.
- **Transitional typefaces** are very clear and well shaped. There is no extreme contrast between the upstrokes and downstrokes. An example of this type is one designed by John Baskerville in 1762.
- In **modern typefaces**, the upstrokes are much thinner than the downstrokes.

Bookman	Aldo Style
Bookman Italic	*Aldo Style Italic*
Bookman Bold	**Aldo Style Bold**
Bembo	Helvetica
Bembo Italic	*Helvetica Italic*
Bembo Bold	**Helvetica Bold**
Garamond	Univers
Garamond Italic	*Univers Italic*
Garamond Bold	**Univers Bold**
Baskerville	Times
Baskerville Italic	*Times Italic*
Baskerville Bold	**Times Bold**

In the lower case alphabet, certain letters have descenders (example: g, j, p) and ascenders (example: b, f, h). The longer the descenders and ascenders of a type, the less vertical height can be used for the other letters without tails (example: a, c, e, i). This vertical height, called the 'x' height, influences linear spacing. For example, Times Roman has short ascenders and descenders so the 'x' height is deep, whereas Perpetua has long ascenders and descenders so the 'x' height is shallow.

Times Roman was designed for the *Times* newspaper in London for use on newsprint and is not very effective on art paper, which is what most magazines are printed on. So, unless you are printing on newsprint, avoid this typeface.

Some typefaces have small cross-lines (serifs) at the end of the vertical strokes. This is called serif type. If there are no serifs, it is called sans-serif type. Sans-serif type is used very often these days. A very popular sans-serif type is Univers.

Bear in mind, also, that not all typefaces are available in italics.

Linear spacing should be visually correct even if it is not uniform. For example, if two lines in a headline have no ascenders or descenders they should be closer together than two lines with ascenders or descenders.

Different typefaces can be used to identify different sections in a publication. For example, a sports feature could have a bold, angular typeface and a babies feature a delicate typeface.

For added variety, the first paragraph of an article or the first word in a paragraph can be set in a bolder type than the rest. Similarly, the first letter may be a dropped capital.

Proofreading

It is very important to proofread any material before it is published to ensure that the content is accurate and that the layout and presentation meet your requirements. When you require changes to be made, it is also important to convey these in a way that is clear to the publishing industry representatives with whom you are working. To this end, it is advisable to familiarize yourself with the basic proofreading signs provided in the following table.

Proofreaders' signs

Instruction	Textual mark		Marginal mark
Insert matter indicated in margin	λ		/
Delete and leave space or insert space	Strike through letters to be deleted		♂
Delete and close up	$\int$	above and below letters to be taken out	♂ /
Leave as printed	- - - -	under letters or words to remain	stet
Change to italic	——	under letters or words to be altered	ital
Change to small (even) capitals	═══	under letters or words to be altered	Sc.
Change to capital letters	═══	under letters or words to be altered	Caps
Use capital letters for initial letters and small capitals for rest of words	═══	under capital letters and under the rest of the words	C. & Sc.
Change to bold type	∼∼∼	under letters or words to be altered	Bold
Change to lower case	/	through letters to be altered	lc.
Change to Roman	Encircle words to be altered		Rom
(Wrong font) Replace by letter of correct font	Encircle letter to be altered		wf.
Invert type	Encircle letter to be altered		⊙
Change damaged letter(s)	Encircle letter(s) to be altered		×
Substitute or insert letters or signs under which this mark is placed, in 'superior' position	/ through character or λ where required		⌣̣
Substitute or insert letters or signs over which this mark is placed, in 'inferior' position	/ through character or λ where required		⌒/ ⌒

Underline word(s)	———	under words affected	*Underline*
Use ligature (e.g. ffi) or diphthong (e.g. oe)	‿	enclosing letters to be altered	‿
Close up – delete space between letters	‿	linking words or letters	‿
Insert space	⅄		#
Make space appear equal between words	/	between words	*equal* #
Reduce space between words	/	between words	*less* #
Transpose	∽	between letters or words, numbered when necessary	*trs.*
Move matter to right	⌐	at left side of group to be moved	⌐
Move matter to left	⌐	at right side of group to be moved	⌐
Begin a new paragraph	⌐	before first word of new paragraph	*np.*
No fresh paragraph here	⊃	between paragraphs	*run on*
Insert omitted portion of copy	⅄		*out, see copy*
Substitute or insert comma	/	through character	
	or ⅄	where required	,/
Substitute or insert full stop	/	through character	
	or ⅄	where required	⊙
Insert hyphen	⅄		/-/
Insert apostrophe	⅄		̓
Insert double quotation marks	⅄		̋

Further reading

Ferreira, T.R. & I. Staude. 1991. *Write Angles: The ABC for House Journals.* Johannesburg: Write Minds.

Jefkins, F. 1998. *Public Relations.* London:

M & E Pitman Publishing.

Sutton, T. 1986. *Creative Newspaper Design: A Manual for Editors and Designers of Corporate Publications.* Johannesburg: Review Press.

Zettl, H. 2000. *Sight, sound and motion: applied media aesthetics.* Belmont, California: Wadsworth.

Chapter 23

Promotional activities

When you have read this chapter, you should:

- be able to set promotional objectives for your organization;
- understand the role of promotion in the marketing context;
- be aware of various objectives set for promotions;
- be familiar with the elements of an efficient promotion;
- be able to identify the role of public relations in a promotional context;
- be familiar with aspects of the law and its impact on promotional activities.

Promotion refers to communication undertaken to persuade others to accept ideas, concepts, or things. A promotional strategy is a controlled, integrated programme of communication methods designed to present an organization and its products and services to prospective customers, to communicate need-satisfying attributes to facilitate sales, and thus to contribute to long-term profit performance. Promotional tools include advertising, personal selling, sales promotion, reseller support (trade promotion), publicity, public relations, and corporate advertising (Engel et al. 1994: 5). It is in this context that every marketing organization should set its promotional objectives.

In the marketing context, promotion is the practice of temporarily offering better value for money. This is done in the hope that the offer of specific benefits will appeal to those to whom they are addressed and that from this will come specific efforts which are beneficial to the brand.

Promotion is thus an extra incentive over and above the product's inherent qualities, established price, advertising, and selling efforts.

This implies a need for planning, measurement, specification – and for subsequent comparison of what was achieved with what was intended. The vast majority of promotions are offered to consumers and traders, but they may be offered to any group which can influence a brand's fortunes.

An efficient promotion achieves its effects speedily – in weeks or at most in a few months, does so just when needed and, if necessary, promptly after the need is realized.

An efficient policy uses promotion to achieve a wide variety of intermediate and ultimate objectives.

Setting promotional objectives

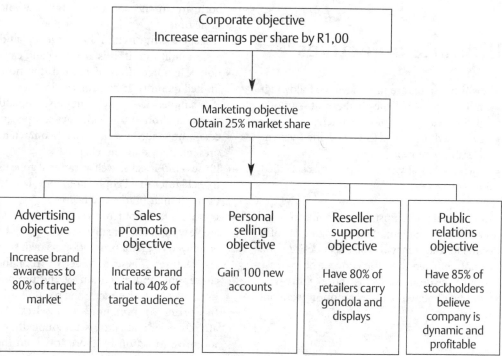

```
┌─────────────────────────────────────────┐
│           Corporate objective           │
│  Increase earnings per share by R1,00   │
└─────────────────────────────────────────┘
                     │
                     ▼
┌─────────────────────────────────────────┐
│            Marketing objective          │
│          Obtain 25% market share        │
└─────────────────────────────────────────┘
```

Advertising objective	Sales promotion objective	Personal selling objective	Reseller support objective	Public relations objective
Increase brand awareness to 80% of target market	Increase brand trial to 40% of target audience	Gain 100 new accounts	Have 80% of retailers carry gondola and displays	Have 85% of stockholders believe company is dynamic and profitable

Adapted from Engel et al. 1983:180.

Intermediate objectives

Intermediate objectives may relate to traders or consumers. The temporary added value which is inherent in the promotion effectively spurs consumers or traders to action which is beneficial to the brand, and which otherwise they would not have been disposed to take at that time.

Traders

Traders may be induced to take the following actions:

- stock the brand or a new pack;
- speed up sales of old stock to make way for new ('improved') stock;
- carry abnormal stocks of the brand;
- display the brand or give it special display;
- specially recommend the brand or make special efforts to sell it;
- act as intermediaries in communicating facts about the brand or about a promotion to consumers;
- cut the price of the brand (or maintain or increase it).

Consumers

Consumers may be induced to take the following actions:

- try a brand – compare a new or improved brand with 'my usual brand';
- buy and use more of a brand – or buy it now instead of later;
- buy a particular pack;
- try a brand for a particular purpose;
- become aware or more keenly aware of a

brand's existence, claimed consumer benefit, or brand image;
- buy it from *this* shop or chain.

Ultimate objectives

The ultimate aims are to achieve the following:
- more users – to a specified extent – among defined categories of consumers;
- increased usage – to a specified extent (users use more);
- increased loyalty from users – to a specified extent.

Under certain circumstances stabilization of usership or loyalty, or the slowing down of a decline in usage, may be the effect desired of a promotion. Even then the concept of increase is valid – the desired effect is 'more'; more than would be obtained if the promotion were not undertaken.

Efficient promotion

The following are some of the characteristics of an efficient promotion:
- It does not attempt to do what other items in the marketing mix do better.
- It is the best promotion for achieving the objectives.
- It gives maximum effect at the lowest cost.
- It is consistent with the behaviour patterns of those to whom it is addressed. Unless there is conclusive evidence that they are ripe for the change, it does not demand that people should change their habits or ways of thinking.

- It is consistent with the brand image. It is necessary that the image of the 'gift' should not do harm to the brand's image when both are in the consumer's mind at the same time.
- It gets attention and has urgency and action built into it. It is arresting and cannot be ignored. It is of limited duration, limited quantity. It demands action now.
- It is simple, clear, easy to understand, and to act on. Promotions which are complicated, or are made to seem so by incompetent presentation, stand no chance.
- It uses emotional as well as rational appeals to self-interest. People are appealed to through their brains and hearts.
- It is unique. Opportunities for uniqueness are very rare, but sensitive creativity can be employed to give a promotion its own special features. These may derive from the conception and execution of the promotion, the name given to it, the reason for it, the prizes or premiums themselves. An attractive individuality is undoubtedly an incentive to action by those to whom the promotion is addressed.
- It is honest – and evidently honest. It must be good value for money. And it must be presented in such a way that its public will not feel that there is any risk of being fooled. Those who accept the offer must also feel that what they get lives up to what they were promised.

It is important to stress that the various elements of a successful promotion – advertising, public relations, publicity, and the actual promotion itself – should be given equal status and be planned together. Experience has shown that advertising alone may not result in a successful promotion.

228

It is very much a team effort and the public relations practitioner's contribution is in the area of originality and overall co-ordination. His or her grasp of the broad overview is often essential for success. This may involve advising on budgets for advertising, in-store promotions, and public relations; providing effective media liaison; arranging fun events, and unusual in-store promotions with top personalities. All this has to be meticulously planned and calls for a wide range of personal qualities and skills.

Promotion work is demanding and requires practitioners who have abundant common sense, first-class organizing ability, good judgment, objectivity, imagination, resilience, a sense of humour, flexibility, and a willingness to work long and inconvenient hours when necessary. A tall order, but the rewards are high and the enjoyment and satisfaction immeasurable ... if you can last the pace.

Key stages of a promotion

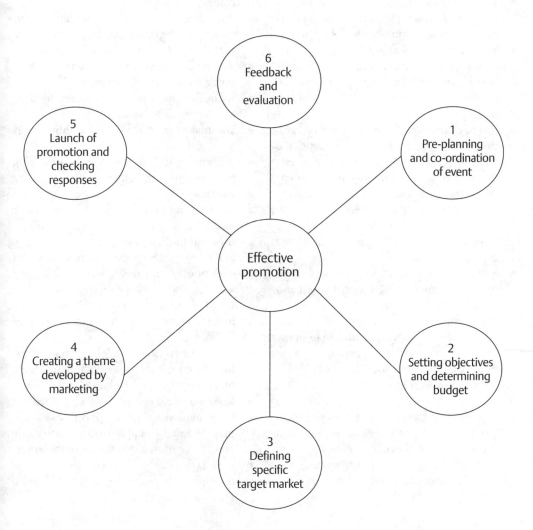

229

Arranging an event

Event management is an important resposibility of public relations. The following guidelines should assist in the co-ordination of a successful function.

- You have an appropriate project plan for the event to be organized.
- You have checked that the date planned for the event does not clash with any other event that will impact on the success of what you are organizing.
- You have decided how much assistance you will need and have confirmed the availability of the people you need to help you.
- You have given careful thought to the choice of venue relative to what the proposed guests will enjoy and what will be appropriate in terms of the impression you wish to create.
- You have arranged the catering with careful thought to the timing of the event, the amount of circulating you want your guests to do, whether they will use fingers or utensils, carrying of glasses or cups, how long you want the guests to stay, and what will work best with the media interviews likely to take place and any speeches during the course of the meal.
- You have sent an invitation, followed up by telephone, sent a written confirmation also confirming the guests' special dietary requirements, and a reminder on the day before the event together with a map showing how to find the venue and instructions on where to park. You have provided a phone number for people to call if they get lost.
- If journalists have accepted, you call them again on the day of the event to check that no big news item has occurred to stop them from attending. If this has happened, you make appropriate arrangements for them to get the story.
- You arrange transport for any important guests who may have difficulty reaching the venue.
- You arrive at the venue in plenty of time to check that all your instructions have been followed.
- You introduce yourself to the banqueting manager and know where he or she is throughout the event so that you can get help quickly if needed.
- If sound or audiovisual equipment is to be used, you check and recheck that it is working perfectly and that you have spare bulbs ready.
- If a client is to do a presentation, you ensure that he or she does a dry run at the venue with the equipment to be used.
- You expect unexpected guests and are well prepared to deal with them.
- Reconfirm the time at which the food or each course is to be served.
- You make sure that the air conditioning is at a comfortable level.
- You ensure that all guests have something to drink or eat before having anything yourself.
- You look out for guests who have no one to talk to and introduce them to someone they will find interesting.
- Make sure that your team understands who is responsible for seeing guests off as they leave and for making sure that all guests who have to leave early are given any gifts or information that they should have as they leave.
- After the event, thank the banqueting staff for their help or, if this has been unsatisfactory, make careful notes for a formal complaint.
- Keep a meticulous list of who attended.
- Send thank you notes as appropriate. These may include a clipping of a particularly good piece of media coverage of the event.
- If it is a client event, arrange a debrief meeting with your account director and a separate one with the client.

Event Planning

ACTIONS

Operational

1. Brief from client
2. Proposal and plan
3. Budget compilation (includes research costs, quotes, and suppliers)
4. Presentation to client for approval
5. Event planning with all suppliers (venue, designer, printers, agency, photography)
6. Compile checklists for individual suppliers
7. Compile individual budgets

Invitations

8. Compile invitation list – client
9. Compile invitation copy
10. Client approval
11. Send invitations (fax, hand-deliver)
12. Set up RSVP lists with staff
13. Revert to client at regular intervals
14. Send confirmations for every RSVP
15. Follow-up on cut-off date
16. Nametags

Venue

17. Source venues and costs
18. Present options to client
19. Recce with client
20. Client approval of venue and costs
21. Finalize menu, flowers, photographer, parking, security, seating, layout, equipment specifications
22. Finalize set up time prior to event
23. Finalize rehearsal, dry run if necessary
24. Post-event thank you

Designer

25. Brief
26. Confirm budget
27. Obtain logos from client
28. Confirm size, colours, materials specifications, deadlines upfront

29. First layout (allow three till internal approval)
30. Present to client
31. Amend layout (if required)
32. Final client approval
33. To final artwork
34. Client to sign-off artwork
35. Designer to hand over artwork (e.g. on disk) to repro-house

Reproduction and printing (if separate company)

36. Brief
37. Confirm budget and specification (deadlines, colour, paper, delivery details, etc.)
38. Hand over artwork
39. Printer to go to final material
40. Client to approve chromalins and check colour before printing
41. Printer to print first sample for client approval
42. Delivery

Media

43. Compile media list with individual angles
44. Client approval
45. Individual media briefings prior to event
46. Arrange interviews
47. Individual press kits for interviews: set up and attend
48. Prepare editorial for individual publications
49. Organize photography for press kits
50. Set up media table at venue and man
51. Attendance list monitor
52. Follow-up with media not attending
53. Post-event thank you
54. Overall media monitoring
55. Compile post-event media report and evaluation
56. Invoice client

Acknowledgement to Baird's Communications.

Conclusion

Promotion is the term used to describe all the methods available for communicating with customers and potential customers. This communication normally contains both information and persuasion. Promotion also refers to the way in which products are presented to customers to match their needs and perceptions. The correct promotional mix is arrived at by considering what has to be communicated to which groups of people and then selecting the most cost-effective media to carry that particular message. A range of methods are used and it is important for them to be carefully planned so that they operate in support of one another in the integrated campaign.

Case study   FIFA World Cup: What it means to South Africa

FIFA World Cup. What it means to South Africa

The right to host the 2010 FIFA World Cup brings South Africa a unique opportunity that extends well beyond football. One of the biggest impacts will come from the phenomenal marketing and communication opportunity it will offer the country and the continent. As world attention focuses on the first African Word Cup, this is an opportunity for Africans to tell their own stories and to showcase South Africa and the continent

National Communications Partnership

To help make this dream possible, a 2010 National Communications Partnership (NCP) was formed in early 2006 through the efforts of the South African Government Communication Information Systems department (GCIS) and the International Marketing Council of South Africa (IMC) together with a group of private sector corporate communicators.

They identified the need for some facility to ensure a well co-ordinated marketing and communication campaign in the build up to 2010 to maximize tourism and foreign investment opportunities for many years beyond 2010, as well as to mobilize South Africans across sectors as hosts and to build national pride.

Membership of the NCP now stands at over 250. These are leaders across sectors and disciplines – marketing, advertising, communication, public relations, creative industries, tourism in the public and private sectors. The work of the Partnership is driven by a task team representative of the various disciplines and sectors which meets monthly.

The Partnership's Role

The Partnership's role is to promote coordinated local and international communication so that the many communication agencies and role players speak with one powerful voice to maximize the benefit of hosting the 2010 FIFA World Cup for the country and the continent.

The Partnership therefore provides a strategic framework for communication – a point of reference for communicators in the period leading up to and during 2010. "Its function is to promote coherence of message and to provide forums of information-sharing and coordination, mutual support for campaigns, strategy formation and to jointly address issues as they arise". (NCP: 2009)

The Partnership should, however, not be seen as a new communication agency. Its many member entities – SA Tourism, the International Marketing Council, South African Airways, Government, 'Proudly South African', the Organizing Committee, private sector and civil society will all embark on communication in the context of 2010 as per their respective mandates and roles. "However, we believe communication will be more powerful because communicators are working together in partnership, sharing a common vision and common message". (NCP:2009)

Economic Benefits

According to a study by Grant Thornton Strategic Solutions in 2008, the 2010 World Cup is set to contribute approximately $5.5 billion to the SA economy and create 415 000 new jobs. "The contribution to SA's gross domestic product (GDP) is made up of the $3.3 billion in direct spending on stadiums and infrastructure, the spectator trip expenditure of $800 million, ticket sales of $600 million and sponsorship deals of $75 million. The expected tax income to government is around $1.9 billion". However, what should also be taken into account is the cost of debt repayment for such an event.

The biggest single benefit is going to be in tourism. The amount of money to be spent by African nationals and foreign tourists is projected to be around $850 million, which is regarded as a conservative figure.

The number of foreign tourists expected to travel to South Africa is estimated to be around 480 000. These include foreign nationals, who will travel from around the globe and 150 000 African neighbours who will come across our borders. Already South Africa hosts in peak summer months almost 870 000 foreign tourists, so the country should easily be able to handle the influx of tourists in June and July, the off peak months, for the six week competition In addition there are the eyes of 35-40 billion TV viewers that will be watching intently for this entire period as the competition unfolds.

The resulting tourism legacy according, to Grant Thornton, will be two fold.

Crucially, the event will make South Africa a better, more widely known and understood destination, with – barring no major problems – an enhanced reputation for service and a quality travel experience. It will also leave behind a greatly improved tourism infrastructure, in the form of increased accommodation (about 35 new hotels will have been built); bigger buses, coach and hire car fleets; better tourism information and destination management; and more efficient tourism supply chains. As far as further long term benefits are concerned South African tourism can expect between 130 000 and 290 000 extra foreign arrivals a year from 2011 through 2015 on account of the World Cup effect.

The legacy of the competition

As a result of the competition

- ten new or redeveloped stadia will have been constructed;
- with an advanced, well developed technical infrastructure in place, visitors to South Africa will have the latest technology at their disposal
- South Africa's national broadcaster the SABC will have broadcast 64 World Cup matches live. Some 300 broadcasters and 18000 journalists will cover the games;
- physical infrastructure will have been upgraded on a major scale in all the main centres where the games have been played
- accommodation will be plentiful and of a very high calibre in all the host cities. FIFA requires 55 000 graded rooms a night for the FIFA family during the tournament.

South Africa has over 100 000 graded rooms in the country and hundreds of thousands of ungraded rooms available to visitors

- pre and post 2010 tourism experience will be exceptional. Tourism SA is in the process of linking 2010 to a range of other tourism experiences throughout the country and the region;
- travel throughout the region will be relatively easy and seamless. Tourists will now have a UNIVSA to travel in the region on a single visa;
- a set of legacy projects of benefit to the continent as a whole will have been executed. These include "Win with Africa, in Africa" the building of 53 'state of the art' synthetic pitches in each country in Africa, "Silencing the Guns" a campaign to facilitate the replacement of guns with radios, "My Game is Fair Play", an initiative to mobilize politicians to sign an undertaking based on fair principles, the launch of a "2010 Peace African caravan" supported by some of the continent's leading soccer players and "My 2010 School Adventure" road show which seeks to promote both education and participation in soccer.

Dr Nikolaus Eberl, author of Brand Ovation:How Germany won the World Cup of Nation Branding believes South Africa too can transform itself just as Germany did in 2006 by hosting a successful FIFA World Cup.

I believe African and South African comunicators and the media, as well as the people of South Africa prior to and during the competition will be responsible for changing international perceptions of the country and the continent. But in order to be successful, South Africa needs to tap into its culture of Ubuntu in order to win the hearts of international visitors in 2010 much as Germany's friendly visitor's campaign did. South Africa and Africa, also needs to make its heroes known to the world.

In the final assessment it will be through the 2010 National Communication Partnership and other initiatives, that the Public Relations profession can play a meaningful role in the successful branding of South Africa and the continent. Both the African Public Relations Association (APRA) with its 15 or so member associations and the South African body PRISA, the Public Relations Institute of Southern Africa, can actively support these initiatives. The challenge is to begin to change the image of the continent from one which is perceived as poverty-stricken and unstable to one that is stable, prosperous and proactive. The 2010 FIFA World Cup is expected to provide that opportunity to start to make the difference.

Cape Town with the new Greenpoint Stadium in the foreground

References

Address by Minister in The Presidency, Dr Essop Pahed, on the occasion of the opening session of the 2010 National Communication Partnership Conference. July 2008: Sandton SA Yearbook 2008/2009. GCIS:Pretoria.
'2010 FIFA World Cup South Africa: Government Preparations 2008'.
Key facts: Government preparations for 2010 World Cup South Africa 2008. GCIS:Pretoria.
Africa's time has come! South Africa is ready South Africa's preparation for 2010 and the impact the 2010 World Cup will have on South Africa 2007. GCIS: Pretoria.
Impact of the 2010 FIFA World Cup. Study by Grant Thornton, November 2008: Johannesburg.

Further reading

Engel, J.F., M.R. Warshaw & T.C. Kinnear. 1983. *Promotional Strategy*. New York: Irwin.
Koekemoer, L. (ed.) 2003. *Marketing Communications*. Cape Town: Juta.
See Chapter 5, on Public relations and marketing, and the PRISA reading list at the end of the book for various other sources.

Chapter 24

Sponsorships

When you have read this chapter, you should:

- know what the essential elements of sponsorship are;
- understand the difference between sponsorship and donations;
- be aware of the origins of sponsorship;
- be able to identify the main objectives of sponsorship;
- be familiar with elements that form the framework on which companies build a systematic approach to sponsorship;
- be able to analyze some of the reasons why companies provide sponsorships;
- be able to draw up selection criteria to judge sponsorships.

Over R6 billion is now being spent by a whole host of companies in the lucrative sponsorship market. It is sometimes difficult for laypersons to link the sponsor with an event, but it should be seen as an investment of shareholders' funds and assessed in the light of returns on that investment.

Such has been the interest in recent years in the range and scope of sports sponsorship that a special South African Sport Sponsors' Association (SASSA) was established. SASSA seeks to encourage and develop the sponsorship of sport to the satisfaction of the sponsors and the sponsored. Its aim is to protect sport through its members' sponsorship, to co-operate with everyone who has the interests of sport at heart, and to disseminate information both in and outside the association.

Sponsorship is not restricted to sport, but is also put to effective use in the promotion of cultural events, for example the National Arts Festival held every year in Grahamstown, part sponsored by Standard Bank and FNB.

Definition

The essential elements of sponsorship are the following:
- a sponsor makes a contribution in cash or kind to an activity which is in some measure a leisure pursuit, either sport or within the broad definition of the arts;
- the sponsored activity does not form part of the main commercial function of the sponsoring body;
- the sponsor expects a return beyond simply creating awareness and publicity;
- the sponsor expects to generate increased sales and, therefore, generate additional revenue.

Background

The difference between sponsorship and donation

The third element mentioned above, that the sponsor expects a return in terms of publicity, distinguishes between sponsorship and donations. However, the terms are sometimes interchanged and it is not unusual to refer to donations by individuals (as opposed to organizations) as sponsorship, as in the case of sponsored walks for charity. In general, however, the term 'donation' refers to financial or material assistance given without the expectation of any return, even in the form of publicity.

Sponsorship is essentially a business deal which is intended to be to the advantage of both the sponsor and the sponsored. If successfully designed and carried out, with properly defined objectives, sponsorship arrangements can be of real benefit to the community in providing events and facilities which would otherwise not be affordable. A number of companies make a clear distinction between their sponsorships and donations, regarding them as quite separate activities to which different criteria apply.

What sponsorship is not

Although for some companies sponsorship expenditure comes out of their advertising budget, it is important to be aware of the distinction between sponsorship and advertising. This distinction is often controversial, especially in connection with television coverage of sport. The amount of direct linking between sponsored activities and advertising allowed under United Kingdom and South African regulations is not nearly as great as in the United States and some European countries – a fact of which international companies operating in a large number of territories are only too well aware.

A broad rule of thumb used by some companies is that if a mention of the company's name or product has to be specifically placed and paid for, it is advertising, whereas if it arises, without a specific fee, from an activity outside its main operations, it is sponsorship. For example, a financial organization would pay to advertise its financial services in the press, but would sponsor sporting events or literary, archaeological, or musical ventures, as a result of which its name would be mentioned in reports on those activities.

Origins

It is usually considered that commercial sponsorship of sport dates back to the nineteenth century. One of the earliest ventures on record is the sponsoring, in 1887, of the first motorsport event by the French magazine, *Velocipède*.

Private patronage of the arts, however, has a much longer tradition. In effect the commercial sponsor of today is the corporate successor to those wealthy and powerful individuals – kings and the aristocracy, princes of the church, and, later, those who acquired wealth from the Industrial Revolution – who used their money to assist artists and provided a living for composers, painters, and poets, who in return would grace their houses, or entertain their households. Both in the past and in modern times, those engaged in the creative arts, unless they were rich, have often had to sacrifice personal creative freedom for commercial considerations. Patronage offered an alternative in that, as long as the patron's taste was not outraged, the artist usually had a free hand. This element of artistic freedom is largely preserved in the most successful commercial sponsorships.

Characteristics of sponsorship

Sponsorship can be effectively used to achieve specific objectives. Characteristics of sponsorship include it being:

- a supplement to, but not a substitute for, already operative direct advertising;
- a means of reaching certain specialized markets directly or indirectly associated with the activity;
- a novel promotional and marketing medium;
- a means of influencing public corporate image and of increasing awareness of product and corporate identity, logos, and symbols;
- an association for fostering relationships, through entertainment, with business associates and the press;
- a beneficial influence on staff relations and morale;
- a means of involving industry in its surrounding community for specific reasons, such as attracting staff and forestalling adverse criticism;
- a vehicle for 'hard sell' promotions, for example personal appearances by sportspeople in their sporting gear selling the sponsor's products.

Guidelines

There are 10 elements which form the framework on which a company can build a systematic approach to, for example, a sports sponsorship. These elements should be considered as key result areas when evaluating involvement in sport via this modern form of patronage. They are the following:

1. the sponsoring company's aims and objectives;
2. the direct and indirect costs of the sponsorship;
3. the type and character of the sponsorship and its arrangements;
4. the structure, both nationally and provincially, of the administrative controlling body;
5. the participants in the sponsorship;
6. the officials in charge of the sponsored event;
7. the venue controllers, where the sponsored event is staged;

8. the degree of interest by the media in the sponsored event;
9. the audience attracted by the sponsored event, both live and through the media;
10. the government's involvement.

Each of these elements should be viewed on its own and collectively in relation to the form and stature of the event. The sponsor must also appreciate that any change occurring in one element will cause a reaction in one or more of the others.

Why companies sponsor

A company's self-awareness determines whether it can benefit from a sponsorship or not. Companies who have entered into sponsorships can be categorized as follows:

- those operating in a highly competitive market needing the stimulus of a novel, supplementary approach outside of their already substantial direct advertising media commitments;
- those who lack an established corporate or product image, or who need to change their existing image;
- recently formed conglomerates wanting to announce their new identity;
- those who rely heavily on an extensive market network that they want to court, mollify, or encourage to remain loyal;
- those experiencing public relations problems;
- those wanting the assistance of the media in order to establish closer links with a specific community;
- those who do not have a tangible product to demonstrate (for example, a service or semi-manufacturing industry), and want to attract wider attention.

Regardless of the category in which a sponsoring company falls, all wish to communicate with predetermined audiences. Looking at

237

more recent sporting sponsorships, the most common messages appear to be aimed at achieving:

- an extension of existing general public campaigns;
- a projection of reinforcement of corporate or brand images to create a climate of goodwill between the company and its important public;
- assistance in the launching of new symbols or logos and in projecting their identities;
- the establishment or improvement of relationships with retail distribution networks;
- an extension of community involvement.

Evaluation and selection criteria

All requests for sponsorship should initially be made in person and followed by a comprehensive written appeal. Companies will view sponsorship in a number of ways, including the following:

- Can the company afford to fulfil the obligation? The sponsorship fee is just the starting point. Count on doubling it to provide an adequate total event budget.
- Is the event or organization compatible with the company's values and mission statement?
- Does the event reach the company's target audience?
- Is there enough time before the event to maximize the company's use of the sponsorship?
- Are the organizers of the event experienced and professional?
- Is the event newsworthy enough to provide the company with opportunities for publicity?
- Will the event be televised?
- Will the sales force support the event and use it to increase sales?
- Does the event give the company the chance to develop new contacts and create new business opportunities?

- Can the company commit to this event on a long-term basis?
- Is there an opportunity for employee involvement? (Corporate sponsorships can promote employee goodwill and teamwork. Employee involvement can also contribute to the success of the event.)
- Is the event compatible with the 'identity' of the company's products?
- Is it possible to reduce the cash outlay for the company and enhance the marketing appeal of the event by trading off products and in-kind services?
- Will management support the event? (If the answer is 'yes' to all the previous questions, the likelihood of management support of the sponsorship is fairly high.)

Sponsorship checklist

The following questions will provide a guide to ensure that all aspects of the sponsorship are carefully considered.

1. Why are you entering into sponsorship?
2. Do your sponsorship objectives match the marketing objectives and contribute to their achievement?
3. Does everyone involved in the sponsorship (internally and externally) clearly understand the sponsorship objectives?
4. Are your objectives realistic and achievable relative to factors such as:
   - your budget allocation?
   - the types of events and activities available to sponsor?
   - your competitors' activities?
5. Is your company fully committed to making the most of the sponsorship in the short term and in the long term?
6. Do your sponsorship objectives provide clear benchmarks by which you can effectively measure sponsorship 'success'?
7. Do you have clear sponsorship selection criteria?
8. Does the proposed sponsorship reach the

target consumers with whom you wish to communicate?

9. Will your sponsorship branding have a reasonable chance of being seen and noted during the broadcast?

10. How does the proposed sponsorship fit in with your corporate marketing needs, product seasonality, and existing or planned marketing communication strategies?

11. Are your competitors involved in sponsorship? To what extent?

12. Is your event high profile enough to result in a dominant association?

13. What is the event profile of the proposed sponsorship (history, previous sponsors)? Can you displace the equity built up by the previous sponsor?

14. How relevant is the proposed sponsorship to your product/service? Is there synergy between the sponsor and the event or activity?

15. Does the proposed sponsorship convey the image you wish to project? Is there 'brand fit'?

16. Is the company prepared to fully market the proposed sponsorship?

17. Is the sponsorship affordable? If so, does it represent value for money?

18. Have you introduced leverage costs into your budgetary calculations? Does your budget for leverage at least match your sponsorship investment?

19. Have you added at least 10 per cent to allow for contingencies and unforeseen expenses?

20. What hospitality opportunities does the proposed sponsorship offer? Are these conducive to entertaining your VIP guests?

21. If the proposed sponsorship involves sport, what level of sports sponsorship does it involve – national team, provincial team, league, club, individual athlete, or development sponsorship?

22. Who are the technical sponsors involved in the proposed sponsorship? What are their branding rights? Will you be able to approve all technical sponsors involved?

23. What licencing and merchandising options are being offered as part of the proposed sponsorship? Do you have a control mechanism in place allowing you to approve all items that will feature your logo or theme piece?

24. What rights to exclusivity will be afforded to you nationally and internationally?

25. If you intend to sponsor a broadcast, what coverage and exposure opportunities are on offer?
- Are your key markets included in the coverage?
- Do you have a clear picture of estimated audience?
- Are audience guarantees included?
- How visible will your logo be during the broadcast? Have you assessed the place-ment and value of your logo's exposure during the broadcast?
- Is advertising space included in the broadcast sponsorship?
- Are there guarantees regarding the placement of your advertisements?
- Does the broadcaster allow the place-ment of your competitor's advertise-ments in and around your broadcast?
- What allowances does the broadcast-sponsorship contract make for product category exclusivity?
- What rights are you entitled to under the broadcast sponsorship contract?

26. Who owns the rights to the event?

27. Have you thoroughly investigated the event/sports marketing agent's credentials? Are you fully satisfied with the credentials?

28. Has a working committee been formed between you and the event organizer? Is there clear identification and agreement on each party's roles and responsibilities in operating the sponsorship?

29. What are the fees involved in the sponsorship and to what rights are you entitled under the contract?

30. What is the duration of the sponsorship and what are your rights to extension and renewal of the contract?

31. Does the contract offer protection from ambush marketing?

32. What is the payment schedule as specified in the contract?

33. Does your contract stipulate the means by which you will measure performance?
34. What cancellation terms for performance clauses are specified in your contract?
35. What geographical and territorial considerations are specified in the contract?
36. What contractual stipulations are there regarding dispute resolution?
37. What efforts have you made to build internal support and agreement across the marketing department, that is with the advertising manager, the sales manager, the public relations manager?
38. How do you intend to gain and maintain the support of senior management and stakeholders in the company?
39. How do you intend to account for and record all expenditure?
40. How do you intend to leverage your sponsorship involvement – what are your leverage objectives and tactics?
41. Have you considered all aspects in planning hospitality at the event – budget, venue, guest list, ticket distribution, programme of events, staff, contingency planning, finishing touches?
42. Do you have a detailed contingency plan?
43. Is your contingency plan funded?
44. Can you plan for any of the possible contingencies in your sponsorship contract?
45. What guarantees do the organizers provide against contingencies?
46. What measurement procedures will you use to evaluate the sponsorship?
47. What key areas will you evaluate?
48. What decisions will you need to make based on the results?
49. Who needs information about the results?

If you can provide informed answers to these questions you will be taking the skilful, well-managed approach to sponsorship enabling you to answer the ultimate question:

50. Has the desired return on investment been achieved?

Conclusion

Sponsorship is an important part of an organization's integrated marketing communication plan offering the opportunity of brand and relationship building and demonstrating relevance and social responsibility to the consumer and society.

It also offers some benefits such as building brand equity and providing good media exposure for the product and the company. However, it is open to ambush marketing, often requires renegotiation of broadcast rights, and could prove expensive for what is ultimately achieved. Above all, when setting sponsorship objectives, the sponsor should include both corporate and product brand objectives.

The main selection criteria for a sponsorship event should include the target market coverage, timing/seasonality, competitor activity, communication factors, event profile, potential media exposure, product relevance, image, budget/costs, and hospitality opportunities.

Often the choice is either sponsoring an existing event or creating an event, but either way it does not automatically ensure the broadcasting rights to the event. These must be negotiated separately.

Broadcast sponsorship is the only form of marketing communication that provides the marketer with an opportunity to dominate the 'stage' without having to share it with competitors. It therefore has the ability to break through the promotional clutter which traditional advertising is often unable to do.

Finally, when implementing the sponsorship, the marketer should gain and maintain the support of senior management and stakeholders, initiate leverage of the sponsorship, carefully plan hospitality for influential people and VIPs, and always have a contingency plan ready.

Case study BMI sports sponsorship: The South African Sponsorship market

Background

No area of marketing and promotion has grown more robustly over the last 20 years than has sponsorship. According to the annual BMI Adult SportTrack™ reports, by the end of 2008, direct sponsorship spend had grown from a base of R63 million in 1985 to R3 503 million, representing an average annual compound growth rate of about 19 per cent. Adding leverage spend, more than R6 billion was invested on local sponsorships in 2008 and that figure will escalate dramatically by 2010 with the FIFA World Cup.

Since 2007 the sponsorship market has been dominated by soccer, with the upcoming 2010 FIFA World Cup stimulating significant price increases for local properties. Led by the Premier Soccer League (PSL) and other 2010-inspired football deals, this trend continued through to the last quarter of 2008, slowed only by the impending global financial crisis.

As more and more companies looked for a way to benefit from the 2010 FIFA World Cup, many tried to get a foothold in the market through football related sponsorships. This in turn rapidly drove up the market price for soccer properties (as well as for other well positioned codes) – a phenomena now referred to as simply the "2010 Tax".

Soccer's impact on the overall sponsorship landscape is best summarized by the following excerpt from the 2007 BMI Adult SportTrack® report:

- media returns for all soccer sponsors alone increased from R1,5 billion in 2006 to more than R3,7 billion in 2008;
- in 2007, sponsors of soccer spent over R1 billion on their sponsorship rights (excluding leverage), representing more than 30 per cent of total direct spend in the overall SA sponsorship market;
- by comparison, Team South Africa went to the 2008 Beijing Olympics without a single sponsor on board;
- whereas year-on-year spend on soccer increased by almost 60 per cent in 2007, all other sports combined increased by less than 10 per cent.

Leverage budgets under pressure

However, it was not all good news for sponsorship as leverage budgets – which were already retracting under the current global financial meltdown - could not possibly keep pace with the 2010 inflationary pressures. As a result, whereas historically South African sponsors have spent more than 80 cents on leverage for every 1 rand directly spent (inclusive of broadcast rights) to acquire the sponsorship property, 2009 has seen this ratio dropping to under 70 cents to the rand.

Segmentation by sport type

More than 80 different sports codes receive at least some sponsorship money each year. In addition, money is also channelled into schools, universities, universities of technology and macro-sport codes, while individual sport personalities are also receiving an ever-increasing amount of sponsorship backing. Significant sponsorship packages are also sold for our participation in major world events. Similarly, naming rights for stadiums and other venues have also demonstrated consistent growth, further adding to the overall investment in the market.

However, despite the breadth of the industry, according to the latest available data the rich are getting richer. Led by soccer, the top five sporting codes as illustrated below now account for approximately 70 per cent of the total sponsorship spend in South Africa.

In addition, of course, to the overall popularity of the above top five codes, broadcast coverage also contributed significantly to their success. Of the codes mentioned, all received a disproportionate amount of the total broadcast coverage for sport. With more than 50 per cent of the total hours of television coverage allotted to the five codes, it is therefore not surprising that they also receive the lion's share of the total sponsorship rights fees in the country.

The major sport sponsors

Although history has proven that sport is, to a certain degree, recession-proof, it is safe to assume that this theory is being tested pretty dramatically right now. The financial crisis is bound to impact on sponsors over the next few years. The international credit crunch has already had an impact on sponsorship spend globally, particularly in the financial sectors, which are the largest sponsorship sector worldwide.

Isolating South Africa financials contribute more than R800-million in direct sponsorship spend a year, or almost 25 per cent of total spend. Together with Telecoms, these two industries account for approx 50 per cent of total spend and represent seven (i.e. 4 banks /3 telecoms) of the top 10 sponsors. They also represent the main sponsors in the biggest codes, namely soccer, cricket, rugby, and golf.

Non sports/music sponsorship trends

Away from sports, there is no doubt that "lifestyle" sponsorships have become a relatively cost effective tool for sponsors seeking to hone in on very specific markets, further creating the ideal platform for deeper emotional bonding and messaging to consumers. More than R300 million was invested by sponsors during the year 2007 on all disciplines within arts and culture. Of this, music in all its forms will account for almost half the expenditure, namely R148 million [up from an estimated R108 million by 2004 and R69 million in 2001].

The music sponsorship market continues to flourish internationally as the industry attempts to reinvent itself in the face of increased pressure from dwindling sales. Reasons cited by a growing number of sponsors who now believe Music to be one of, if not the best of alternatives to sport include:

- it offers significant numbers of followers and high entertainment value;
- it is also something that many consumers feel emotional about, which allows for that special connection to be created between a sponsoring company and consumers;
- music sponsorship is a way of connecting with the notoriously hard-to-reach 18- to 34-year-olds in a way that is genuinely engaging;

- music offers a strong platform for experiential marketing opportunities;
- music offers strong content opportunities and is not surprisingly becoming the battleground for cellular companies in Africa;
- lack of clutter/competition = Value for money on sponsorship spend.

Sponsorship measurement and strategy

As a result of the global economic woes, we are seeing a sharpening of below the line budgets, and a move to base more and more sponsorship decisions on measurable objectives. Additionally, the core key issues of any sponsorship investments are being examined under a microscope for conformance to legal, corporate governance, financial best practices and corporate marketing objectives. The new reality for sponsorships will be dominated, however, by one thing: a return to value

The strongest managerial implication to come from the wealth of available research is that it is no longer enough to consider exposure alone when selecting and evaluating sponsorships. More and more sponsors now understand that measuring and quantifying the amount of media exposure they are generating through the sponsorship is in fact, not Return on Investment (ROI).

While media exposure will always be an important benchmark, there is a continued realization of the importance of measuring - and increasing – levels of association and impact (i.e. awareness, image and engagement tracking). Therefore, working closely with your target market through the practise of qualitative market research to uncover opportunities, which can demonstrate fit and sincerity, will become a key part of sponsorship management going forward.

It is no surprise, therefore, that over the last five years many different tools and highly sophisticated techniques have been designed specifically to measure, evaluate, and maximize any association with a major sponsorship.

The measurement debate

Over the last few years, the new buzz word in global sponsorship measurement circles has been 'ROO' – or 'Return on Objectives'. While not a new concept, it has evolved and now often advocates leaving behind the "old-school approach" of logo counting, media equivalencies, impressions, "good corporate citizenship", and the like. Instead, it focuses strictly on measuring against objectives. Some proponents of ROO even go so far as to question whether it matters at all if a million people saw your logo – but not one of them changes their perception of your brand or their behaviour towards it? They claim that it does not matter because the objective is to measure changes in perceptions and behaviours.

While it is tempting to jump on this bandwagon and simply write off media tracking and awareness as irrelevant measures in this new world, there is, however, just one small problem... clearly only consumers that are aware of the brand or product can actually be influenced in any way.

Make no mistake; ROO is as relevant today as it has ever been. But evaluating only a single link in the marketing chain is misleading and will severely limit any real strategic insights that might otherwise have been gained.

In this regard, the South African market is in some aspects leaps and bounds ahead of their international counterparts, when it comes to sponsorship evaluation. Marketers here have for more than a decade, already been increasingly embracing a holistic approach to determining sponsorship effectiveness. To further enable the growth and maturity of the sponsorship industry, and more specifically to address the expressed needs of both sponsors and rights holders alike, BMI introduced SponsorMatch™. Offering analysis spanning areas such as property assessment, strategic fit analysis, target market penetration, rights audits, and fee assessment, the service is aimed at accommodating this shift in philosophy, providing both clients and rights holders alike with a step by step strategic process specifically tailored to channel sponsorship spend up front, to maximum effect and benefit in line with overall marketing and corporate objectives.

Ultimately, sponsorship research requires a more holistic approach that considers multiple points along the marketing chain. Different metrics provide different inputs on sponsorship effectiveness – whether it is exposure, consideration, engagement, brand impact or consumer equity. All of these factors are measurable and when combined, the resultant research is extremely valuable in obtaining a more thorough view of a sponsorship's overall effectiveness.

As rights fees continue to climb, only those willing to take a more strategic approach to sponsorship, fully integrating brand, and communication objectives with sponsorship objectives will unlock the true potential value sponsorship investments can deliver.

David Sidenberg
Head of Strategic Consulting & Rights Commercialisation, BMI Sport Info.
e-mail: sponsorvalue@mweb.co.

Further reading

Association of Marketers. 1997. *Sponsorship Guidelines*. Johannesburg.
Koekemoer, L. (ed.) 1998. *Promotional Strategy: Marketing Communication in Practice*. Cape Town: Juta.

Sponsorship is covered in the various texts on marketing management.

Individual companies heavily involved in sponsorships, such as South African Breweries, Vodacom, FNB, ABSA, and MTN in sport; and Standard Bank and Rembrandt in the arts, could be approached for further information.

Chapter 25

Exhibitions and trade fairs

When you have read this chapter, you should:

- be aware of some of the reasons for exhibiting;
- be able to prepare an exhibition budget;
- be able to draw up a public relations campaign for an exhibition;
- understand some of the problem areas you may encounter when exhibiting;
- be able to provide guidelines for staff manning an exhibition.

Even in this modern age of technology, the value of face-to-face communication cannot be underestimated. The slogan of the United States exhibition industry is that 'there are some things you just can't dotcom'.

In the United States, exhibitions have become a more important part of the business marketer's tool-kit. A study shows that among nine marketing approaches used by American companies with annual sales of more than $50 million, exhibitions have jumped from fifth place to third place in the past two years.

The increasing number of exhibitions and trade fairs now being held in South Africa is a sure sign of the growing importance of this medium as a means of presenting new products and services to both a select and a mass public.

Before a decision is taken to exhibit or not, it is important for a company to establish its objectives. Objectives may include:

- generating sales leads and making new contacts;
- achieving immediate sales;
- launching a new product or service;
- meeting existing customers or building customer loyalty;
- changing and enhancing company image;
- carrying out market research;
- generating press coverage;
- recruiting new agents or distributors;
- obtaining competitive intelligence.

The cost factor

It is the cost factor which finally determines whether to exhibit or not. Large exhibitors have enough money in their promotional budget to exhibit, but many smaller exhibitors only find out the true cost of exhibiting at the end of the exercise. The total cost is made up of items under the following headings:

- Rx per square metre for the floor rent;
- fees to stand designers, including erection staff;
- cost of constructing the stand;
- transportation of exhibits, panels, photographs, furniture, and fittings to the exhibition;
- insurance;
- cost of promotional literature;
- staff costs and general administration expenses.

It must be stressed that it is essential to draw up a budget carefully and to do everything possible to keep the cost of each item within the allotted amount. It is also general practice to allow a substantial sum, say 10 per cent, to cover contingencies.

Public relations for an exhibition

Your public relations policy for an exhibition should be based on the answer to the question, 'Why are we exhibiting at this show?' The public relations campaign should help attract the right type of audience to the stand, one whose composition and purchasing power are suited to the products being displayed. It should provide liaison with all media, particularly the press, to ensure maximum coverage of your participation prior to the exhibition and maximum attendance of members of the press at the stand. It should also provide the vital co-ordination between you as an exhibitor and the exhibition's own public relations department. Combined public relations campaigns can be extremely effective and therefore it makes sense to use all available resources.

Public relations and the organizers

The exhibition organizers' publicity campaign will be far broader in scope than your individual campaign, but you must know precisely how the organizers plan to carry out their campaign, so that you know how to plan your own promotional activities. You should try to co-ordinate your efforts with theirs and thereby save on expenses. An exhibitor's manual will probably be made available to you by the organizers. This manual provides details of the organizers' functions and services for the exhibition period, possibly including some of their publicity activities, and can serve as your handbook before, during, and after the exhibition.

The public relations methods that the organizers use could include visitors' leaflets, direct mail, advertisements in the press, a comprehensive catalogue, press receptions, posters for display outside or inside the exhibition hall, television and radio interviews, liaison among hotels, railways and airways, a daily news leaflet for exhibitors during the show, press releases, a conference programme, invitations on opening day, and special events to attract the press, trade, and public.

Direct mail

Direct mail is one of the most useful ways to promote your participation in an exhibition. Various types of printed material can be sent out to prospective visitors to encourage them to come to your stand, including letters giving general information about the exhibition; information in the form of a leaflet about the exhibitors on your stand and their products; an exhibitors' directory or a set of information sheets; a reply card that potential clients can fill in and return to you for more information; invitations to any special events you are staging in connection with your exhibit, such as a reception and free admission tickets to the exhibition, if this can be arranged with the exhibition organizers.

The first mailing should be sent to your prospective visitors about five weeks before the show opens. The mailing could include a general letter about the exhibition, a leaflet or brochure with information on your exhibits, and an admission ticket. A second mailing could be sent out approximately three weeks before the opening. It might consist of a letter giving more details about the exhibition, an exhibitors' directory, an invitation to a reception you will be holding at your stand, and a reply card.

Not everyone on your mailing list should be sent all of the direct-mail material you have prepared. Some potential visitors will be more important than others, so they should receive special consideration, such as invitations to your reception or a free entry ticket. The best way to handle the list of names for your direct mailings is to divide it into two or three groups, according to the degree of influence the person has on buying decisions in his or her company. Those in the top category should be sent the most complete set of material, including any special invitations you are sending out.

Press publicity programme

A press relations campaign can be one of the most effective ways to publicize your participation in an exhibition if your funds are limited. Press releases are one of the main features of a press campaign.

About two to three months before the opening of the show you should send out a general press release containing information about the exhibition (name, location, and date), your exhibits (what products are being shown) and your stand (main theme, number, location). This first general press release can be followed up by more specific press releases dealing with products to be displayed or the general development of your industry in this field. These more specific press releases should be sent out every week or two until the show starts. You can also put out press releases during the exhibition, covering such events as sales of your products made during the show and visits of important people to your stand.

All press releases that you send out should name the person to be contacted for more information, and include his or her address and telephone number. They should also give the name, location, and date of the exhibition

and your stand number. Even if some of this information forms part of the text of the press release, it should also be stated separately.

As with direct mail, press releases should be sent to a select audience. A major task in carrying out a press release programme is to develop a list of appropriate newspapers and journals to send your press releases to.

Make sure that you know the frequency of the publications to which you are sending press releases, as well as their copy deadlines, so that your press releases can be well timed.

Press conferences are another avenue for publicity that you should be able to use to your advantage. One possibility would be to organize a press preview of your exhibit just before the show opens and arrange for a government official to make a statement to the press. Before organizing a preview be sure to check with the show organizers about the timing, so that it does not clash with any similar events hosted by competitors. It should also be timed so that journalists can get away in time to meet their copy deadlines.

Other types of publicity

You will probably have limited funds for advertising your participation in the show. It is therefore advisable to pick out a few key publications in which your advertising will be most effective. The exhibition catalogue is perhaps your best advertising medium, because it also acts as a sales and reference book for visitors to the exhibition long after it ends. Another publication in which you might place an advertisement is the special issue that a leading trade journal might be running for the show. This type of advertisement could mention the products you will be showing, state your purpose (seeking agents, perhaps) and ask readers to write to you if they are interested in receiving more information on your products.

Receptions at your stand for clients are another means of publicizing your participation in the exhibition. One reception might be held at the end of the first day of the show. Others might be scheduled later on during the show for particularly important clients contacted during the show.

You should be able to generate additional publicity by co-ordinating your own publicity efforts with those of the organizers of the exhibition. Seminars, film screenings, VIP visits, and other events sponsored by the organizers may offer opportunities to make your products better known and initiate new contacts.

Personal approach

Public relations for an exhibition is an intricate communications exercise that relies as much on personalities as on a systematic and well-timed approach. You should not neglect the personal approach if you want to achieve the desired public relations results.

For instance, before the exhibition opens you should meet the exhibition organizers and make contact with their public relations staff, including their press officer, to establish your lines of communication with them. You should also get to know the editors of the main trade journals related to the products on exhibition. Good contacts with all these people will help make your public relations job easier.

Problem areas

Experience and research have shown that results do not always repay the time, cost, and effort involved in preparing for an exhibition. Lack of success may result from any one or a combination of the following:

- no defined objective, or too nebulous an objective;
- failure to establish a target group (which group do we wish to reach?);
- lack of staff communication on the objectives and benefits of the show and exhibiting techniques;
- no or inadequate staff training;
- lack of contact with visitors by staff or poor opening remarks;

- failure to establish visitor identity or potential;
- avoidable last-minute panics;
- understaffing;
- underselling or failure to use appropriate sales techniques;
- poor stand design with regard to objectives and accessibility;
- poor stand management;
- exhibiting the right products at the wrong time.

The most attractive exhibit will fail miserably if staff are not properly motivated. Sadly, this is the one vital area that is often neglected in the total exhibition build-up.

Many company directors would be appalled by the image that some of their staff project to potential customers.

It may be necessary for companies to offer incentives to members of staff who are alert, attentive, and thoroughly professional in looking after their interests at exhibitions. It could pay off handsomely.

Preparing for the exhibition: points to remember

Careful preparation is essential. The requirements for a successful exhibit are now discussed.

Decide objectives

New product launch? Public relations purposes? Make new contacts? Meet old clients? The exhibitor's objectives will clearly influence the design of the stand. For example, if a new product launch is planned, a good-sized demonstration area is needed, with facilities for the swift taking and following up of leads. There should also be plenty of both technical and sales staff on hand for queries.

Set a budget

The cost of the following items should be included in a budget:
- space cost, design, construction;
- preparation and transport of exhibits;
- graphic for display panels;
- on-site entertaining;
- personnel transport and accommodation;
- promotional plans surrounding the show.

Draw up a comprehensive written design brief

This is essential before commissioning a designer or contractor. It should include stand objectives, outline of the budget, overall dimensions of the stand, requirements for stand services such as water and waste, weights and sizes of any product or machinery to be displayed, details of company colour schemes to be followed, and special product features.

A written brief gives all parties involved a chance to comment before any money is spent, reduces the 'subjective' factors, and provides a benchmark against which the design can be evaluated.

Do not change the brief without telling the designer or contractor, or judge the work against anything other than the brief, which all concerned parties should agree before it is commissioned.

Devote time to briefing your designer and contractor. It generally saves a lot of telephone calls later! Make sure they agree on the brief, are happy with it, and think it is feasible. Encourage them to make suggestions. Apart from the value of ideas, they will identify more with the end design.

Appoint a reputable contractor and designer

Many contractors operate their own in-house design service, but will generally be happy to work with an outside designer of your choosing if you so wish. Ensure that your constructor is a member of the Exhibition Association of South Africa (EXSA). A full list of members can be provided by the organizers.

Set a high priority on good communications

Ensure that all personnel involved with the exhibition – both internal and external – are clear on relevant developments as they occur and on their part in them.

Hold briefing sessions – particularly on stand staffing and rotas so that everyone knows who does what on the stand. Are all those overseas representatives aware of the latest product modifications? Do the works manager and foreman appreciate that those samples have got to be in show condition four weeks before the exhibition to allow for plinths to be made?

Write short but informative reports after major meetings.

Appoint a stand manager early

If you are not to manage the stand yourself, make sure that a stand manager is appointed and the appointment is known early on. Ensure there is a deputy in his or her absence. It is essential that pre-show co-ordination and decisions about operations on the stand have one arbitrator whose authority is unchallenged, before as well as during the show.

Pay attention to detail – at all times

A grand design can be spoiled by something as mundane as difficult-to-read small type on your display panels. Constant vigilance will avoid these small but significant pitfalls. It is not pernickety. It is professional.

During the exhibition: points to remember

Careful preparation needs to be followed by disciplined hard work during the exhibition. What is needed is now discussed.

Measure

The following arrangements should be made to measure the effectiveness of your exhibition presence and the success of your stand objectives:

- Keep accurate records of all enquiries and follow them through.
- Establish, if possible, whether you would have got that order if you had not been at the show.
- Keep the analysis going. Sometimes contacts begun at an exhibition take time to flourish, but with careful nourishing they often do.
- Carry out a post-exhibition survey, either through a research house or via your own staff, with a simple postal or telephone questionnaire. It is worth establishing how widely you were seen; if your sales messages are noted; what customers liked or disliked, and did or did not understand.

Measure your effectiveness within a few days of the exhibition – you will be surprised how useful it can be.

Treat exhibitions seriously

Your show programme should be regarded as an integral and important part of your sales and marketing plan. Consider exactly what you want to get out of the exhibition and what you need to put in to get it.

Do not let your staff be put off by the change of surroundings or the 'glamour' of the show. You would not send three or four employees to lark about in a customer's reception hall; doing it on-stand is the same thing.

Staffing behaviour

Staff behaviour can make or break all the hard work done to prepare and build the exhibit. Stand staff should not:

- sit reading, or look bored;
- congregate into groups where a potential visitor feels embarrassed about interrupting;
- 'hover' or 'pounce' on people. 'Can I help you?' is the easiest way to get rid of visitors – it evokes the automatic response 'No, thank you.'

Stand staff should:

- be presentable and alert at all times (not just on the first day);
- treat every visitor like a VIP, whether he or she looks like a customer or not;
- take regular breaks (if they want to sit down and drink coffee they should do it off-stand, or in the stand lounge if there is one);
- keep two pairs of shoes on the stand. Manning an exhibition stand can be very wearing on the feet and it is amazing what a lift a change of footwear can give.

Staff should cultivate the art of unobtrusive observation, so they can tell, by the way a visitor begins to look around for a stand staff member, when he or she is ready to talk, or ascertain exactly what the visitor is studying. Then, in a relaxed manner, the staff member can offer information, for example, 'I see you're looking at our model XI. That's the one with independent suspension, but of course it's just one of the range. The others are over here if you'd like to see them ...'

With acknowledgement to Reed Exhibitions, SA.

Further reading

The organizers of national and regional exhibitions and trade fairs can be approached for literature. Individual exhibition organizers and consultants are also sources of information. A checklist is provided in Part IV.

Chapter 26

Conferences and seminars

When you have read this chapter, you should:

- be familiar with the guidelines to be followed in planning a successful conference or seminar;
- be able to draw up a master checklist to run a successful conference;
- be able to plan an internal staff conference at an outside venue;
- be aware of the advantages of video-conferencing.

At the outset, it is important to differentiate between seminars to which delegates are invited by a company or organization in order to promote its products and services, and commercial seminars or conferences arranged by professional organizers on behalf of institutes, associations, and trade bodies.

In both cases it is absolutely vital that the delegates come away with new-found knowledge and experience that can be applied to their own work situation. Gone are the days when companies were prepared to spend a great deal of money to send staff along to hear a 'big name' and allow them the luxury of a convivial atmosphere away from the office. Nowadays the content of all seminars must be well thought out, well presented, and relevant.

There are generally fewer problems when the company organizes and runs its own promotional seminars. It is not a question of how many delegates will be interested, but how to keep the numbers down to manageable proportions. The venue will determine the size of the audience, but from a general communications point of view it is better to have a series of seminars rather than have hundreds of delegates packed in for one special performance. A small cover charge for refreshments and lunch is perfectly fair since anything that is offered free of charge somehow loses credibility ... it might smack of propaganda!

Attention to detail is vital. It is rare for organizers to be given a second chance. We have all heard of a number of occasions where the public address system failed at the crucial moment, the late arrival of a key speaker upset the whole timetable, and the catering arrangements did not coincide with the planned breaks.

Guidelines to successful functions

The guidelines to be followed in planning a successful function are now discussed.

Research and development

It is important to define the goals of the event and the target audience right from the start. Even if the audience is made up of staff members (your own sales staff, accounts department, production people) it is necessary to define it carefully to determine the approach you should use to achieve your goals. This is also a good time to determine whether you need help. Your best ally is often the staff at the venue where you are holding your conference. It is vital to take them into your confidence. They know what resources and facilities are available at the venue. They also have considerable experience and have probably orchestrated your type of event many times before.

Finances

The next step is to predict costs, establish a budget, and stick to it. Again it is important to enlist the help of the venue staff, to check the completeness of your figures. Always allow at least 10 per cent for contingencies. Generally this will suffice to cover any items left out, emergencies, and special requests.

Dates and venues

The desired date, duration, and venue of the event must be determined and the venue inspected. During your inspection, choose the meeting rooms and check the ventilation, accommodation, and eating areas. Also check the access to these rooms. Go through the menus with the venue staff and determine what service delays you are likely to encounter.

Programme development

Get help in preparing your programme. Build in variety: move speakers around on a schedule, have sessions of different time spans, create diversions. Watch out for 'danger times', particularly the sessions immediately after morning tea and lunch. Also consider housekeeping requirements: conference rooms require fresh water and peppermints.

Publicity

If the conference is for internal staff, keep the participants informed with regular releases and updates. If the conference requires delegates to be away from home, make sure that spouses are informed in sufficient time for them to make their own alternative arrangements. Also ensure that contact phone numbers of the venue are available to all concerned. If the conference is a public affair and the delegates are drawn from outside, prepare news releases and distribute them well in advance.

Conference material

Most conferences require support material. It is wise to develop a central theme and use the same layout, heading, or colour paper for all announcements, brochures, notes, registration cards, and name tags. Develop a conference identity in much the same way you would develop a corporate identity. You will also need to consider the more personal handouts, such as air tickets, bus coupons, badges, name tags, briefcases, and special programmes for spouses.

Three-dimensional thinking

The message here is very clear. Try to 'live' the conference. Sit back, close your eyes, and run through the entire day. Go through all that will be required. Get your delegates there. Look after them while they are there and then get them back. Look at every activity slowly and carefully. For example, is there enough time to register the delegates? What will happen if many delegates arrive late – will you be able to cope with the rush? Can the dining room handle the meals in the time allocated? How busy is the venue generally? What will happen to the toilets during a rush time? Where will delegates park? Is the security adequate? Ask yourself these questions over and over again.

Think, too, of contingencies. What plans do you have to make in the event of bad weather? Think about the support staff. If, for example, you are having staff working overtime, what will you do about their meals and how will they get home? If staff have to prepare the venue in advance of delegates' arrival, have you allowed time for them to clean up and change?

Layout

Good physical arrangements can go a long way to making your conference successful. There are a number of ways in which a presentation can be laid out. These include:

- auditorium style;
- classroom style with straight desks;
- classroom style with herringbone desks;
- U shape;
- oval shape;
- the cocktail style (desks placed strategically around the room);
- the syndication style (separate rooms with table/s or grouping of tables and chairs in each room to facilitate discussion).

There can be variations of these styles, particularly when one uses trapezoidal tables, but these will generally be used in very specific learning situations. The important thing is to establish exactly why you require a particular style and to consider the applications, especially the use of visual aid equipment.

Avoid clutter. It is sufficient to have on the tables just the essentials: water, glasses, and peppermints.

Seating

Seating must be comfortable and not cramped – front to back or left to right. Provide plenty of aisles. Make sure that delegates know where the toilets are before you start your conference.

Look at items such as the positioning of lecterns in relation to the seating, and bear in mind that if the room is going to be darkened, the speaker may require some lighting to read notes.

Equipment

The most important item at any conference or seminar is the public address system. It is also often the piece of equipment that gives the most problems, so test it, check it, try it, and practise using it. When you test it, move around with the microphone. You may find that there are some areas where the microphone picks up other sounds. Nothing kills a production quicker than microphone squeal or feedback.

The next most common item of equipment is the overhead projector. Most suppliers have good booklets and instruction material on the correct use of an overhead projector. It can be most effective as a training tool. Apply the following hints to ensure success:

- Avoid putting the projector right in the middle of the room. People will have difficulty in peering around it and invariably the lecturer will stand next to it, which will also cause an obstruction. The most effective area for the screen is in the right-hand corner of the room with the overhead projector in the front and to the side.
- The screen should be equipped with an anti-keystone device and the image should fill the screen. Avoid having too small a screen, because the image will project beyond it and you will get distracting flashes of light on the wall. An equally bad alternative is having too large a screen, with a small scribble-filled circle in the centre that delegates are expected to read.
- Make sure the writing is legible.

Each piece of projection equipment should be carefully placed. Consider the obstruction it may cause for people sitting at the back of the room. You should place projection equipment as far back as possible, but ensure that it is still convenient for the speaker. Often the lenses on these pieces of equipment make it impossible for them to be placed as far back as you might like. Make sure that you, as well as the opera-tor, are familiar with all equipment and that you know where light switches and curtain controls are located.

Finally: never, never leave home without a conference kit. This is your lifeboat.

Conference kit

Super cleaning cloths	Safety pins	Matches
Masking tape	Drawing pins	Torch
Scotch tape	Paper clips	Band-aids
Double-sided tape	Ball of string	Screwdriver
Self-adhesive labels	Scissors	Pliers
Shorthand notebooks	Stapler	Knife
Ballpoint pens	Staples	Hammer
Pencils	Elastic bands	Glue
Erasers	Felt pens	Extension cord
Sharpeners	Whiteboard pens	Double adaptors
Prestik	Overhead projector	Plugs
Pritt	Pens	Coins or phone cards
Straight pins	Chalk	for public telephones

Master checklist

A master checklist is an essential feature of a successful conference. The secret of success is a detailed blueprint that covers every possible requirement. The task of drawing up a master checklist should be delegated to a single person who will then be in charge of all physical details.

Master checklist provided by hotel

A. Accommodation (agreement to be reached with hotel before conference)
1. Approximate number of guest rooms needed
2. Stipulate whether single, double, or suite
3. Room rates
4. Confirmation of reservations
5. Copies of reservations to those concerned
6. Date on which majority of group is arriving
7. Date on which majority of group is departing
8. Date on which uncommitted guest rooms are to be released
9. Hospitality suites needed or not; how many
10. Check rooms, bars, snacks, service time

B. Meetings (check with hotel before conference)
1. Floor plans furnished
2. Correct time and date for each session
3. Room assigned for each session, and rental
4. Seating number, seating plan for each session, and speakers' tables
5. Equipment for each session
6. Other special requirements (check immediately before meeting)
7. Cooling, heating system operating
8. Public address system operating, microphones as ordered
9. Recording equipment operating
10. Water pitcher, water, glasses for those attending
11. Overhead projector and screen
12. Pencils, note pads, paper
13. Lighting as ordered
14. Flowers, plants as ordered

15. Direction signs if meeting room is difficult to locate
16. Photographer present

C. Equipment and facilities
1. Special notes to be placed in guest boxes
2. Stage size
3. Chalkboards
4. Chart stands and easels
5. Film projector or videocassette recorder
6. Printing or photostat facilities
7. Dressing rooms for entertainers
8. Parking, garage facilities
9. Decorations
10. Agreement on total cost of extra services
11. Telephones
12. Stenographer
13. Flags, banners
14. Closed-circuit TV
15. Insurance on equipment taken out or security provided

D. Registration
1. Signs for registration desk
2. Registration cards: content, number
3. Tables, number, size
4. Computers
5. Personnel – own or hotel's
6. Bulletin boards
7. Telephones
8. Hospitality desk
9. Waste-baskets
10. Duplicate registration lists

E. General
1. Timetable of events: lunch, tea, dinner
2. Menu to be finalized
3. Special requirements for delegates
4. Special give-away souvenirs to mark the conference
5. Private bar facilities
6. Name tags for each delegate
7. Travel arrangements
8. Invitations sent out in time

Internal sales or marketing conference

Public relations staff are often called on to arrange internal conferences for staff at outside venues. Some of the planning considerations are now discussed:

Theme

It is important to choose the correct theme for a conference. For example, you cannot have a theme like 'The Winners' if, in fact, the sales team did not even reach half the target.

The theme should therefore be chosen with great care and can be emphasized by having it printed on:

- gimmicks and hand-outs;
- the invitations;
- banners which are part of the décor in the conference rooms;
- folders for documents;
- correspondence to be used as a follow-up after the conference.

Conference programme

The ideal conference combines the elements of involvement, humour, discipline, learning, control, and relaxation. All these factors, mixed correctly, can provide a most satisfying result – but above all, delegates must be kept alert and on their toes, because when aware of what is going on around them they are most receptive to the message one is trying to get across.

Participation by the delegates is therefore critical to the success of any conference. Guidelines for the 'working programme' are given below.

General

To maintain interest, start the second morning with a short film or audiovisual presentation. This should be about 15 minutes long – time enough to let all those who had a heavy night the previous evening think they have time to catch up on a few minutes' sleep. Then switch on the house lights and ask someone in the middle of the room a pertinent question about the presentation. Half the room will turn and

---

Working programme

A. Preparation (before conference)
1. Select participants
2. Collect data and audiovisual aids
3. Appoint leader and recorder

B. Approach to decision-making (during conference)
1. Define real problems and motivate group
2. List all possible solutions to problems
3. Eliminate, rearrange, and combine possible solutions
4. Select best solutions or combinations of solutions
5. Assign responsibilities for action: most assignments should be voluntary and no assignments should be assumed by the leader, who should be free to give advice and assistance

C. Follow-up (after conference)
1. Recorder to distribute minutes to participants
2. Participants to fulfil assignments and keep leader posted
3. Leader to assist participants with individual assignments and reports

---

watch, and everybody who was contemplating a quick nap will definitely think twice about it.

Delegates could also be given some task to accomplish during the evening recess. Make sure that it is followed up the following morning. This, hopefully, will keep most of the delegates out of the bar and ensure reasonably clear heads the next day. It will also give management an added incentive to get the people to their rooms at a reasonable hour. It is amazing how many people do not want to be seen the next morning as having let their side down.

Entertainment programme

From a motivation point of view, the entertainment programme should be well planned in order to maintain interest. In this instance, participation from delegates could provide a lot of fun. If the conference is a week or longer, the programme should leave at least one afternoon and evening free for delegates to do something of their own choice. The entertainment programme could include guest speakers, the final dinner, and light entertainment.

Guest speakers, if required, should be invited well in advance. The following aspects should be attended to (this checklist could be used for arranging any special entertainment):
- inform them of the time available to them;

- inform them of the type of talk you want them to give;
- will a fee or expenses only be charged?
- when is payment to be made?
- will the speaker require special equipment?
- has he or she been furnished with the programme as early as possible?
- has someone been designated to meet the speaker on arrival?

Generally, conferences are closed with a dinner or banquet. It is normally a formal function which has to be well planned. The following procedure should be followed:
- discuss the date, time, number of persons attending, and menu with the hotel personnel;
- send invitations to delegates and special guests, and receive their replies;
- print the menu and programme;
- make seating arrangements;
- provide name cards for tables;
- order décor and flowers;
- arrange for a band or music;
- determine special drink requirements;
- see to it that cups and prizes are engraved and available;
- appoint a master of ceremonies;
- inform all people who are expected to make speeches;

255

- arrange for a photographer to be present;
- identify people who follow a particular diet (halaal, vegetarian, kosher).

Light entertainment would largely depend on what the hotel has to offer and should be investigated when searching for a venue. Hotels offer the following in the line of entertainment:
- cabaret;
- sports facilities (could be used for competitions);
- disco;
- casino.

All of these could be used very effectively or special arrangements could be made. A few ideas for special entertainment are given below:
- a fancy-dress dinner or a dinner with a specific theme, for example an Eastern Evening at which people dress accordingly and Eastern food is served;
- competitions such as a darts competition or mixed hockey;
- a beach braai or a party on a boat;
- a medieval evening;
- a prominent television personality to do a solo show.

Photographs are a must at these functions. They can be given to delegates after the conference and used for house journals or just serve to provide a laugh and to bring back happy moments of a successful conference.

Video-conferences

The 1990s saw a new kind of conference emerge in the United States: video-conferences. Proponents of this technological brainchild cite several advantages, which can all be summed up as cost- and time-effectiveness. For example, instead of having top executives spend hours travelling to conference venues (remember: time equals money) and having companies foot hefty hotel and expense bills, the executives stay put and the conference is 'brought' to them by means of a sophisticated, full-function video-conferencing unit. Although a video-conferencing unit is by no means cheap, the money spent on purchasing one will be recouped relatively soon through savings effected through its use.

Still, there are disadvantages to this method of conferencing. It cannot be denied that the immediacy, the sense of 'being there', is lost with video-conferencing. Another significant, universally reported drawback is the loss of body language feedback. Since body language contributes at least as much to communication as the spoken word, there is a definite danger of losing some of the finer nuances of what is being communicated.

Potential drawbacks include anything from accidentally hitting the wrong control button, to deliberately pressing the mute button when a conflicting opinion is being expressed, to power failures. But then, unless proper control is exercised, technical problems can sink practically any 'conventional' conference as well.

Useful tips when video-conferencing are the following:
- Be on time and stick to the agenda. Telephone lines are booked in advance, requiring fixed start and stop times. Benefit: Video-conferences tend to be more productive because of the time limitations.
- Introduce yourself and wait your turn. Jumping in while others are talking creates confusion. Most video-conferences have one camera at each location, so you're not seen when offering offhand comments. Advice: If you need to interrupt, introduce yourself and look up to see if you are on or off camera.
- Use a normal tone of voice and speak clearly. The microphones used in video-conferences are sensitive, but the audio portion can have a short delay. Beware: If you subconsciously tap pencils, drum your fingers on the table, or rustle papers, you will play havoc with the audio.
- Prepare graphics, but make them easy to understand. Use large type, limit charts to bar and pie formats in a horizontal format, and don't crowd the page. Acid test: Put

graphics on the floor. If you can read them from a standing position, they will transmit clearly.

- Some corporates have very fast connections, but realize that video speed can be disconcerting. Do not be surprised that the video runs at 15 frames per second (television images run at 30 frames per second), giving the impression of swimming under water. How to handle: When you are on camera, do not jump around or use your hands a lot. You will quickly adjust to viewing the slower speed video.

- Rely less on body language. Asking for a wider camera angle helps those who are animated when speaking. Strategy: Depend on facial expressions and your voice to communicate.

- Appearance counts – this is television. Shiny noses, foreheads, bald spots, and jewellery reflect light. Plan ahead: Use a tissue in private to blot perspiration; dress simply in unpatterned pastels and dark colours.

- Anticipate problems and be considerate. Fax copies of your presentation materials to participants in advance. Follow up with a report, minutes, or a to-do list. Remember: video-conferences are still new for most people, so make the participants comfortable and prepare for what can go wrong with your presentation.

Although there will always be a place for lavish conferences hosted in state-of-the-art conference centres across the world, video-conferences are certainly here to stay. The prudent public relations practitioner will be aware of this and see to it that his or her company is properly prepared to meet the challenges presented by this new medium. By adhering to the principles outlined above you will go a long way towards mastering the art of video-conferences.

Case study Business tourism

The business tourism industry contributes an estimated R20 billion per year to South Africa's GDP. This represents around quarter of a million jobs, with R6 billion being paid in salaries each year, and more than R4 billion in taxes. In short, the sector is a highly lucrative one, which contributes enormously to economic development and poverty alleviation.

Business tourism is the highest yielding and one of the fastest growing sectors in the world. Working on increasing South Africa's slice of the pie, South African Tourism has rolled out its business tourism initiative – the Business Unusual global marketing campaign in Amsterdam, London, and Singapore. The aim of the campaign is to see South Africa break into the top 10 by 2010.

According to research published by Grant Thornton, South Africa hosts around a thousand international conference events annually, drawing more than 150 000 foreign Meetings,

Incentives, Conferences and Exhibitions (MICE) participants.

Overall, the local and international MICE industry is estimated at 101 000 events a year, attended by 11 million participants, and representing almost 15 million delegate days.

South Africa's world class facilities, like the International Convention Centres in Durban, Cape Town, and Sandton make it possible to host both large and small gatherings with the expertise of conference managers ensuring each event is run professionally. Additional convention centres are being planned for other centres in South Africa to tap into this lucrative market.

The ICC Durban has now completed a R406 million expansion and now stretches over a kilometre in length and is over 60 metres wide on a single, column-free level. Able to host an expanded International Tourism Indaba, it makes it the biggest conference facility in the country.

The Cape Town International Convention Centre (CTICC) is also having great success in attracting some of the world's major medical and scientific conferences.

The Sandton Convention Centre and other smaller centres, strategically placed at the heart of the country's business hub in Gauteng, are also benefiting from expansion in this market sector.

When one considers that the average business visitor spends as much as three times more money than his or her leisure counterpart, it is clear that this sector holds enormous growth potential for South Africa. It is estimated that by 2010, business tourism will account for more than a third of the world tourism market.

Please also consult the Southern Africa Conference, Exhibition and Events Guide: *gomesi@iafrica.com*; (SAACI) the Southern African Association for the Conference Industry: *www.saaci.co.za*; (EXSA) Exhibition Association of Southern Africa: *www.exsa.co.za*; ISES-Europe, Middle East (EMEA) Affiliate branch of the International Special Events Society (ISES): *www.iccaworld.com*.

Sources: *www.capeconvention.com*; *www.icc.co.za* and *www.saconvention.co.za*.

International Convention Centre, Durban, that can now host over 13000 indoor delegates for major events.

Further reading

The various associations listed above, together with individual hotels and conference centres, will be happy to provide potential clients with details of their facilities. These can be researched through their various websites.

Chapter 27

Plant openings and open days

When you have read this chapter, you should:
- be aware of the main considerations in planning a plant or factory opening;
- be able to plan the event;
- be familiar with some of the reasons for having an open day;
- know what to do at an open day.

There are many occasions at which a company can present its products or services to its public – open days, exhibitions, cocktail parties, in-house seminars, and so on. However, the opening of a new plant is a very special event, not only as a symbol of progress for the company but also for employees, the customer, or user of the product, the industry in which it operates, the local community, and of course the country.

Before drawing up the programme for such an event, the public relations practitioner must first do an assessment.

Plant openings

Assessment

Doing an assessment entails asking the following questions:
- Why is the plant being opened – is it new, a transfer, or an extension?
- What are the reasons for building the plant in South Africa and in that specific community (economic, pollution, labour, transport, market proximity)?
- What progress has the company made to date in South Africa, and overseas, if applicable?

Checklist for planning and organizing the event

What
1. Guest list – employees, press, customers, government officials
2. Printing of invitations and reminders
3. Display signs for tour areas
4. Red-ribbon tour route on floor
5. Caterers arranged
6. Tents or canopies provided
7. Provision for rain
8. Ample parking – police assistance or attendants

9. Traffic directions (AA signs)
10. Adequate toilet facilities
11. First-aid room with nurse or doctor
12. Tour guide or hostess (uniform, number stationed, and who)
13. Identification of hostesses
14. Supervisors in work areas
15. Name tags (quantity, printed)
16. Designate out-of-bounds areas
17. Thorough cleaning – inside and garden
18. Company and national flags
19. Reception line
20. Public address system
21. Invite press – issue pre-printed speeches (press kit)
22. Samples of company products, if applicable
23. Product display
24. Overtime payment for workers who do extra work
25. Photographs
26. Printing of company house magazine to commemorate the event
27. Corsages for women
28. Safety clothing and hats, if necessary
29. Insurance – all guests to be covered in case of accidents
30. 'After the party's over' – cleaning, dismantling, traffic plans

How
1. Do a 'dry run' to see if everything flows smoothly.
2. Is a VIP from 'outside' to open the proceedings?
3. Is company chief (local or overseas) to open the proceedings?
4. How many speeches?
5. Cutting ribbons, turning on the machinery, opening of gates and doors
6. Will it be recorded?
7. Is there a theme, e.g. 'Partners in Progress'?
8. Give out programmes of the event to all guests.
9. Set up a work committee.
10. If children are present, consider entertainment, a crèche and suitable refreshments.

Where
1. Outside or inside the plant
2. If the event takes place away from the premises, provide suitable transport.

When
1. Date
2. Exact time
3. Expected weather conditions
4. Check public, religious, and school holidays.
5. Consider having an open day for employees and their families, perhaps the Sunday before the opening.

Implementation of specific activities

- set up work committee;
- assign responsibilities;
- draw up a strategy and action plan with responsibility and timing.

Follow-up (measurement)

- meet with work committee and other helpers;
- ask for feedback from employees;
- request salespeople to question customers who attend;
- evaluate press reports and coverage;
- send a questionnaire to a selected few and ask for comments.

A detailed checklist can be found in Part IV.

Open days

In contrast to plant tours, special conferences, news conferences, or other special events, an open day provides the opportunity for company officials to meet the company's 'public'.

Why have an open day?

These are some of the reasons for having an open day:

Function planner: Plant opening

Guest List	Invitations	RSVP	Venue	Welcome desk
Media	Media invitations	Call-backs	Décor – flowers	Labels arranged alphabetically
Guests for plant opening	Media follow-ups	Final number of guests	Seating arrangements	Staff to greet guests on arrival
Guests for post-event		Confirmation to caterers	Security	Media table

Equipment	Parking/Security	Catering/Bar	Press kits	Entertainment
Sound System (Amp) x 2	Parking attendants	Tea and coffee	Press release compilation and approval	Tour arrangements
Cabled mic and stand x 2	Entry permits	Menu selection and approval	Photographic material sourcing	Guides
Radio lapel microphone	Arrange security	Full bar or wine and malt	Press kit folder	
Lecturn	Sign posted	Special dietary requirements	Fact sheet	
9 x 6 screen x 2				
Video machine				
Video projector				

Speeches	Printing	Décor	Signage	Gifts/Give-aways
Number	Invitations	Flowers/plants	Welcome display	VIPs
To provide background material	Programme of events	Welcome desk	Display stands	Guests
Keynote address	Folders	Buffet tables	Banners	Staff
Welcome	Literature	Bathrooms	Lecturn signage	
Thank you	Media kit		Directional signage	
MC			Bathrooms	
			Media boards	

Source: Umbogintwini Operations Services

- *Community relations.* Local goodwill is important, particularly if the community provides labour and essential services (transport, sport, water, fire prevention). A company with a good reputation attracts better workers. A good relationship with local authorities can assist in obtaining better co-operation (parking, taxes, labour regulations). An open day provides the opportunity for influential people in the local community to get acquainted with your company.
- *Customers.* A new product, special equipment, or a revolutionary process can attract customers to your company at an open day. Regular open days can allow for a group of customers with similar or even different interests to visit your facilities and meet senior employees. Certain organizations, such as mines and the Council for Scientific and Industrial Research (CSIR), prefer a scheduled open day to plant tours since this is less disruptive. Furthermore, an open day can be more lavish, operations can be better explained, and models and films can be used to greater effect.
- *Company employees.* Your employees are your greatest asset. To keep them motivated is to keep them involved and make them feel that they are part of the organization. Their work environment is more than just a place to work. Spouses, children, and family all have a special interest in where Dad or Mom works.
- *General public.* This is more applicable in the case of municipalities, universities, and institutions such as the South African Bureau of Standards (SABS) where it is important to show taxpayers what is being done with their money.
- *Shareholders.* They are the actual 'owners' of a company and as such they have a right to see what is being done with their money.
- *Media.* Unless the event is really of great significance, media publicity and news conferences should be avoided. On the other hand, if you want to highlight an important event without resorting to the ordinary news conference, an open day (provided it is really unique) can help gain more editorial attention.

When and how long?

An open day can be held at any suitable time. Morning, afternoon, all day – it depends on what you have to show. An all-day event can be too lengthy for a business or the press, and to suit them it may be better to opt for a half-day event. An all-day event is fine for families (10:00 to 15:00) and Saturday is often a good choice. Organizations such as the SABS, CSIR, or universities and technikons may prefer a half to a full day.

Who is the public?

The nature of the business or institution determines the target public, among whom are the following:
- shareholders – associated with listed companies;
- employees – important to all organizations;
- customers – dealers, distributors, wholesalers;
- general public – students, schoolchildren, housewives, institutions, clubs;
- media – general lay press, technical press, radio, television;
- financial institutions;
- local community.

What happens at an open day?

Much depends on the reasons for holding the day, but the following ideas could be expanded upon:
- an exhibition of the company's products;
- a talk by one or more senior officials (welcome, history, objectives, policy);
- the presentation of awards (performance, sports, long service);
- film or slide shows,
- a product launch (particularly for customers and the media);
- a tour of the plant and facilities;

- demonstrations of new equipment and techniques;
- sporting events (such as soccer or athletics);
- picnic, luncheon, cocktails, tea and biscuits;
- entertainment for the children (for example pony rides);
- give-aways (presents, gimmicks, souvenirs, samples).

An open day must not be "just another one of those days" which one feels obliged to attend.

It is important to make it different, and above all, to ensure that it will be a success by making it a professional affair.

Further reading

Major companies or consultants who have handled such events could be a good source of additional information.

Chapter 28

Corporate image and corporate identity

When you have read this chapter, you should:

- know the difference between corporate image and corporate identity;
- be familiar with some of the changes in corporate design;
- understand how to implement a new corporate identity programme;
- be familiar with a corporate identity checklist;
- be aware of some of the factors that affect corporate image.

All companies need to market themselves, and marketing can take many forms of which advertising is but one. In marketing anything, whether a company, product, service, country, even a person, it is necessary to define the touchpoints, where interaction takes place with stakeholder.

Corporate image is the impression created by 'how you look, what you say, and what you do'. Corporate identity is the visual system for controlling how you look.

Since 'image' is the result of all communication, whether deliberate or not, it is impor-

tant for companies to set standards for themselves which truly measure their reputation.

The problem in most cases is that businesses leave the design of their products to engineers, the design of their factories and stores to architects or contractors, their advertising to advertising agencies, their letterheads and business cards to printers, their packaging and signs to suppliers, and so on. Each one, while doing their best to communicate the identity of the business as he or she sees it, develops a different corporate identification. The result is a totally confused picture.

Research has shown that a company with a good corporate image and reputation has the following advantages:

- it attracts the best employees;
- it is trusted as being ethical and behaving with integrity;
- products or services provided by the company can command premium pricing;
- a strong brand delivers emotionally and functionally, so creating loyal customers and consumers and buyers (Proctor & Gamble defines end users in this fashion).

As a result of the above, the listed shares of a company with strong brand(s) will outperform those that do not.

Image development

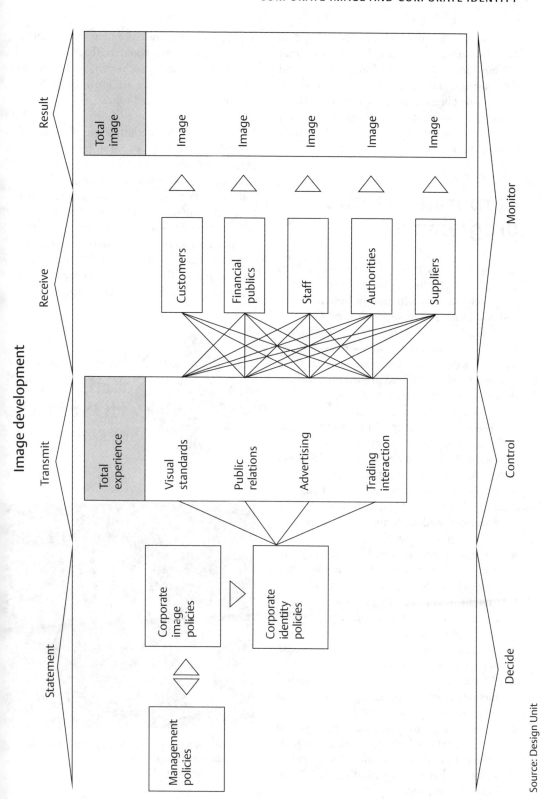

Source: Design Unit

The British publication Brands & Branding (The Economist/Interbrand) records: 'that Warren Buffet, the world's most famous (and least sentimental) investor, told a group of investors that brand is the most important factor in deciding where to invest. His criteria: 1) brand; 2) good management team; 3) a strong balance sheet.

Corporate identity programme

An organization's image – its reputation – is among its most valuable corporate resources. It is a priceless asset which must be both nurtured and readjusted in keeping with events and the times, and with changing business realities. When an organization has to reposition its image, it is critical for future success that these changes are efficiently and professionally introduced, and that the ultimate results reflect management's new or desired image.

The success of a corporate identity programme is dependent on several factors:
- total commitment and active participation on the part of senior management;
- the development and selection of suitable and relevant visual concepts, which can be promoted and communicated to achieve the desired objectives;
- the quality and standard of the design of the visual elements, which in turn are themselves dependent on an accurate establishment of objectives, adequate research, and a systematic and creative approach in the actual design process;
- the impact and clarity of the messages being communicated;
- the standard of control both in the implementation of the programme and in the ongoing management of the programme;
- the institution of systems and processes to ensure that the communicated image is reflected in all the activities of the organization – that the organization is, in fact, how it views itself;

- the ongoing measurement and analysis amongst all stakeholders that the desired effects are being achieved, and that the brand(s) continue to grow both brand equity and financial value.

With reference to the last point, it should be appreciated that a corporate identity programme which is properly planned and developed can play a significant role, right from the start, in improving staff performance and attitudes. It should be conducted in conjunction with systematic and relevant training in communications. Even the best conceived, planned, and executed programme cannot, in the long term, persuade the world that an organization is something that it is not in practice.

An ambitious programme by Rotary International to "Kick Polio out of Africa". This is their logo.

Corporate structure

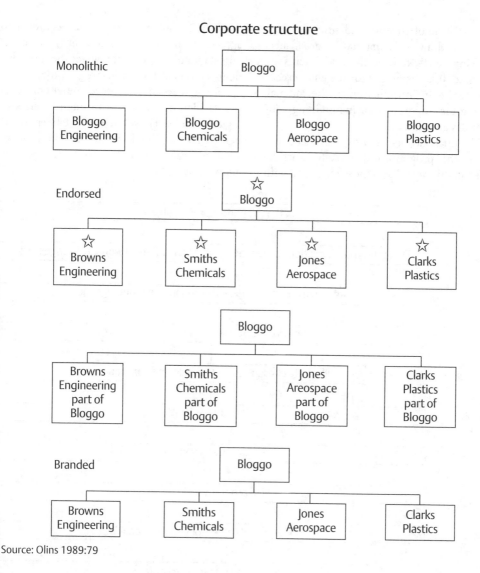

Source: Olins 1989:79

Implementing a corporate identity programme

To lay the foundation for a corporate identity programme, it is important to find out a number of things about the particular company, for example its background and activities, its long-range plans, the image to be projected, and the audiences to be addressed. All existing items that have been designed need to be studied and

a close look must be taken at the competition. Perhaps most important of all, the lines of communication within the company, from the shop floor to the chief executive, must be re-examined. This initial briefing and research phase is concerned with gathering information, conducting a visual audit, and evaluating all the various factors.

The second phase looks at design and conceptual work. In design, the elements to be evaluated are the company name, trademark, logo or signature, typeface, type style, and house colours.

267

The next stage of corporate identity development is to draw up a manual or broadsheet specifying exactly how all the visual items are to be used. It is customary for the chief executive to write an introduction in the manual, stressing the importance of maintaining consistent design standards.

The final stage is the actual implementation of the programme. All staff must be briefed in this regard and those entrusted with the actual implementation must conform to agreed specifications and standards. To maintain standards is probably one of the most difficult aspects of the whole programme.

To be successful, the development of a corporate identity must run through a series of logical phases. However, it must be remembered that this should be an ongoing process, what we call a Brand Cycle™, the process adopted by BMW.

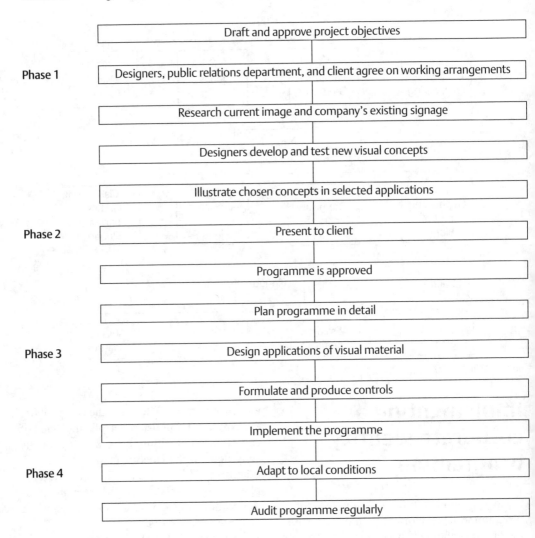

	Draft and approve project objectives
Phase 1	Designers, public relations department, and client agree on working arrangements
	Research current image and company's existing signage
	Designers develop and test new visual concepts
	Illustrate chosen concepts in selected applications
Phase 2	Present to client
	Programme is approved
	Plan programme in detail
Phase 3	Design applications of visual material
	Formulate and produce controls
	Implement the programme
Phase 4	Adapt to local conditions
	Audit programme regularly

Factors that affect corporate image

Corporate image is developed through the composite effect of a variety of factors. These include:

- size of business (conglomerate or backyard operation);
- standing (national or international);
- action of overseas parent and home country (fights for human rights, the environment);
- nature of business (electronics, undertakers);
- performance of products (low quality or high quality);
- employees and sales staff (pleasant or unpleasant);
- type of management (stagnant or progressive);
- labour relations (excellent or poor);
- share earning record (no dividends paid or steady increase in dividends paid);
- value for money offered (expensive and good or cheap and nasty);
- pricing policy (cheap or expensive);
- premises;
- public relations activities (low profile or high profile);
- action of competitors (no competition – a monopoly, or one or more strong competitors);
- national identity (English, Afrikaans, African);
- service (slow or fast);
- corporate logo (none or well known);
- advertising (none, or very frequent and easily recognized).

Size of the business

If you are buying paint, would you rather buy Parthenon, a Plascon paint made in one of their six factories, or 'Housebrite', made at Plot No. 6, Pofadder?

But being largest is not always an advantage. Sometimes being second largest is better, as in the case of Avis – 'We try harder.' Being small

and being able to give personal service may be better still. For each type of business the advantage or disadvantage of size must be measured.

Standing: national or international

If you are shopping for computers, IBM, Lenovo or Apple have the background and size, and are international as well.

Action of overseas parent and home country

The action of international pharmaceutical companies to protect their patent rights with regard to the sale of HIV/Aids drugs on the South African market has generated a lot of anger and frustration. Depending on your standpoint, you may either support or boycott these companies.

Nature of business

The nature of the business a company is in will affect its image and the support it gets from the public.

Huletts Sugar can promote a tennis circuit but how many will support one sponsored by Spectre, Posthumous, and Kin Undertakers?

Performance of products

The Rolls-Royce logo on the engines of the jet plane you are boarding provides reassurance. So does the General Electric logo on the next jet you board. Both are good engines, but given a choice, would you prefer to be kept aloft by Rolls-Royce or by General Electric? Or would it not be important to you?

Employees and sales staff

The impression that employees make on the public is a major image builder. Junior staff, such as the receptionist, sales force, and messengers, frequently have the greatest interaction with the outside world. The receptionist is one of the front-line staff of a company.

Compare the well-dressed, well-groomed sales staff of Avis to, say, a local pawn shop.

Type of management

Does management have an image of old-fashioned stagnation or is it geared towards the future and progressive?

Good management is the lifeblood of a company. The reputation of directors and other senior personnel for stability, skill, and dynamism plays an important part in creating a favourable image. Johan Rupert, Njabulo Ndebele, and Raymond Ackerman are a few examples of people whose personalities permeate their organizations' images.

Labour relations

Does the company have a reputation for paying low wages? The handling of labour issues, the way in which applicants for employment are received, and staff training are all factors that affect a company's image among outsiders, but particularly among its own staff.

Stock earning record

Companies quoted on a stock exchange are continually in the public eye. A steady increase in dividends paid over many years inspires confidence in the company.

When a take-over bid is imminent, awareness of the degree of loyalty of your shareholders could be vital.

Value for money offered

The product may be expensive but the quality high. Many companies purposely maintain an image of high cost and quality. Some low-cost products are also good value for money. Consider Mercedes and Volkswagen – almost opposite ends of the price scale but both good value for money. Is it because both are German products? Some stores deliberately create an expensive image. Is this good policy?

Pricing policy

Pick n Pay and Shoprite Checkers are local examples of companies that used low-price policy in its public relations activities to fight inflation, to help the consumer. But is cheaper always better? Today the debate is about the delivery of value.

Premises

The appearance of offices and factories is also a factor. An impression of security, cleanliness, modernity, efficiency, and success are good image builders.

Many companies today are investing in imposing buildings and tasteful furnishings. How important are these to your publics?

Public relations activities

Some firms purposely keep themselves in the public eye through their public relations activities. Woolworths is one of the best examples. Whereas some firms keep a high profile, others either by design or through ignorance prefer to remain invisible. Which is the best policy for your company?

Action of competitors

The action of competitors has an effect on the corporate image of a company. The cellphone market is one of the few product fields today where fierce competition has forced prices down dramatically. Retailers such as Shoprite Checkers, Pick n Pay, and Spar are all trying to create a favourable image with their customers.

National identity

In South Africa some companies are seen to be English and some Afrikaans. Both groups probably try to become South African, but despite all the Afrikaans-speaking counter staff First National Bank may have, and all the English-speaking counter staff ABSA may have, the language group image of the two is not easy to dispel.

There are strong moves afoot to translate the concept of the 'rainbow nation' into a strong national brand which can compete on world markets. Special promotional campaigns to attract tourists, business, and investment have been successfully launched in the United Kingdom and Europe, the United States, Japan, and the Far East. See the case study on Proudly South African at the end of this chapter and visit the website for the International Marketing Council of South Africa: www.imc.org.za.

Service

One of the biggest problems of industrial companies is slow service. Most manufacturers today are under-utilizing their plants and equipment. There is little excuse for slow delivery. Yet many quote up to eight weeks' delivery when two-week deliveries are being called for. Consequently, any firm that can build up an image of fast delivery will find a place for itself in a competitive market.

Corporate logo

There has been a rash of corporate logos lately. Some are well known to us, others are mysterious. A logo is a useful way of linking the names of various companies which belong to conglomerates (such as companies belonging to ABSA, Murray & Roberts, Bidvest, and Anglo American).

Logos displayed on delivery vans and trucks, messenger uniforms, stationery, buildings, and products are strong image builders.

Bear in mind that the image built could easily be negative, instead of positive.

Marketers

The most frequently raised question heard among marketers is: do we promote the product or the company? The answer is probably both in different ways in different media.

Financial journals like *Financial Mail*, *Finweek*, and *Business Times* are usually chosen for corporate advertising in an attempt to influence top management in buying and influencing organizations. National and regional newspapers and trade journals are aimed at the consumer and are more suitable for product advertising, but there is no hard and fast rule. Maybe you would do better with a full page in the *Sunday Times*. Maybe you should channel the money to consultants to ensure your brand is well defined, focused and delivering its promise.

Conclusion

The brand(s) is probably the single most important asset of most concerns. Its protection and improvement should receive constant attention. Periodic measurement gives management the opportunity to evaluate changes that have taken place against company policy and leads to a deeper understanding of how actions are perceived by the different publics the company serves, who serve it, or whose attitudes and opinions are important for the success of the company.

Case study Proudly South African

South Africa attained its political freedom in 1994, but the challenge still remains to achieve economic freedom which translates into prosperity and a better life for all South Africans.

The Proudly South African Campaign originated from the deliberations of the 1998 Presidential Jobs Summit, called by former president, Nelson Mandela. Proudly SA is much more than a marketing/branding instrument. It is a key domestic resource in the national effort to promote national pride and patriotism, contributing to business competitiveness, and employment creation (protection and creation of jobs). This is achieved by promoting Proudly South African member companies and by stimulating consumer demand for quality, locally-produced products and services – **buy local**!

Proudly South African defines who we are as a nation – the essence of PSA's brand is national pride and patriotism.

As a national campaign with the challenge to create top-of-mind awareness and stimulate a behavioural change amongst consumers – '**buy local**' – Proudly South African has to sustain a continuous media presence, directed by a strong marketing/promotional strategy to ensure success.

Maintaining stewardship of a campaign that in essence demands adherence to the principles of good corporate governance requires that Proudly South African sets a good example of openness and transparency through effective communication and dialogue. These factors guide and inform the campaign's approach to its marketing, promotions, and communication initiatives.

The Proudly SA campaign strategy can be summarized as follows:
'To build a **credible and sustainable country-of-origin brand** and license this brand to **qualified member organizations**, supported by strategic business and social partner relationships, a media education campaign to **encourage consumer and procurement support**, as well as the delivery of **value-added services** to members which enable them to **leverage their association with the campaign** and improve their **competitiveness**.'

The initial focus of the campaign – building overall awareness – has now shifted to sustaining (and building) awareness, stimulating uptake of Proudly SA member products and services, while actively encouraging a behavioural change – '**buy local**' – as part of the second phase of the campaign's business model.

A number of marketing objectives have been developed to ensure that Proudly South African achieves its purpose:

- to educate South African consumers about buying local products and the impact it has on economic growth, job creation, the retention of jobs, and quality of life (prosperity);
- to claim the highest position for the Proudly SA brand/logo as the most recognized and best-known brand in South Africa;
- to retain and grow Proudly SA membership;
- to add value to and support the marketing initiatives of Proudly SA members;
- to encourage extensive support for the Proudly South African Campaign by retail chains and all participants in the value chain, including ongoing point-of-sale and promotional support by the retail members;
- to gain ongoing support from stakeholders/sponsors, and ensure their involvement in the campaign (as 'brand ambassadors') wherever possible.

A variety of flagship projects serve as vehicles for the campaign's strategic marketing objectives:

- Proudly SA Endorsement Campaign – this campaign utilizes thought-leaders who share the Proudly South African ethos to enhance brand association/loyalty in niche markets. In essence it represents a call to the public to '**buy local**'.

- Consumer Education Outreach Campaign – this is a cyclical campaign (programme) through which Proudly SA aims to increase its footprint across all provinces in South Africa. Both conventional mass media (national radio campaign advertising in all official languages and print media) and community media such as industrial theatre are utilized. This campaign gives effect to Proudly SA's repositioning strategy and utilizes the **Nca!** concept (meaning 'lekker', appealing, nice...). **Nca!** is captured in different permutations such as **Nca!**tion and the pay-off-line: Buy local and support the pride and prosperity of the Nca!tion. Formative research has confirmed that the word is well received and understood across all language and cultural groups in South Africa.
- Clothing and Textiles Strategy, including measures to optimize buy local/advance the competitiveness of the local clothing industry in the two-year window period created through the quota system implemented in respect of clothing, textiles, and footwear products imported from China. This flagship project complements the campaign's efforts to assist and help develop capacity in manpower-intensive economic sectors, that have been prone to large-scale job losses – by working with the industry and promoting '**buy local**' – quality clothing, footwear, and textiles produced by local manufacturers, utilizing talented local designers, and on sale/available from local retail stores. This relatively short window of opportunity to resuscitate this important industry demands a partnership approach and Proudly SA will continue to work with all major stakeholders to optimize its contribution to the creation of sustainable jobs and the protection of jobs in this industry. This includes participating in events such as the Cape Town Fashion Festival and similar initiatives that promote the best interests of this industry.
- Development of Proudly SA towns and cities – aimed at empowering local initiatives, businesses and communities to optimize/capitalize on the unique, Proudly South African assets of the selected or deserving town, city or township, in partnership with a variety of strategic stakeholders. Preference is given to those unique, local industries and sectors, such as Tourism and Agro Processing which show the best potential to deliver on both the campaign's aims and the development aims envisaged for ASGISA.
- Proudly SA Homegrown Awards – this is a prestigious annual Proudly SA member competition, aimed at acknowledging, promoting, and enhancing South African innovation and entrepreneurial excellence.
- Proudly SA Week/Month – this campaign, which runs in September and coincides with Heritage Day, utilizes a broad spectrum of media to focus attention on the purpose of the campaign, and locally-produced products and services, while building consumer loyalty and pride in the Proudly South African brand – **buy local**!
- The Christmas, Back-to-School, Easter, and Winter Buying Campaigns focus on promoting Proudly South African products and services, and the buy local message through, and in collaboration with, the retail sector and all members of the value chain. It is linked to the national buying and retail cycles.
- Youth Campaign – the youth is a niche market for Proudly SA – they are reached by working with Proudly SA schools and educational institutions, together with other stakeholders, and through the development of special projects, linked to suitable national days such as Youth Day. The campaign also spearheads youth development initiatives such as the planned Nca! Youth Arts Awards.
- Proudly SA Loyalty Card – this initiative, which is in the assessment and due diligence stage, will add another powerful tool to the campaign's marketing bouquet, offering an opportunity to promote the Proudly South African brand, while simultaneously creating additional value for members and all Proudly South African consumers.

The campaign has adopted a partnership approach in building the capacity of companies, including SMMEs to continuously aspire to higher standards of quality and efficiency, in order to enhance their competitiveness in local and global markets. The campaign would like to partner with provinces and municipalities to promote buy local in the context of 2010 – by encouraging them to consider 'Buy Local' opportunities in their procurement processes for events such as the 2010 FIFA World Cup.

CEO Network Forums, environmental scanning, media intelligence, and regular consumer research; ongoing assessment of internal systems and processes, and a commitment to quality and excellence (Proudly SA is ISO9001:2000 compliant) ensures that Proudly South African stays in touch with its environment and continuously adapts to serve the needs of members and consumers. This approach is assisted through regular and effective communication with staff, stakeholders, constituencies, members, and consumers through the mass media, and dedicated communication tools such as *PROUD!* (the Campaign's official quarterly magazine); **Nca! News!** (monthly electronic newsletter); staff newsletters, and the Proudly South African website which is in the process of being reviewed to enhance its functionalities and usability.

By fulfilling its mandate, the Proudly South African campaign is contributing towards inspiring and consolidating our national pride in support of the country's socio-economic objectives. As one of a number of tools with the economic well-being of our country at heart, Proudly South African is making its impact felt in terms of the protection of jobs and the creation of quality job opportunities – '**buy local!**'

Source: http://www.proudlysa.co.za

Further reading

Gray, J.G. 1986. *Managing the Corporate Image – The Key to Public Trust.* Westport: Quorum Books.

Olins, W. 1989. *Corporate Identity – Making Business Strategy Visible Through Design.* London: Thames & Hudson.

Brands and Branding 2009. (The Economist/ Interbrand) 2nd edition.

Penguin *Dictionary of Marketing* – Phil Harris (2009)

Chapter 29

Corporate social investment

When you have read this chapter, you should:

- understand the social responsibility of business;
- be aware of the history and new policy directions on corporate social investment (CSI);
- be aware of some of the latest research trends;
- be familiar with the elements of good practice in the field;
- know how to establish a community relations programme.

Corporate social investment

The field of corporate social investment has evolved out of a broader field called corporate social responsibility. Corporate social responsibility can be defined as an area of management action which has developed in response to the changes and demands of society at large and involves business, government, and communities in the following areas:

- socio-economic, ethical, and moral responsibilities of companies;
- compliance with legal and voluntary requirements for business and professional practice;
- CSI/CSR now forms part of the BBBEE Scorecard and companies are able to score points to enhance their ability to do business with government and others by being 'good' corporate citizens;
- the company and its employees;
- the natural environment;
- the challenges posed by the needs of the economically and socially disadvantaged;
- responsible management of business activities.

Thus corporate social responsibility encompasses the responsibility of a company to ensure it:

- produces safe products for human use;
- manages itself responsibly and to the advantage of its employees and society;
- contributes to the sustainable development of the natural environment;
- contributes towards the development and upliftment of disadvantaged people;
- is managed within the moral, ethical, and legal frameworks and rules of society.

Corporate social investment itself is defined as the funding of, and involvement in, socio-economic upliftment. It excludes employee benefits and sport sponsorships, and usually concentrates on the following areas of involvement:

- education;
- housing;
- health;
- welfare;
- job creation;
- community development and empowerment;
- small business development;
- arts and culture;
- environmental conservation;
- rural development.

Brief history of corporate social investment

Corporate social investment in South Africa has had a short, dynamic history. With very little recorded involvement before 1972, it was given a massive boost with the introduction of the Sullivan Principles in 1977 and a major drive in the 1990s to assist in the new government's Reconstruction and Development Programme, to bring about real development change and a better life for all.

This has resulted in a drastic shift in private sector attitudes towards corporate social investment from the realm of 'nice to have' into one of 'must have', with organizations working alongside Government, albeit independently, in an effort to meet the demands of the transformation envisaged for the country. Simultaneously, there is a growing awareness by the private sector that being seen as a socially responsible and caring corporate citizen, is an important aspect of a company's public relations and corporate image profile.

Trends are away from 'responsibility' and into 'investment' and 'community development'. Inclusivity in terms of representative committee decision-making, decentralization, and unbundling are becoming increasingly popular. Employee involvement either formally, informally, or on a voluntary basis is being encouraged and even rewarded. Ad hoc donations have given way to more focused approaches into specified sectors within expressed criteria.

The shift away from a hand-out philosophy into a more developmental approach, brings with it the concepts of empowerment and sustainability. This also necessitates a new approach to corporate social investment, requiring partnership building with communities and other role-players, and increased networking and communicating between corporate donors, in order to maximize the impact on development.

Along with the increased openness and inclusivity apparent throughout the country, the last few years have seen corporates starting to publish more information about their corporate social investment expenditure and project support. Articles about corporate social investment are beginning to appear more widely in the mainstream press. While some are public relations announcements trumpeting projects that companies had funded, others are critical examinations of the role of corporate social investment in South Africa's development process. In 1991, the *Weekly Mail & Guardian* launched what has become an annual 'Investing in the Future' supplement to analyze trends in corporate social investment. This supplement was accompanied by an award honouring South Africa's 'Most Caring Companies'. *People Dynamics* magazine published occasional articles on the subject. The *Innes Labour Brief*, which targets industrial relations and human resources managers, ran articles on this topic and also published the *CSI Letter*.

In 1995, Myra Alperson published *Foundations for a New Democracy: Corporate Social Investment in South Africa*, a corporate social investment book exclusively for the South African environment. It provides a brief background on corporate social investment in South Africa, an examination of socially responsible investment, and a resource on organizations and publications pertaining to the sector. In the same year Mersham, Rensburg, and Skinner published *Public Relations Development and Social Investment: A Southern African Perspective*. This work draws together and examines the relationship between public relations, development in the southern African context, and corporate social investment, using South African case studies to examine the notion of corporate social investment from multiple viewpoints. It also provides practical guidelines for introducing, developing, and evaluating corporate social investment programmes.

With the endorsement and support of many role-players in corporate social investment, the *Corporate Social Investment Handbook*, published by Trialogue, was launched in 1998. It is now the most authoritative guide to the CSI arena and has become an invaluable decision-making instrument for corporate and non-profit development practitioners, while offering government a bird's eye view of CSI initiatives.

CSI trends

Over the past decade the CSI sector has changed considerably. It has moved from voluntary philanthropic pursuit to one that is beginning to be recognised as an important business consideration. Over the same period, CSI funding has escalated considerably – from R1.5 billion to over R4.1 billion annually – making it a significant contributor to social development.

Whilst this might suggest a dynamic and growing industry, recent research has revealed a state of flux that has been considerably worsened by a calamitous global financial situation which is having a huge impact on both a company's ability and willingness to contribute to CSI

"CSI in South Africa is struggling to find its place between the corporate and development spheres, and lacks capacity to achieve meaningful developmental impact among beneficiary communities despite the substantial financial resources pouring into it.

In part, this was seen to be due to the lack of developmental expertise, professional skills and qualifications of many CSI personnel" (*Introduction to the CSI Handbook*. 11th edition. 2009).

The report also mentions that it believes the root cause of the sector's ills "is that few South African companies are making CSI a strategic business imperative. Despite throwing more money at it, too many companies continue to conduct business 'almost as usual' where CSI is no more than a BEE scorecard necessity"

The severe financial downturn has also thrown CSI into sharp focus because funding, based as it is on a sharing of between one and two per cent net profit with beneficiaries, has been seriously undermined. In a loss situation companies do not have the luxury of allocating funds they do not have and so the CSI budget is the first to be cut.

Way forward

In addition to conducting annual primary research, the publishers of the *CSI Handbook*, Trialogue, also conducted 14 in-depth interviews with key stakeholders, who, between them, hold a wealth of knowledge and informed opinion about this complex subject. This is a summary of their findings divided into six themes.

First principles

There is a wide variation in how business and different industry sectors with diverse contexts interpret, approach, and apply social responsibility. Some believe that an ethical paradigm should motivate businesses to help redress the apartheid legacy of deprivation and inequality. For others, the basis for "right action" is enlightened self interest. Others think that a "big-stick" approach of Government prescriptions and sanctions is the only way to ensure that corporate resources are harnessed for the public good. "Whatever the point of departure, it is widely accepted in South Africa that business is an important agent of social and economic development and that it is explicitly required to contribute to national development objectives".

The corporate environment

CSI is not widely regarded as a strategic business imperative, and many companies continue in a state of 'business as usual'. The result is that CSI is still regarded as charitable giving - or at best, a BEE scorecard prerequisite – and is often not taken seriously by many boardroom executives. Thus CSI remains a sideshow that is peripheral to core business.

The CSI sector also occupies an uncomfortable, difficult space between the corporate, its development partners (which may include government), and beneficiary communities. CSI practitioners are required to wear many different hats to straddle these three spheres, each with a different agenda, divergent priorities, and different language. "This is no easy task, and an already complex function is made more challenging by the fact that, within their own organisations, CSI Units are often relegated to the periphery".

CSI Units must also navigate the tension between the marketing and developmental functions of the business. "In many instances, this internal dynamic is exacerbated by the fact that CSI is housed within the marketing department. Thus until social responsibility thinking is internalised within the business and CSI has a clearly defined developmental role, it is likely that companies' social investment will be conflated with PR, cause- related marketing and sponsorship".

The developmental role

In the South African context, it is considered appropriate for companies to align themselves with government policies and priorities. This is especially so given that the state's capacity to implement has proved weak and CSI can play a complimentary role in augmenting state programmes or filling critical delivery gaps. But when engaging in public-private partnerships, the CSI sector treads a very fine line. On the one hand, CSI departments run the risk of becoming a corporate tool to lobby for and secure state tenders; on the other, they risk being driven by the need to enhance corporate or government reputation rather than serving community interests. "Even if initiatives are aligned with state priorities, CSI units need to be clear about their objectives and to retain their own developmental integrity".

As the CSI sector moves away from ad hoc funding to a more strategic approach, there is a growing emphasis on partnerships for development. Increasingly therefore, CSI departments are engaging in working partnerships with NPO service providers to implement their programmes. "For many CSI practitioners, the key to achieving results is to choose effective development partners and to be instrumental in facilitating development, rather than 'doing development'. The overall result to all these initiatives is, however, disappointing".

The general opinion is that while there are pockets of excellence within the sector, on the whole, the sector is not using CSI funding to best effect. "Too frequently, CSI initiatives are ill- conceived and poorly implemented. In other cases, CSI strategies are well- conceived but never implemented. The majority of companies still see themselves as donors, with little consciousness about the long term enduring impact on the people and programmes they support".

Achilles heel of CSI practice

It is widely acknowledged that impact assessment is not yet a priority for the CSI sector. "In the current context, very few corporate grant makers engage seriously in debates about assessing the developmental impact of their programmes. Among those that do conduct impact assessments, measurement tools and processes are, generally speaking, superficial". To step up a gear, more CSI players need to conduct impact assessments on all their programmes and publish the results. This is the key to increasing the rate of learning within the CSI sector.

The professional status of CSI

The report states that there is little doubt that CSI is more professional than it was a decade ago and the level of skill and knowledge within CSI departments is growing. "Leading CSI companies have realised the need for greater professionalism among CSI staff, and have, in the past few years, actively recruited CSI personnel with development qualifications. But while this is a notable shift, it will take time for professionalism to feed through the system and translate into sector-wide expertise and better development on the ground".

Strengthening the CSI sector

In summing up, the report concludes that over the years, CSI has evolved in a way that has included charity, welfare, PR and cause-related marketing to varying degrees. It believes that the industry has now reached a point where it needs to disassociate from this hold-all basket and to embrace the development agenda wholeheartedly. "This process has to gather momentum on many fronts. The sector must strengthen its institutional footing within corporate structures; it must mobilize corporate leadership to move beyond a compliance mentality to one that embraces the development imperative of CSI; and it needs the support of the country's institutions of higher learning to instil deeper corporate understanding of the relationship between business and society".

"It also needs to forge greater consensus around the ethos of grant making, so that practitioners themselves don't confuse marketing with CSI; it must equip CSI personnel with recognised qualifications and proper skills; and it needs a professional body with standards of practice and platforms for knowledge-sharing and capacity-building".

Above all, it exhorts corporate leaders to engage seriously with CSI. "Our top companies need to apply the same resources to this function as they would to other strategic areas of the business, so that the CSI sector is given the institutional platform it requires to address the task at hand. In doing so corporate South Africa must start showing a greater willingness to collaborate with other companies and to set aside narrow interests for the greater good"

CSI Funding

Estimates for the expenditure on corporate social investment in South Africa for the 2007-2008 financial year amount to R4.1 billion according to the CSI Handbook (2008).This reflected more than a 22 per cent increase over the previous year.

However, these figures and those projected for 2008–2009 and beyond will be severely distorted by the downturn and recession which South Africa and its main trading partners are currently experiencing.

In these circumstances it was felt that a detailed discussions of the breakdown of CSI expenditure would serve little purpose based as they are on historical figures. For comparison purposes, however, the allocation of funds by development sections is included in the table on the following page.

The earlier discussion focussed on the Achilles heel of CSI practice must be seen in the light of the general global economic downturn which is affecting all decision making at government and private sector levels.

How companies determine the size of their CSI budgets.

Irrespective of the current financial crisis, it is interesting to note how companies determine the size of their CSI budgets. The CSI Handbook again provides some useful pointers. Whereas it would seem that a number of different formula-based methods are in use, the 'percentage of net profit after tax' approach is gaining most traction because it is the one prescribed in the BEE Codes of Good Practice. "Code 700 of the BEE Codes stipulates that companies should spend one per cent of profit after tax (NPAT) on socio-economic development (SED) and whilst the interpretation of SED is not yet entirely clear, it includes many of the initiatives formerly defined as CSI." It would appear that some companies already spend at least one per cent of NPAT on CSI. But for many it constitutes a new benchmark towards which they now need to aim.

SI expenditure by sector (R4,1 billion) 2008

Education	Supported by 88% of CSI programmes ... receives 31% of total CSI budget.
Health	Supported by 76% of CSI programmes ... receives 11% of total CSI budget
Social development	Supported by 78% of CSI programmes ... receives 16 % of total CSI budget
Job creation	Supported by 65% of CSI programmes ... receives 13% of total CSI budget
Training	Supported by 62% of CSI programmes ... receives 7% of total CSI budget
Sports development	Supported by 29% of CSI programmes... receives 2% of total CSI budget.
Environment	Supported by 56% of CSI programmes ... receives 6% of total CSI budget
Arts and Culture	Supported by 32% of CSI programmes ... receives 2% of total CSI budget.
Safety and Security	Supported by 27% of CSI programmes ... receives 2% of total CSI budget
Housing	Supported by 20% of CSI programmes ... receives 2% of total CSI budget

Source: *The CSI Handbook*. 11th edition. 2008

Good practice guidelines

According to the *CSI Handbook*, CSI practitioners should strive to create a more focused and targeted corporate social investment programme which allows for improved evaluation,

more efficient controls, and the opportunity to make a greater impact and enhance visibility. It is infinitely wiser for corporate social investment practitioners to be guided by the maxim 'fewer but better' rather than be pressurized into a scatter-gun approach. Investing in a few quality projects would in the long term make communities, and employees, see companies in a much more favourable light and generate sustainable development. Practitioners should review the size and number of grants they are making each year, in relation to how many they receive and in terms of their corporate social investment strategy. Whilst there is a trend towards making bigger grants to fewer organizations, practitioners may wish to undertake a more balanced approach, making a handful of larger grants to carefully selected areas, such as education and job creation, and supporting more projects with smaller grants in other areas.

Proactive

CSI practitioners should aim to find the right balance between being proactive and being responsive in their corporate social investment activities. One possibility is to adopt a proactive approach with a few major projects, which are aligned to the programme's goals and in which resources are focused, and then keep a discretionary or general fund for responding to other projects. Increasing the level of proactive activities of the corporate social investment programme allows for greater control over the outputs, improved relationships, enhanced impact and communication, and most importantly, encourages sustained development. However, it needs to be remembered that whilst a proactive approach provides numerous benefits, it requires a particular style which includes:

- having the competencies to prepare the community for self-help;
- spending the required time with the project;
- being willing to take risks;
- understanding that corporate social investment mileage comes with a clear focus, hard work, and a readiness to be rendered redundant when communities achieve self-reliance.

Continuum of giving

Make a conscious decision about the motivation of the corporate social investment programme and where on the continuum of giving your activities lie, from philanthropic to commercially driven. Whilst the most popular corporate social investment motivation currently is one of community investment, there has been a significant shift in the last few years for corporate social investment programmes to align their activities to the corporate's core business and away from pure philanthropy. However it is possible for CSI practitioners to align the major portion of the corporate social investment programme to company goals whilst keeping a certain portion available for pure philanthropy – effectively positioning themselves on two points of the continuum.

Strategic business function

The corporate social investment programme should be viewed as a strategic function that adds value to the business and the communities it operates in, creating a conducive economic environment, whilst at the same time facilitating good corporate citizenship. Like any business function, corporate social investment should prove its worth via added value and the bottom line, and must be vigorously monitored to measure its return on investment. For the corporate social investment activities to be in line with the group's business objectives, it is imperative to have absolute clarity as to the company's goals and its internal and external target audiences. This approach makes the programme responsive to the company's needs whilst upholding its commitment to communities. As CSI practitioners find themselves under increasing pressure to justify their position, the international and local trend is to balance community needs with company needs, ensuring they are beneficial to both communities and companies. The key strategy is increasingly to align the corporate social investment programme with corporate goals, adding value to the company and to communities. The potential, in terms of both business benefit and social impact of programmes which embody a win-win philosophy, are substantial. Strategic corporate social investment programmes include:

- clearly defined goals and operating criteria;
- the cultivation of partnerships and joint ventures;
- the completion of needs assessments to ensure the viability and sustainability of each project.

Get involved

Whilst corporate social investment contributions have tended to favour financial interventions, CSI practitioners are increasingly recognizing the importance of non-cash contributions in order to sustain and increase existing corporate social investment commitments, as well as to leverage the impact of their support. Non-financial support can be provided in many forms including:

- the provision of products;
- secondment of staff to projects;
- skills transfer;
- the provision of venues;
- services;
- employee involvement;
- most importantly, time.

It is the provision of non-financial contributions to projects that will make the difference between an ordinary corporate social investment programme and an outstanding programme, a fact that is recognized by many corporates, by government, and non-profit organizations. Therefore, in light of the substantial benefits to the company, its employees, and the communities, it is recommended that an increase in non-cash contributions is a strategy that commands high priority.

Top management support

Top management should not only sanction the corporate social investment activities but also be aware of the issues surrounding the programme and its social context. Like all key functions the onus is on corporate social investment management to ensure that top management recognizes the value of the programme, its impact, and contribution to the business, by presenting its performance reports and influencing decision-making at executive level.

Decentralized and departmental involvement

Wherever possible, regional contribution to the corporate social investment programme should be encouraged. This includes creating clear corporate social investment policy guidelines which involve managers in decentralized operations and the co-operation of company divisions, each contributing their own particular expertise. On the whole, CSI practitioners should consider enhancing the role line management has in corporate social investment: buy-in and support of line management is likely to have a positive spin-off for the programme. Stronger ties with regional and other departments will help CSI practitioners to create a more effective and localized corporate social investment programme.

Ongoing corporate social investment debate

Corporate social investment practitioners should be aware of and engage themselves in the current debates around corporate social investment and development, specifically the definition of corporate social investment, as it influences programme evaluation as well as communication efforts. The debate centres on the inclusion and exclusion of various items from the corporate social investment budget, seeking parameters for corporate social investment, and defining its role in business. An understanding of all the activities of business that have the potential to produce public good is necessary in order to clarify the dividing lines of what corporate social investment actually is. A key element to this discussion is to avoid a uniform or prescriptive approach to corporate social investment, as the individual styles and approaches undertaken by various CSI practitioners are pivotal to their contributions.

Partnerships

There are few CSI practitioners today that do not recognize the value of developing partnerships with the various role players, including the government and civil society organizations, in order to enhance the impact of their investment and to maximize efficiency and effectiveness. For many organizations, particularly those involved in social development, partnerships emerge as the most expedient way to obtain resources, gain knowledge, achieve objectives, and ultimately foster strategic growth and development.

This approach also enables CSI practitioners to participate in more ambitious projects than their own financial resources will allow. Whilst there is no simple definition or clear-cut formula for partnerships, the question of balance remains central and monitoring the balance of effort and reward is important. One method of doing this is to maintain a contribution and reward sheet for each of the partners.

Employee involvement programmes

One of the most strategic methods of leveraging the corporate social investment programme and generating buy-in from corporate staff is the use of employee involvement programmes. International studies have also proven that employee community involvement directly contributes to enhanced corporate image and reputation, as well as employee loyalty, whilst providing an additional opportunity for companies to make a real difference to their communities. Whilst many corporates claim to have employee programmes in place, very few have established policy that entrenches these programmes or have set up formal programmes. It is advised that corporate social investment practitioners rally for the establishment of policy guidelines for employee involvement programmes and include them as a vital element of the business response. It is also important for the staff participation programme to be tied into the organization's vision and culture, and linked with the company's core business. Furthermore, corporate social investment practitioners would be wise to formalize recognition procedures for employee involvement in community efforts, as they provide an excellent opportunity for building morale. The most compelling argument for companies to introduce or enhance employee support programmes, lies in the many benefits that these programmes provide the communities, the employees, and the company, and therefore it is recommended that CSI practitioners view these programmes as a top priority.

Communications strategy

With corporate social investment programmes expected to provide a return on investment and to contribute to the promotion of the company's image in the marketplace, it is essential that CSI practitioners have a communications strategy in place that is aligned to the programme's mission and strategic objectives. Effective communication of the corporate social investment activities plays an important role in the projection of the company as a caring citizen and is often not given the priority it deserves, until things go wrong. Communicating your corporate social investment says you take it seriously, you are willing to share your experiences and models, and you are acknowledging the important role played by the various parties. It is important that the corporate social investment programme works closely with the marketing or public relations departments to ensure there is effective co-operation.

Corporate social investment practitioners should consider the full spectrum of communication tools including: internal newsletters, and quarterly or annual reports; CD-ROM; videos; promotional material such as banners, logos, flags, and signboards, press releases in both national and local press; adverts and advertorials; specialist press such as the *Corporate Social Investment Handbook*; and the Internet. The Internet is becoming an increasingly useful communication tool for corporate social investment, and although at present it is predominantly used for public awareness, there are many more creative and effective ways in which it can be used to enhance the corporate social investment programme.

Whilst there are many mechanisms for promoting the company's corporate social investment activities, the power of open dialogue with the targeted communities should not be underestimated. Another critical factor is giving internal communication of the corporate social investment programme the same emphasis as external efforts.

Budget determination

The method used to determine the corporate social investment budget should be carefully assessed and CSI practitioners should strive to move away from arbitrary and discretionary methods, towards a more guaranteed and stable method of determination. A strategically aligned programme should ensure benefits for both the business and community, and therefore position the corporate social investment programme in a less precarious position where it is viewed as an important business function rather than an add-on.

Internal versus external corporate social investment

CSI practitioners should examine the extent to which their corporate social investment programme is inward- or outward-looking, and review whether this is the best strategy for their company, both in terms of impact and reputation. Benchmarking this specific aspect of the corporate social investment programme would enable practitioners to assess whether they are in line with current thinking and best practices.

Corporate social investment structures

CSI practitioners should take cognizance of how the corporate social investment programme is positioned in the company, assessing the extent to which this influences the nature of the programme and if this is in line with the corporate social investment strategy. The location of the corporate social investment programme is a strong determinant of the character of the programme activities and therefore impacts on the image and impact that the CSI practitioner will make on communities. This means that the position of the corporate social investment programme should be carefully considered when any restructuring or strategizing takes place. It is not adequate to palm the corporate social investment programme off to the public relations person to undertake in his or her 'spare time'. Whatever the structure of the corporate social investment programme, it should allow and encourage integration with other relevant departments in the company, including marketing and communications, for the maximum advantage of both the programme and the other departments.

Corporate citizenship

Thus a new universal model for corporate citizenship is emerging that goes beyond current corporate social investment and introduces a value system that brings together the self-interests of business and its stakeholders with the interests of society. The benefit of being committed to the pursuit of being a good corporate citizen is that all stakeholders realize that a company's values are deep-seated and relevant, and will therefore reap the financial and additional benefits of this commitment. Part of this challenge, and an integral part of corporate citizenship, is the need to align South African business practice with international moves to develop corporate social investment as a cornerstone of company activity. This means linking corporate social investment to the increasing need to develop skills in a range of areas such as diversity management, cross-cultural leadership development, and reputation and values-based management. Fostering a wider tradition of corporate citizenship throughout the company is a key recommendation, with corporate social investment playing a pivotal role in this transformation. Discussion is being encouraged on all these topics and reference is made to the publishers of the *CSI Handbook*, Trialogue, for further information. They can be contacted through their website at www.trialogue.co.za.

The JSE SRI Index

Stakeholders play a key role through engagement in influencing company behaviour. Increasingly, issues such as climate change and escalating oil prices are being put on the agenda as matters of global interest for companies to take note of and address.

Corporate responsibility is well established as an imperative in South Africa. This is due to the country's unique history and need to address socio-economic issues as a matter of urgency, and the fact that a company plays a central role in the economy as an immediate presence to the people. More recently there is a growing realization that upholding sustainability principles is important in the overall non-financial risk management of a company.

The JSE sought to leverage its unique position within the financial services environment to focus the growing debate on responsible investment. The Socially Responsible Investment (SRI) Index was thus launched in May 2004. The SRI Index provides a measurement of the triple bottom line performance of participating companies. Companies that are constituents of the FTSE/JSE All Share Index are invited annually to participate in the assessment and performance is measured against criteria based on the environmental, social, and economic pillars of the triple bottom line, with a central base in good corporate governance principles, which is measured separately.

The Index has made some inroads since its inception with a record success rate in 2006. A total of 58 companies out of 62 applicants met the Index criteria evidencing that triple bottom line considerations are becoming part of the way that companies do business.

The Index offers incentives for compliance as it provides an aspirational benchmark for organizations which incorporate triple bottom line best practice into business operations. It further serves as a tool facilitating responsible investment, which calls for investors to be vigilant about investment decisions and closely considering responsible companies. The concept of responsible investment is a burgeoning one globally, especially following the release of the UN Principles for Responsible Investment (PRI) in April 2006.

The SRI Index is not the first Index of its kind. Internationally there is already the FTSE4Good and the Dow Jones Sustainability indices. The SRI Index was however the first of its kind to be sponsored by an exchange and the first in emerging markets. This sets the JSE apart in championing measurement of ESG principles. More significantly, the SRI Index provides a framework for non-financial risk management for companies and investors alike.

For further information about the Index, please consult www.jse.co.za/sri or email sri@jse.co.za.

Community relations programmes

Sound community relations are not built on promises or propaganda. They are the product of responsible policies and actions that are well publicized. A community relations programme must identify the company with the interest and welfare of the community. It must consist of actions that demonstrate the company's sincere recognition of its responsibility to the society in which it operates. These actions will reflect most favourably on the company if the community and public are informed of them, modestly and subtly, through normal channels of information.

The first step in establishing a community relations programme is to evaluate the company's policies. This needs to be done to ensure that they are in accord with the public interest. It is useful to be aware of society's attitudes towards an organization, and until you know how informed (or misinformed) the public is, you cannot know how to plan an effective public relations programme.

For this reason, many companies begin by doing community surveys to determine the attitude of the general public towards them. They are then able to determine the direction of their community relations programme, as well as its objectives.

Such a survey can be accomplished by means of a questionnaire sent to a cross-section of the community. Some of the questions the survey will hope to answer are the following:

- What is the general feeling about the job the company does as a member of the community?
- How much information does the average citizen get about the company?
- Where does the public get most of its information about the company?
- What is the perception of the company as an employer?
- Is the public aware that company executives and employees are involved in local civic affairs?
- Are people aware that the company contributes to local charities?
- What does the community like about the company?
- What does the community dislike about the company?

Once the study of local opinion has been concluded, it is important to know the 'personality' of the community.

This is done by analysing the population and determining its composition, the number of residents, race, age, sex, religious beliefs, economic status, and occupations.

Then determine the primary social problem of the community. Find out all you can about those characteristics of your market that are likely to influence the direction of your community relations programme.

With this information, you will have a sound basis on which to base specific objectives and develop an effective programme of community activities to increase public approval of your company.

Some of the activities that might feature in a community relations programme are:

- open-house days and factory tours;
- financial and executive involvement in community programmes;
- meetings with opinion-makers to exchange views;
- membership of community organizations;
- exhibits and displays in public places;
- service to the youth, including schools;
- loaning of equipment for special projects;
- financial assistance to social and welfare bodies;
- conservation projects;
- sport, cultural, or recreational sponsorships;
- financial assistance to universities and universities of technology;
- bursary and scholarship schemes;
- assistance with environmental issues;
- career counselling at schools;
- publishing a booklet telling the community about your internal and external social responsibility programmes.

Community Liaison Forums (CLF)

Because of the needs of communities, many companies are now considering setting up their own CLFs to understand and resolve community concerns. They believe these forums have a positive role to play in the development of local communities through a range of opportunities such as jobs, learnership, and by being a good neighbour.

It would appear that social investment works best when it is carried out as a joint effort with local organizations that have the capacity to implement sustainable projects. It is also most effective when more than one company, or industry player is involved and when it is aligned with government programmes and objectives.

According to one of the major players in the South Durban basin SAPREF, who have successfully created a CLF over the past few years: "we believe the solution is to seek out the right partnerships with local organizations and to develop the capacity of these organizations

to gain access to the resources that government, companies and also SAPREF have available to support community development."

There are indeed resources available for community development from other sources, namely the municipality, so establishing a separate institution for grant making would not allow partnerships to develop to the same extent, 'even if we had a trust to administer social investment funds, we would still have a problem of not having an ability to implement projects'.

Further reading

Alperson, M. 1995. *Foundations for a New Democracy: Corporate Social Investment in South Africa.* Johannesburg: Random House.
Corporate Social Investment Handbooks. 1998 – 2009. Cape Town. Trialogue Publications.
Corporate social investment information can be found on www.trialogue.co.za.
Culbertson, H.M. & Chen, N. (eds.) *International Public Relations. A Comparative Analysis.* Mahwah, N.J.: Lawrence Erlbaum.
'Global Reporting'. http:/www.globalreporting.org.
Levin, R. 1987. *An Assessment of Corporate Social Responsibility, Ideology, and Action.* Johannesburg: Wits University Press.
Mersham G.M., R. Rensburg & C. Skinner. 1995 and 2004. Public relations, development and social investment: *A Southern African Perspective.* 2nd edition. JCS & Associates.
Zadek, S., M. Foster & P. Raynard. 2002. 'Social Development and the Role of the Private Sector: Corporate Social Responsibility'. Unpublished Working Paper, United Nations Department for Economics and Social Affairs: Division for Social Policy and Development. New York.
Zadek, S. 2002. 'Exploring the Business Case', in *Ethical Corporation*, May 9:33.
Most of the leading newspapers and financial journals now publish annual CSI surveys.

Chapter 30

Public relations and crises

When you have read this chapter, you should:

- understand the rationale behind crisis communication;
- be aware of the different types of crisis;
- be able to draw up a crisis management plan;
- be able to implement a crisis management plan;
- be familiar with some of the standby measures in the event of an emergency.

Every large organization must be prepared to handle enquiries from the media or other interested parties arising from a variety of crisis situations. These may range from accidents to environmental problems, strikes, work stoppages, product recalls, employee misconduct, and even terrorism.

Situations such as these will never produce good publicity, and no organization expects its representatives to be able to turn a bad situation into good news. However, a bad situation will always be made worse by ignoring the news media or mishandling their enquiries.

The media have a right to report the news – good or bad. A socially responsible company accepts this principle by responding to media enquiries promptly and accurately. It is in the company's interest to release information, rather than have the media use material obtained from a secondary source because such information is often inaccurate and detrimental to the company.

When the news is bad, it is best to release accurate information as fast and as fully as possible, rather than try to hide the facts. "No comment" is not an acceptable response. A better response would be, 'I will get accurate information and come back to you as soon as possible.' Refusing to provide information can result in sustained bad news over several days, as the press uncovers new information and disseminates new accusations from uninformed and possibly unfriendly secondary sources.

What is a crisis?

Traditionally, a crisis is a critical situation, a turning point. It is that moment of drama when hostile forces are at the height of their opposition.

> There are physical, mental,
> financial, and religious crises.
> The point is that a crisis can
> be almost anything you
> perceive it to be.

South African companies and institutions are not immune to crises. In the last few years we have witnessed tragic mining disasters, incidents of labour unrest, and violent confrontations.

More than a century ago, the British prime minister, Benjamin Disraeli, wrote: "What we anticipate seldom occurs. What we least expect generally happens."

A company's reputation is hard won and the true gravity of a corporate crisis must obviously be measured in terms of human suffering – not in terms of corporate image or profit and loss statements. Yet the impact of a major public crisis on an organization's interests can be devastating.

However, if a crisis is professionally managed, damage can be minimized and sometimes, through prompt, constructive action, the organization's reputation may even be enhanced.

Types of crisis

Whereas public relations practitioners cannot always predict when and where a specific disaster or crisis will occur, they must determine the type of crisis they may have to deal with. Crises fall into three broad categories:

- **Immediate crisis**. This is the most dreaded type, which happens so suddenly and unexpectedly that there is little or no time for research and planning. Examples include a plane crash (Concorde), product tampering (Tylenol), fire, earthquake (Turkey and India), terrorism (World Trade Centre, New York), bomb scare, and workplace unrest or shooting. To deal with

this type of crisis, a consensus among top management should be worked out in advance so that a general plan on how to react is in place. This will help to avoid confusion, conflict, and delay.

- **Emerging crisis**. This type of crisis allows more time for research and planning, but may suddenly erupt after brewing for long periods. Examples include general employee dissatisfactions and low morale, substance abuse on the job, overcharging, and poor service. The challenge is to convince top management to take corrective action before the crisis reaches the critical stage.

- **Sustained crisis**. This type of crisis persists for months or even years, despite the best efforts of management. Examples include persistent rumours of downsizing, retrenchment and closure of operations, mergers and takeovers. Once again, senior management must take the lead in providing a clear and unequivocal statement of intent.

The key to anticipating and avoiding crises is assessing what can go wrong, what can affect people or the environment, and what will create visibility.

A crisis management plan

Unnecessary withholding of information during a crisis encourages public speculation about its extent, cause, and who is to blame.

In the absence of hard news, rumour can magnify an incident out of all proportion.

Effective crisis management depends on the following four key elements:

- a clear definition of the organization's policy and procedures for handling a crisis;
- assigning responsibility to specific personnel who would be the most likely to be involved in the event of a serious crisis;
- training key personnel to respond on the organization's behalf on television and in

radio interviews, at press conferences, and on the telephone;
- establishing a communications system and preparing appropriate facilities and equipment.

These key elements should form the basis of the crisis management plan.

Although even the most deftly executed risk management strategy may fail to avert a crisis, adequate preparation greatly improves an organization's chance of communicating effectively in, and surviving, an unexpected crisis.

The following guidelines are part of a crisis management plan developed by Traverse, Healy, and Regester of London, and are currently used by a number of multinational companies around the world.

Planning for crisis

The initial points to consider are the following:
- Faced with disaster, assume the worst possible scenarios – and act accordingly.
- Have a crisis management plan prepared.
- Be prepared to demonstrate human concern for what has happened.
- In communication terms, be prepared to seize early initiatives by rapidly establishing the company as the single authoritative source of information about what has gone wrong and what steps the organization is taking to remedy the situation.
- Whenever possible, look for ways of using the media as part of your armoury for containing the effects of the crisis.
- At the outset of the crisis, quickly establish a 'war room' or emergency control centre, and staff it with senior personnel trained to fulfil specific roles designed to contain and manage the crisis.
- Set up telephone hotlines to cope with the flood of additional incoming calls that will be received during the crisis, and have personnel trained to man the hotlines.

- Win your opponents over to your side by getting them involved in resolving the problem.
- Add credibility to your cause by inviting objective, authoritative bodies to help end the crisis.
- In communicating about the crisis, avoid the use of jargon – use language that shows you care about what has happened and clearly demonstrates that you are trying to put matters right.
- Know your audience and ensure that you have a clear picture of their grievances against you – if possible use research to verify your standpoint.
- Whenever possible, seek outside expert advice when drawing up crisis contingency plans.
- When the dust has settled, look to see what lessons you might be able to teach the rest of industry from your experiences.

A crisis plan methodology

Responsibilities

- Operations and safety. These are the responsibilities of operational and safety management who have to develop procedures that will minimize risk to lives and property. These procedures must be developed alongside communication procedures, since successful implementation of the latter will depend largely on the effectiveness of operational and safety procedures.
- Communication. This is the responsibility of corporate affairs and public relations personnel or others charged with responsibility for communication. They have to develop emergency communications procedures that will both protect the company and project it as sympathetically as possible during a crisis.

Analysis of parameters

Define areas of risk (people, operations, products) and the following areas of social and physical impact:

- employees and concerned relatives;
- local community;
- media;
- branch offices and head office;
- shareholders;
- trade unions;
- business partners;
- government departments, municipalities, civil defence.

Scenario preparation

Jointly with operations and safety people, prepare 'What if?' scenarios of anything and everything that could go wrong. Without a full understanding of what could go wrong the correct practices and procedures cannot be developed and put into place.

Procedure preparation

- establish call-up procedures for all personnel;
- describe operational procedures (plant shutdowns and office closures);
- describe product procedures (product recall, relabelling, etc.);
- describe communication procedures (who says what to whom, and when);
- determine what technology, facilities, and resources are available;
- draw up a transportation plan – make sure you can get your resources to the crisis;
- inter-link with police, defence, or civil defence procedures;
- describe casualty procedures involving ambulances, hospitals, doctors, firefighting, paramedics, etc.

Procedure and facilities testing and modification

- develop a detailed scenario, using as few people as possible to ensure secrecy;
- against a detailed scenario, run a full-scale mock 'emergency' to test each of the procedures and facilities which have been put in place;
- have each stage of the emergency monitored by qualified observers;
- conduct a detailed debriefing by qualified observers of everyone involved;
- institute modifications to the procedure as required; improve facilities, develop specialized training programmes;
- test, re-test, and test again.

Implementation of the crisis plan

Essential actions during a crisis

- say that you are an authorized spokesperson if asked;
- assume that everything you say will be printed;
- defend your colleagues and company at all times;
- record details of all enquiries;
- ring back if you promised to do so;
- refer relatives of any casualties to the human resources department;
- give out official information only;
- if in doubt, first check with the co-ordinator who knows the answer;
- use only the public relations department as your source of information;
- always try to sound helpful – express concern, but do not accept blame;
- give your name to journalists or reporters when asked.

What not to do during a crisis

- do not disclose your 'normal' position;
- do not promise to ring back unless you absolutely have to;
- do not answer any questions of which you are unsure without first checking with the co-ordinator;

- do not withhold information which is readily available;
- do not give unauthorized information.
- never lose your temper;
- do not be trapped into speculating;
- do not forget to be helpful;
- do not give information 'off the record'.

Know who the media are

- national press;
- regional press;
- local press;
- trade business publications;
- television and radio;
- news agencies;
- international press (if appropriate).

Know what the media look for

- up-to-date information;
- background statistics and filler material;
- dramatic pictures;
- human interest stories;
- diagrams, maps, and technical drawings;
- explanations of possible causes of the crisis.

Biggest news stories as presented by the media

- loss of life;
- danger to individuals or the community;
- major political scandal or embarrassment;
- pollution or major damage to the environment;
- disaster involving major loss of facilities, equipment, or money (for example, theft or major forex crimes).

Checklist of facilities and equipment required

- dedicated press room with pre-ordered press release list;
- telephone lines;
- computers and fax machines;
- bleepers or radio contact equipment;
- emergency travel arrangements;

- stocks of press release forms and general documentation;
- fact books and information sheets for responding personnel;
- relief staff;
- senior management spokesperson, trained to handle the press and television;
- video footage for media use – photographs and location maps.

Crisis training

As an integral part of planning to deal with a crisis, look at possible specialized training programmes that should be instituted to ensure that you have a team of 'professionals' to handle the company's external communications. Regrettably, because of our all too human tendency to think that "this won't happen to me", this aspect of training is the most difficult to implement.

Senior management will need training in handling television and radio interviews and holding press conferences.

Middle management will need to learn telephone answering techniques.

The human resource department will need training in procedures for contacting and managing staff and extra resources; handling calls from relatives and friends; liaising with the police; and informing the next of kin of victims.

Switchboard personnel need to be informed how to handle initial press queries, from whom to expect calls, and to whom calls should be routed.

Your company will inevitably fall victim to a disaster of some kind sooner or later: a fire, an industrial accident, an explosion, a product recall. The manner in which the situation is handled will have a major effect on the public's image of the company and its management. It is therefore important for the public relations department to establish a crisis communication programme, for which the recommended measures to be taken are set out on the next page.

Standby measures in the event of an emergency

Strategy

1. Designate an authorized company spokesman in advance, who will be the management representative on site.
2. Provide information on personnel casualties to the families involved as quickly as possible.
3. Provide information to the press and to authorities as quickly as facts can be verified.
4. Refrain from speculation on a subject that is not verified, such as the cause of an accident.
5. Take the initiative in informing the press if they are not already aware of the situation.
6. Take the initiative in informing appropriate government officials or local authorities.
7. Allow reporters and photographers immediate access to company property within the limits of safety and national security.
8. Refrain from releasing information on personnel casualties until families have been notified.
9. Refrain from estimating damage or construction costs until they can be accurately assessed.
10. Immediately release company decisions relating to special employee or community relief or plant reconstruction.
11. Emphasize the company's safety record and the continuing precautions that have been taken to avoid accidents.
12. Use every means of communication to present the facts that will offset rumours or false statements.
13. Inform as quickly as possible, all the company's interested publics, including employees' families, shareholders, suppliers, dealers, members of the community, neighbouring companies, industrial associations, banks.
14. Designate an emergency site where victims can be cared for. Provide meals if necessary. Provide facilities for the press and radio and television personnel.
15. Install special telephone facilities on the designated site.
16. Personal information on senior executive – if a victim – is to be issued if requested by the media.
17. Legal and insurance officials are to be notified. This could be linked with 14 above, both with regard to facilities and responsibility.
18. Group public relations department to keep current information and photographs.
19. Managing director, financial director, tax and insurance manager, or administration manager.

Responsibility

1. The managing director, plant manager, or nominated person. This could be the responsibility of the human resources manager or officers, or the nominated person.
2. This information should be cleared with divisional chief executives and channelled through the group public relations department.
3. Insist that nobody other than yourself, divisional chief executive, or group public relations manager speak to the press.
4. Nominated person.
5. Managing director or nominated person.
6. Approval must be given by managing director or nominated person.
7. Nominated person. This can only be made known to the press after legal and insurance assessors have given the clearance.
8. Managing director to advise local staff, group human resources, group public relations, and divisional chief executives.
9. This information should be readily available from the human resources department.
10. To be initiated by the managing director or chief executive and executed by nominated person.
11. Press releases, house journal, notices on bulletin boards, meetings, personal letters, and, in cases of urgency, telefax and telephone calls.
12. This is the responsibility of the safety or security officer or the personnel officer or manager.

Questions to expect regarding fires or explosions

- number of deaths;
- number of injuries;
- damage (fire chief will give estimate in rands; give yours in general terms, for example what was destroyed);
- what burned or collapsed;
- time;
- location within plant (for example paint room, laboratory, office);
- names of dead and injured (after relatives have been notified);
- victims' addresses, occupation, ages, and length of service with the company;
- number of employees, products manufactured, or nature of the business.

Incidents and questions to treat with caution

- *Delivery or construction delays.* Emphasize positive aspects as soon as information is available.
- *Cause.* Let police officials release this – chances are that the story will die before their report is completed.
- *Specific damage estimates as well as what was destroyed.* Take care since this information could be extremely valuable to competitors.
- *Layoffs.* Disclose the situation as soon as you can; delay breeds rumour.
- *Plant shutdown.* Gather forces and fully assess damage before making a statement regarding the situation. Once the decision is taken, however, release details to the press.
- *Violation of a safety regulation by the victim.* Keep quiet – the penalty has already been paid; pointing out negligence appears callous.
- *Do not make speculative statements.*

Notification of employee-victim's next of kin and personal assistance

The manner in which an employee's family is notified of injury or death reflects on the company. The speed with which you inform a vic-

tim's family of the accident and the way in which you do this can help ease the pain, give the family strength to face the crisis, and comfort them when they need it most. Your attitude will quickly become known to other employees and their families.

1. Assign an executive in upper management to notify next of kin – either the immediate supervisor, managing director, or human resources manager.
2. As soon as the emergency becomes known, determine as accurately as possible the extent and nature of injuries.
3. Find out immediately where the victim is being taken.
4. Dispatch a member of the management staff, possibly the same person as in 1 above, to the victim's home as soon as you know where the victim has been taken.
5. In cases of injury rather than death, give the person going to the victim's home a head start by having someone from top management call the victim's spouse and explain that an accident has occurred and he or she has been injured. If questioned, say you are waiting to hear from the doctor, that someone is already on the way to the house to help in any way possible and will be there shortly.
6. Keep someone at the office in contact with the hospital to learn as much as possible about the victim.
7. On reaching the home, the management representative should first call the office to hear of any new developments. Depending on the situation, he or she should offer to take the spouse to the hospital, find someone to take care of the children, or make any telephone calls.
8. In cases of death, the management representative, after informing the spouse of the accident, must offer to assist in any manner possible. It is helpful to know the name of the family doctor and the family minister.
9. The management representative should remain at the house until other family members arrive or as long as possible. It is his or her duty to protect the family from calls or visits from the press.

10. Be prepared to make special arrangements. If necessary, make reservations through the company for the parents to visit. Order food. Be ready to assist in any manner possible.
11. If release of the estate of the deceased is delayed it is advisable to make a cash advance or donation to tide the family over.
12. Get the name of a close friend or close relative of the family and maintain constant contact with them until the funeral. This will provide a good opportunity to identify any needs of the family.
13. Consider providing educational assistance (such as a bursary) for the children of the deceased.

Case study African Centre for Disaster Studies

1. Setting the context

Disaster risk management in Africa consists of a labyrinth of cross cutting facets requiring the participation of a host of sectors and disciplines not only from within the spheres of Government (national, provincial and local), but involving the private sector, the civil society, non-governmental organisations (NGOs), community based organisations (CBOs), research institutions, and institutions of higher learning, to name but a few. In the context of disaster risk management, none of these role players can act in isolation. The cornerstone of successful and effective disaster risk management is the integration and co-ordination of all of the above role-players and their activities into a holistic system aimed at disaster risk reduction.

The subject of disaster risk reduction draws its relevance from earlier contributions and previous practices in the disaster management fields, where traditionally the focus has been on preparedness for response. Disaster risk reduction emphasises a new global thinking in the management of disasters and disaster risk through a multi-disciplinary approach. Disaster risk reduction can be see as the systematic development and application of policies, strategies and practices to minimise vulnerabilities and disaster risks throughout a society, to avoid (prevention) or to limit (mitigation and preparedness) adverse impact of hazards, within the broad context of sustainable development (ISDR 2002:25).

Disaster reduction strategies include, first and foremost, vulnerability and risk assessment, as well as a number of institutional capacities and operational abilities. The assessment of the vulnerability of critical facilities, social and economic infrastructure, the use of effective early warning systems, and the application of many different types of scientific, technical, and other skilled abilities are essential features of disaster risk reduction.

Through multiple efforts, the importance and uniqueness of hazard and further risk reduction for the future have become evident. In contrast to the earlier concepts of disaster management, hazard and risk reduction practices relate to significantly larger professional constituencies, and depend on much more diverse information requirements. While there is no doubt that emergency assistance will remain necessary, the potential consequences of increasingly severe hazards indicates that much greater investments need to be made to reduce the risk of social and economic disasters. The challenge for risk and disaster management in the coming years is to find effective means by which a much more comprehensive, and multi-sectoral, participation of professional disciplines and public interests can contribute to disaster risk reduction. Accomplishing this goal requires both a political commitment, as much as public understanding to motivate local community involvement. It is in no one's interest to continue to accept the rationale that the resources on which all societies depend must first be lost to hazards and disasters before their value is deemed worthy of protection, replacement, or repair.

An African regional consultative meeting of experts hosted by the AU/NEPAD (2-3 June 2004) reiterated the importance of disaster risk reduction towards sustainable development. The meeting emphasized the importance of investment in current centres of excellence in Africa focussing on issues of disaster reduction, and that concerted efforts should be made to engage public and private entities as partners in these initiatives (Van Niekerk, 2004; AU/NEPAD, 2004a; AU/NEPAD, 2004b).

In terms of South Africa, on 15 January 2003, the President signed into power the Disaster Management Act 57 of 2002 (DMA). The DMA heralds a new area in the proactive management of hazards and vulnerability, thus contributing to disaster risk reduction. It calls for the establishment of Disaster Management Centres at all three spheres of government, and aims to incorporate a clear focus on disaster reduction into developmental planning. The above-mentioned act came into operation through a phased approach over a two-year period from 1 July 2004.

It is against the above background that the activities of the African Centre for Disaster Studies (ACDS) as a research entity within the North-West University (Potchefstroom Campus) should be viewed. The contribution of the ACDS towards the understanding of disaster risk, in South Africa but also Africa, is growing but can and should be expanded to address the ever-growing need for research, education, training, capacity-building, and consultancy on the African continent.

2. Background on the African Centre for Disaster Studies

The African Centre for Disaster Studies was established in January 2002 within the School for Social and Government Studies, Faculty of Art at the North-West University, Potchefstroom Campus (previously Potchefstroom University for Christian Higher Education). The initial aim of the ACDS was to generate third stream income for the university through tenders, projects, contract research, and short courses.

The ACDS functioned under the School of Social and Government Studies, but was never incorporated into the organogram or administrative functioning of the School. This can largely be ascribed to the fact that much of the managerial and financial decisions that were taken in terms of the ACDS and its projects happened at Faculty level. This was largely due to the nature of the ACDS work and the university policy on financial management.

In January 2007, after the appointment of a new Director for the research focus area 7.2: Sustainable Social Development, the ACDS was moved to function under the new director. In that year, the ACDS was also given a more specific research focus within the Research Focus Area with the establishment of the research sub-grouping: Water and Disaster Studies. Since 2007 the ACDS has grown significantly in its staff component as well as its research and consultancy offerings. Its website (www.acds.co.za) enjoys considerable international Internet traffic with most searches on disaster risk reduction in Africa being routed to the site by search engines (such as Google). In 2008 the ACDS produced the first African e-journal for disaster risk reduction (called *Jàmbá*). In the same year the ACDS implemented a Masters degree in Sustainable Development with a focus in disaster risk reduction. The strategic focuses of the ACDS are contained in the following sections. These focuses are driven by its vision and mission.

3. Vision, mission, and aims of the ACDS

3.1 Vision of the ACDS
A leading academic and research centre for disaster risk reduction on the African continent.

3.2 Mission of the ACDS
To provide internationally relevant academic courses, conduct world-class innovative research, outstanding consultancy services, community-based and locally relevant outreach programmes, and groundbreaking disaster risk reduction projects for the African continent, in order to encourage and stimulate sustainable development.

3.3 Aims of the ACDS
The ACDS aims to:
- develop world-class academic courses in disaster risk reduction with a particular emphasis on the African continent;

- stimulate and conduct high-quality inno-vate research on disaster risk reduction;
- provide consultancy services for disaster risk reduction in line with current needs and realities;
- develop and engage in community-based outreach programmes to address risk perception;
- obtain and deliver disaster risk reduction projects in order to generate additional income for outreach, research and academic purposes;
- contribute to the ideals of sustainable African development.

4. Strategic focuses of the ACDS

The ACDS is ideally positioned to address a wide variety of disaster risk reduction challenges on the African continent. As primarily an academic and research centre, the ACDS is experiencing an increasing need for the services that the centre offers. The logical step for the centre was to expand its offerings in order to address the disaster risk reduction needs in Africa more effectively. For this purpose certain strategic focus areas can be identified. The following section will elaborate on the future strategic focus areas of the ACDS.

4.1 Focus area 1: Research

Research forms the foundation of knowledge. Without research, current and historical phenomenon cannot be explored and new methods and solutions cannot be discovered. Current research on disaster risk reduction is severely limited.

It is envisaged that the ACDS will expand its current research initiatives in order to address pressing issues on a macro as well as micro scale. This will include research into:

- better and more accurate risk, hazard and vulnerability assessments;
- best practice guidelines for Disaster Risk Management Centres;
- community-based participatory disaster risk reduction;
- the innovate use and application of "leap frog" technology in disaster risk reduction and mapping (e.g. remote sensing and

application of satellite technology and geographical information systems);
- policy, legislation and strategy development;
- protection of critical infrastructure through risk reduction;
- disaster prevention and mitigation;
- emergency preparedness and response;
- disaster assessment and loss estimation;
- scenario planning;
- risk perception;
- livelihoods assessments;
- food security in sub-Saharan Africa;
- sustainable social development; and
- HIV/Aids.

The research focus area of the ACDS will further ensure a constant publication record including accredited articles, books, working papers, project reports, research findings, and newsletters in order to stimulate African thinking in disaster risk reduction.

The current ability of any given university in Africa to provide adequate and world-class post-graduate mentorship is severely lacking. Through the expanded human resource base, the ACDS will ensure the appointment of individuals that have contributed to the field of disaster risk reduction in Africa and that can provide outstanding post-graduate supervision. The expansion of academic programmes will contribute to the disaster risk reduction body of knowledge through the inherent cutting-edge research of these programmes.

4.2 Focus area 2: Academic programmes

In order to incorporate research findings into the learning process, it is imperative to establish a link between academic programmes and the practical reality. The ACDS provide input to the following qualifications:

- M.A. Sustainable Development: Disaster Studies; and
- PhD. Development and Management: Disaster Studies.

All of the programmes have a unique African focus and incorporate components of research and practical experience.

4.3 Focus area 3: Capacity-building and skills development

Besides concentrating on the formal educational needs in Africa, the ACDS also aims to develop capacity-building and skills development training interventions. Such initiatives are aimed at professionals at all levels of government and the private sector that contribute to disaster risk reduction though their activities. The ACDS aims to address the following challenges in capacity-building and skills development:

- facilitate experiential learning opportunities through the development of a disaster risk management learnerships;
- establish a disaster risk reduction internship/mentorship programme for student exchange between different countries and regions (though the GOLFRE initiative and South-North Cooperation Project with Lund University, Sweden);
- councillor training interventions;
- ward committee capacity training in hazard and vulnerability assessment.

4.4 Focus area 4: Disaster risk reduction projects

Disaster risk reduction projects have been the heartbeat of the ACDS since its inception. Projects in which the ACDS pursue include:

- hazard, risk and vulnerability assessments;
- development of disaster risk management plans;
- policy and strategic disaster risk reduction framework development;
- establishing institutional disaster management capacity;
- development of standards and guidelines for the application of disaster risk reduction on all levels of government;

- development of contingency plans;
- development and facilitate emergency response exercises and scenarios.

4.5 Focus area 5: Consultancy

The ACDS currently provide a number of consultancy services. These services include:

- assistance in setting up disaster management centres;
- guidance on organisational arrangements for disaster risk reduction;
- skills and gap assessments in disaster management centres;
- development of disaster risk management and contingency plans;
- disaster risk management plan implementation;
- evaluation of hazard, risk and vulnerability research findings;
- facilitate disaster risk management strategic planning and framework development;
- observation and evaluation of disaster response exercises;
- assessment of disaster management and contingency plans.

4.6 Focus area 6: Community outreach and awareness programmes

Through community outreach and awareness programmes the ACDS is able to apply its knowledge on disaster risk within vulnerable communities. The following activities enjoy attention:

- girls in risk reduction leadership;
- livelihoods assessments;
- participatory rural appraisals;
- community-based disaster risk reduction;
- newsletters and posters; and
- primary and secondary schools programmes.

Further reading

Creichton, S. & A.L. Jamotte. 1992. *How to Avoid the Corporate Nightmare*. Johannesburg: Write Minds.

Regester, M. 1987. *How to Turn a Crisis into an Opportunity*. London: Hutchinson Business.

Regester, M. & J. Larkin. 1998. *Risk Issues and Crisis Management*. London: Kogan Page.

Skinner, J.C. & G. Mersham. 2009. *Disaster Management: A Guide to Issues Management and Crisis Communication*. Durban: JCS and Associates.

Other case studies have been documented in newspapers and magazine articles, both locally and internationally.

Chapter 31

Public relations and industrial relations

When you have read this chapter, you should:

- be aware of the new legislation impacting on industrial relations;
- know the objectives to be aimed at when handling potential labour unrest or a strike;
- be familiar with the guidelines for dealing with serious unrest where a strike has not yet occurred;
- be familiar with the guidelines for dealing with strike actions.

In times of sociopolitical change, no company, however advanced its policies may be, is exempt from industrial relations problems.

The companies that cope best with labour unrest and strike action are those that are prepared for it. It is essential to handle each situation with flexibility, to take account of personalities, and to deal with circumstances as they arise. Action should only be taken after consultation and careful reflection on all possible consequences.

New legislation

The enactment of the Labour Relations Act in 1995 signified the beginning of major changes within labour relations. Since then, we have seen the passing of various other pieces of legislation such as the Basic Conditions of Employment Act of 1997, the Employment Equity Act of 1998, and the Skills Development Act of 1999. Every employer in South Africa should keep abreast of these changes for fear of falling foul of the law.

The Labour Relations Act of 1995 was intended to make conciliation between employer and employees the 'heart' of the new industrial relations dispensation. The Act created the Commission for Conciliation, Mediation, and Arbitration (CCMA). This is an independent body financed by the state, that can charge for its services.

The CCMA has the right to administer mediation and arbitration. There is no appeal against arbitration awards; non-compliance is equivalent to contempt of court. In order to promote grassroots conciliation, that is, conciliation at the level of the disputing parties, no legal representatives are allowed without consent. Exceptions to this rule are permitted in complex cases where the imbalance of representation would naturally demand equity.

The Labour Relations Act is in the process of being amended. The amendments to the Act focus mainly on the following contentious issues: disputes surrounding the disclosure of information; the extension of collective agreements; representation of parties at CCMA hearings; retrenchments; compensation for procedurally unfair dismissals; and transfers of contracts of employment. These issues have been debated at length between business and labour.

The Basic Conditions of Employment Act of 1997 regulates certain minimum conditions of employment such as working hours, overtime pay, and leave. Employment contracts may not contain conditions which are less favourable than those contained in this Act.

Another key piece of legislation is the Employment Equity Act of 1998. This act aims to redress demographic imbalances in organizations. The Act will have a significant impact on organizational climate and culture as it deals with two key areas, namely unfair discrimination and affirmative action. Failure to comply with the provisions of this Act could result in severe financial losses for most organizations as fines begin at R500 000. Businesses are required to draft an employment equity plan that will be monitored by the Department of Labour.

Tied to the Employment Equity Act is the Skills Development Act of 1999 which aims to co-ordinate industrial training in a more structured and purposeful manner. The Skills Development Act should be seen as supportive of the Employment Equity Act in that it wishes to encourage employers to develop people who were previously disadvantaged. By obliging all employers to contribute to regionally based training funds and by providing that funds for training may be released only for approved programmes, it aims to ensure that money spent on training has the necessary effect.

Industrial relations practice

Industrial relations practice aims at establishing formalized structures for the regulation of relationships between management and employees.

It is an accepted fact that the management-employee relationship is a dialectic one and that it holds inherent conflicts of interest. Industrial relations practice attempts to channel this as constructively as possible.

Whether the workforce is unionized or not, it is essential for formalized upward and downward communication structures to be in place. Typically there are employee committees and grievance procedures for upward communication and a disciplinary procedure and briefing for formal downward communication.

In a unionized environment, management and the union enter into a negotiated recognition agreement which lays down the rules and procedures for handling the relationship, that is, election and appointment of shop stewards; meetings between shop stewards and management; disciplinary, grievance, and retrenchment procedures.

Enlightened managerial practice attempts to build constructive relationships with unions and to be proactive in resolving employee grievances as quickly as possible. However, the collective bargaining process is a power game and sometimes strikes and lock-outs do occur. The consequent loss of production and negative impact on relationships and corporate image can be substantial. This is where the roles of public relations and industrial relations overlap. Informed management will involve their public relations practitioners when negotiations break down and strikes or lock-outs occur.

The public relations practitioner should attempt to inform the company's customers, and other publics who may be affected, of impending disruptions.

Managing the media is an important part of maintaining the moral high ground. An ably-led media campaign can reduce negative impact on the corporate image and put pressure on employees to accept the offer and return to work.

Employer representatives should use every opportunity to advance the company's case in the appropriate media. Refusing to comment to the press immediately raises questions regarding the management's bona fides.

Unions have generally been proactive in using the media to support their case. A carefully orchestrated media plan on the part of the company, with press releases giving maximum disclosure, is advantageous provided that the company's stance is defensible and reasonable.

Workplace forums

The Labour Relations Act of 1995 set up joint problem-solving structures called workplace forums to meet this need for participative communication. The statutory model for a workplace forum is formally structured for large organizations with over 100 employees. Smaller organizations are nevertheless encouraged to develop participative committees voluntarily, based on the model in the Act.

The objectives of both voluntary and statutory workplace forums are:
- to promote the efficiency of the enterprise;
- to meet the needs of all the people in the enterprise;
- to shift away from adversarial industrial relations;
- to avoid the unproductive industrial action indulged in each year in the past during protracted negotiating.

The operating principles of workplace forums are:
- representatives from all levels of employees have equal votes;
- meetings must be on a regular basis. There should be a general meeting with senior management at least once a year for company disclosure on the financial state and future prospects of the enterprise;

- facilities are to be provided for representatives to be able to hold report back and feedback sessions for employees after forum meetings;
- union officials can be invited to attend forum meetings;
- disputes on forum procedures or issues are to be referred to the Commission for Conciliation, Mediation, and Arbitration for advisory awards or statutory decisions.

Collective bargaining

The social thrust of the Labour Relations Act of 1995 is to balance adversarial collective bargaining (the distribution of wealth – a downward flow from employer to employee) with participative collective agreements (the creation of wealth – a joint process between employer and employee).

Adversarial collective bargaining and participative collective agreements develop two different kinds of relationships between employers and employees.
- Adversarial collective bargaining has emotional spin-offs in work-to-rule, go-slows, strikes, lock-outs, and alienation (the 'cold shower').
- Participative collective agreements lead to joint problem-solving and constructive engagement, which results in identification, commitment, motivation, and inclusion (the 'warm bath').

However, can management negotiate wages one week (where employees do not achieve their optimistic expectations) and then have a participative session in the next week and still expect contribution, motivation, and commitment from the same employees? Whether we like it or not, collective bargaining issues and workplace related issues overlap; these issues cannot be clearly separated and there will always be grey areas.

Public relations and labour unrest

Objectives

The objectives in dealing with potential labour unrest or a strike are the following:

- to ensure that employees remain at work or return to work at the earliest possible opportunity;
- to ensure that management retains the initiative in dealing with labour unrest;
- to prevent injury to persons and damage to property;
- to get to the root of the problems causing dissatisfaction and to gain a full picture of the situation;
- to negotiate with employees once the exact nature of the problems is known;
- to arrive at a settlement which is acceptable to both management and employees, and which conclusively settles all issues that gave rise to the unrest or strike.

Warning signs

Labour unrest and strikes do not usually occur out of the blue, without any advance warning to employers. Warnings may come from consultative committees as a result of unresolved matters, from shop stewards or supervisors, or they may be manifested in increased friction on the shop floor, assaults, refusal to accept instructions or company discipline, and so on.

Companies should develop a system to ensure that management is aware of, receives, and records reports of any warning signs. Management should be alert to potential labour unrest or a strike situation, and preventive action should be taken immediately so that workers are aware of management's desire to avoid confrontation.

Guidelines for action before labour unrest occurs

- Obtain a list of work and home telephone numbers of people and bodies who will have to be contacted.
- Contact a senior officer in the police, explain company policy for dealing with labour unrest, and, if possible, keep in touch with him or her.
- Get to know neighbouring companies, and try to establish understanding about what you or they intend doing.
- Identify vulnerable spots (such as buildings and equipment) on the premises, and decide how they can be adequately protected in case of violence. Make a plan to ensure that facilities such as furnaces can be safely shut down if labour is withdrawn.
- Make security arrangements for staff not involved to leave the premises in the event of a strike. This is particularly important where female staff have to walk some distance to bus stops or taxi ranks, or have to pass in the vicinity of strikers.
- Prepare a strategy for dealing with customers during a work stoppage.
- Proper radio communication (by means of walkie-talkie radios) with communication between managers and between management and security is essential at all times.
- A proper public address system, powerful enough to address the whole workforce, must be available. Companies in close vicinity of each other could possibly invest in one portable system and share the costs.
- Since it may be necessary to allow some staff to leave the premises, sufficient staff must be trained to handle the telephone switchboard and to project an image of competence during a crisis.
- A 'crisis centre' must be identified in advance and a competent person appointed to head it during a strike. Take care to select the best site for this centre and ensure enough telephones are available. All decisions must be taken at the centre.

- Fire-fighting equipment must be checked regularly to ensure that it is in working order at all times.

Guidelines for dealing with serious unrest where a strike has not yet occurred

Where confrontation has taken place and there is a possibility of a strike, it is vital for a company to have a manager or responsible person who has full authority to:

- make the necessary decisions;
- negotiate with employees;
- issue any press statements deemed necessary;
- ensure that arrangements made in a settlement are implemented;
- ensure that a full written record of all discussions and agreements is kept.

The responsible person should communicate with the following parties to obtain advice and instructions. This may be:

- the senior executive officer of the company;
- the senior industrial relations manager or human resources manager;
- the head office labour division;
- representatives of relevant trade unions;
- the Department of Labour;
- the South African Police Service.

As soon as he or she becomes aware of unrest within the establishment, the responsible person should call a meeting of the workplace forum, works council, or employee representative body to discuss the specific grievances or, if these are not yet evident, to establish what the grievances are.

Should the employee representative body not be in a position to negotiate on behalf of employees because of fear of victimization or because it is unacceptable to employees, the responsible person should seek to hold meetings with small groups of employees, if possible by department or section. He or she should listen to their grievances and request them to submit these through the workplace forum or works council. If this is not acceptable, the responsible person should ask employees to elect one or more spokespersons to put their grievances to management.

It is vital to assure employees that there will be no victimization of workers' representatives, and that these representatives will be given the opportunity to report back to the workers.

No attempt should be made to prescribe which representatives would be acceptable to management. Where trade unions are involved and labour unrest is apparent, the unions' local organizers or general secretaries should be contacted immediately, unless the unrest results from a purely internal matter, in which case union participation is neither necessary nor desirable.

Mass meetings

The Labour Relations Act of 1995 confers the right of employees to assemble. A representative trade union is entitled to hold meetings with employees outside working hours at the employer's premises. (This right to assembly is, however, subject to any conditions as to time and place that are reasonable and necessary to safeguard life or property or to prevent the undue disruption of work.)

Nevertheless, the responsible person should try to avoid mass meetings, as they are inevitably emotionally-charged and ineffective as a method of communication. Instead, every effort should be made to speak to a small delegation of worker representatives. However, where management acknowledges that an injustice has been done and is willing to rectify it, the matter should be settled as soon as possible, even if this means meeting employees *en masse*. Management should never attempt prolonged negotiations at a mass meeting. The responsible person should limit discussion to assuring workers of management's genuine desire to get to grips with workers' problems; workers should be asked to return to work while investigations are in progress and an undertaking should be given to provide feedback by a set and agreed time.

If workers do not have effective spokespersons as yet, the responsible person should invite the election of spokespersons (immediately or later, if the workers are not yet ready) and leave the meeting.

The responsible person should ensure that feedback is provided promptly and accurately at the agreed time, and that employee representatives play their part in the process.

If language is a problem, the responsible person should make use of an impartial interpreter, not an employee representative. A public address system or loudspeaker should be used to ensure that all workers hear the message.

In case of an agreement

If agreement is reached with workers and strike action is avoided, the responsible person should ensure that:

- all arrangements made are implemented immediately;
- all arrangements and promises made are kept to the letter;
- every worker is advised of the agreement by the appropriate method, in the language normally used by the worker;
- the appropriate authorities are advised of the outcome.

Intimidation of workers

Numerous employers who have experienced labour unrest have observed definite attempts on the part of some workers to influence the perceptions and behaviour of their colleagues through intimidation and violence. Employers must therefore be aware that these tactics could be used in their establishments and are strongly advised to do everything in their power to protect workers who do not want to participate in organized labour action. This protection should definitely be exercised on all company property and areas of work, and should preferably extend to the usual approaches to the place of work and even to residential areas.

If intimidation is allowed to occur through default or lack of awareness on the part of employers and authorities, acceptable industrial relations practices and procedures will never be effective in resolving labour problems.

Guidelines for dealing with strike action

The definition of a strike in the Act includes partial or complete failure to work, retardation, and obstruction of work.

The Labour Relations Act of 1995 decriminalized strikes. Strikes are no longer legal or illegal. Strikes are now 'protected' (striking employees cannot be dismissed) or 'unprotected' (striking workers who have no legitimate reason, or who are striking for a rights issue, for example the dismissal of a fellow worker in contravention of the Act, are liable to dismissal). Protected strikes are those embarked on for any matter of mutual interest with the employer, for example a wage increase at the annual review time.

The right to strike is entrenched in the new Act. Employers have recourse to lock-out. (Recourse is a right with limitations in terms of the Constitution.)

If a strike occurs it is essential to appoint a responsible person, as outlined above, to deal with all situations involving the action by the workers, and to contact:

- the senior executive officer of the company;
- the senior industrial relations manager or the human resources manager;
- the head office labour division;
- representatives of relevant trade unions;
- the Department of Labour;
- the South African Police Service.

The responsible person should maintain contact with the police at a senior level throughout the strike. This does not mean, however, that the police should be asked to be present. Police intervention should generally be seen as a last resort where the situation has deteriorated to such an extent that injury to persons or damage to property seems imminent. The visible presence of police should be avoided during negotiations with strikers if the negotiations, even if noisy, are peaceful.

A strike tends to generate panic and excitement, which may make it difficult to communicate effectively with the strikers. The responsible person must nonetheless try to negotiate with leaders and spokespersons of the strikers, preferably through the workplace forum, works council or employee representative body or, failing that, with trade union officials or ad hoc representatives of the workers.

A strike can be greatly eased if the employees elect spokespersons, but this suggestion is often resisted because of fear of victimization or manipulation. In order to allay these fears, the responsible person must be ready to give public assurance to the strikers that spokespersons will not be victimized and will be given means to report back to the strikers after discussions with management.

The responsible person should meet with employee spokespersons and inform them that as soon as strikers return to work, negotiations with their spokespersons will get under way. Workers must be assured that the matters that gave rise to the strike will be investigated immediately, provided that they return to work. A request to return to work will have a much greater chance of success if it comes from the workers' elected spokespersons, and these people should therefore be asked to convey that request. An undertaking should be given to provide feedback by a set and agreed time.

A company's main objective during a strike is to secure a return to work. This should not, however, be insisted on during the early stages of a strike, when it may be necessary to live with a stoppage until a negotiating body has been appointed by the strikers and the nature of their grievances is known.

Staff not involved in strike action should not be permitted in or near the strike area. Unauthorized persons, who will undoubtedly congregate at the strike area to watch proceedings, should not be allowed to remain there. Employees who do not wish to strike should be permitted to work, and should be protected from intimidation.

Managing a strike is a form of negotiation and, as in any bargaining situation, the overhasty use of ultimatums generally limits the options. Likewise, threatening language heightens conflict while seldom yielding any tangible benefit. Ensure that nothing is done to widen or change the area of dispute.

If the responsible person decides that an ultimatum is to be issued to strikers, it must be possible for them to meet the ultimatum and for the company to carry out its part of the ultimatum.

Workers' anger tends to be immediate and intense. It is seldom sustained over weeks, or even days. Patience is normally a valuable ally in defusing crises and resolving problems. During negotiations workers should be made to feel that progress is being made, and should be kept informed.

If negotiations are unsuccessful and the responsible person comes to the conclusion that the strike or work stoppage should no longer be tolerated, he or she should convey the following messages to the strikers in writing (direct handouts and notices on notice boards), and verbally in a language that they understand (through an interpreter):

- Strikers will not receive payment for the time they have been on strike.
- Their grievances will be investigated and discussed with their representatives only after they have returned to work. Hence, if they wish negotiations to continue, a return to work is essential.
- They are to return to work by a particular time on a particular day, failing which they will be considered dismissed (in unprotected and illegal strikes only).
- Strikers who fail to return to work by the appointed time must collect all monies due in terms of the industrial agreement (wages, pro rata leave pay, and pro rata holiday bonus) at a particular time and place.

Strikers who do not resume work will not be permitted on company property after the appointed time. Employees who do return to work will be accepted by management and protected against victimization.

Having decided on the above actions, the company should adhere to them. If the strikers choose to ignore instructions to return to work, or if a mob gathers on company property, and refuses to leave, or if their actions lead to violence, the police must be called and allowed to disperse the strikers. It is most important for the company not to be seen to be party to the use of force in dispersing strikers.

Liaison with the media

Ensure that management and staff are fully aware that they have no authority to speak on behalf of the company, but can refer any enquiry to a person specifically designated to speak to the media. Only the designated person should make statements.

A statement should contain factual information only and not express opinions which may prejudice negotiations. If possible, issue the statement in writing, and avoid discussing the strike over the telephone.

After the strike

Management must implement every detail of whatever was agreed with the minimum of delay. If it was agreed to negotiate with employees, this must be done as soon as working conditions have returned to normal. Management must not be seen to be dragging its heels on agreements reached during the strike.

Tact and diplomacy will ensure a return to normal working relationships. Avoid incidents that could spark off a recurrence of unrest, such as taking retribution, and re-establish formal channels of communication if these were ruptured by the strike.

In its 15 years of existence, the CCMA has effectively rewritten the dispute resolution landscape in South Africa. In 1996, the South African labour market was fractured, divided by race, class, sector, and even ideology. Little was held in common between competing interests. There was no uniform dispute resolution system and the old Industrial Court was inaccessible, unaffordable, and unable to meet the requirements of the changing workplace. It did not enjoy the sanction or legitimacy of the majority of workers.

In contrast today, the CCMA is regarded as a role model on social dialogue, partnerships, and collaboration. It has processed over one million cases, 10 000 a month, 500 per day, in every corner of the country with a combined resolution rate of over 70 per cent. By any indicator in the dispute resolution chain therefore, the CCMA has proven the strength of the idea, and the success of its business model.

Case study   Corporate and industrial theatre

---

*The play's the thing in which
I'll catch the conscience of
the King!
(Hamlet, William Shakespeare)*

The tradition of using song, dance, mime, and theatre to transfer learning is as old as the history of civilization. In the Middle Ages, travelling players moved around Europe telling of the king's exploits in wars, stories about knights and their lady loves, as well as passing on general information.

In Africa this tradition is deeply rooted in the culture of its people.

Professor Lovemore Mbigi said, 'In Africa you cannot introduce change with a memo – you have to get the people emotionally involved in the process.' He calls this using 'the burning platform', a process of problem-solving used in African cultures, which are far more group and process oriented than traditional Western societies.

Communication theory tells us that to successfully transfer a message we must use signs and symbols which are real to the receiver. In Africa today it is imperative that we begin to use communication media using codes that really speak to the people.

The cost of failing to communicate successfully in business is prohibitive. According to statistics from the Department of Labour's Health and Safety section, six out of 10 accidents in the workplace stem from management failure. They regard failure to adequately inform and instruct on safety and health issues as one of the major contributing factors. Many companies feel that they have communicated these messages to the workforce – at great cost. However, if the message is not received, duplicated, understood, and accepted, then all we have done is run into the barriers to effective communication.

Communication through theatrical techniques

Human beings learn most effectively in a creative environment. The proliferation of books on this subject has taught us to use creativity in many spheres. Tony Buzan's seminal work on mind-mapping shows how to achieve vastly improved retention of messages through the use of art and colour. The right brain learning experience comes into full play when using theatre as a communication medium.

At a seminar for a large corporation on the power of a learning organization and the need to train and develop people in the organization, two methods were used to communicate the message: an excellent international speaker, using lots of audiovisual material, and a 40-minute piece of corporate theatre.

Six months later the retention of the message from the speaker was in the region of 10 per cent while retention from the play was close to 90 per cent!

Theatre as a communication medium is a high-impact, cost-effective solution that works because it:
- taps into the cultural framework of the participants;
- provides an emotional and then a cognitive experience;
- facilitates recall of the relevant messages;
- engages the target audience;
- utilizes everyday situations;
- combines effectively with educational drama-related workshops.

Through the use of techniques such as humour, parody, dramatic irony, and exaggeration one is able to 'speak the unspeakable' and deal with highly sensitive issues without causing offence. These techniques create a safe space in which people can view their shortcomings and fixed ideas. They allow people to rehearse for real life and make it safe for them to change.

Applications of theatrical techniques

Ambush theatre

Ambush theatre is a carefully scripted process used where there is resistance to an issue, as in the following example.

A board of directors at a leading financial institution experienced conflict within the group. The chief executive officer wanted to have a conflict resolution seminar but the rest of the board were extremely resistant to the idea. They were not willing to face the issues and stated that they did not need this seminar as there was in fact no conflict in the group.

A Friday afternoon workshop was set up and a consultant came in as a 'traditional corporate trainer'. A complicated overhead slide was put up and the group was told they would be discussing this slide for the next two hours. The meeting was then 'ambushed' by two actors who came in, posing as pest control workers, authorized by the chief executive to spray the room for fleas and cockroaches at 16:15 that day!

The actors were well primed to 'push the buttons' of the group and its latent conflict instantly surfaced. After allowing this scenario to run for 15 minutes in order to bring all the issues out into the open, the process was halted and the actors' identities revealed.

A very successful workshop was then conducted with the delegates, who were now willing to co-operate.

Theatre in training

Theatre in training creates a safe space to view yourself and your flaws.

A training session on image and presentation skills is complemented by the use of theatre in which body language and personal image is graphically and humorously demonstrated.

Delegates who experience this training regularly comment that, although they already know the theory, this piece of theatre hits home so dramatically that certain aspects which had previously been only intellectually understood are now accepted – resulting in a change of behaviour.

Vision and values campaigns

Theatre is extremely powerful at changing the hearts and minds of people, as it is firstly an emotional experience and then a cognitive one. By framing the messages in terms and references that communicate directly with the reality as perceived by the target audience, fast acceptance and retention of the messages are achieved.

When two major companies merge, the new culture and identity have to be communicated to and accepted by the staff. Illovo

Sugar used theatre as a medium after they bought the Lonrho interests in southern Africa. The new corporate culture and values were communicated through two plays performed in five southern African countries.

Inco Labs (Innoxa) used theatre as a medium to get the 'buy in' of their factory staff for the implementation of ISO 9000 standards.

Industrial theatre

A powerful tool to communicate on issues that have traditionally been perceived as difficult to get acceptance on. The following are examples:

- Health and safety issues. Major manufacturing plants are using theatre to reinforce safety and good housekeeping issues. In plants where they have had problems with these issues for many years, changes in behaviour were achieved.
- Business understanding and wage negotiations. A very successful programme using theatre gets the understanding of how a business operates and the need for profit. One major company reported that after this theatre intervention they had a wage negotiation with no problems. One factory worker was overheard to say to another, 'Don't do those things – you are putting up our overheads!'

Social responsibility

A powerful tool for addressing sensitive issues such as Aids awareness, environmental awareness, substance abuse, and other social issues.

With acknowledgment to Sally Falkow and Bradd Kietzmann & Associates, Durban.

Further reading

There are many sources available for information on South African labour legislation. Consult your Human Resources and Industrial Relations Specialists for advice.

Bendix, S. 2008. *The Basics of Labour Relations*. Cape Town: Juta.
http://www.labourline.co.za
The Institute of People Management (IPM) will be able to supply a list of books, magazines, and articles for further reading.

Chapter 32

Our multicultural market

When you have read this chapter, you should:

- be aware of the dynamics of our multicultural market;
- understand some of the religions practised in South Africa;
- be aware of how these trends and policies could have an effect on the communication specialist.

South Africa is a country rich in cultural diversity, languages, and traditions. A population of around 48 million is made up of a few remaining members of the San people; Nguni people, who constitute about two thirds of the population and speak Xhosa, Zulu, Swati, and Ndebele; Sotho-Tswanas, among them the South, North, and West Sotho (Tswana) people, each with their own language; the Tsonga people; the Venda people; coloured people; Indians; white Afrikaans and English speakers; and immigrants from China, the Netherlands, France, Germany, Portugal, Italy, and many other European countries, who still maintain their own traditions, languages, and cultures.

Religions and culture

I love you when you bow in
your mosque, kneel in your
temple, pray in your church.
For you and I are sons of one
religion, and it is the spirit.
(Kahlil Gibran, The Voice of the Poet).

We are proud of our multi-cultural society, even though we still mainly socialize within our own race groups. But we have all certainly learned a lot about tolerance and accommodation over the past 16 years. On a business level, we function pretty well and race and gender issues are worked out when they arise. But what about religion?

What do we know about each other's religions – that absolute core element of many people's lives? It is not enough to simply respect each other if we want to function effectively in the business community in our multicultural society. We need to understand where people are coming from, how they function, and what they believe.

> We have just enough religion to
> make us hate, but not enough
> to make us love one another.
> -Jonathan Swift, essay
> 'Thoughts on various subjects'.

African traditional religion (ATR)

African traditional or African religion has been practiced for thousands of years across the continent in various ways. It is clan-based and independent of the Western understanding of religion. Religion among African people is not treated as an isolated entity. It is dealt with in a broader context as it permeates all sections of life of both an individual and society. There is no line of demarcation between 'believers' and 'non-believers', and in fact such a distinction is inconceivable since everyone in that society is born into his or her religion.

The religious beliefs and practices are believed to have originated from the spiritual world and handed down both by word of mouth, and also practically by the forebears. Africans, whether in West, East, and Central of South Africa, believe in both the spiritual and physical world. They believe in the creator of the universe, who is also named according to his attributes, like greatness, holiness, benevolence, etc.

Communication between the creator and the living is believed to be through those who have already died, the ancestors. Africans believing in this religion, also practice religious activities called amasiko (religious rituals). The Creator, ancestors and rituals are common to all believers of this indigenous religion of the African. Hence it is called a 'religion' and not 'religions'.

Despite the onslaught of colonialism, African traditional religion has survived. The very cornerstones are myths; the role of ancestors; rituals; the meaning of sacred places; practicing a moral code; and respect for life as in ubuntu. Certain Africans prefer not to be Christians because they believe that missionary colonialists forced Christianity upon them.

In African traditional religion, individualism is discouraged. It is regarded as inhuman. The communal way of life is central whereby human beings share joys, blessings, sorrows, and burdens, hence the saying 'I am because we are, and since we are, therefore I am' – ubuntu.

African Traditional Religion has no founder. It is believed to have been divinely revealed to the first generation which is believed to have been directly created by the supernatural Power or God. The main groups all have different names for God.

An important focus of African religion is the belief that people who have died – the ancestors – continue to have an influence on living people. The ancestors are seen as the mediators between the living and the spiritual world.

Sangomas or spirit mediums, play a big role by channeling the ancestors for the living.

An inyanga is a herbalist, whose medicine is known as muthi. Muthi is mainly of vegetable origin although animal substances are used.

African traditional religion has no sacred texts; religion is written in the minds and actions of the people and passed on by oral tradition.

There is no special holy day. Every day can be holy. People celebrate many special festivals – to encourage rainmaking, to ask for blessing for ploughing and planting, and to say thank you for harvests. At these festivals they eat and drink and often sacrifice an animal. The cry of the animal indicates the ancestors' acceptance of the sacrifice.

Birth, death, and becoming an adult are also important ceremonies celebrated in these festivals.

African Independent Churches (AIC)

Also known as the African Initiated Churches or African Indigenous Churches these are Christian churches, which started to emerge by the turn of the 19th century, growing from African concerns in an African idiom, rather than on the initiative of foreign missionaries. It is estimated that today perhaps 38 per cent of South African Christians belong to the group of African Initiated Churches.

Since 1980 they have increased by about 25 per cent, which makes them the fastest growing sector of Christianity in South Africa. There are around 4000 different churches, mostly Apostolic, Pentecostal, and Zionist.

Zion Christian Church

By far the largest of the African Initiated Churches is the Zion Christian Church, with a membership of perhaps two million. This Church has its headquarters at Mount Moria, near Pietersburg in the Northern Province.

The Zion Christian Church (ZCC), led by the Right Reverend Bishop Dr. Barnabas E. Lekganyane, was founded in 1910 by Engenas Lekganyane, a farm worker. It is a family dynasty of succession.

The highlight of the ZCC religious calendar is the Easter celebration, which draws more than 1 million church members for several days of religious services at Zion City. Zionist beliefs emphasize the healing power of religious faith, and for this reason, ZCC leaders sometimes clash with the traditional healers. Despite occasional conflicts, however, the ZCC respects traditional African religious beliefs, in general, especially those concerning the power of the ancestors to intercede on behalf of people.

The ZCC proscribes alcoholic beverages, smoking, and eating pork. It condemns sexual promiscuity and violence. The followers of this religion usually wear an identifying badge on their clothing.

Shembe

Members of the Nazareth Baptist Church are popularly known as Shembe. The Shembe church in KwaZulu-Natal is divided between the factions, eKuphakameni and eBuhleni. Both believe they are the 'real' Shembe. The church started in 1909 by Isaiah Shembe and currently there are three Shembe church leaders, two in Durban and one in Johannesburg. The Shembe Sabbath falls on Saturday.

Near Inanda, north of Durban, is a sacred site called Ekuphakameni, the 'Place of Spiritual Upliftment.' It was named by Isaiah Shembe, prophet and founder of the Shembe Church. A major festival is held in mid-January at an equally sacred location, the mountain dubbed Nhlangakazi, some 30 kilometres north of Ekuphakameni. The Shembe Church is well known for its spectacular dance festivals and the church's structure is a mixture of Christian doctrine and the tenets of Zulu culture.

According to Durban journalist, Themba Nyathikazi, 'Some worshippers travel very long distances to reach the holy mountain, where they participate in ritualistic song and dance. During the exodus to the mountain, the Shembe take part in a hypnotic, trance-like dance, with the men leading the way. The married women follow, carrying furled umbrellas and tiny ceremonial shields in the same colours as their church clothing. They are, in turn, followed by young maidens in full traditional regalia. A constant stream of vehicles and barefooted worshippers walk along the dusty road to the holy site. Praising the Almighty on top of the mountain, and executing traditional Zulu dances, the Shembe reflect an alternative version of Christianity, which has evolved based on the Old, rather than the New Testament.'

The two factions alternate the use of the site for their rituals.

Christianity

History tells us that Jesus of Nazareth was born a Jew from the line of David. After his baptism, by his cousin John the Baptist, he preached a whole new doctrine of salvation through love and faith.

A church is the building in which come together to pray to and worship God through his Son Jesus Christ. The rituals and services used for worship differ enormously from church to church. The Catholic and Orthodox Churches are very different from the

Protestant and the charismatic churches, but they are all Christians. They all believe that Jesus Christ is the Son of God, who died on the cross for the sins of mankind, and that he is the Saviour of all people.

Christians believe that one day Jesus will return and everyone will be judged. Those who accept Jesus as their Saviour will live forever with God in Heaven. They believe that the Bible is the uniquely inspired and the fully trustworthy Word of God. It is the final authority for Christians in matters of belief and practice, and though it was written long ago, it continues to speak to believers today.

Christians also believe human beings only die once and after that face judgment. In Adam's sin, the human race was spiritually alienated from God. Those who are called by God and respond to His grace will have eternal life. Those who persist in rebellion will be lost eternally.

Jesus is God incarnate, according to Christians and, therefore, the only sure path to salvation. Many religions may offer ethical and spiritual insights, but only Jesus is the way, the truth, and the life.

Sunday is the holy day for Christians and they usually go to church on this day to worship God, pray, sing, and listen to sermons from their priests/ preachers/ ministers or pastors. Some services are held in tents, stadia, or homes.

The main Christian Festivals are Christmas (25 December) and Easter (March or April), the days that Christ was born and was crucified, according to their religion.

Hinduism

Hinduism made its first appearance in 1860 in South Africa, when indentured labourers were shipped in from India to work on the sugar plantations of KwaZulu-Natal. They brought with them their religions and soon started to build shrines and temples. The most famous Hindu with South African connections was the Guajarati Mahatma (Great Soul) Gandhi, who arrived in 1893, and eventually spent 20 years in the country.

Today there are minor differences regarding practices of worship between various groups of South African Hindus. The religion of most Hindus revolves around family life, the temple, cultural activities, and annual festivals. Yet Neo-Hindu movements such as the Arya Samaj, Ramakrishna and Divine Life Society, Hare Krishna's (International Society of Krishna Consciousness), and Sai Baba's followers also have a strong impact on South African Hinduism. Hindus live throughout the country, especially in urban areas, with the overwhelming majority in KwaZulu-Natal.

Most Hindus do not eat beef and do not wear leather and many are strictly vegetarian.

There are four main linguistic groups of Hindus in South Africa: Tamil-speaking, who originate from South India; Hindi-speaking, who originate from North-India; Gujarati-speaking who also originate from north-India and the Telegu-speaking who originate from central India. There are also Gujarati-speaking Muslims in South Africa.

For Hindus, the attainment of spiritual perfection and freedom is the aim of life and the purpose of human birth. Hinduism sees man as being a combination of body (action), emotions (feelings), will (thoughts), and intellect (discrimination). Each of these facets of an individual's personality can be made perfectly attuned to the Divine – this is called Yoga or union of the individual soul with the universal Soul.

Hindus believe in the divinity of the Vedas, the world's most ancient scriptures, in one, all pervading God and believe in respecting all other religions.

They also believe in Karma, the law of cause and effect, by which each individual creates his own destiny by his thoughts, words and deeds.

Hindus believe that the soul reincarnates, evolving through many births until all Karmas have been resolved. Not a single soul will be eternally deprived of this destiny. Hindus also hold the belief that divine beings exist and that that all life is sacred.

The Festival of Diwali or Deepavali is the most significant of the Hindu holy days

Swami Shivananda, The Divine Life Society, Rishikesh explains that Hinduism is extremely inclusive, liberal, tolerant, and elastic. 'This is the wonderful feature of Hinduism. A foreigner (visiting India) is struck with astonishment when he hears about the diverse sects and creeds of Hinduism. But these varieties are really an ornament to Hinduism. They are certainly not its defects. There are various types of minds and temperaments. So there should be various faiths also. This is but natural. This is the cardinal tenet of Hinduism. There is room in Hinduism for all types of souls – from the highest to the lowest – for their growth and evolution.'

Islam

Islam was the second of the 'world religions' to have settled in South Africa, having arrived at least as early as 1658 with the Dutch settlement in the Cape. Because of very repressive conditions during the first century and a half, the first mosque could only be erected in 1804.

Islam received a new injection with the arrival of Indian labourers in KwaZulu-Natal from 1860 onwards. Today Islam has entered a new phase of its history and Muslims play an important role in society across the country.

Currently, about 650 000 South Africans, or less than 2 per cent, are Muslim. They are mostly members of the country's Indian and coloured communities. Christianity – practised by 80 per cent of the country's 45 million population – is still the dominant religion among black South Africans. But an estimated 75 000 Africans are now Muslim, compared to fewer than 12 000 in 1991 during apartheid white rule, according to research by the Human Sciences Research Council.

Prophet Mohammad (pbuh) was born in 571 CE. He was not called to the prophetic life until he was about 40 years of age. Allah is the name of God in the Arabic language. The Muslim belief is that the last Prophet that God sent was the Prophet Muhammad (pbuh). When Muslims hear, say or read the name of the Prophet Mohammed they are urged to say either silently or aloud 'Saiallahu 'alauahi wa

sallam'; Peace and blessings of Allah be upon him (pbuh).

The Qur'an or Koran is the sacred book of Islam, and was originally written in Arabic. Muslims believe it is the infallible word of God and was dictated to Mohammad (pbuh) through the medium of the Angel Gabriel (Jibra'il).

Festivals and religious holidays are important for observant Muslims, especially Ramadan and Eid.

The full connotation of the word 'Islam' is "the perfect peace that comes when one's life is surrendered to God".

The following are known as the Five Pillars of Islam which constitute the 'straight path' the Muslim is to follow in order to be assured salvation.

1. Repetition of the creed (Shahadah)

'There is no god but Allah, and Muhammad (pbuh) is His prophet.' This is the creed which every Muslim must believe and repeat.

2. Prayer (Salat/Salah)

The act of regular prayer consists of a ritual of ablution, prostrations and recitations from the Qur'an. The main themes of prayer are expressing praise and gratitude and also supplication to Allah (pbuh). The five times of prayer are at dawn, midday, mid-afternoon, sunset, and bedtime. Friday is the special day of public prayer where all assemble in the mosque.

3. Charity (Zakat/Zakah)

This is a free-will offering made to the poor, the needy, debtors, slaves, wayfarers, beggars, and charities. It is calculated at two and half percent of the accumulated wealth of a man or his family at the end of each year.

4. The Observance of Ramadan – Saum

This is the fast undertaken during the holy month that commemorates Muhammad's (pbuh) receiving his initial commission as a prophet, and 10 years later, his historic Hijraj from Mecca to Medina. Those who are able, fast from daybreak to sunset. Fasting also makes one think, teaches self discipline, reminds one of man's frailty and dependence on God, and makes one feel for the hungry and needy.

5. Pilgrimage (Hajj)

Once in a lifetime every Muslim, man or woman, is expected, unless it is impossible, to make a pilgrimage to Mecca in the 12th month of the Islamic year.

There are many different sects of Islam, the chief two being the Shias and the Sunnis. Islamic mysticism is known as Sufism. Devotion, meditation, and prayer form important parts of the Sufi way of life.

If an animal is slaughtered and Allah's name was not taken, that animal is regarded to be carrion. It is prohibited to eat the meat of such an animal. Ritual slaughtering of animals, under the supervision Muslim authorities produce food, labeled Halaal. Muslim dietary restrictions also include abstinence from pork products, gelatin, and also alcohol (see Catering for official functions).

Judaism

Judaism arrived on South African shores, in the early 19th century, when practicing Jews (mainly from England, Germany and Holland) sought a new home in this country. The first synagogue was established in Cape Town in 1841. Today, about 85 per cent of Jews are Orthodox, falling under the jurisdiction of the Union of Orthodox Synagogues of South Africa, while only about 15 per cent belong to the Reform movement. There are also a few ultra-Orthodox groups.

The one great theme of the Jewish religion is that a single, righteous G-d is at work in the social and natural order, and He has revealed His will in history. There are many different forms of Judaism. Some conservative, some intellectual, others mystical etc. – all are different approaches to the basic beliefs which are as follows:

The covenant – G-d (Yahweh*) continues to give Himself in goodness to his people if they in turn pledge themselves to keep His commandments. Please note for Judaism, that the term 'Yahweh' is an academic reconstruction, and it is considered blasphemous to

attempt to pronounce the word written YHWH by all religious Jews.

There are various names for G-d in Hebrew, the Jewish language, but they are so holy that they can only be pronounced during prayers, and his most holy name is never spoken. Rabbis are teachers of Jewish law. They often call G-d, Hashem which means 'The name'. One writes G-d because Jews do not write or say his holy name.

According to Jewish belief, G-d gave his law to Moses on Mount Sinai. Moses was a direct descendent of Abraham. This law is called the Torah. The Law (the Torah) contains the ritualistic and ethical prescriptions, which make man's collective life, endure. There are some 613 commandments regulating human behaviour (Mitzvoth) but the Ten Commandments have had the greatest impact on the world (Exodus 20). Baby boys are circumcised when they are 8 days old as an outward symbol of the covenant formed between Moses and G-d.

Friday evening at just before sunset, the Jewish Sabbath (Shabbat) begins. Shabbat ends just after sunset on Saturday. On Saturday, Jews go the synagogue or Shul to worship G-d. Children born to Jewish parents are considered Jewish by birth.

Jewish people are only allowed to eat kosher food. This is meat that is slaughtered according to religious ritual prescriptions. Other dietary regulations also apply (see Catering for official functions). The Jewish calendar is different from the Roman lunar calendar that we use for months and years. Jews also celebrate New Year in late September/ early October, on a day called Rosh Hashanah. This is the day that Adam and Eve were created. Festivals and holidays are very important for the Jewish community. Yom Kippur is another important holy day.

Other religions

There are many other religions, mostly branches or sects of the major ones like Baha'i, Buddhism, Sufism, Hare Krishna, Chinese Religion etc. For further information on this topic please consult the various sources provided.

Case study   Civil Society in South Africa

Definitions and Terminology

Civil society has been described as "*the sphere of organizations and/or associations of organizations located between the family, the state, the government of the day, and the prevailing economic system, in which people with common interests associate voluntarily. Amongst those organizations, they may have common, competing or conflicting values and interests.*"[i]

The most commonly-used terms in South Africa are:

- Non-governmental organization (NGO);
- Non-profit organization (NPO);
- Community-based organization (CBO);
- Civil Society Organization (CSO).

After 1994 the first democratic government invested considerable effort in dismantling apartheid legislation inimical to effective civil society functioning. A new regulatory framework designed to 'enhance the capacity of non-profit organizations to perform their functions' was created. This set of legislative reforms aimed to establish a progressive public space in which state-civil society relations could be managed, and the non-profit sector funded.

Why do we need a Strong Civil Society Sector in South Africa?

"The truth is that we are not yet free, we have merely achieved the freedom to be free, the right not to be oppressed."

Nelson Mandela

In the 14 years since South Africa's first non-racial and democratic election, there has been a strong drive to alleviate the poverty and marginalization of apartheid. Significant strides have been made at policy levels towards the transformation of the lives of ordinary South Africans. However, poverty and inequality is still very much present in South Africa. Unemployment stands at 23,5 per cent, and is actually much higher if those who have given up looking for work are counted.

The Gini Coefficient, used to measure income inequalities and associated inequities, shows that South Africa has overtaken Brazil and is now the most unequal society in the world.[ii]

These challenges are currently exacerbated by the global economic crisis. While 13 million people have now been included in the safety net of social grants, poverty remains a daunting challenge.

About 40 per cent of households still live below a poverty line estimated by the National Treasury to be about R480 per person per month. Poverty is closely linked to the structural problems of unemployment and the lack of skills; unemployment affects poor households most severely.

Hunger remains a common denominator among poor people in South Africa. Inequality has increased among African people and apartheid racial patterns have remained roughly the same. The rapid growth of the black middle class has meant that inequality, as measured by the Gini Coefficient, has risen among black people, from 0.55 in 1994 to 0.59 in 2008.[iii]

In spite of an enlightened Constitution, discrimination and inequity still abound in South Africa. Women, people of colour, indigenous peoples, migrants, homosexuals, and people living with HIV and Aids, are among particularly vulnerable groups.

There has been some progress in racial, ethnic, and gender equality since apartheid was dismantled.

However South Africa remains a society where the means of production, employment, property and the distribution of wealth remain concentrated in the hands of a small minority.

Women still suffer discrimination in the world of work, and experience a high rate of sexual and gender-based violence.

Contract migrant workers are excluded from the reach of labour laws and some human rights protections, and other Africans living in

South Africa are subjected to many forms of xenophobia, including the violence which swept the country during 2008. [iv]

In at least ten 'development sectors' organizations of civil society are working to alleviate the socio-economic problems delineated above. These organizations work to alleviate poverty, to skill the unskilled, to provide health care to the marginalized, and to challenge the effects of discrimination and human rights abuses.

Dimensions and contributions of civil society

We are currently hampered by the lack of current national data on civil society. The most recent and reliable estimates are from 2002 study which showed:

- there were 98 920 NPOs in South Africa of which 53 percent were less formalized, community-based, often staffed by volunteers, and providing a range of essential support services within poor and marginalized communities;
- South African civil society is as large, in proportional terms, and as vibrant, as in all but a handful of advanced industrialized countries;
- a focus on the developmental role of civil society organizations has been widespread. South Africa's Civil Society Sector has traditionally advocated for social and economic justice, especially under apartheid. In addition organizations of civil society have provided some relief from the detrimental effects of poverty and marginalization.

However the sector is anything but homogenous, and has been authoritatively characterized as a combination of NGOs (which deliver formal services, sometimes in partnership with government), community-based or survivalist agencies (which provide basic support such as home-based care within marginalized communities), and social movements (which are currently challenging state policy and non-delivery).

The more formal NGOs' collaborative relationship with the state is largely a product of the services they render on behalf of the state. In a society still confronted with massive back-logs and limited institutional capacity, this role can only be to the benefit of democracy, since it facilitates and enables service delivery to ordinary citizens and residents. [vi]

A survey of the voluntary sector identified NGOs and CBOs as having an important role to play in filling the gaps left by the government, especially in poor communities. This role, it was argued, was earned 'through the strategic location of NGOs, their access to communities and the credibility they enjoy from these communities. Further, their organizational flexibility and capacity to identify development alternatives make them the missing link in many of the state's development ventures.' [vii]

Although there is little current national information about the civil society sector currently available, we do have information about the critical work of organizations within the different sectors of civil society. For example:

A 2008 report commissioned by the National Development Agency found that: "In South Africa, many civil society organizations are filling the gaps by providing socio-economic and basic services that the state is unable to provide and in some cases have taken over the functions of the state. An example of this is the child protection sector, in which social workers at Child Welfare organizations carry out statutory services which are the responsibility of the state. Civil society organizations are seen as an important mechanism in assisting the state with service provision and poverty alleviation at the margins of society, because CSOs (and CBOs in particular) usually arise organically in response to needs within a community and are able to reach areas where there is little formal organization but where the need is often greatest." [viii]

A new study by the South African Institute of Relations shows that between 2002 and 2007 the number of child-headed households in South Africa increased by 25 per cent – from 118 000 in 2002 to 148 000 in 2007. The study shows that most of these children live in 'income poverty' and that in many cases the only support provided to these households is provided by civil society organizations of various kinds. [ix]

315

Current challenges facing civil society

As described above, organizations of civil society in South Africa play a crucial but often under-valued role. One of the challenges currently faced by this sector is that of financial sustainability.

Whereas under apartheid the sector was generously funded by the international donor community, since the dawn of democracy international funding has been channeled through an often ineffective state apparatus.

While we do not have current and reliable statistics on funding to the sector, a variety of sources show that most organizations rely on a combination of (diminishing) international funding, corporate social investment, donations from individuals, and a degree of income-generation, often via government contracts. The support of government is erratic at best, and international funding is gradually diminishing. This situation is greatly exacerbated by the current economic recession.

The civil society sector represents the third element in South Africa's development equation. The other two sectors, the state and the market are regularly monitored and reported on by various government institutions including Stats SA and the National Treasury.

The same cannot be said of the civil society sector, despite the fact that this sector represents the bridge between the citizenry, the state and the market. The state's commitment to poverty alleviation and development cannot be realized without full participation and resourcing of this sector.

In order for civil society to effectively fulfill the important roles outlined above, a supportive policy, funding and institutional environment is critical. Currently the state is not meeting its responsibilities to the sector, either in regard to the legislative environment, or the functioning of the several agencies set up to ensure that the sector is properly funded, monitored and included in ongoing policy and planning processes.

Further discussion on this important sector can be obtained from CAF Southern Africa at www.cafsouthernafrica.org or by contacting Colleen Du Toit at info@cafsouthernafrica.org who researched and wrote this case study.

[i] www.sarpn.org.za/documents/d0000990/index.php.

[ii] Dinokeng Scenarios, 2009 (page 20).

[iii] Danish Institute for Human Rights Human Rights and Business Project. South Africa Country Risk Assessment (page 10) [Online]. Available: aiccafrica.org/cra-sa.

[iv] Swilling, M & Russell, B. The Size and Scope of the Non-Profit Sector. Centre for Civil Society (undated); Giving and Solidarity, 2008. HSRC Press. Review of the State of Civil Society.

[v] Habib, A. 2008. In Prodder, NGO's and Development in South Africa, 2008.

[vi] Boulle, J. 1997. 'Putting the Voluntary Sector Back on the Map'. Development Update 1,1.

[vii] Review of the State of Civil Society Organizations in South Africa, compiled for the NDA by CASE, Planact and Africa Skills Development, 2008. (page 23).

[viii] Fast Facts. 2009. 7: July 2009. The Institute of Race Relations, South Africa.

[ix] Swilling, M. & Russell B. op cit; and Review of the State of Civil Society Organizations in South Africa, compiled for the NDA by CASE et al, 2008.

Conclusion

An emergent growing economy such as South Africa is labour intensive and the consequences of HIV/Aids are staggering. It has been predicted in the 'Love Life' campaign that the number of employees lost to Aids over the next 10 years could be the equivalent of 40 to 50 per cent of the current workforce in some South African companies.

The impact of Aids from a national perspective could result in:

- a slower economic growth;
- decrease in international competitiveness;
- increased demands in state health;
- redirection of state funding away from essential expenditures;
- reallocation of resources from savings and investment to cash (redirection);
- illness and death of productive people and a fall in overall productivity;

- a shift from labour intensive to capital intensive markets.

While the KwaZulu-Natal market is likely to be most affected by HIV/Aids, some of the national marketing implications could include:
- a decrease in the number of potential customers;
- changes in the demographic profile;
- a decrease in discretionary spending;
- an increase in the default of long-term credit granted;
- growing terminations of insurance policies;
- an increase in medical and funeral policies;
- change in overall priorities.

Marketers have been exhorted to build brand equity and relationships of trust with consumers. The current growth phase is expected to flatten out and competition will increase. Weaker, less competitive brands are not expected to survive the 'stake out'.

Products expected to be negatively affected include furniture, electrical appliances (especially colour televisions, irons, kettles, fridges),

and savings accounts. The number of defaulters on long-term loans is expected to increase as people get too sick to work and eventually stop earning. Even people who buy furniture and clothing on account are more likely to default – especially those who are very materialistic and deeply in debt. Beauty and other products positioned to the emerging female market are likely to take one of the biggest knocks as their target market is going to be most affected. The number of people taking advantage of incentives like free funeral cover can be expected to increase as Aids-related deaths increase.

Aspirational messages are likely to become less effective as people's needs move down from higher order needs (like prestige, status, and keeping up with the Joneses) to more basic needs of food, warmth, and shelter. As people become focused on mere survival their obsession with materialism and the glamour associated with 'soaps' is likely to become less powerful as a selling proposition.

Being seen to be associated directly with HIV/Aids is fraught with potential problems for most marketers due to its 'taboo' nature

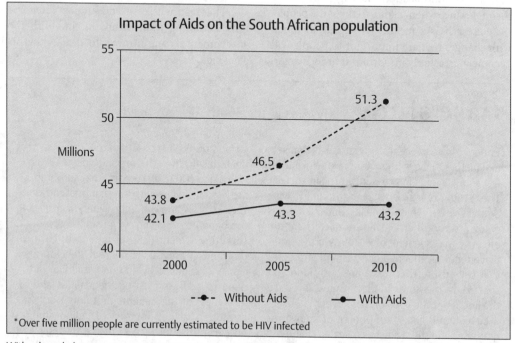

Impact of Aids on the South African population

*Over five million people are currently estimated to be HIV infected

With acknowledgement to Futurefact 2000, Unilever Institute, School of Management Studies, University of Cape Town

among many people. Social responsibility programmes, where appropriate and possible, may be a viable way of making a difference in the world and in some way safeguarding target markets through prevention as well as building customer loyalty. The issues that face people as a result of the disease offer endless possibilities for marketers both in terms of new product opportunities and communication messages.

As people become increasingly informed about the disease, their concerns should start turning increasingly towards health issues. Remaining healthy and keeping up your body's immunity could offer consumers solutions to their new concerns.

There is no doubt that HIV/Aids is going to take the lives of many young South Africans. This is likely to cause growing markets to contract in numbers. As more people lose their income as a result of Aids-related illnesses, disposable income is expected to decline so competition will increase as brands fight over market share in smaller, poorer markets. The scourge of Aids is expected to alter people's priorities, values, and aspirations; effective, well-targeted communication messages may lose their relevance when talking to the same people.

Research as a means of keeping in touch with changes that are important to people will become increasingly important if brands are to survive the next 10 years in South Africa. The threats ahead look serious. While there may be a turning point in the not too distant future, as there is with most trends, survival is going to be a real challenge for the immediate mid-term future.

The Department of Health has developed the National Strategic Plan (NSP) for HIV and Aids for 2007-2011. The plan emphasizes treatment and prevention. It also spells out clear, quantified targets, and places a high priority on monitoring and evaluation.

The primary goal of the NSP is to reduce the rate of new HIV infections and to mitigate the impact of Aids on individuals, families, and communities.

The NSP aims to achieve a 50 per cent reduction in new infections by 2011 and provides an appropriate package of treatment, care, and support services.

The package includes counselling and testing services as an entry point; healthy-lifestyle interventions, including nutritional support; treatment of opportunistic infections, antiretroviral (ARV) therapy; and monitoring and evaluation to assess progress and share research.

The treatment, care, and support intervention is gaining momentum in line with the government's commitment to deal with this challenge.

Case study HIV/Aids in the South African society

Evidence from a recent study suggests that several factors that are important and relevant for CSI and HIV/Aids in the South African society. The study revealed that companies with aggressive HIV/Aids policies and strategies enjoy a surge in employee morale. Therefore effective management of HIV/Aids in the workplace requires effective policies and strategies that will ensure that there are both long and short term measures in place that will reduce the impact of the virus on employees.

Education is a key component of many programmes and the study has revealed that most corporations have co-ordinators or clinics that deal specifically with the pandemic.

Rockey (2002: XIV) reports that corporations are keeping in line with international corporate social trends and are increasingly recognizing the benefits of having an advanced corporate social investment (CSI) programme. CSI programmes have taken on real development challenges, driven by an understanding of the need to address existing inequalities and an awareness of the benefits that flow from successful social development. Leading companies in South Africa treat CSI as a strategic and not as a superficial feel-good form of charitable giving. Evidence from this study suggests that large corporations are leading the way in terms of broad development challenges. Business plans have now become impossible to consider CSI without the inclusion of HIV/Aids. Additional pressure has been placed on the CSI practitioner to deliver in the area of HIV/Aids.

Nilsson (2005: 94) comments that 'business is admittedly making serious efforts as regards the pandemic, both internally as well as in the broader community.' Strong evidence from this study suggests that the South African corporate sector have accepted the problem of HIV/Aids and have realized that the problem can be addressed and have adopted the approach that community equals workplace. Business is now actively supporting the issue of HIV/Aids in South Africa. Companies have begun to recognize the seriousness of HIV/Aids and the impact it has on the workplace as well as the social and economic life of employees. Evidence also reflects the degree of commitment displayed by large corporations towards the development of policies on HIV/Aids. Companies are therefore committed to addressing HIV/Aids in a positive, supportive, and non-discriminatory manner with the informed support and co-operation of all employees. New company strategies have a two-pronged approach, with the focus on prevention and positive living. The prevention aspect involves the avoidance of new infections by encouraging employees to make informed choices and decisions and take responsibility for their own lives. Part of this strategy includes training and development, awareness campaigns, information, and knowledge sharing. Some companies have elected HIV/Aids committees representing staff, members of management, human resources staff, trade unions and peer educators. These strategies also extend to the broader community, and in most cases are facilitated by a foundation.

Findings also reveal that the South African business community is serious about HIV and they are serious about educating their staff and are therefore guided by South African legislation which provides strict instructions on HIV/Aids testing procedures. The results reported in this study help South Africans understand the stimulus faced by the private sector when dealing with the problem of HIV/Aids. Many large corporations have implemented effective workplace policies and are ensuring that their employees are given the best in terms of education and medical assistance to help curb the spread of the virus. However, this is not so in the case of the smaller companies, where only a small percentage of SMEs have implemented HIV/Aids policies. This shows that smaller companies still lack a strategic response to the pandemic. Although most of the large companies indicate they have policies/strategies in place, it is not certain whether employees have seen or are aware of these policies. It is also not certain exactly how much is being done in terms of communication, care and assistance to employees.

The reality of the HIV/Aids problem is affecting all facets of our South African Society and has especially challenged the corporate world. The investment in human resources has come to the forefront, and why not? If collectively the corporate world does not take responsibility for its manpower, it will not only be detrimental to the company, but also to innocent affected employees that assist the corporate sector in achieving its many commitments.

The absence of investment in mitigation will result in labour becoming a non-renewable resource. The challenge is to effectively link corporate social investment and HIV/Aids policies, in order to optimize impact, both for business and for the community.

Sources

Dr Renitha Rampersad.

Nilsson, S. 2005. 'Translating Corporate HIV/AIDS Activities. A Case Study of HIV/Aids Strategies, Policies, and Programs in Four South African-based Companies'. Stockholm: Unpublished Masters Thesis in Organization and Management.

Rockey, V. 2002. *The Corporate Social Investment Handbook*. 5th edition. Cape Town: Trialogue.

Further reading

All Media Products Survey (AMPS). 2007–2009. Johannesburg: SAARF.

Beck, D. & G. Linscott. 1991. *The African Crucible: Forging South Africa's Future.* Denton: New Paradigm Press.

Green, W. & R. Lascaris. 1988. *Third World Destiny.* Tafelberg: Human & Rousseau.

Langschmidt, D.T. 1996. *SA to Z – South Africa from A to Z: The Decision-maker's Encyclopaedia of the South African Consumer Market.* Johannesburg: SA to Z.

Mytton, G. (ed.) 1993. *Global Audiences: Research for Worldwide Broadcasting.* Johannesburg: New Paradigm Press.

Race Relations Surveys. 2000–2009. Johannesburg: SA Institute of Race Relations.

South African Yearbooks. 2000–2009. Pretoria: GCIS.

SABC. 1992. *Reaching Critical Mass.* Johannesburg: Market Research Report.

Whiteside, A. & C. Sunter. 2000. *Aids: The Challenge for South Africa.* Cape Town: Human & Rousseau.

In addition to these books and reports, leading research bodies and private companies have done extensive research into the multi-ethnic, multicultural market in South Africa.

There are also a number of websites that monitor HIV/Aids and provide up-to-date information on a variety of research projects and programmes.

Part IV

Doing it right: a practical guide to protocol, business etiquette, and handling special events

Protocol

The government of South Africa

The Constitution

The Constitution of the Republic of South Africa, 1996 (Act 108 of 1996), was drawn up by the Constitutional Assembly and reaffirms South Africa as a constitutional and republican state.

The Constitution is the highest and most important law of the land. No other law or government action can supersede the provisions of the Constitution. Fundamental rights are contained in Chapter Two and seek to protect the rights and freedoms of individuals.

The Constitutional Court guards these rights and determines whether or not actions by the State are in accordance with constitutional provisions.

Government

Government is structured at national, provincial, and local levels. The powers of the lawmakers (legislative authorities), governments (executive authorities), and the courts (judicial authorities) are separate from one another.

Parliament

Parliament is the legislative authority of South Africa and has the power to make laws for the country in accordance with the Constitution. It consists of the National Assembly and the National Council of Provinces. Parliamentary sittings are open to the public.

National Assembly

The National Assembly consists of no fewer than 350 and no more than 400 members elected through a system of proportional representation. The National Assembly, which is elected for a term of five years, is presided over by a Speaker, assisted by a Deputy Speaker.

The National Assembly is elected to represent the people and to ensure democratic governance as required by the Constitution. It does this by electing the President, by providing a national forum for public consideration of issues, by passing legislation, and by scrutinizing and overseeing executive action.

National Council of Provinces

The National Council of Provinces consists of 54 permanent members and 36 special dele-

gates, and aims to represent provincial interests in the national sphere of government.
Delegations from each province consist of 10
representatives.

The National Council of Provinces gets a
mandate from the provinces before it can make
certain decisions. It cannot, however, initiate a
Bill concerning money, which is the preroga-
tive of the Minister of Finance.

In October 1999, NCOP Online! was
launched, which links Parliament to the
provincial legislatures and local government
associations. Utilizing a website, e-mail, and a
fax-broadcast and cellphone messaging
system, NCOP Online! provides information
on, among other things, draft legislation
and allows the public to make electronic
submissions.

Law-making

Any Bill may be introduced in the National
Assembly. A Bill passed by the National
Assembly must be referred to the National
Council of Provinces for consideration. A Bill
affecting the provinces may be introduced in
the National Council of Provinces and after it
has been passed by the Council it must be
referred to the Assembly. A Bill concerning
money must be introduced in the Assembly
and must be referred to the Council for consideration and approval after being passed.

If the Council rejects a Bill or passes it subject to amendments, the Assembly must recon-
sider the Bill and pass it again with or without
amendments. There are special conditions for
the approval of laws dealing with provinces.

The President

The President is the Head of State and leads
the Cabinet. He or she is elected by the
National Assembly from among its members
and leads the country in the interest of national unity, in accordance with the Constitution
and the law.

The Deputy President

The President appoints the Deputy President
from among the members of the National
Assembly. The Deputy President must assist the
President in executing government functions.

The Cabinet

The Cabinet consists of the President, as head
of the Cabinet, the Deputy President, and
Ministers. The President appoints the Deputy
President and Ministers, assigns their powers
and functions and may dismiss them.

The President may select any number of
Ministers from among the members of the
National Assembly and may select no more
than two Ministers from outside the Assembly.

The President appoints a member of the
Cabinet to be the leader of government business in the National Assembly.

The President may appoint Deputy
Ministers from among the members of the
National Assembly.

Traditional leadership

According to Chapter 12 of the Constitution,
the institution, status, and role of traditional
leadership according to customary law, are recognized subject to the Constitution.

The Chief Directorate: Traditional Affairs
in the Department of Provincial and Local
Government gives support to traditional leadership and institutions.

The Chief Directorate is responsible for
the formulation of policy on traditional leadership and institutions, the determination of
the remuneration of traditional leaders and
their capacity-building, the maintenance of a
database, and giving support to the National
House of Traditional Leaders.

A discussion document has been finalized.
Uniform remuneration of traditional leaders
has been determined and was published in the
Government Gazette No. 19901 dated 1 April
1999.

Provincial boundaries

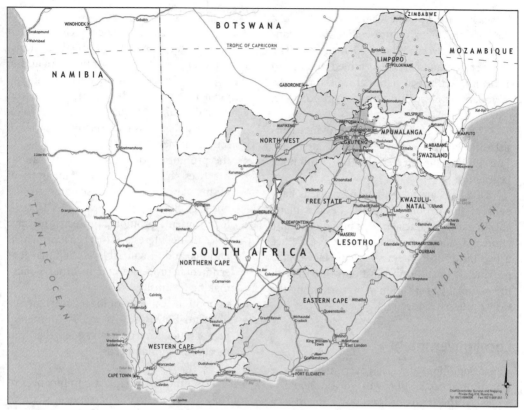

The Chief Directorate has also been involved in the issue of the constitutional position of communities who view themselves as indigenous, such as the Griqua. The National Griqua Forum was established to represent these groups.

Houses of Traditional Leaders

The Constitution mandates the establishment of Houses of Traditional Leaders by means of either provincial or national legislation.

Provincial houses of traditional leaders have been established in all six provinces where traditional leaders are found, namely Eastern Cape, KwaZulu-Natal, Free State, Mpumalanga, Northern Province, and North-West.

The National House of Traditional Leaders was established in April 1997 in terms of legislation passed by Parliament. Each provincial House of Traditional Leaders nominated three members to be represented in the National House, which then elected its own office-bearers.

The National House advises the national Government on the role of traditional leaders and on customary law. It may also conduct its own investigations and advise the country's President on request.

Volkstaat Council

The Volkstaat Council presented its final report to the President in April 1999. The Volkstaat Council Act, 1994 (Act 30 of 1994), formalized the body set up by the 1993 interim Constitution to investigate the concept of a nation-state for Afrikaners.

325

Provincial government

In accordance with the Constitution, each of the nine provinces has its own legislature consisting of between 30 and 80 members. The number of members is determined in terms of a formula set out in national legislation. The members are elected in terms of proportional representation.

The Executive Council of a province consists of a Premier and a number of members. The Premier is elected by the Provincial Legislature.

Decisions are taken by consensus, as happens in the national Cabinet. Besides being able to make provincial laws, a provincial legislature may adopt a constitution for its province if two thirds of its members agree. However, a provincial constitution must correspond with the national Constitution as confirmed by the Constitutional Court.

Local government

The recognition of local government in the Constitution as a sphere of government has enhanced the status of local government as a whole and of municipalities in particular, and has given them a new dynamic role as instruments of delivery. The relationship between the three spheres of government is outlined in Chapter Three of the Constitution, which, among other things, requires Parliament to establish structures and institutions to promote and facilitate intergovernmental relations. According to the Constitution and the Organized Local Government Act, 1997 (Act 52 of 1997), which formally recognizes the South African Local Government Association and the nine provincial local government associations, organized local government may designate up to ten part-time representatives to represent the different categories of municipalities and participate in proceedings of the National Council of Provinces.

South African Local Government Association

The South African Local Government Association (SALGA) has a mandate to transform local government in South Africa and to represent the interests of organized local government primarily in the country's intergovernmental relations system with a united voice.

SALGA's business plan sets out a series of objectives, namely:
- the promotion of sound labour relations practices that can achieve high levels of performance and responsiveness to the needs of citizens;
- to represent, promote, protect, and give voice to the interests of local government at national and provincial levels, in inter-governmental processes and in other policy-making forums;
- to build the capacity of local government;
- to contribute towards a developmental democratic governance system that can meet basic human needs.

SALGA is funded through a combination of sources. These include a percentage share of the national revenue allocated to local government, membership fees from provincial and local government associations that are voluntary members, and donations from the donor community that funds specific projects.

Municipalities

The Constitution provides for three categories of municipalities.

As directed by the Constitution, the Local Government: Municipal Structures Act, 1998 (Act 117 of 1998), contains criteria for determining when an area must have a Category A municipality (Metropolitan Municipalities) and when its municipalities fall into Categories B (District Municipalities) or C (Local Areas or Municipalities). It also determines that Category A municipalities can only be established in metropolitan areas.

The Municipal Demarcation Board, appointed by the President, determines the areas that have metropolitan municipalities by designating the nodal points of such areas. According to the Board's determination, Johannesburg, Durban, Cape Town, Pretoria, East Rand, and Port Elizabeth are metropolitan areas.

Metropolitan councils have a single metropolitan budget, common property rating and service tariffs systems, and a single employer body. They move towards integrating service delivery in metropolitan areas through service utilities or agencies.

The Board, which began its work in March 1999, finalized the redrawing of municipal boundaries in 2000. The process reduced the number of South Africa's municipalities (previously 843) drastically. The Board also determined ward boundaries. Wards are used in the determination of electoral rolls and in sub-local government functions. A councillor, who looks after the interest of the residents in the area and through whom residents can raise issues, represents each ward.

Existing municipalities are rationalized into the three categories prescribed by the Constitution, namely Categories A, B, and C.

The Local Government: Municipal Structures Act, 1998 provides for the allocation of powers and functions to Category B and C municipalities and deals with the electoral system that will apply to future municipal elections. The Act defines a new system for local government in South Africa. According to the Act, all metropolitan councils should be transformed into single municipalities or unicities.

The metropolitan council may decentralize powers and functions. However, all original municipal, legislative, and executive powers will be vested in the metro council.

In metropolitan areas there is a choice of two types of executive systems: the mayoral executive system where legislative and executive authority is vested in the mayor, and the collective executive committee where these powers are vested in the executive committee.

Non-metropolitan areas consist of district councils and local councils. District councils are primarily responsible for capacity-building and district-wide planning.

The Judiciary

The Constitution provides for a judicial system with a powerful Constitutional Court. This court is the highest authority on constitutional matters and can override the Legislature. It is regarded as the guardian of the Constitution and especially the Bill of Rights. The Supreme Court structure at provincial and local levels continues to exist.

The Constitutional Court has the final say on matters relating to the interpretation, protection, and enforcement of the provisions of the Constitution at any level of government. Its decisions are final and binding, which means that no other court has the power to interfere with its decisions.

Bill of Rights

The Constitutional Court also has the function of protecting the rights and freedom of citizens. These are contained in a Bill of Rights which extends the democratic rights and freedom of all citizens and protects them against possible abuse by the State. These rights include fundamental liberties such as equality, life, human dignity, freedom and security of the individual, religion, belief and opinion, freedom of association, freedom of movement, citizens' rights, and political rights. The Bill of Rights also protects the individual against servitude and forced labour.

The courts have the responsibility of breaking new ground in defining the exact nature and limits of many of the first, second, and third generation rights included in the Bill of Rights.

The current *South African Yearbook* provides an excellent update on all these matters and should be consulted for further details.

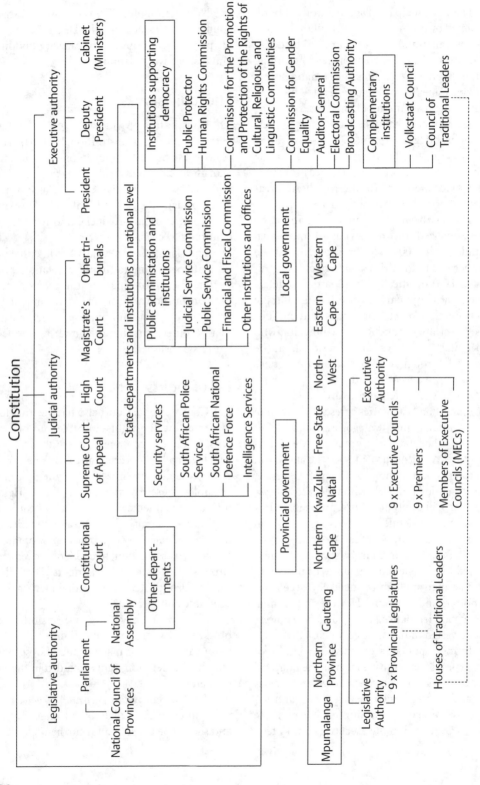

Protocol guidelines

It is surprising how few organizers are aware of protocol requirements when dealing with a government minister or other important figures, and yet ignorance of the correct procedure may cause offence to important guests and considerable embarrassment to your organization.

The guidelines which follow will smooth the path and ensure a gracious occasion. For additional information on specific details of the personal preferences of dignitaries it is wise to check with the relevant protocol officers or private secretaries of government departments or mayor's offices immediately before an important event.

Order of precedence

The Official Table of Precedence is a guide to determining seniority accorded to the different dignitaries of the Republic of South Africa at official functions. Other institutions, for example, sports organizations, churches, and the diplomatic corps have their own order of precedence. Failure to adhere to the Table leads to the embarrassment of both the host and the guest.

The President of the Republic of South Africa and his or her spouse or companion are in all instances accorded the highest precedence in the country at all functions, public or private.

This Table of Precedence should be strictly adhered to in:

- seating arrangements for all official (public and private) functions;
- presenting dignitaries to the President or to visiting dignitaries on formal occasions;
- arranging arrival and departure times for dignitaries at functions – the most senior dignitary is the last to arrive and the first to leave;
- serving meals at formal dinners, buffets, luncheons, and so forth. The most senior is served or serves him- or herself first.

Official Table of Precedence

1. The President of the Republic of South Africa or the Acting President.
2. The Executive Deputy President and the President elect (for the period between his or her election and assumption of office).
3. (a) The Chief Justice or the Acting Chief Justice;
   (b) President of the Constitutional Court or the Acting President of the Constitutional Court;
4. (a) Former Presidents of the Republic of South Africa, in order of seniority;
   (b) Former Executive Deputy Presidents, in order of seniority.
5. Cabinet Ministers, the Speaker of the National Assembly, the Chairperson of the Constitutional Assembly, and Premiers of the respective provinces, in order of seniority (see Rule 2 on page 334).
6. (a) Ambassadors, in order of seniority;
   (b) Envoys Extraordinary and Ministers Plenipotentiary, in order of seniority;
   (c) Chargés d'affaires en titre, in order of seniority;
   (d) Heads of other permanent diplomatic missions, in order of seniority.
7. (a) Deputy Minister, Members of the Executive Councils, and Speakers of provincial legislators, in order of seniority.;
   (b) Deputy Speaker of the National Assembly and the Deputy Chairperson of the Constitutional Assembly, in order of seniority;
   (c) The Chief Whip of the majority party in the National Assembly and Deputy Speakers of provincial legislators, the Chairperson of the Standing Committee on Public Accounts in the National Assembly, and the Parliamentary Counsellor of the President, in order of seniority.
8. The Secretary of the Cabinet and the Chief of the South African National Defence Force (see Rule 3 on page 334).

9. (a) Chargé d'affaires ad interim of embassies, in order of seniority;

(b) Chargé d'affaires ad interim of legations, in order of seniority;

(c) Chargé d'affaires ad interim of other permanent diplomatic missions, in order of seniority.

10. (a) The leader of the official opposition;

(b) Leaders of the different political parties in the National Assembly, in order of seniority.

11. (a) Deputy President of the Constitutional Court;

(b) Judges of Appeal, in order of seniority;

(c) Judges of the Constitutional Court, in order of seniority;

(d) Judges President, in order of seniority;

(e) Deputy Judges President, in order of seniority;

(f) Judges of the Supreme Court, in order of seniority.

12. Former Chief Justices, in order of seniority.

13. Chairpersons of the Commissions established by or under the Constitution of the Republic of South Africa, 1993 (Act No 200 of 1993), in order of seniority.

14. (a) Members of the National Assembly, in order of seniority;

(b) Members of the provincial legislatures, in order of seniority;

(c) Local royalties, in order of seniority;

(d) Chairperson of the Council for Traditional Leaders;

(e) Chairpersons of the provincial Houses of Traditional Leaders, in order of seniority.

15. The Auditor-General, the Governor of the South African Reserve Bank, the Chairperson of the Public Service Commission, and the Public Protector, in order of seniority (see Rule 4 on page 334).

16. (a) Mayor of the capital of the province in which the function is held;

(b) Chairpersons of the metropolitan councils of the region in which the function is held.

17. Mayors of provincial capitals, with seniority according to the grade in which the local authority was categorized.

18. The spouses of the foregoing persons (or in the case of single, divorced or widowed persons, the persons officially recognized by the Government as their hosts) enjoy the precedence of their spouses or the persons for whom they act as hosts.

19. Persons who do not appear in this Table may, on special occasions, be accorded courtesy precedence (as defined in Rule 7) by the President of the Republic of South Africa.

Provincial Table of Precedence

- The Premier;
- Members of Executive Councils, in order of seniority;
- Provincial Speaker;
- Members of the Provincial Legislature;
- Chief Whips of political parties;
- Judges, in order of seniority;
- Former judges;
- Chairpersons of commissions;
- Royal families;
- Chairperson of the traditional leaders;
- State Institutions, for example Auditor-General, Public Protector;
- Directors-General;
- Former Members of Executive Councils, Speaker, and so forth;
- Former chairpersons of Standing Committees;
- Mayors (seniority according to grading);
- Spouses of the aforementioned persons.

Note: The President precedes everybody. The Premier precedes Cabinet Ministers in matters relating to his or her province.

Local government Table of Precedence

- Mayor;
- Chairpersons of the Metropolitan Councils;
- Deputy mayor;

- Chairperson of the Executive Committee;
- Deputy chairperson of the Executive Committee;
- Chairpersons of Standing Committees;
- Councillors;
- Members of the Standing Committee.

Note: Each municipality differs regarding the total number of councillors, Standing Committees, and so forth.

- Chief Executive Officer/Town Clerk;
- Deputy Chief Executive Officer;
- Heads of departments.

Rank structure: South African National Defence Force

SA Army	SA Air Force	SA Navy	SA Medical Service
General (Gen.)	General (Gen.)	Admiral (Adm.)	General (Gen.)
Lieutenant-General (Lt Gen.)	Lieutenant-General (Lt Gen.)	Vice-Admiral (V. Adm.)	Lieutenant-General (Lt Gen.)
Major-General (Maj. Gen.)	Major-General (Maj. Gen.)	Rear-Admiral (R. Adm.)	Major-General (Maj. Gen.)
Brigadier (Brig.)	Brigadier (Brig.)	Commodore (Cdre)	Brigadier (Brig.)
Colonel (Col)	Colonel (Col)	Captain (Capt.) (SAN)	Colonel (Col)
Lieutenant-Colonel (Lt Col)	Lieutenant-Colonel (Lt Col)	Commander (Cdr)	Lieutenant-Colonel (Lt Col)
Major (Maj.)	Major (Maj.)	Lieutenant Commander (Lt Cdr)	Major (Maj.)
Captain (Capt.)	Captain (Capt.)	Lieutenant (Lt) (SAN)	Captain (Capt.)
Lieutenant (Lt)	Lieutenant (Lt)	Sub-Lieutenant (S. Lt) (SAN)	Lieutenant (Lt)
Second Lieutenant (2 Lt)	Second Lieutenant (2 Lt)	Ensign (Esn)	Second Lieutenant (2 Lt)
Candidate Officer (CO)	Candidate Officer (CO)	Mid-Shipman (Mid.)	Candidate Officer (CO)
Warrant-Officer Class 1 (WO 1)	Warrant-Officer Class 1 (WO 1)	Warrant-Officer Class 1 (WO 1)	Warrant-Officer Class 1 (WO 1)
Warrant-Officer Class 2 (WO 2)	Warrant-Officer Class 2 (WO 2)	Warrant-Officer Class 2 (WO 2)	Warrant-Officer Class 2 (WO 2)
Staff Sergeant (S. Sgt)	Flight Sergeant (F. Sgt)	Chief Petty Officer (CPO)	Staff Sergeant (S. Sgt)
Sergeant (Sgt)	Sergeant (Sgt)	Petty Officer (PO)	Sergeant (Sgt)
Corporal (Cpl)/ Bombardier (Bdr)	Corporal (Cpl)	Leading Seaman (LS)	Corporal (Cpl)
Lance-Corporal (L. Cpl)/Gunner (Gnr)	Lance-Corporal (L. Cpl)	Able Seaman (AB)	Lance-Corporal (L. Cpl)
Private (Pte) Rifleman (Rfm.) Trooper (Tpr) Sapper (Spr) Signalman (Smn) Pioneer (Pnr)	Airman (Amn)	Seaman (Sea.)	Private (Pte)

Protocol for the Arms of the Service

- South African Army;
- South African Air Force;
- South African Navy;
- South African Medical Service.

Rules to be observed in connection with the Official Table of Precedence

1. The order of precedence laid down in the Table of Precedence shall be observed at all official functions and the host may deviate from it only with the approval of the President of the Republic of South Africa.
2. When foreign relations or interests are the main focus of an official function, or when precedence above office bearers in Rubric 5 (see page 331) is given to the doyen or doyenne of the diplomatic corps in terms of international protocol, the Minister of Foreign Affairs shall be given precedence above the doyen or doyenne and the office bearers in Rubric 5.
3. When foreign relations or interests are the main focus of an official function, the Director-General of the department hosting the function shall enjoy precedence after the Secretary of the Cabinet, the Chief of the South African National Defence Force, and the Director-General of Foreign Affairs.
4. Rubric 15(a) (see page 332): Should the Public Protector already hold a higher position in the Official Table of Precedence, he or she shall retain his or her personal higher precedence for all official functions.
5. Rubric 15 (see page 332) is included, provided that Chairpersons of State Corporations are invited when the function concerned relates to their specific fields or according to the choice of the host, should he or she wish to invite all or any of the Chairpersons.
6. Persons not appearing in the Table shall not be placed above persons appearing in it, unless they have either been accorded ad hoc precedence in terms of Rubric 19 (see page 332) of the Table or are invited as guests of honour.
7. Courtesy precedence is restricted to persons who are not normally resident in the Republic of South Africa, but includes church dignitaries within the Republic, and other dignitaries, office bearers and functionaries for whom specific provision has not been made in the Table.
8. Amendments to the Table shall be effected only by the President of the Republic of South Africa and shall be published in the Government Gazette.

Forms of address

The President has no form of address. He or she is simply Madam or Mr or Dr or Professor as the case may be. He or she may be addressed as Mr or Madam President in speaking. When addressing a letter it is simply addressed, in the present instance, to:

Mr J Zuma
President of the Republic of South Africa
Plus address

The written salutation is 'Dear Mr/Madam President' and the letter-ending is simply 'Yours faithfully', as opposed to the old order 'Yours most respectfully'. 'Yours faithfully' may be preceded by 'I have the honour to be'. The same is applicable to the Deputy President.

'The Honourable' is only used for Rubrics 3, 11, and 12, that is the judiciary. Cabinet Ministers Plenipotentiary are still referred to as 'His/Her Excellency' as it is an international diplomatic title.

The forms of address for heads of the diplomatic corps are as follows: a letter is addressed to 'His/Her Excellency the Ambassador Extraordinary and Plenipotentiary of … (or High Commissioner); the written salutation is 'Excellency' or 'Mr/Madam Ambassador' or 'Dear Ambassador'; the letter-ending

Office	On envelope	In written salutation	Letter ending	In speaking	On invitation
Charge d'Affaires – as Head of Mission (e.t.) or ad interim (a.i.)	The Charge d'Affaires e.t./a.i. Embassy of ...	(Dear) Mr/Madam Charge d'Affaires, or (Dear) Sir/Madam, or Dear	I have the honour to be, or Yours faithfully	Mr/Madam Charge d'Affaires, and then Sir/Madam	Mr/Ms ...
Head of other permanent diplomatic missions	Mr/Ms ... 1. Representative of ... 2. Head of Office of Interest of ...	Dear Mr/Ms ...	Yours faithfully	Sir/Madam	Mr/Ms ...
Chief Whip	1. Mr/Ms ..., MP, Chief Whip: National Assembly 2. Senator ..., Chief Whip: Senate	1. (Dear) Mr/ Madam Chief Whip, or (Dear) Mr/Ms ..., or (Dear) Madam/Sir 2. Senator ... or Madam/Sir	Yours faithfully	1. Mr/Ms Chief Whip; then Sir/Madam 2. Senator ... or Madam/Sir or Mr/Ms ...	Mr/Ms ...
Chief of the South African National Defence Force	General/Admiral ... (Decorations), Chief of the South African National Defence Force	(Dear) General/Admiral (...)	Yours faithfully	General/Admiral	Mr/Ms ...
Judge of Appeal	The Honourable Mr/Ms Justice (Note: No initials)	(Dear) Sir/Madam or (Dear) Judge	Yours faithfully	Judge/Sir/Madam In court: My lord/My Lady or His Lordship/Her Ladyship	The Honourable Mr/Ms Justice
Judge President, Deputy Judge President	The Honourable Mr/Ms Justice ... Judge President/Deputy Judge President of the ... Division (Note: No initials)	(Dear) Sir, Madam, Judge	Yours faithfully	Judge/Sir/Madam In court: My lord/My Lady or His Lordship/Her Ladyship	The Honourable Mr/Ms Justice
Judge	The Honourable Mr/Ms Justice ... (Note: No initials)	(Dear) Sir, Madam, Judge	Yours faithfully	Judge/Sir/Madam In court: My Lord/My Lady or His Lordship/Her Ladyship	The Honourable Mr/Ms Justice

Note: Initials are not used. For correct identification of judges with the same surnames, the initials of the junior judge are used and he or she is addressed as Mr/Ms...

Office	On envelope	In written salutation	Letter ending	In speaking	On invitation
Members of the Executive Council	Mr/Ms ... MEC	(Dear) Sir/Madam or (Dear) Mr/Ms	Yours faithfully	Sir/Madam/Senator or Mr/Ms ...	Senator or Mr/Ms ... MP
Member of Parliament (National Assembly and Senate)	Mr/Ms ... MP or Senator	Sir/Madam/Senator or Mr/Ms ...	Yours faithfully	Sir/Madam/Senator or Mr/Ms ...	Senator/Mr/Ms ... or Mr/Ms ... MP
Heads of Government Departments and Institutions	Mr/Ms ... Official designation, i.e. Director-General: Foreign Affairs	(Dear) Sir/Madam or (Dear) Mr/Ms ...	Yours faithfully	Sir/Madam or Mr/Ms ...	Mr/Ms ...
Mayor	His/Her Worship, the Mayor of ... or Alderman/Councillor ... or Alderman/Councillor Mr/Ms ...	(Dear) Mr/Madam Mayor or Dear Councillor/Alderman	Yours faithfully	Mr/Madam Mayor, and then Sir/Madam	Councillor/Mayor/Alderman ... (and Ms/Mr ...)

from an official is 'Please accept, Mr/Madam Ambassador, the (renewed) assurance of my highest consideration' while a member of the public uses 'Yours respectfully'; in an address 'Your Excellency' or 'Excellency' or 'Mr/Madam Ambassador' is used. The spouses or partners are merely referred to as Mr or Ms as the case may be.

Please note that Cabinet Ministers and their deputies, the Provincial Premiers, and MECs (or Provincial 'Ministers') are not entitled to any form of address.

As a courtesy and a sign of respect, we refer to the King of the Zulu nation as 'His Majesty' both in writing (in the address) and in speaking. The salutation is 'Your Majesty' and the letter-ending 'Yours most respectfully'. This is not officially prescribed but obviously custom dictates. The full written address on the envelope will be:

His Majesty
King Goodwill Zulu Zwelithini
Private Bag 5023
3950

Defence Force forms of address

- All Generals/Admirals as General or Admiral;
- All Colonels/Lieutenants-Colonels as Colonel;
- Lieutenant-Commander as Commander.

Meals, meetings, and functions

Invitations and appointments

All invitations to and appointments with a Minister should be arranged with his or her private secretary. Invitations should be issued well in advance.

The space at the top of the invitation is to allow the guest's name to be written in (not typed in).

The Minister of Public Service and Administration
requests the pleasure of the company of

Mr J. C. Skinner and Dr. Skinner

at a Cocktail Reception
at the Sheraton Hotel, 24 Church Street, Pretoria
on Monday 17 September   at 18:00 to 20:00
RSVP before 6 September   Dress Code: Lounge Suit, Traditional

Nomsa Dube, Tel.   012-555-5555
            Fax.   012-555-5556
            e-mail nomsad@telkomsa.net

Dress code

Only the men's dress is given on the invitation card. Women dress according to the instructions given for men. There are four options:

- *Black tie*. Men wear a black evening suit, white evening shirt, and black bow tie. Women wear a short or long evening dress or suit, according to fashion.
- *Dark suit*. Men wear a dark coloured suit and women wear a cocktail-type dress or suit.
- *Day suit*. Men wear a lighter suit and women wear a day dress or a suit.
- *No jackets and ties*. This is the correct terminology for informal clothing.

If hats are to be worn, this should be indicated on the invitation.

The terminology formal/informal/casual/smart casual/sport should not be used.

There are opportunities for traditional dress to be worn on all occasions.

Formal meals

If the Minister is the host, he or she will either be seated at the head of the table or at the middle on one side. If the Minister is seated at the head of the table, his or her co-host will sit at the foot of the table. If the Minister is seated at the middle on one side, his or her co-host will sit opposite him or her.

For purely social meals, the head and foot arrangement of the table is best. If a very large number of people are present at a social occasion, it sometimes works better to place the minister (or host, if the minister is a guest) in the middle, because this arrangement places all the most important people together at the middle of the table, rather than in two isolated groups at the ends. The accompanying diagrams show the proper seating arrangements for formal meals.

Working meals

The above arrangement also works best at working meals, especially where more than

eight people will be present. Opposite the host or Minister will be a co-host, usually the person next in importance among the colleagues of the host.

Meetings at a table

These can be divided into two groups:

- discussions and negotiations between two or more groups with the Minister as the head of one group; or
- a meeting of a group, whether uniform or assorted, where the Minister is the chairperson or a guest speaker.

In the second group, the Minister will sit at the head of the table if he or she is the chairperson or host. If he or she is a guest speaker, the Minister will sit to the right of the chairperson of the meeting.

In the first group, the Minister will sit at the middle of the table with the members of his or her group on either side of him or her, arranged alternately to the left and right according to precedence. The leader of the visiting delegation will sit opposite the Minister with his or her delegation arranged in the same way. Sometimes, special circumstances arise with regard to the placement of the group. For example, if one has a delegation from a neighbouring state consisting of Ministers and officials with various portfolios, an attempt should be made to place persons with similar interests opposite each other if this is at all possible (see diagram on page 340).

Cocktail functions and buffet meals

On such occasions where the Minister is the host, he or she will act like any other host.

Where a Minister has been invited as a guest to such an occasion, possibly as a speaker, he or she will be accompanied by a security officer and often by a member of his or her personal staff. Do not serve the Minister separately, as this will defeat the purpose of the exercise, which is to have people meet one

Formal meals

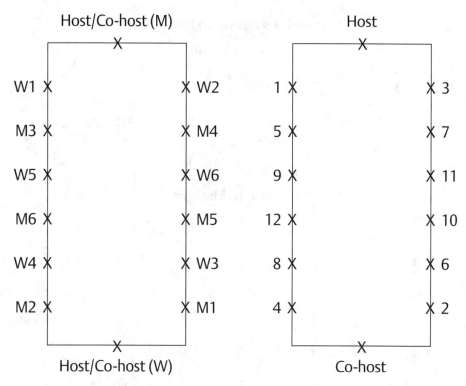

Host/Co-host (M)

W1 X	X W2
M3 X	X M4
W5 X	X W6
M6 X	X M5
W4 X	X W3
M2 X	X M1

Host/Co-host (W)

Discriminatory: differentiates between
male and female guests

Host

1 X	X 3
5 X	X 7
9 X	X 11
12 X	X 10
8 X	X 6
4 X	X 2

Co-host

Non-discriminatory: usually men or
women only, or a working meal

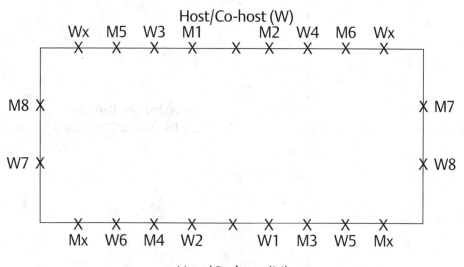

Host/Co-host (W)

Wx M5 W3 M1   M2 W4 M6 Wx

| M8 X | X M7 |
| W7 X | X W8 |

Mx W6 M4 W2   W1 M3 W5 Mx

Host/Co-host (M)

This arrangement is suitable for very long tables.

W = woman
M = man

337

Discussions between two groups

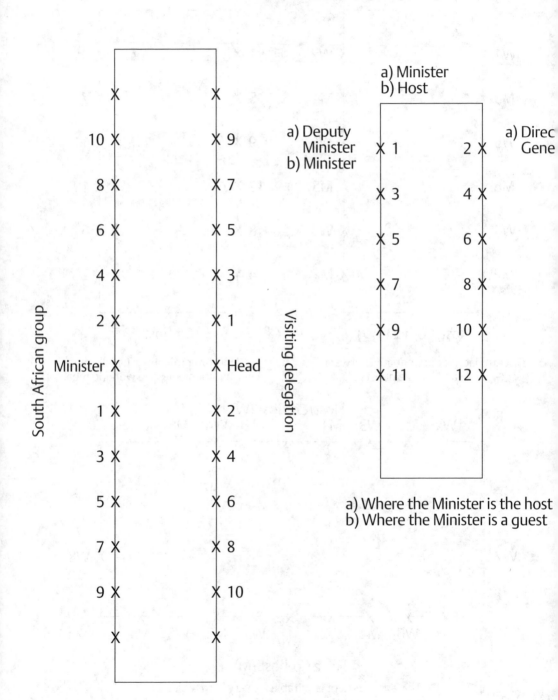

a) Minister
b) Host

South African group

Minister X — X Head

10 X — X 9

8 X — X 7

6 X — X 5

4 X — X 3

2 X — X 1

1 X — X 2

3 X — X 4

5 X — X 6

7 X — X 8

9 X — X 10

a) Deputy
   Minister
b) Minister

Visiting delegation

X 1 — 2 X

X 3 — 4 X

X 5 — 6 X

X 7 — 8 X

X 9 — 10 X

X 11 — 12 X

a) Direc
   Gene

a) Where the Minister is the host
b) Where the Minister is a guest

another, including the minister. It should be the task of the host of a function to ensure that no one person or group monopolizes the minister's attention during the function.

Speeches and press conferences (public appearances)

Security is always an important factor when ministers or other dignitaries are present at a public meeting. The fact that security is strictly applied does not mean, however, that access to the minister should be totally restricted.

At public meetings there is usually a main table where the host, the main guest such as the Minister, and other important people sit. As a rule, try to have as few people as possible at the main table; between four and eight is preferable. Try to balance the main table with the number of people in the audience; for example, apply a ratio of 1:10. VIPs to be seated at the main table could include the chairperson of the organizing committee, the local Member of Parliament, prominent business people, and possibly their spouses. If there are other speakers, they may be invited to sit at the main table unless there are too many of them, in which case they can be called from the audience when it is their turn to speak.

At a press conference, a decision must be taken on who is to act as chairperson and which advisers should be present to assist him or her in answering specific questions. Often, after a prepared statement has been made by the chairperson, the media are invited to ask questions. Some questions may concern this statement, but the occasion also provides journalists with an opportunity to closely question the Minister or spokesperson on other matters. Under these circumstances both the Minister and organizer must be prepared for anything: organizers need to be prepared for some difficult and controversial questions to be put and answered.

Table settings

The following guidelines are applicable:
- *Tablecloths.* The tablecloth should be long enough to reach the seat of the dining-room chairs. White cloths are best for official functions. However, colour can be introduced for daytime occasions.
- *Table napkins.* These should not be starched. They should be set on the small plates provided to the left of the place settings or can be folded to decorate the table. At the end of the meal, guests put their table napkins on the table. If a guest leaves the table during the meal the table napkin is left on the chair.
- *Cutlery.* Cutlery should be set two centimetres from the bottom edge of the table. Guests use cutlery from the outside inwards as the different courses are served. The bread knife is placed on the right, furthest away from the plate or on the small plate to the left of the place setting.
- *Glasses.* Glasses are grouped above the knives on the right.
- *Bread.* Bread is placed on the small plates or in a basket on the table.
- *Salt cellar, butter dish, and menu.* There should be one of each for every two guests.
- *Flowers or other decorations.* These should not obscure cutlery, glasses and plates, or the view.

Table plans

On occasions where both men and women are present, the host and his or her usually sit at the head and foot of the table, opposite each other. This is so that one of them can co-ordinate the meal and see that everything runs smoothly.

The rule is that the most important guest sits to the right of the female host or co-host if he is male, and vice versa. This guest's partner sits to the right of the partner of the host or co-host.

The accompanying diagrams illustrate the table arrangements for different numbers of guests.

Public appearances

Minister as main speaker

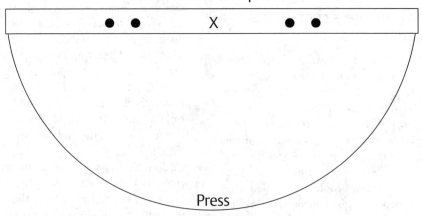

Press

Minister with delegation leader

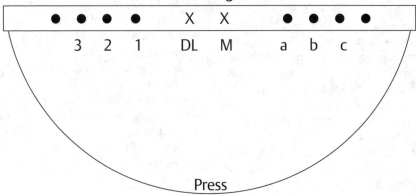

Press

Minister with multiple delegations

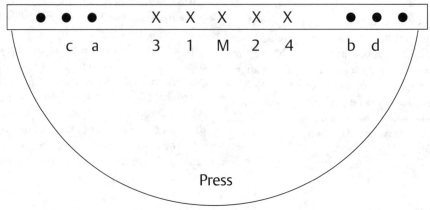

Press

Both men and women present

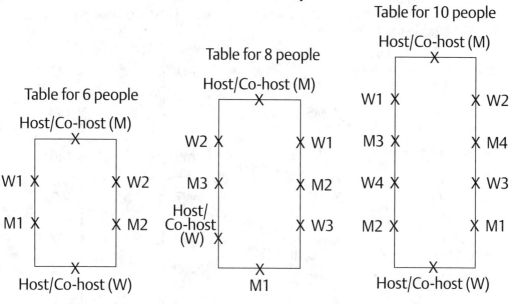

Table for 6 people

Host/Co-host (M)

W1 — W2

M1 — M2

Host/Co-host (W)

Table for 8 people

Host/Co-host (M)

W2 — W1

M3 — M2

Host/Co-host (W) — W3

M1

Table for 10 people

Host/Co-host (M)

W1 — W2

M3 — M4

W4 — W3

M2 — M1

Host/Co-host (W)

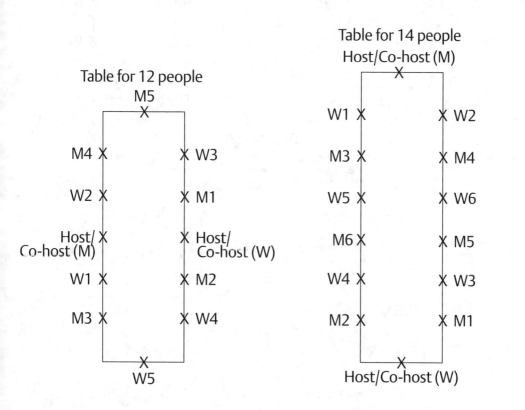

Table for 12 people

M5

M4 — W3

W2 — M1

Host/Co-host (M) — Host/Co-host (W)

W1 — M2

M3 — W4

W5

Table for 14 people

Host/Co-host (M)

W1 — W2

M3 — M4

W5 — W6

M6 — M5

W4 — W3

M2 — M1

Host/Co-host (W)

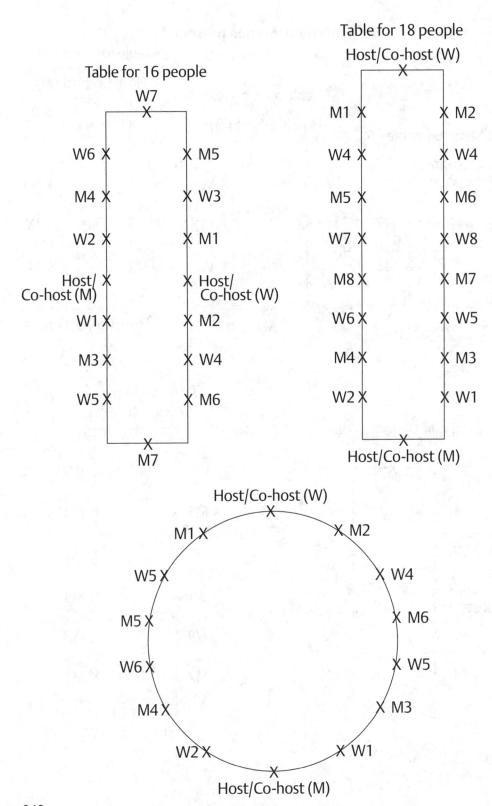

Table for 16 people

Table for 18 people

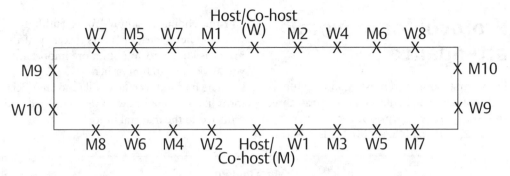

Host/Co-host (W)

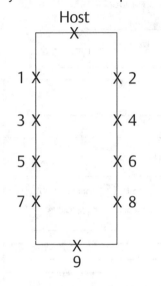

Only men or women present

Guests seated on one side of the table only

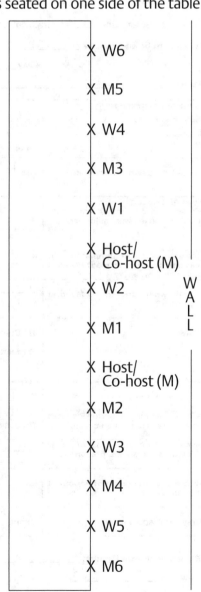

Protocol for mayoral attendance

It is first and foremost good manners and considerate to invite a mayor at least three (preferably six) weeks prior to your function.

The salutation is 'Dear Mr/Madam Mayor'

and the ending is simply 'Yours faithfully' if you have never met, or 'Yours sincerely' if the mayor is known to you but more importantly, you are known to him or her.

The mayoral secretary will send an official form like the one below to be completed and returned to the mayoral office.

**Mayor's Parlour
Invitation Advice Form**

Please complete and return to the Mayoral Secretary, Mayor's Parlour

Function to be attended by _____

Day _____ Date _____

Venue_____

Name of organization	
Person to contact	
Telephone	Bus. ———— Home ———— Fax————
	Email ————————————
Should spouse/partner attend?	Yes ☐ No ☐
Type of function Please advise whether any other function is linked with main event	_____ Meal ☐ **Snacks** ☐ _____ Please tick if applicable
Names and designations of persons on hand to meet Mayoral dignitaries on arrival	
Exactly where should the Mayoral car arrive?	
Time	a) Specific time of arrival—— a) Duration of function ——— b) Start of function —— b) Convenient time of departure ——
Is a speech required? (Tick appropriate box) **NB:** A minimum of 5 working days notice is required for a speech.	Yes ☐ No ☐ Other active participation Time allocated ————
Name and designations of other distinguished guests present	
Who will be the guest of honour at this function?	
Dress(Tick appropriate box)	Casual ☐ Lounge suit ☐ **Dinner suit with bow tie** ☐

Signature and designation _____

Date _____

Protocol and arrangements for the attendance of the mayor

1. Time	The mayoral car will arrive at the venue exactly on time.
2. Arrival and departure	The reception party should always meet the mayor at the car and should be on the pavement or at the entrance to the building as the mayoral car arrives. They should step forward when the chauffeur opens the door of the car and introduce themselves and any other persons in the party. At the conclusion of the function the chauffeur should be informed of the imminent departure of the mayor and part- ner, and they should be accompanied to their car. Note: In the event of the State President, a Cabinet Minister, or senior personage also being present, the mayor and partner should be scheduled to arrive five min- utes beforehand. After the customary greetings, the mayor will wait with the reception party and should be the first to greet the President, Cabinet Minister, or senior personage. The mayor will then introduce the host to that personage. The host introduces the personage to the rest of the members of the reception party.
3. Form of address	The correct form of address is 'Mr/Madam Mayor'. When referred to in the course of a speech, it is 'His/Her Worship the Mayor'. The correct form of address of deputies is 'Mr/Madam Deputy Mayor'.
4. Speeches	If required, the mayor's role is frequently to give a short word of wel- come or congratulations, or officially open a function. At least five working days' notice is required if a speech is given. The average dura- tion of a mayoral speech is three minutes, the maximum being four minutes.
5. Dress	It is important to be quite specific on dress requirements for the mayor and his or her partner. The mayoral couple are sometimes required to attend more than one evening function and they could be present in formal dress despite a request for informality.
6. Seating arrangements	The mayor is always on the immediate right of the host if he or she is the senior guest present. Where feasible, the mayor's partner is on the left of the co-host. However, the mayoral couple can be seated togeth- er if required. Guests are presented to the mayor and partner, not vice versa. In the event of the State President, a Cabinet Minister, or senior personage also being present, the main table arrangements may be discussed with the mayoral secretary.
7. Mayoral programme	Any extensive tours or a lengthy period of standing which may be required of the mayoral couple should be discussed with the mayoral secretary beforehand. To avoid any possible embarrasment during the function, a person should be designated to watch that the mayor is never left alone.
8. Presentations	It is suggested that in the case of a charity hosting a function, no gift or memento should be presented to mark the occasion.

Business etiquette

It is often asked if there is a difference between social and business etiquette. There are differences. Gender and class are less important in the workplace than in the social context. Good manners, however, should always prevail.

Business etiquette guidelines

Seniority

One needs to be aware of the status, titles, and seniority of people in an organization. The general rule, however, is that the visitor, client or customer always comes first and should therefore be accorded VIP status.

Greetings

In welcoming someone to your company, department, or office, it is important that you make the first move. Do shake hands with everyone; don't worry about age, rank, or gender. Maintain direct eye contact, smile, and give a firm handshake.

Forms of address

It is important that you address individuals by their correct title – Professor, Dr, Mr, or Ms. It is preferable not to use the titles Miss and Mrs any longer. Often a person is simply introduced by name and position in the company, for example Elize Taylor, our human resources consultant.

Be careful in using first names. Don't call your manager (or any other senior person) by his or her first name until asked to do so. The onus is on the senior person to be proactive in this respect.

Introductions

This is quite a complex subject where protocol is concerned, but in the business environment some general rules apply. Always taking seniority into account:
- a peer in your own company is introduced to a peer in another company;
- a non-official person is introduced to an official person;
- a junior executive is introduced to a senior executive;
- staff are introduced to a customer or client;
- a visitor is introduced to an employee.

The most important person's name is generally said first. It is important to practise the pronunciation of people's names. Do not assume that you may use first names in initial briefings or meetings with clients.

Respecting the line of command

Always be aware of the line of command. Be careful not to overstep the mark and don't be the one to initiate friendship with your manager. Allow him or her to make the first move.

Respecting other people's space and privacy

Be guided by good manners. Don't barge into an office without announcing your presence. It is important to respect other people's space and privacy.

Disagreements or reprimands

Always try and respect the dignity of the individual. Try to discuss matters without rancour or bitterness and, above all, keep your cool. Things said in anger could have a long-term detrimental effect on relations.

Always allow for feedback or sharing of problems and different perspectives. Reprimand someone in private rather than in the presence of a third party.

Toilet etiquette

Don't freshen up in public. If necessary, do this in the rest room. Also don't eat in public or reception areas where visitors can see you. Food often leaves a lingering smell after being eaten.

Dress codes

Remember that your dress reflects your professionalism but be guided by the environment in which you work. Dress should always be 'appropriate to the occasion'.

Gifts

It is necessary to check company policy about receiving and giving gifts. Always try to understand the motivation behind the present. Does the giver want something from you and will you be at all compromised if you accept the gift?

Courtesy

Receiving visitors or callers

- Alert reception if you are expecting a visitor.
- Ask your secretary to go down to reception to meet your visitor or go down yourself.
- Do offer your visitor refreshments and something to read.
- Whoever arrives at a door first, whether the person is male or female, should hold it open for the others and keep it open until all have passed through.
- It is common courtesy to stand when a visitor comes into your office. If possible, you should also come out from behind your desk to shake the person's hand.
- When your visitor leaves, you should rise and escort him or her to the door, shaking hands at the conclusion of the interview.
- If you happen to be in the general reception area, do greet any visitors who may be there, even if they are not calling on you.
- When you see visitors wandering around the building, ask them if you can help by directing them to the correct office.
- No matter how busy you are, and even when you are running late, don't keep visitors waiting.

Showing appreciation

Two very important words are 'Thank you'. Thanks can be expressed personally or by letter. It is usually the thought that counts.

Gender courtesy

The usual norms for courtesy apply when men and women interact at work, but do not take advantage of the work situation where your position gives you certain leeway.

A person's gender should not influence the way he or she is treated at work.

Sexual harassment

Both men and women have the right to reject any sexual harassment. Be firm and make your views known. If the harassment continues discuss the problem with your immediate superior.

Your personnel or human resources department should be able to advise you about what action to take in difficult or compromising situations.

Responding to telephone calls and letters

Telephone etiquette

- Most people are notoriously bad at returning phone calls. Many secretaries seem to spend their days making excuses for managers who never get round to returning phone calls.
- Research reveals that as many as 50 per cent of calls handled by a manager are queries that could have been answered by an efficient secretary or receptionist.
- As a general rule, calls should be returned within 24 hours if at all possible.
- If secretaries know that their individual managers are going to be unavailable, or out of town or on holiday for an extended period, it is good business etiquette to advise the caller of this. Offer another person's assistance if you are not able to help the caller yourself.
- A basic knowledge of the company is a prerequisite for any person who wants to show efficiency and professionalism in his or her

job. It is important that relevant files and details are readily accessible to secretaries so as to avoid wasting time when particular questions are asked.

- Do leave messages on telephone answering machines. If your call has not been returned within 48 hours, call again.
- If both parties are unable to make contact, secretaries can arrange 'callback appointments' to suit their individual managers.
- It is important that your telephone be answered, even if you are not in your office. Inform switchboard of any difficulties, delays, or problems. Arrange for other people to handle your calls if you are away from the office.
- Always be conscious of your tone of voice when returning calls. Try and put a smile into your voice.
- If anyone has difficulty in expressing themselves in whatever language, be patient and understanding. Repeat any request made so that there is no misunderstanding.

Responding to letters

- It is essential to answer promptly, preferably within 48 hours.
- Check layout, design, and spelling of all correspondence.
- If an answer is required and you can't handle it immediately, respond telephonically and tell the writer that you will deal with the matter as soon as possible.

Meetings

Guidelines for meetings

- Plan. The meeting must have a purpose and a well-prepared agenda, with a copy for each participant, despatched to all concerned in good time.
- Inform. The agenda must be self-explanatory and leave no possibility for misinterpretation of any of the items listed on it.

- Prepare. Have all the required facts at hand and the necessary people present.
- Structure. Structure your discussion in problem-solving order:
  - establish facts first;
  - check that the interpretation of facts is clear to all those present;
  - find a solution.
- Control. Place important items first on the agenda; less important items, though urgent, should follow. Balance the input of conversation.
- Record. The secretary should take minutes of the entire meeting so that there is a formal record of what was agreed on by all present.

Serving refreshments

This depends largely on the context. At a formal function it could be the responsibility of the public relations department. Normally tea or coffee is passed around after orders have been placed. The question of who pours the tea at a formal meeting can be easily resolved if the chairperson delegates this responsibility to an individual either before or during the meeting. Don't ask the secretary who is taking the minutes to perform this duty.

Smoking etiquette

New smoking legislation now bans smoking except in designated areas in public places such as airport lounges and restaurants. It is an offence to smoke outside these areas and individuals themselves can press charges against offenders who disregard official warnings.

In the work environment, smoking is also banned and smokers are requested to refrain from smoking in offices, corridors, boardrooms, and canteens.

If you are a smoker it is suggested you smoke before entering a building, in your car, or outside where your smoke can cause no offence.

Special events

The aim of special events is to improve communication with target publics in order to achieve one or a combination of the following:
- create awareness;
- raise funds;
- obtain publicity;
- promote products;
- build personal relationships;
- establish favourable dispositions;
- promote the organization's role in the community.

Most special events can probably be classified under the following headings:
- Opening ceremonies, inauguration ceremonies, ground-breaking ceremonies, dedication ceremonies, and cornerstone-laying ceremonies, which are symbols of progress for the organization, its employees, the customer or user of the product, the industry in which it participates, the local community, and the country as a whole.
  Example: The opening of the uShaka Marine Park, Durban.
- Open-house days, functions, visits, and tours aimed at employees, the local community, opinion leaders, or other specialized publics such as the media or customers. These are aimed at improving employee or community relations.
  Example: Open day at the Durban Institute of Technology, Durban Campus.

- Meetings, symposia, seminars, workshops, conventions, conferences, and congresses, including those to which delegates are invited by an organization in order to promote their own products and services, and those arranged on behalf of institutes, associations, trade bodies, and so on.
  Example: The PRISA Congress and National Annual General Meeting.
- Exhibitions and trade shows or fairs, including both general shows and specialized exhibitions. These are aimed at improving the company's image and increasing sales.
  Example: The Royal Show, Pietermaritzburg.
- Sport and cultural sponsorships aimed at creating favourable relationships, obtaining publicity, and improving the organization's image.
  Examples: FNB Arts Awards; Standard Bank PRO 20 Series.
- Miscellaneous events, for example special days and weeks, where a programme is built around the particular day or week in order to make the public aware of a certain cause.
  Examples: The Heart Foundation's Heart Week; Aids Day.
- Anniversaries, which offer the organization the opportunity to communicate with its publics on progress, achievements, and contributions made by the organization.

These are aimed at developing trust in and prestige for the organization.

Examples: Shopping centres such as Fourways, Sandton.

- Special awards made to employees, shareholders, dealers, and consumers. These serve to acknowledge contributions made by individuals to the organization and present an opportunity for the organization to build its own image.

Example: Business Partners Limited and Ithala awards to small businesses.

- Parades and processions aimed at displaying an organization's force and improving relationships with the community.

Examples: Rag days; SPCA 'wag' processions.

- Also considered as events would be competitions, receptions, and functions, promotions such as those presented in shopping centres during Easter and on Valentine's Day.

General guidelines

A good public relations programme makes provision for dozens of secondary ideas which back up the essential primary ideas. In fact, the public relations professional can create his or her own public relations opportunities through holding special events such as openings, celebrations, anniversaries, seminars, and competitions.

This section of the book will give you practical suggestions for achieving success with these.

Remember that it is important to see the part every event (big or small) will play in your overall communications strategy.

- It is important to brainstorm with colleagues from the marketing, sales, human resources, and other relevant departments to develop ideas for such events.
- How will this event be integrated into the wider communications strategy for the year? Even if it is a one-off affair it must serve to communicate your organization's image.

- How can the event be developed so that it is relevant to the broadest possible audience?
- Does the event spark off ideas for other occasions which might lend themselves to special treatment in order to generate interest and news?

Keeping these general points of policy in mind, you can go on to consider the following particular questions:

- When, during the campaign, might it be beneficial to get the services of a celebrity?
- Could a celebrity be involved with a whole series of related activities rather than just one event?
- Has a proper briefing session been arranged with the celebrities so they know exactly what role they have to play in the detailed programme for the day?
- For more formal occasions, is the event of such significance that you could approach a leading public or political figure? Would this be acceptable to your identified key audience?
- Have the details of the event and programme been arranged?
- Has each activity been costed and an overall budget prepared?
- Have the media been advised of the programme and will they be given the opportunities they may require for special pictures and interviews?
- Have you established how you will monitor success in meeting the objectives concerning the event and how this might affect decisions and budgets in the years to come?

Planning the event

Efficient organization is essential in planning any major public relations event. Whatever the event, some basic factors and decisions have to be taken into account. These include:

- *Date and time.* Use a calendar to check that there is no clash of dates. Be aware of public holidays and religious festivals. Opt for alternative dates to ensure VIP attendance. Decide on the time the event should start and finish.

- *Critical path.* Prepare an overall master plan and develop a critical path plan. Identify decision dates for all key elements.
- *Theme.* Try to identify a theme. Brief designers who will interpret this theme in displays, printed matter, and exhibitions. Select relevant speakers, celebrities, or special guests.
- *Invitations.* Draw up an invitation list identifying all important internal and external guests.
- *Venue.* Book a suitable venue and make all the necessary hotel arrangements for lunches and overnight accommodation. Confirm these arrangements in writing well in advance and provide final numbers by telephone 48 hours before the function.
- *Media relations.* Prepare and issue press invitations with details of the preliminary programme. Check who is likely to attend. Make arrangements for media kits, news stories, special travel, telephones, press office, background material, and photographs.
- *Printing requirements.* Decide on the printed items you require. Prepare the brief and appoint a printer or designer. Obtain quotes and detailed production schedules for each item.
- *Displays.* Agree on the displays or exhibition material you require. Appoint designers or contractors. Brief them thoroughly and give them instructions regarding co-ordination with print and theme elements. Obtain quotes.
- *Presentations.* Agree on speakers and prepare a brief for each. Put the programme together. Check the physical resources including the public address system and closed circuit television, audiovisual aids, recording facilities.
- *Papers.* Request copies of speeches in advance. Make copies as required. Distribute these during or after the event.
- *Hospitality.* Confirm who will meet your guests and look after them. Check whether

there are any VIPs who require special attention. Confirm arrangements for visitors' books, presentations to senior guests, bouquets, and gifts.

- *Facility inspections.* Check on the guides, their briefing, the tour itineraries, display items, noise level, safety and security aspects, lapel badges, rehearsals, and timing.
- *Staff briefings.* Talk to all support staff and contractors. Brief them on the theme, style, policy, and objectives. Stress the importance of attention to detail.
- *Consistency.* Make sure that the theme is carried through consistently, including the colours, selection of flowers, displays, and presentation sets. Check that staff are wearing the right badges and overalls, that there is special clothing and headgear for visitors where required, and that vehicles, badges, signs, visitors' flags, and banners have been prepared.
- *Travel.* Confirm all travel arrangements, particularly for VIPs. Make sure guests have location maps and that there are suitable AA signage and adequate parking facilities. Advise the local police of the event. Provide any necessary back-up transport if required.
- *Catering.* Check final numbers and advise caterers accordingly. Discuss menus, special dietary requirements, wines, special service, table settings, the master of ceremonies, music, and toilet and cloakroom facilities.
- *Information.* Prepare the required material for other media such as advertisements, posters, exhibits, product displays, and visual aids. Liaise with other bodies and associations for assistance and possible participation.
- *Photography.* Select and brief your own photographers. Respond to their requests, as well as to those of invited media, particularly television and radio reporters.
- *Memento.* Choose a suitable memento of the occasion for guests (such as a photograph or product).

- *Run-through.* Check the final plan for discrepancies in timing and budget. Organize any progress-report meetings. Confirm individual staff responsibilities.
- *Contingency.* Plan as far as possible for any likely contingencies, for example wet weather, travel delays, or the late arrival of guests of honour.
- *Budget.* Prepare final costings on all the agreed activities. Compare with the original budget. If there are any budget anomalies, advise management. Either cut back on activities or amend the budget with management's approval.
- *Follow-up.* Issue appropriate material to those unable to attend. Determine any further media requirements. Obtain press cuttings and broadcast transcripts. Express thanks and appreciation. Check bills against quotes and settle accounts.
- *Assessment.* Hold a final debriefing session immediately after the event. Analyse the successes and failures. Prepare a written report on these so that a similar subsequent event can benefit from this experience.
- *Overseas requirements.* Now that South Africa is re-entering the international arena it is important to arrange for interpreters, translation facilities and press kits, captions and displays in appropriate languages. Check that no material is unintelligible or offensive to foreign nationals. Confirm arrival times and dates and plan for delays or cancellations. Advise caterers of any special requirements.

By working systematically through each of these key elements, an event of whatever size, nature, and complexity can be successfully staged. As stated in the introduction, the preparation of a detailed checklist should go a long way towards ensuring a successful function.

Planning and staging a conference or convention

Attention to detail, planning, and professionalism are essential ingredients in organizing a successful conference or convention.

It is important to appoint an organizer and a committee right from the start to run the event. As their first priority they need to analyze the aims and objectives of the conference and the type of image they would like to project.

Suitable venues must be investigated at least a year in advance. Once the venue has been decided on and arrangements discussed and agreed to by the functions manager, all arrangements must be confirmed in writing.

A budget also needs to be drawn up detailing all costs likely to be incurred.

The committee then needs to set out a flow chart or work schedule detailing all the proposed activities, who is responsible for what, and the date by which the various activities should be completed.

In order to allocate responsibilities, a number of subcommittees should be formed to handle the various activities. These include:
- compiling the programme;
- registration and hostessing;
- tours and visits;
- press liaison and publicity;
- budgeting and financial arrangements.

Initially, regular monthly meetings should be held. During the last month before the conference weekly meetings should be held. Daily meetings are necessary during the build-up to the conference.

A great deal depends on establishing a close, cordial relationship between the organizers and the functions manager of the hotel where the conference or convention will take place. The 'conference planner' drawn up between the two parties should act as a blueprint for the event.

353

Conference planner

Conference planner
Type of function
- ❑ meeting
- ❑ convention
- ❑ presentation
- ❑ exhibition
- ❑ other

Estimated number of participants:_____

Function date(s):_____
(Avoid dates that clash with public holidays or other events.)

Bookings   *Booked*
- Book function space
  (including set-up time if required)
- Seating arrangements
  (tick where appropriate)
- ❑ schoolroom
- ❑ theatre
- ❑ U shape
- ❑ boardroom
- ❑ head table
- ❑ other:_____   *Booked*

- Book catering requirements
- ❑ breakfast
- ❑ tea/coffee
- ❑ lunch
- ❑ dinner
- ❑ cocktail reception

Guest speakers   *Booked*
- Book speaker(s)
- Book accommodation
- Book hospitality suite
- Book storage space
- Name of speaker:
- Schedule:
  Date:_____
  Time on:_____
  Time off:_____
  Speaker's audiovisual requirements:_____
  _____

Confirmation details   *Confirmed*
- Finalize programme
- Reply system set up
- Invitations sent

- Written confirmation of bookings:
- ❑ function space
- ❑ accommodation
- Accounting requirements
- Arrangements for settling accounts made
- Deposit settled
- Cancellation clause
- Gratuity
- Transport requirements
- Parking requirements
- Menus selected and approved
- Wines selected and approved
- Bar facilities
- ❑ cash
- ❑ account

Audiovisual requirements   *Confirmed*
- See list below
- ❑ overhead projector
- ❑ 16 mm projector
- ❑ slide projector
- ❑ video equipment
- ❑ screen
- ❑ public address system
- ❑ blackboard/whiteboard
- ❑ spotlights
- ❑ flip chart
- ❑ data link-up
- ❑ other:

Miscellaneous meeting requirements *Organized*
See list below
- ❑ note pads
- ❑ pens/pencils
- ❑ iced water/juice
- ❑ podium/lectern
- ❑ waste basket
- ❑ coat rack
- ❑ movable partitions
- ❑ other:

Registration   *Arranged*   *Confirmed*
See list below
- ❑ registration table
- ❑ name tags
- ❑ telephone
- ❑ typewriter
- ❑ manpower
- ❑ conference kits
- ❑ press kits

❑ rooming list
❑ seating plan
❑ pre-registration (accommodation)
❑ other:

Countdown

- D-30   Finalize rooming list
- D-30   Copy rooming list to venue
- D-3   Communicate final guaranteed members to venue and adjust bookings if necessary
- D-2   Confirmation of:
  programme timing
  venue
  speaker(s)
- D-2   Final briefing of helpers

D-Day

- Meet with functions manager and discuss arrangements
- Check pre-registration arrangements
- Check hospitality suite set-up

Function venue:

- Check set-up and seating arrangements
- Check microphone
- Check audiovisual and lighting equipment
- Check speaker's requirements
- Liaise with functions manager on all aspects of function programme prior to execution time

Evaluation

- D+7 Post function evaluation
- D+30 Outstanding accounts cleared for payment

Feedback to hotel

- Complete questionnaire (see below).

Questionnaire

1. Were your initial enquiries handled efficiently and professionally by the functions department?
   Yes ❑   No ❑
   Comments:_____
   _____

2. How do you rate the parking facilities?
   Poor ❑   Good ❑   Excellent ❑
   Comments:_____
   _____

3. On arrival at the function, were you welcomed and attended to by the banqueting manager?
   Yes ❑   No ❑
   Comments:_____
   _____

4. Was the venue suitable for your requirements?
   Yes ❑   No ❑
   Comments:_____
   _____

5. Was the room layout to your specification?
   Yes ❑   No ❑
   Comments:_____
   _____

6. How do you rate the standard of service?
   Poor ❑   Fair ❑   Average ❑   Good ❑   Excellent ❑
   Comments:_____
   _____

7. How do you rate the quality and presentation of food?
   Poor ❑   Fair ❑   Average ❑   Good ❑   Excellent ❑
   Comments:_____
   _____

8. Were food and beverage services:
   Efficient ☐   Prompt ☐   Courteous ☐
   Comments:_____
   _____

9. Was the equipment you required of a high standard?
   Yes ☐   No ☐
   Comments:_____
   _____

10. Was the room temperature comfortable?
    Yes ☐   No ☐
    Comments:_____
    _____

11. Was your room tidied up and refreshed after each break?
    Yes ☐   No ☐
    Comments:_____
    _____

12. Did tea and coffee breaks occur timeously?
    Yes ☐   No ☐
    Comments:_____
    _____

13. Would you consider holding your next function/conference at the hotel?
    Yes ☐   No ☐
    Comments:_____
    _____

14. General comments:_____
    _____
    _____

Checklists

Dinners and banquets

Dinner/Banquet	Assigned to	Date/Time assigned	Date/Time completed
A. ADVANCE PLANNING			

A. ADVANCE PLANNING
1. Agree with chief executive officer regarding date and venue to coincide with special event (anniversary, launch, special promotion).
2. Make sure this date is suitable for guest of honour and other VIPs. Agree on number of speeches and provide deadline for their receipt.
3. Appoint co-ordinator and planning team.
4. Allocate responsibilities to members of team:
   - planning of programme;
   - media and publications;
   - exhibitions.
5. Prepare a preliminary cost estimate based on agreed numbers.
6. Submit time schedules and deadline dates. Necessary to hold monthly meetings with team for regular updates.
7. Investigate protocol requirements.
8. Finalize invitation list. Prepare invitations and send out. Provide RSVP contact and final acceptance date. Follow up those who have still not replied for answer.
9. Discuss with hotel suitable menu, wines, gratuities. Confirm final numbers 48 hours before function.
10. Arrange photographer to cover event.
11. Prepare brochure/literature to be sent out in advance to invited guests.
12. Arrange invitation cards, programme, menu, table seating, and registration cards.

Dinner/Banquet	Assigned to	Date/Time assigned	Date/Time completed

13. On receipt of acceptances, plan seating arrangements, and table hosts.
14. Make arrangements for exhibition and audiovisual presentations.
15. Book accommodation for VIPs for night of function.
16. Co-ordinate media representatives and their requirements.

B. ON AND BEFORE THE DAY OF THE FUNCTION
  1. Arrange for telephone and telephone number to be made available at hotel for contact purposes throughout the day.
  2. Staff briefing prior to banquet including registration procedure.
  3. Purchase of suitable souvenirs and gifts.
  4. Agree on security arrangements with hotel and local police.
  5. Supervise construction of exhibits.
  6. Run through audiovisual programme.
  7. Liaise with media attending and confirm what facilities they will require (especially television).
  8. Be present at laying out of banquet room. Arrange table numbers, place cards, menus and programmes, lecterns, and flowers.
  9. Check public address system and arrange for audio-recording of main speeches.
 10. Set up registration tables and assign staff responsibilities.
 11. Brief photographer regarding specific requirements.
 12. Check final protocol arrangements.
 13. Arrange for staff to be on duty at least half an hour before function commences. Final briefing session.
 14. Appointed hosts to meet guests and escort them to registration tables where they will receive their table allocation seating plan. They will then be personally introduced to guest of honour and other VIPs.
 15. Banquet commences. Co-ordinating team to make sure that all arrangements run according to schedule.
 16. Press conference arranged at end of function.
 17. Retire for well-deserved nightcap!

C. AFTER THE FUNCTION
  1. Check banquet room for any articles that may have been left behind.
  2. Oversee dismantling of exhibition and equipment.
  3. Settle costs for overnight accommodation with hotel.
  4. Ask table hosts and officials for comments on function (e.g. reaction of guests).
  5. Complete budget and arrange for settlement of various accounts.
  6. Write thank you letters to all who participated in the event.

Dinner/Banquet	Assigned to	Date/Time assigned	Date/Time completed

7. Monitor press for any media coverage.
8. Send photographs and covering letter to invited guests, thanking them for their attendance.

Exhibitions and trade fairs

Although exhibitions and trade fairs are still relatively new in South Africa, exhibits should be an integral part of any public relations or marketing plan, since they communicate your message to prospective buyers via the exhibit structure, graphic images, sales personnel, and collateral support materials.

Exhibitions are without doubt the most cost-effective promotional tool in the marketing mix and certainly constitute one of the strongest known sales media. If approached correctly, exhibitions can be an extremely effective sales tool. Exhibiting can be broken down into three fairly clearcut sections:
- deciding which exhibition to support and to what degree;
- preparing a brief and organizing the construction of the stand;
- staffing and controlling the stand for the duration of the exhibition, including the period prior to the opening and during the dismantling of the stand.

There are a number of details to be attended to at various stages in the preparation for an exhibition. It is therefore desirable to draw up a detailed timetable listing all the items that have to be attended to, giving the final dates in each case. The schedule will include such items as insurance, transport, briefing of staff, telephones, stand cleaning, photography of stand, preparation of literature, entries in the exhibition catalogue, advertising or other publicity, arranging press conferences, fire precautions, security, and possible travel and accommodation for staff.

Exhibitions and trade fairs	Assigned to	Date/Time assigned	Date/Time completed

A. CHOOSING THE EXHIBIT TO SUPPORT
1. What is the exact scope of the exhibition, expected attendance, and type of visitor it attracts?
2. What are the general conditions of exhibiting?
3. How much space is needed to adequately display the articles or services that are to be exhibited?
4. What is the overall budget for exhibiting?
5. Can the company afford not to exhibit when strong competitors will be present?
6. Is the timing of the exhibition convenient in respect of new product launches, production schedules, and other events?
7. What additional sales are likely to result from exhibiting compared with other promotional channels?

B. ORGANIZING THE STAND
1. Consult all interested parties to ascertain their requirements.

Exhibitions and trade fairs	Assigned to	Date/Time assigned	Date/Time completed

2. Draw up a written brief setting out clear goals and objectives.
3. Unless a company has its own exhibition design staff, appoint a contractor who provides a design service or engage the services of a specialist architect/designer.
4. Initial design brief presented to client and agreed to.
5. Plans and specifications put out to tender. Contracting firm appointed.
6. Stand is erected in accordance with the specifications and in time for opening.
7. After the exhibition is over, designer/organizer to check all contractors' accounts, agree or disallow any extras and certify the final accounts for payment.

C. STAFFING AND ADMINISTRATION OF STAND
1. In planning staff requirements, it is desirable to have a few general staff members plus sufficient technically or otherwise qualified personnel to deal with difficult questions.
2. Build up a staff register of people who have proved to be absolutely reliable.
3. At overseas fairs, it is always necessary to have multilingual staff.
4. If the hours are very long, it may be necessary to allow for twice the staff required to be on duty at any one time.
5. Appoint a stand manager and a deputy to prepare staff roster, monitor staff behaviour, inspect the stand for cleanliness, and to take immediate action to remedy any damage or interference with the lighting or working models.

D. REVIEW PARTICIPATION IN THE EXHIBITION
1. Submit a written summary of the show and your company's participation to the pertinent division or heads of department and the chief executive officer:
- Include your reactions and those of your staff.
- Get reactions of show-goers (official and unofficial questionnaire).
- Assess cost-effectiveness.
- Include recommendations for improvements.

Budgeting for exhibitions

Main category	Subcategory		Action		Budget	Actual	Notes	Date
1 Stand costs			1.0	Make bookings				
	1.1	Space cost	1.1	Note payment deadlines				
	1.2	Shell scheme	1.2	Are items in 1.3 included in shell? Avoid duplication of costs				
	1.3	Stand fittings Displays Graphics/signage Plans and models	1.3	Get quotes in early. Watch cost escalation				
	1.4	Services Electricity Telephone Water Cleaning Fridge and furniture Plants Security Carpet hire	1.4	Do organizers arrange? Check meter readings before and after exhibition				
	1.5	Insurance Third party Inventory	1.5	If additional to company policies				
	1.6	Consulting/design fees Design company Architect	1.6	Can be worthwhile for peace of mind and increased effectiveness				
	1.7	Contingency	1.7	Add 15 per cent for non-contractual items				
2 Exhibit stand material	2.1	Internal	2.1	Inform relevant staff timeously				
	2.2	Purchased	2.2	Stay with standard sizes – specials may not fit or be available in time				
	2.3	Stand assembly	2.3–2.5	All take time				
	2.4	Storage						
	2.5	Equipment testing						
	2.6	Transport	2.6–2.7	Inform (to and from expo) of dates and times. Is labour available?				
	2.7	Lifting equipment						
	2.8	Contingency (peace of mind and increased effectiveness)	2.8	10 per cent should suffice				

Main category	Subcategory		Action	Budget	Actual	Notes	Date
3 Visitor promotion	3.1	Advertising Press Radio/television Posters Point of sale Direct mail	3.1 Supplement organiz- er's plans targeting own audience. Agency to incorporate men- tion of expo in prior ads				
	3.2	Catalogue/buyers' guide Adverts Editorial Additional copies	3.2 Buyer's guide can be used later				
	3.3	Specialist press Editorial Adverts	3.3 Special ads? Ensure press release is sent out in good time. Must be professionally written				
	3.4	Literature Catalogues Leaflets Technical informa- tion Point-of-sale material Other printing	3.4 Do we have what we need? Is reserve mate- rial available? Is new product literature available?				
	3.5	Press kits Editorial Releases Photographic Public relations agency fees	3.5 Tie in with organizer's plans. Issue own pics and releases? Post- exhibition releases also provide good cov- erage				
	3.6	Entertainment VIP visits Meals Cocktails Refreshments	3.6 Get organizers to han- dle pre-registration of VIPs. Are special facili- ties available? Will cocktails be served on the stand? Who will be invited?				
	3.7	Special events	3.7 Competitions – prizes. Publicity before and during show				
	3.8	Contingency	3.8 Allow up to 20 per cent because good ideas often come late				
4 Staff costs	4.1	Internal staff	4.1 Is training needed for reps? New product experience?				
	4.2	Temporary staff	4.2 What staff needed for overflow? What train- ing?				

Main category	Subcategory		Action		Budget	Actual	Notes	Date
	4.3	Training/films	4.3	Contact organizers re training films				
	4.4	Pre-exhibit training	4.4	Make sure everyone knows what to do. Do it before the opening day				
	4.5	Hotel expenses	4.5–4.8	Plan in advance and make bookings early				
	4.6	Travel and air fares						
	4.7	Meals and parking						
	4.8	Care hire						
	4.9	Uniforms	4.9	Can look smart – corporate image				
	4.10	Identity badges	4.10	Important visitors like to know to whom they are talking; include name and position in company				
	4.11	Parking/exhibitor passes	4.11	Contact organizers				
	4.12	Interpreters	4.12	Are foreign visitors expected? What have organizers laid on for interpreters?				
	4.13	Contingency	4.13	Between 5 and 10 per cent should cover the unexpected				

TOTAL BUDGET AND COSTS

Criteria when judging a stand

The Exhibition Association of South Africa has provided the following list of criteria when judging a stand. This list was drawn up after careful consideration, keeping the main objectives of exhibiting in mind at all times. The weighting of points was based on a total of 100.

- design impact and lighting (20 points);
- information, message and theme, literature available (15 points);
- construction, finish, and neatness (5 points);
- presentation of merchandise or story (15 points);
- originality and initiative (10 points);
- staff attitude, appearance, and product knowledge (15 points);
- language use and multilingualism (5 points);
- movement or animation and demonstration (10 points);
- traffic circulation and accessibility (5 points).

Opening ceremonies, plant tours and visits, other special events

Plant openings, buildings, and expansions	Assigned to	Date/Time assigned	Date/Time completed

A. ADVANCE PLANNING

1. Planning committee to be formed. Appointment of chairperson, secretary, treasurer.
2. Agreement with chief executive officer regarding main aims and objectives of the opening.
3. Date to be agreed at least six months ahead.
4. Invitation to be extended to Minister/VIP to attend function and to perform opening.
5. Invitation list to be drawn up to include all key stake-holders including media.
6. Arrange to send out invitations at least three months in advance. Monitor replies.
7. Make provisional bookings with caterers, equipment hire specialists, arrange marquee, platform, chairs, and plants.
8. Arrange for commemorative plaque.
9. Arrange with AA to have signs to direct visitors to venue.
10. Mark out appropriate parking spaces that show ease of entrance and exit without interfering with local traffic.
11. Check insurance policy for any company liability for accidents on the day.

B. PLANNING FOR ACTUAL DAY

1. Check all prior arrangements and set up venue day before.
2. Be there with your team early to attend to last-minute arrangements.
3. Station appropriate security guards inside and outside plant.
4. Arrange for welcoming committee which should include plant manager, other directors, and chief executive officer.
5. Plan various tours of the office and plant. Stanchions, ribbons, and signs are imperative. Signs should indicate what work takes place in each area. Various tours should be arranged starting at different points to avoid congestion. Appoint competent tour guides to lead the different tour groups.
6. Prepare an information kit which includes: short history of company, selected fact sheets, prepared speeches, sample of product(s).
7. Handle the media contingent: provide media kit, copy of speeches, pictures, maps, and plans. Minister's speech will be handled independently.
8. Arrange for photographer to record the official opening and take social pictures.

9. Oversee all catering arrangements:
   - Check with caterers on time and arrangements for tea and lunch.
   - Monitor bar facilities.
   - Make sure lunch is served on time, plates are cleared, and guest speaker is not delayed.
   - Provide gift for speaker and mementoes for guests.
10. Check microphone and sound system and test just before official opening.
11. Arrange to usher any VIPs off the plant after function.

C. AFTER THE EVENT
1. Check that all hired equipment is returned.
2. Check for any loss or damage.
3. Send thank-you letters to all who contributed to the success of the function.
4. Work out final budgets and settle accounts.
5. Have a special function for key personnel to thank them for their efforts.

Regular plant tours and visits	Assigned to	Date/Time assigned	Date/Time completed

A. ADVANCE PLANNING
1. Consider establishing a regular programme of plant tours/visits.
2. Get go-ahead from chief executive officer and senior management.
3. Appoint a co-ordinator for project to provide written proposals.
4. Look at feasibility of what to see in limited time frame.
5. Identify target audiences (visitors), e.g. schools, clubs, shareholders, clients, national and local government officials, media.
6. Invite other employees and their families for a first tour.
7. Recruit guides for the tour and train them for the task. They should familiarize themselves with tour routes.
8. Set days and times should be arranged and advertised.
9. Arrange parking. Notify security.
10. Arrange catering.

B. PLANNING FOR ACTUAL DAY
1. Arrange to meet at a central point at appropriate time.
2. Check whether all guests have arrived.
3. Provide name tags.
4. Have tour guide to welcome the party.
5. Do audiovisual presentation if available.
6. Arrange tea/coffee en route or at end of tour.
7. If necessary, prepare stanchions, ribbons, and signs for identification and directions.
8. Spot and place directions and signs well before visitors arrive.
9. Keep groups to a manageable size (12–15 maximum).

Regular plant tours and visits	Assigned to	Date/Time assigned	Date/Time completed
10. Prepare and present a small printed take-away flyer to each visitor, including other mementoes where appropriate.			
11. For media tour, arrange for interview with chief executive officer, provide fact sheets, media releases, brochures, and suitable photos.			

C. AFTER THE EVENT
1. Provide questionnaire for visitors to complete.
2. Escort visitors off premises.
3. Arrange letter of thanks/gratuity for tour guides for their services.

Visitors/special functions	Assigned to	Date/Time assigned	Date/Time completed

A. ADVANCE PLANNING
1. Draft letter of invitation for signature by person hosting visit.
2. Once invitation is accepted, organizer makes contact with visitor. Diarise to keep in touch with visitor while arrangements are made.
3. Who is paying? Confirm with guest exactly for what we have arranged to pay.
4. Compile budget.
5. Get background information – CVs, information on the company. This information goes to relevant people involved in the programme.
6. Draft a programme for approval by host.
7. Go through programme and book venues, arrange appointments.
8. Go through programme and diarise deadline dates for action, checking finalising, dry run, etc.
9. Sightseeing, pre-, and post-event tours.
10. Arrangements for companion/family.
11. Catering arrangements – teas, lunches, drinks, dinners, printing of menus, invitations, music, etc.
12. Transport arrangements – who will meet visitors and where, flight and other transport arrangements.
13. Hotel arrangements.
14. Audiovisual arrangements – videos, microphones if necessary, slide projector, overhead projector, flip charts.
15. Arrange photographer.
16. Check whether any special protocol is necessary. In the case of government officials and overseas guests, check with Department of Foreign Affairs or embassies.
17. Publicity.
18. Gifts, publication packages, etc. If gifts are given at a dinner or reception, arrange a special table.
19. Dry runs and rehearsals where necessary.

Visitors/special functions	Assigned to	Date/Time assigned	Date/Time completed
20. Final programme and relevant information (e.g. route map to venue) to guest.			
21. Confirm and double check all arrangements. Ensure that all those involved have programmes and other necessary documentation.			

B. PLANNING ON ACTUAL DAY
1. Flowers in venue(s).
2. Security.
3. Parking arrangements.
4. Prepare name badges, names on discussion tables.
5. Dinners: have seating plan approved where relevant. Check protocol with Department of Foreign Affairs (protocol section). For large dinners, guests are to be given a card on arrival with the number of the table where they will be seated. Helpers at the door to indicate where tables are.
6. Identify whether assistance is needed for registration, ushering people to their seats, etc. Carefully brief helpers and all others involved.
7. Arrange permits in access-controlled areas.
8. Check venue, seating arrangements and all details down to the smallest, e.g. music to be switched off during speeches, how the public address system works, someone to guard gifts.
9. Have extra copies of programme, name cards, publications, etc. available. Also have an emergency kit with important telephone numbers, scissors, pens, working files, etc.

C. AFTER THE EVENT
1. Debriefing after event to look at lessons learnt, discuss feedback, and update checklists.
2. Write thank-you letters.
3. Finalise finances.

What emerges from this brief review is that attention to detail, meticulous planning, and control are essential ingredients of any successful function or special event.

The one sobering thought is that organizers have only one chance to make an impression, and human nature being what it is, it is the things that went wrong which will always be remembered – the microphone that did not work, the guest speaker who did not arrive on time, the food that was served cold …

At the same time, a successful, professionally run function can achieve a great deal for an organization, enhancing its reputation as a first-class company with which to do business.

So remember, if in doubt, check it out. This will save a lot of heartache in the long run. There are no short cuts to excellence.

We conclude this section with a detailed Public Relations-Marketing checklist and an Integrated Marketing Communication checklist. These explore the relationships within an organization to see how each department can work more closely together for greater efficiency and publicity. We have also included an outline of a basic business plan to help entrepreneurs in setting up their own business.

Public relations-Marketing checklist

Since marketing and public relations work very closely together, the following checklist will be helpful in planning a joint strategy involving both departments.

A1 Concept and function – marketing

- What is the marketing concept and function of the organization being advised?
- What part does marketing play in corporate planning?
- How is the marketing policy evolved?
- How is the marketing budget determined?
- What is the organization's marketing mix?
- What are the marketing strategy and tactics?
- Is there market segmentation?
- What is the marketing structure?

A2 Concept and function – public relations

- Does public relations play a part in the marketing mix?
- Who has the key responsibilities for marketing planning?
- Do they take into account public relations activity or concepts?
- Is liaison satisfactory to produce co-ordinated campaigns?
- Is there a critical path analysis?
- How are the staff informed of the marketing concept, policy, and plan?
- Does the market itself have any public relations potential?
- Is the market declining/static/growing/new?
- Are there any seasonal variations/trends?
- Are there any regional biases/strengths/weaknesses?

B1 Market research – marketing

- Is market research used by the organization?
- How important a part does it play in the marketing plan?
- What is the market research brief?
- What use is made of internal business records?
- Which sampling techniques are used?
- Which field techniques are used?
- How is the questionnaire constructed?
- How is the data tabulated, analysed, and updated?
- How is the data used generally?
- Is market research used for any of the following?
  - marketing policies and methods;
  - markets in terms of consumer segmentation;
  - channels and methods of distribution;
  - products – goods or services;
  - product use development;
  - publicity – all forms;
  - selling activities and performances;
  - competitive products, methods and publicity;
  - international development?

B2 Market research – public relations

- Is market research used for public relations?
- To what extent does market research indicate attitudes towards the organization?
- What are the criteria for defining and reaching customers?
- Can any mileage be got out of the research project itself?
- Would the research be of interest to the industry through its trade or professional associations?
- Are there any opportunities for 'piggyback' schedules – by teaming up with other organizations and doing joint marketing research?

C1 Advertising – marketing

- Is there an advertising campaign?
- What is the overall campaign plan?
- How have market survey results been applied?
- Does the plan include a corporate campaign?
- Does the plan include campaigns aimed at particular sections of the public?
- What is the appropriation for the campaign?
- Which media will be used?
- Is there any below-the-line expenditure? If so, on what? Why?
- How will the campaign be evaluated?
- What do the staff think of it?

C2 Advertising – public relations

- Does the campaign have public relations potential with the trade press, staff, etc.?
- Is the advertising campaign linked to a public relations campaign?
- Is liaison satisfactory between all concerned – client, agencies, customers, and public relations counsel?
- Who are the advertising agents?
- Do they have any public relations ideas?
- Do they feel involved in the marketing campaign?
- Are they kept informed of its progress/success/failure?

D1 Product/service planning – marketing

- To what extent are the market research results applied to product/service planning?
- What are the sources for new product/service ideas?
- What are the product/service cycles?
- How is the product/service plan to be implemented?
- Is there any test marketing?
- What are the factors affecting product/service planning?
- How did the packaging evolve?

D2 Product/service planning – public relations

- In what ways can public relations help product/service planning?
- Is ecology or conservation taken into account? Are raw materials involved?
- Does the proposed product have any public relations potential?
- How will it be launched?
- Are technical institutes involved?

E1 Distribution – marketing

- How is the distribution organized?
- How is the product/service distributed/supplied?
- How were the channels of distribution chosen?
- How are data on the whole distribution line, from raw material to consumer, collected, analysed, and acted on?
- Where are the outlets located? Why?
- Are the goods exported? Where? Why? How? When?

E2 Distribution – public relations

- Can public relations solve any distribution problems?
- How does the public view the organization's distribution?
- Is there public relations potential in any of the following?
  - overcoming distribution problems
  - regional, national or international demand
  - method of transportation – own or others
  - people involved
  - traditional/ultramodern techniques/service
  - documentation
  - handling, storage, dispatch, receipt?
- Have any of the transport agencies public relations facilities which can be incorporated in the organization's public relations programme?
- Do those who carry know what they are carrying – and feel proud to do so?

369

F1 Pricing – marketing

- What is the pricing policy?
- How did it evolve?
- What are the pricing objectives?
- Is it a sellers' or buyers' market – supply/demand?
- How does the price affect the consumer's motivation?
- What are the industrial purchasing motives?
- Are there any alternative pricing policies?
- What place has pricing in the marketing mix?

F2 Pricing – public relations

- Can public relations solve any problems created by pricing?
- How does the purchaser regard the organization's pricing policy?
- How is the price communicated?
- Has the price itself any public relations potential, for example:
  - lowest;
  - fairest;
  - promotions;
  - exclusive value?

G1 Sales forecasting – marketing

- How is sales forecasting used in organization planning and control?
- What are the factors influencing forecasting?
- What are the information sources?
- What techniques are employed?
- What is the method of projection?
- How accurate has sales forecasting been?

G2 Sales forecasting – public relations

- What are the public relations factors involved in failing to meet, or exceeding, the forecast?
- Are there any contingency plans?

H1 Sales force – marketing

- What are the policies/objectives of those who market or sell?
- Are they aggressive/defensive/weak/strong?
- How is the sales force organized?
- How are staff recruited?
- How are staff trained?
- How do they implement the marketing concept, i.e.:
  - How are they motivated?
  - What are their targets?
  - What are the incentives?
  - Do they have marketing/sales manuals?
  - Do they hold marketing/sales meetings?
  - How effective are these meetings?
  - What form do they take?
- What use is made of performance standards?
- What are the systems of communication and control?

H2 Sales force – public relations

- How much do the marketing/sales staff know about public relations?
- Do they understand it?
- What experience have they had of it?
- What is their attitude towards it?
- Do they practise it?
- What are their individual basic problems?
- What can public relations do to solve them?
- Do other departments appreciate their work and difficulties?
- Can other staff assist directly by public relations involvement, for example engineers, lawyers, accountants, professionals, technicians, clerical – in fact, all personnel in the organization, in various ways?
- Do the employees feel involved in the marketing campaign?

J1 Selling – marketing

- What selling techniques are employed?
- What are the factors influencing marketing/sales?
- What is the effect of a buyer's/seller's market?

- What is the cost-effectiveness of promotional alternatives?
- What are the effects of scale of promotion?
- What is the influence of the market share?

J2 Selling – public relations

- Are there any special factors in the sales techniques which would be of interest to any industrial or management journals?
- What visual aids will be employed?
- What is the selling environment?
- Where are the customers (in town/country/at home/abroad)? Is there a public relations angle?
- Who are the customers? Are there any well-known personalities among them?
- Why do they buy? Are there repeat orders – is there a 'regular customer', 'brand loyalty over many years' angle? Why are they loyal?
- Are the goods/services sold to wholesalers?
- Is there a story in quality?
- Are the goods/services sold to retailers?
- Is there a story in type, location, numbers?
- Is there a supermarket or hypermarket story?
- What is the public relations analysis of point-of-sale support technique and practice?
- What about displays? Are they impressive/effective?
- What about complaints?
  - Do complaints affect sales?
  - Who deals with complaints?
  - How are complaints dealt with?

K1 Finance – marketing

- Is the company viable?
- If a public company, is it growing financially?
- If another type of organization, has it adequate finance?
- What are the financial aspects of the marketing campaign?
- How are financial decisions made?
- How are the marketing and production plans integrated into the overall budgetary control system?
- How is the budget arrived at and controlled?

- How is the target profit planned?
- How are marketing costs analysed?
- Is there a break-even analysis?
- How is performance/return measured?
- What is the share/stock performance?
- What is the price-earnings ratio?

K2 Finance – public relations

- Is there public relations in the assets?
- Is there public relations in property, investments, etc?
- Is there a financial public relations campaign?
- Is there a cash flow success story?
- What is the attitude of the JSE and financial institutions?
- When is the end of the financial year?
- How are the annual report and accounts presented and how effective are they? Do they get positive press coverage?
- What interest do the shareholders take in the company?
- How many attend the annual general meeting? What form does it take?
- Does the organization support community projects financially?
- Has it a charity policy?
- What is the organization's international financial reputation?

L1 Production – marketing

- What are the unique marketing advantages of the organization's production?
- What is the relationship between the marketing department and the production or service departments?

L2 Production – public relations

- Has public relations counsel actually seen the production line or service operation?
- What kind of history has it?
- Is it free of industrial disputes?
- If it has been troubled, has the solution any public relations potential, or is there a public relations solution?

- Are there any personalities at any level involved in production who, if publicized, can help build up confidence in the organization's product or service?
- Have the producers of the product ever met the producers of the raw materials?
- Have they met the retailers, or the customers at home or abroad?
- What are the conditions of work like – clean/healthy/safe/interesting/attractive?
- What is the attitude towards publicity visits? Are the visitors of value to the company as possible investors/buyers?
- Is there public relations potential in the production process itself?
- In production, how and where are raw materials and products stored? Is there a public relations angle to scale, size, safety, unique method, care?
- Do documentation, checking, systems, quality control, offer public relations opportunities?
- Are there any technical features of production which can be written up and be of interest to a wider public?
- Is there a special method, process or system of work?
- How are the goods packed/wrapped? What materials are used? Is there a public relations point – best designed/safety/convenience – of interest to wider public?
- Where are the goods produced, or the services offered/rendered?
- Has the building a public relations story – its lighting, heating, ventilation, drains, accommodation, décor, facilities, landscaping, or history?
- What machines are used?
- Is shift work involved? If so, are there any public relations problems or plus factors?
- What wages are involved? Are there any public relations problems or plus factors here? Do negotiations present problems?
- Staff: how are staff recruited/trained/pensioned?
- Is there a good work safety record?
- What about welfare/social activities?
- Are there any canteen facilities?

- What are the conditions of work?
- How much useful information reaches the shop floor from management and by what means?
- Does top management know what really happens on the shop floor?
- Is ecology/the environment affected by production?

The media and public relations

Like the questions on marketing and its public relations aspects, the following points should also be kept in mind:

A General

- Can this information be used in itself, or does it suggest other ideas for public relations action? Is it of historical importance?
- What media can be used?
- In what way?
- Who pays?

B Spoken word

- Is there any material available to compile speech notes for anyone speaking anywhere at any time on behalf of the organization?
- Should anything said be recorded?
- Is there subject matter for internal talks to involve the staff?
- Is there a possible topic for a paper to be read to an outside audience?
- What speaking engagements can be arranged?
- Is there a topic that lends itself to a conference session?

C Film

- Should a film be made? Is there an audience? If there is one, define it.
- If so, should an 8 mm or 16 mm film be made in-house?

- Or should a 16 mm or 35 mm film be made professionally?
- Can useful video or film slides be made?

D Photographs

- What about photographs? What is the potential? What is the demand?
- How good is the client's photographic library?

E Printed material

- What printed material is available?
- Is the material being produced so that, in addition to being a sales aid, it can be used by a wide audience?
- Should there be a direct mail shot, but perhaps in another direction, to other groups?
- Could a poster be produced on an ancillary theme?
- Is there a news bulletin item internally or externally?
- Is there a paper/house journal for workers?
- What use is made of notice boards?
- Are newsletters sent out?
- Would a brochure on an ancillary theme be useful?
- Should writers be commissioned to produce special articles, features?
- What can be communicated in the house journal?
- Is there material for the annual report?
- Is there scope for good visual aids, such as maps, plans, diagrams?
- What about house style?
- Is there a history of the firm? What part will the marketing campaign have in it?

F Press

- Would the local, national, technical, or professional press be interested either in the product, the people who make it, technology, or any other aspect of the company's activities linked to the marketing campaign?

- Are press releases satisfactory?
  - Is there feedback from editors about press releases?
  - Has a press release been requested?
- Should a press briefing be held?
- Should a press conference be held?
- What about press facility visits?
- Are press distribution lists up to date?
- Is basic background material updated and given to the press regularly?
- How are people in the company informed about press comment?
- How far down line management do executives actually meet and know the press?
- Are facts about the organization in press reference books accurate and up to date?
- Is the press-clipping service well organized, but not overemphasized?

G Radio and television

- Is there a radio news item or feature at home/abroad/locally/nationally?
- Is there television material? Have all types of television programme been considered?
- Is closed circuit television applicable?
- Are video tapes or other audiovisual techniques applicable?
- Do the organization's spokespersons come across well on television?
  - Are they the best available?
  - Can they take criticism?
  - Can they be trained?
  - Can they improve?

H Exhibitions

- Is there anything that could form part of an exhibition of any kind – marketing/trade/commercial/permanent/annual/scientific/local/international?
- What about models – are there any? Could any be worth while?
- Would artists' impressions be of use?
- Should the organization sponsor any event or commission a work of art for private or public viewing?

J Personal public relations

- How important are community relations and the community's use of the organization's media?
- Does the local community ever visit the organization to see what happens?
- Are staff involved in the wider issues of the day?

K Special events

- Can any of the following special events be of use?
  - openings;
  - VIP visits;
  - anniversaries;
  - open house;
  - record breaking;
  - facility visits;
  - new methods of production;
  - overseas visits;
  - industry events;
  - banquets;
  - significant achievements;
  - reunions;
  - product launches;
  - presentation of scholarships;
  - community events;
  - customer functions;
  - national events;
  - awards.

Public relations invariably has a corporate responsibility embracing stakeholder relations, social involvement, and employee relations, among others. However, in a marketing environment, public relations should also aim to contribute to the sales and marketing objectives of the company.

Integrated marketing communication strategy

The consumer

Target buying incentive
- How does this group perceive the products in the category?
- What do they buy now? How do they buy and use the product(s)?
- Lifestyles, psychographics, attitude towards category
- Key group insight
- What does the group want from the product category that they are not getting now?

Target buying incentive: I will buy a product that gives me better value for money than any other product in the category.
Recommend target buying incentive for group. Why?

Does the product fit the group?

The reality of the product:
- What's in it?
- Why is it different?
- How does the consumer perceive the product?
- How does it look, feel, taste, etc.?
- How does the consumer perceive the company behind the product?
- The 'naked truth'.
- Does the product fit the group? Recommendation.

How will the competition affect our objectives?

- What is the network, the competitive frame? Why?
- What do competitors now communicate to the consumer's way of life?
- How are competitors perceived by the consumer?

- How will competition retaliate against our programme?
- How vulnerable is competition? From whom will we take business?

What is the competitive consumer benefit?

- must be a benefit – solve a consumer problem, improve the consumer's way of life;
- must be one benefit;
- must be competitive – 'better than' the competitive frame;
- must not be a slogan or ad phrase;
- must be one sentence.

How will marketing communications make the benefit believable to the consumer?

- product reason why;
- perceptual support;
- communication support.

What should the personality of the brand be?

What unique personality will help define the product and differentiate it from the competitive frame?

Objectives

What main point do you want the consumer to take away from the communication?

What action do you want the consumer to take as a result of the communication?

- try product;
- send for more information;
- use product more often;
- other.

Perceptual effect

If communication is successful, ... months/ years from now the consumer will perceive the product as ... compared to the competition.

Consumer contact points

To most effectively reach the consumer with a believable, persuasive message, the following consumer contact points should be considered. Why?

Future research

List types of research needed in the future to further develop the communications strategy. Why?

With acknowledgement to Schultz, DE, SI Tannenbaum, and RF Lauterborn. *The New Marketing Paradigm – Integrated Marketing Communications*, p. 85–86, 1966.

The business plan

Drawing up a business plan is essential if you wish to set up your own business. Statistics show that there is a higher success rate among new businesses who have embarked upon this course. You can draw up a business plan yourself or hire a professional consultant to assist you. It is important that it is technically correct and professionally presented, as your ability to raise finance may depend upon it.

What is a business plan? It is a comprehensive feasibility study or action programme outlining every area of your venture. It forces an entrepreneur to translate a business idea into practical terms. It prepares the entrepreneur for the future, as he or she has anticipated possible problems and already looked at alternative solutions.

When applying for finance, banks insist upon a detailed business plan. Banks use the plan to assess the risk associated with the new enterprise and then decide whether or not they will extend a loan.

Business Partners Limited list the following points to show the importance of a business plan:

- it forces you to arrange your thoughts in a logical order;
- it forces you to simulate reality and anticipate pitfalls before they occur;

- it should be your working action plan or guideline when your business is up and running;
- it is an essential aid when applying for financial assistance or trying to sell your idea because it will assist in determining the viability of your business;
- it can eliminate potential flaws in your idea;
- it is an essential decision-making tool.

There is no set format for a business plan. What you will find is a list of guidelines to ensure that it is a comprehensive (detailed) document and does not leave out anything of importance.

Business Partners views the following as the important components of a business plan:
- a definition of the business;
- the objectives of the business;
- a 'people plan';
- a marketing plan;
- a resources plan;
- assumptions made about terms of trade, interest rates etc.;
- a profit and loss budget;
- a cash flow forecast;
- your methods of monitoring the business plan.

It further breaks down the business plan into a number of easy steps.

Step 1: Make a good first impression

The front page should include the following:
- the name of the business;
- the type of business;
- the name(s) of the owner(s);
- the address, telephone and fax numbers, and email address of the owner(s) of the business;
- the logo or emblem;
- the date presented.

The contents page should be divided into clearly numbered headings with corresponding page numbers.

Step 2: Introduction

Start off with an interesting introduction. It should include:
- a description of the product or service you intend selling or manufacturing;
- why you believe your venture is viable;
- your short, medium, and long-term business goals and objectives.

Step 3: Description of business

Provide a comprehensive description of your proposed business venture, including:
- the type of business ownership;
- legal requirements such as licensing permits and tax regulations;
- a comprehensive outline of the products or services you intend selling or manufacturing;
- a technical outline containing details and capabilities of your machinery and equipment;
- a description of your location, features, floor layout, proximity to competitors, leasing, and purchasing conditions;
- a comprehensive outline of your educational qualifications, work experience, and training courses attended;
- a comprehensive and objective SWOT analysis of the business;
- a description of your competitors and their products.

Step 4: Marketing plan

Comprehensively outline your proposed marketing plan and strategy. It should include:
- a description and substantiation of your specific target market;
- the percentage of market-share that is aimed for in the medium and long term;
- a description of your competitors' marketing strategy and the potential effect on your business;
- a description of your purchasing, costing, pricing, selling, and sales promotion strategy.

Step 5: 'People plan'

This deals with staffing requirements, and should include:
- a description of the manager's or managers' background;
- a description of the skills required by staff;
- an outline of possible training of staff.

Step 6: Resources plan

- a list of people, machinery, stock etc. needed to set up the business;
- decisions to be made regarding purchasing or leasing of equipment.

Step 7: Financial plan

Comprehensively outline your financial plan and strategy. This should include:
- a detailed income statement or profit and loss account for a projected period of 12 months;
- an indication of the break even point calculated as total expenses divided by gross profit percentage;
- a detailed cash-flow for the projected 12 month period;
- a detailed balance sheet;
- a sensitivity analysis showing what would happen if business were good, average, or poor;
- an outline of one's own financial contribution;
- an outline of the necessary financing required – when and how much;
- an outline of the security available.

Step 8: Operating plan

Comprehensively outline your business structure or operating plan and strategy. This should include:
- a description of the staff you intend employing and how you are going to recruit them;
- a description of the management and staff structure including qualifications, number of staff, and remuneration;
- a description of the administrative or record-keeping system;
- a record of staff policy concerning working hours, fringe benefits, overtime, etc.

Step 9: Conclusion

End off with a positive and motivating conclusion. Include:
- a summary of why your business plan will work;
- why you believe finance should be granted;
- a motivating factor for other people to have faith in your proposed venture.

Once created, a business plan should not be discarded but should be used to monitor progress.

Further reading

Lloyd, P.H. 1984. *Public Relations*. London: Hodder & Stoughton.
Mersham, G.M. & P. Morrison. 1996. *How to Start Your Own Business*. Johannesburg: Heinemann.
Nieuwenhuizen, C., E.E. le Roux, & J.W.S. Jacobs. 1996. *Entrepreneurship and How to Establish Your Own Business*. Small Business Management series. Cape Town: Juta.
Sargent, D.J. *Your Business Plan: A Workbook for Owners of Small Businesses*. Canada: College of New Caledonia.
Business Partners Limited. *Drawing Up a Business Plan*.
Schultz, D.E., S.I. Tannebaum, & R.F. Lauterborn. 1996. *The New Marketing Paradigm*. Chicago: NTC Business Books.

PRISA library list

Anna-Mari Honiball Library List

A service for PRISA registered individuals only.

Advanced Communication Skills, Liesel Erasmus-Kritzinger, Marietta Swart, and Vusi Mona

Advertiser's Desk Book, Admark Publishing Company Limited

Advertising – Its Role in Modern Marketing, S W Dunn

Advertising for Free (1, 2, 3, 4), Chris Skinner and Richard Cluver

Advertising Law in South Africa, Tanya Woker

Affirmative Action – a Guide for Managers, Thea Wingrove

Africa Media Review (1994 Vol. 8 No. 2, 3), Charles Okigbo

African Way (The), Mike Boon

Age of Participation (The), Patricia McLagan and Christo Nel

All about Public Relations (1, 2), Roger Haywood

Analysis for Improving Performance, Richard A Swanson

Applied Strategic Planning (1, 2), Leonard D Goodstein, Timothy M Nolan, and J William Pfeiffer

Art of Persuasive Communication (The), Johann C de Wet

Aspects of Business Communication, Ronel S Rensburg, and Christien Bredenkamp

Aspekte van Massakommunikasie, Marais, Engelbrecht, Groenewald, Puth, and Breytenbach

Assertiveness at Work: A Practical Guide to Handling Awkward Situations, Ken Back, Kate Back, and Terry Bates

Assertiveness: A Positive Process, Barrie Hopson and Mike Scally

Australian Public Relations Manual (The), Candy Thompson and Bill Sherman

Bedryfsielkunde (Verpligte praktiese werkopdrag), Wolfaardt and Viviers

Bedryfsielkunde Studiegids (Narvorsingsmetodiek en sielkundige meting), Wolfaardt, Viviers, Coetzer, and Tustin

Bedryfsielkunde Studiegids (Organisasie en beroepsielkunde), Watkins, Cilliers, Coster, and Theron

Bedryfsielkunde Studiegids, A L Theron and Z C Bergh

Bedryfsielkunde Studiegids, Bergh, Theron, and Coster

Bestaanskommunikasie, Martinus van Schoor

Beware the Naked Man Who Offers You His Shirt, Harvey Mackay

Better Business Writing, Susan L Brock

Bluff Your Way in PR, Basil Saunders and Alexander C Rae

Body Language, Allan Pease

Brands and Branding in South Africa, Tom Peters

Brands and Branding in SA: Advertising and Publishing (1, 2, 3), various authors

Business Day Directory, Politics and Business in SA, Adrian Hadland

Business Economic (Hons) Study Guide (PR Management), Unisa

Business Economics Study Guide (PR Management), B A Lubbe

Business Sponsorship, Caroline Gillies

Celestine Prophecy: An Experiential Guide, James Redfield and Caroline Adrienne

Charis-Magic in Public Speaking: The Power to Move People, Dick Milham

Commitment-Led Marketing, Jan Hofmeyer and Butch Rice

Common-Sense Time Management for Personal Success, Barrie Pearson

Communicare V 1 (2), V 2 (2)

Communicate, C N Parkinson

Communicating – a Guide to PR in Japan, JDW Associates

Communicating (for the Professions), G Stewart, C De Kock, M Smit, R B Sproat, and G Storrie

Communicating Change, T J Larkin and Sander Larkin

Communicatio, J P Fourie

Communicatio, Hennie Swanepoel and Frik de Beer

Communication, D F du Plessis

Communication and Public Relations, Gary Mersham and Chris Skinner

Communication by Objectives (1, 2), H P Fourie

Communication for Development (1, 2), Hennie Swanepoel and Frik de Beer

Communication for Work, Carol Carysforth

Communication Management

Communication Media, Gary Mersham and Chris Skinner

Communication in the New Millennium, Argyle

Communication in the Organisation, Thomas Blatt

Communication in the Third World: Seizing Advertising Opportunities in the 1990s, Nick Green and Reg Lascaris

Communication Works, Teri Kwai Gamble and Michael Gamble

Communitas Vol 2: 1995

Community Capacity Building (1, 2), Hennie Swanepoel and Frik de Beer

Company Courtesy, Christopher Ward

Company Image and Reality, David Bernstein

Competitive Green, Dennis Kinlaw

Complete Entrepreneur – a Guide to Survival for the Small Business (1, 2, 3), David Oates

Concise Communicator, Clive Simpkins

Conquer the Job Market (Five Steps to Win the Job) (1, 2, 3), Thebe Ikalafeng

Consultants Guide to Proposal Writing, H Holtz

Consultants Manual (a Complete Guide), T L Greenbaum

Consumer Behaviour: a South African Perspective (1, 2), P J du Plessis, G G Rousseau, and N H Blem

Contemporary Advertising, William F Arens

Contemporary Conversations, Linda Human

Contemporary Social Problems 4th Edition, Robert K Merton and Robert Nisbet

Content Analysis of Communications, Budd, Thorp, and Donohe

Corporate Communication, Paul Argenti

Corporate Communications Handbook, Timothy R V Foster and Adam Jolly

Corporate Communication Strategy (1, 2, 3, 4), Benita Steyn and Gustav Puth

Corporate Culture in a Changing Society, Unlisted

Corporate Culture Sourcebook, Bellingham, Cohen, Edwards, and Allen

Corporate Cultures: The Rites and Rituals of Corporate Life, Terence Deal and Allen Kennedy

Corporate Identity, Wally Olins

Corporate Reputations: Strategies for Developing, Grahame R Dowling

Creating Effective Marketing Communication, D Yadin

Creating the High-Performance Team, S Buchholz and T Roth

Creative Newspaper Design, Tony Sutton

Creativity Factor: Unlocking the Potential of Your Team, Edward Glassman

Creativity in Public Relations, Andy Green Institute of Public Relations

Credibility Factor, Lee Baker

Crisis Communications Planning Guide, Manual

Crisis Counselling, Norman Wright

Crisis Marketing, Joe Marconi

Crisis Response, Jack Gottschalk

Crisis Response, T Forster

Critical Arts, K Tomaselli

Critical Perspectives in Public Relations, J L'Etang and M Pieckza

Customer Driven Company (1, 2), Richard C Whitely

Customers as Partners: Building Relationships that Last, Chip R Bell

Cutting Costs, Harry Figgie Jr

Dealing With an Angry Public, Lawrence Susskind and Patrick Field

Democratic Corporation, Russell L Ackoff

Desk Research, Peter Jackson

Design Management

Die Afwykende in die Gemeenskap: 'n Kriminopatologiese Benadering, G Cronje and P J van der Walt

Die Samelewingskritiek van C Wright Mills, Nerina Jansen

Diplomacy Protocol, J K Mollo

Diplomatic Handbook, R G Feltham

Don't Do What I Did, Allen Berkowitz

Don't Say 'Yes' When You Want to Say 'No', Herbert Fensterheim and Jean Baer

Discovering the Essence of Leadership, Tony Manning

Dynamic of Public Relations, Chris Skinner

Ecquid Novi (2)

Effective Business Writing, Michael Fielding

Effective Communications – a PR Viewpoint, Chris Skinner

Effective Communication in Organisation, Michael Fielding

Effective Group Communication, Ernest Stech and Sharon A Ratcliffe

Effective Internal Communication, Lyn Smith and Pamela Smith

Effective PR Management, Paul Winner
Effective Press Releases (1, 2, 3, 4, 5, 6), Ralph
    Cohen
Effective Public Relations 5th, 6th (1, 2), and *7th*
    Edition, Cutlip, Center, and Broom
Effective use of Sponsorship: Marketing in Action
    series, David Wragg
Effective Media Manager, Carel van der Merwe
Elements of South African Marketing, Norman
    Blem
Empty Raincoat, Charles Handy
Encyclopaedia of Brands and Branding in SA:
    Millennium Edition
English for Law Students, C van der Walt and AG
    Nienaber
Enhancing the Volunteer Experience, Paul J Ilsley
Essentials of Effective Public Relations, S M Cutlip
    and A H Center
Essence of Leadership (1, 2, 3, 4), Edwin A Locke
Ethical Dilemmas
Evaluation of Public Speaking, Johann C de Wet
    and Ronel S Rensburg
Event Planning, Judy Allen
Excellence in Public Relations and
    Communications Management (1,2) James
    Grunig
Excellence in Public Relations and
    Communications Management (3) David M
    Dozier, Larissa A Grunig, and James Grunig
Executive at Work, F DeArmond
Executive Guide to Strategic Planning, P Below
Facts and Fallacies
Fifty Years Ahead of the News, John Sattler
Film Propaganda: Soviet Russia and Nazi Germany
    (file), Richard Taylor
Finance for Managers, Derek Thorn
First Things First (1) Patrick Forsyth
First Things First (2) Stephen R Covey
Flawless Consulting, Peter Block
Flawless Consulting 2nd Edition, Jenis Nowlan
Focus on Business Management, Ma Igee Mayhem
Focus Press Freedom in South Africa, A S de Beer
Fraudbusting – How to Deal with Corporate Fraud
    (1, 2, 3) David Price
From Executive to Entrepreneur, Gilbert Zoghlin
Frontline Customer Service, Clay Carr
Fundraising and PR: A Critical Analysis, Kathleen
    Kelly
Future South Africa: Visions, Strategies, and
    Realities, Bobby Godsell
Getting New Clients, Dick Connor
Getting the Best from Agencies, Geoffrey Smith
Going Green, E Harrison

Governare Le Relazioni, Toni Muzifalconi
Government Public Relations
Group Dynamics 3rd Edition, Marvin E Shaw
Guidelines for Successful Conference Organising,
    Tony Carlile
Guide to the Law 5th Edition, Bell, Dewar, Kesley
    Stuart
Guts – Advertising from the Inside Out, John Lyons
Handbook of Financial PR, Pat Bowman
Handbook of Modern Marketing, V P Buell
Handbook of Personnel Management Practice (A),
    Michael Armstrong
Handbook of Public Relations 3rd Edition, Chris
    Skinner and Llew von Essen
Handbook of Public Relations 4th Edition (1, 2)
    (blue), Skinner and Von Essen
Handbook of Public Relations 5th Edition (green),
    Skinner and Von Essen
Handbook of Public Relations (Revised: 1, 2)
    (grey), Skinner and Von Essen
Handbook of Public Relations (1982) (red),
    Skinner and Von Essen
Handbook of Public Relations 3rd Edition (1, 2, 3)
    (yellow), Skinner and Von Essen
Handbook of Public Relations 3rd Edition (4),
    Skinner and Von Essen
Handbook of Public Relations and
    Communications (1, 2), Phillip Lesley (editor)
Handbook of Public Relations, Ellis and Nigel
Hardcastle's Money Talk, Bob Hardcastle
Healing Management, William Lundin and
    Kathleen Lundin
Help Directory (a Guide to SA Services and
    Resources), Pat Barton and Hilary Bassett
High Income Consulting (1, 2) Tom Lambert
Hitchhiker's Guide to the Internet, Arthur
    Goldstruck
Horizontal Management: Beyond Total Customer
    Satisfaction, K Denton
How to Audit the Human Resources Department
    (file), John H McConnell
How to Avoid the Corporate Nightmare (1, 2) Sue
    Creithton
How to Build a Successful Career, Alan Jones
How to be a Successful Exhibitionist, J Donovan
How to be an Assertive (not Aggressive) Woman in
    Life, Love, Job, Jean Baer
How to Get Published in South Africa, Basil van
    Rooyen
How to Manage Public Relations, Norman Stone
How to Organise Effective Conferences and
    Meetings, David Seekings
How to Run a Successful Meeting, Anthony Jay

How to Run Seminars and Workshops, Robert Jolles

How to Select and Manage Consultants (1, 2, 3), Howard Shenson

How to Think on Your Feet, Patrick Quin

How to Understand and Manage Public Relations (1, 2), Dr John White

How to Write a Million, Wood, Reed and Bickham

How to Write a Million (More about), Dibell, Scott, Card, and Turco

How to Win in a Job Interview, Jason Robertson

Human Resources Management, P D Gerber, P S Nel, and P S van Dyk

Iacocca Management Technique, Maynard M Gordon

I and Thou, Martin Buber

I Was Your Customer: A Survival Kit for World-Class Customer Care, Peter Cheales

Identity and Branding-Design, Design Management Journal

Image at the Top: Crises and Renaissance in Corporate Leadership (Life), Richard S Ruch and Ronald Goodman

Image Factor, Eleri Sampson

Leading Managers 2003 Edition

In Search of Excellence, Thomas J Peters and Robert H Waterman Jnr

Industrial Adman's Desk Book, Admarks Publishing Company Limited

Industrial Public Relations, Paul I Slee Smith

Industrial Relation in the New South Africa 3rd Edition, Sonia Bendix

Influencing – Marketing the Ideas that Matter, Chip Bell

Inleiding tot Bestuurswese, G de Cronje

In All Labour Profit, Frans Rautenbach

Innovative EA Employee Communication, Alvie L Smith

Inside Organizational Communication 2nd Edition, Carol Reuss and Donn Silvis

Interactive Public Relations, Wole Adamolekun, Tayo Ekundayo

International Business Communication, David A Victor

International PR Case Studies 1993 (1, 2), Sam Black

International Public Relations in Practice, Margaret Nally

Introduction to Advertising and Promotion, an Intergrated Marketing Communication Perspective 3rd Edition, George E Belch, Michael M Belch

Introduction to Communication, G M du Plooy

Introduction to Marketing, J M Strydom (editor)

Introduction to Public Relations, Sam Black

Is Anyone Out There Listening? (Essential Reading to Understand the Future of Women in Business), Sandra van der Merwe

Joernalistiek Vandag, A S de Beer

Journal of Communication Studies (Vol. 4), Grisham

Journal for Journalists in S A (Vol. 1), (I A J) July 1995

(Book review: *Writing for the Media*) (1)

Journalism – Truth or Dare (I A J) July 1995

(Book review: *Writing for the Media*) (2)

Juran on Quality by Design (1, 2, 3), J M Juran

Kierkegaard en Kommunikasie (1, 2), Marthinus van Schoor

Kommunikasie in Kleingroepe (1979) (1), H C Marais and L J Nieuwmeijer

Kommunikasie in Kleingroepe (1989) (2), H C Marais

Kommunikasiekunde Studiegids (Oorredingskommunikasie), De Wet and Rensburg

Later Years – PR Insights, E L Bernays

Law of Defamation in South Africa, Jonathan M Burchell

Lead to Succeed (1, 2, 3), Michael Beer

Leading Managers (2003)

Leadership the Human Race, Guy Charlton

Liberation Management, Tom Peters

Live for Life Avoid the Stress Mess, Dr Brian Jude

Look out: A Survival Guide to the International Business Onslaught, Peter Cheales

Major Film Theories: An Introduction, J Dudley Andrew

Make the Other Half Work Too (1, 2), Mark Barenblatt and Roger Sinclair

Making Your Case, Anthony Jay

Making the Media Work for You, Ryland Fisher

Mampudi (100 Mindsparks to light up your head, heart, body and soul), Mike Lipkin

Management and Practice of Public Relations, Norman Stone

Manager's Guide to Excellence in PR and Communication Management, David M Dozier, Larissa A Grunig, and James E Grunig

Manager's Guide to Solving Personnel Issues, Isobel Emanuel

Manager's Guide to Staff Incentives, John G Fisher

Managers Talk Ethics: Making Tough Choices (1, 2) Barbara Toffler

Managing Assertively, Madelyn Burley-Allen

Managing Brand Equity, David Aaker

Managing Change and Making it Stick, Roger Plant

Managing Differences, Daniel Dana

Managing in the New Team Environment, Larry Hirschhorn

Managing Knowledge: Channels, Changes, and Choices

Managing Perceptions, Gillian Goldman

Managing the Professional Service Film, David H Maister

Managing Problem Loans, Michael Groves

Managing Public Relations (1, 2), James Grunig

Managing Successful Projects, Philip Baguley

Managing to be Green, Marian Propkop

Managing Transition: New Ways of Thinking About Your Business, Ruth Tearle

Marketing Success Stories (1, 2), A van der Walt

Marking Success Stories, Robert Pritchard

Marketing to Black Townships, Robin Morris

Master of Ceremonies, Franscois Marais

Mastering Decision Making: The Step-by-Step Approach for Success, Unlisted

Maverick, Ricardo Semler

Maximised Marketing, Shirley Grady

Media are American, Jeremy Tunstall

Media Studies (Vol. 1) Theories and Issues, Pieter J Fourie

Media Science, J B Freyssen, R M Briel, C Potgieter, E S J van Graan, L J van Niekerk

Media Virus, Douglas Rushkoff

Media Write, Fritz Spieegl

Mediareg, Klopper, Strauss, and Strydom

Mediation – Principles, Process, Practice, Lauren Boulle, and Alan Rycroft

Meet the Media, Barrie McMahon and Robin Quin

Memory Vision, James Liebig

Mike Bike Story, Nico Venter

Millions from the Mind, Alan Tripp

Mind of the Strategist, Kenichi Ohmae

Mind Traps – Change Your Mind, Change Your Life, Tom Rusk

Monitor: Globalising Public Relations – Considerations in South Africa, R Singh (editor)

Movies as Social Criticism, I C Jarvie

Moving up to Supervision 2nd Edition (1, 2) Martin M Broadwell

Multicultural Communications, Debrea Miller

Munisipale Verhoudings, Thomas du Toit

Naked Manager for the Nineties, Robert Heller

Natal Story: 16 Years of Conflict (1, 2, 3), Anthea Jeffrey

Navigating Change, Donald Hambrink, David Adler, Michael Tushman

Negotiation: Methodology and Training, Louise Nieuwmeijer

New Insights into Communication and Public Relations, Gary Mersham and Chris Skinner

New Media Developments, Jo Groebel

Newsman's English, Evans and Harold

Newspaper History of South Africa, Vic Alhadeff

Newspaperman's Guide to the Law, Bell, Dewar, and Hall

New Zealand Handbook of PR, Joseph Peart and Jim R. Macnamara

Numberwise: How to Analyze Your Facts and Figures (1, 2), Michael C Thomsett

Online Public Relations (1, 2) David Phillips

Oor Samelewings en Samelewingseksistensie, C J Alant, A M Lamont, F A Maritz, and I J van Eeden

Openbare Skakelwese in Suid-Afrika (1, 2), J P Malan and J A L'Estrange

Organization Development (1, 2), W Warner Burke

Organizational Behaviour, Robert Kreitner and Angelo Kinicki

Organizational Vision, Values, and Mission, Cynthia D Scott, Dennis T Jaffe, Glenn R Tobe

Organizing for the Creative Person, D Lehmkuhl

Parliamentary Lobbying, Ellis, Nigel

Passages: Predictable Crises of Adult Life, Gail Sheehy

Passion Makes Perfect, Peter Cheales

Patterns of High Performance, Harry Fletcher

People and Projects in Development

Personal Management Handbook, John Mulligan

Personality Rights and Freedom of Expression, Jonathan Burchell

Persuasive Business Presentations, Nick Robinson

Persuasive Communication, Erwin P Bettinghaus

Pictorial Communication, J M Peters

Piet Fiets Verhaal, Nico Venter

Plan or Die, Timothy Nolan, Leonard Goodstein, J William Pfeiffer

Planning for Development and Growth: The Key to Business Development, David McKeran

Planning and Marketing a Public Relations Campaign (IPR Series), Anne Gregory

PR and Communications Theory, Chris Skinner

Practical Guide to Labour Law (A), Du Plessis, Fouche, Jordaan, Van Wyk

Practical Guide to Meetings (1, 2), Oscar Britzius

Practice Development for Professional Firms, Audrey Wilson

Practice of Public Relations 5th Edition, Fraser P Sietel

Presentation of Self in Everyday Life, Erving Goffman

Presenting Yourself, Mary Spillane

Press Freedom in South Africa, A S de Beer

Preventing Chaos in a Crisis, Patrick Lagadec

Principles of Professional Management, Louis A Allen

Print Media Advertising, Dr C L Koekermoer

Private Life of Public Relations, Richard Kisch

Proceedings of the 2nd World Public Relations Festival (1, 2)

Professional Adviser's Guide to Marketing, Geoff Humphrey and Norman Hart (editors)

Professional Image, Susan Bixler

Professional's Self-Assessment Kit, Michele Eckenschwiller

Profiel en Professie: Inleiding in die Teorievorming van PR, A van der Meiden, G Fauconnier

Profit From Pro-Active Public Relations (1, 2), Skinner, Von Essen

Project Management, Joan Knutson, Ira Bitz

Projecting Your Image, Pat Roberts

Promote Like a PRO, Linda F Radke

Promotional Strategy Management in Practice, Ludi Koekermoer

Protocol Manual, M L Tabane

Public Relations and Communication, C V Narasimha Reddi

Public Relations 3rd Edition, Frank Jefkins

Public Relations Client Service Manual, Gable Group

Public Relations, Development and Social Investment, G M Mersham, R S Rensburg, J C Skinner

Public Relations for Leisure and Tourism, Y French

Public Relations Handbook 1st Edition, R W Darrow, D J Forrestal and A O Cookman

Public Relations in Action, Robert Reilly

Public Relations in Local Government, Tom Richardson

Public Relations in Practice (IPR Series), Anne Gregory

Public Relations in South Africa (1, 2, 3), B A Lubbe and G Puth

Public Relations Management, Raymond Simon, Frank W Wylie

Public Relations Possibilities 4th Edition, Allen H Center, Patrick Jackson

Public Relations Practices in South Africa, 4th Edition, J P Malan, J A L'Estrange

Public Relations Strategy, Sandra Oliver

Public Relations Strategies and Tactics (1986) (1) Wilcox, Ault, Agee, Check

Public Relations Strategies and Tactics (1989) (2) Wilcox, Ault, Agee, Check

Public Relations Strategies and Tactics (1992) (3) Wilcox, Ault, Agee, Check

Public Relations Techniques, Frank Jefkins

Public Relations Techniques 2nd Edition, Frank Jefkins

Public Relations Writer's Handbook, Merry Aronson, Don Spetner

Public Relations Writing 3rd Edition, Doug Newsom, Bob Carrell

Public Relations Writing and Media Techniques, Dennis Wilcox, Lawrence Nolte

Public Relations, Development, and Social Investment – a South African Perspective, Mersham, Rensburg, Skinner

Public Speaker's Treasure Chest

Putting Pressure to Work, Ivan Hatvany

Psychology of Customer Service

Rainbow – Your Guide to a Bright Future

Research 2002 (Vol. one)

Reconstruction and Development Programme, African National Congress

Reklame vir die Sakeman, J H Picard

Relationship Marketing, Mary Nowensnick

Reputation Management: Realizing Value from the Corporate Image, Prof. Charles Fombrun

Running Public Relations Department, Mike Beard

Secrets of Successful Speaking and Business Presentation, Gordon Bell

Self Development in Organizations, Pucker, Burgoyne, Boydmi, Wilshman

Service Please, South Africa (1, 2, 3, 4) Norman Blem

Seven Habits of Highly Effective People (1, 2) Stephen Covey

Shaping Strategic Planning (1, 2), Pfeiffer, Goodstein, Nolan

Sight, Sound, Motion: Applied Media Aesthetics, Herbert Zettl

Slovian PR Theory and Practice 1999–2000, Pedja Asanin Cole, Dr Dejan Vercic

Smiling Pawpaw, Ronel Engelbrecht, Chris Rademeyer

Social Responsibility in Public Relations, Zarine Smit

Social, Political, and Economics Contexts in Public Relations, H M Culbertson, D W Jeffers, D B Stone, M Terrell

Sociological Theory 4th Edition, Nicholas S Timasheff, George A Theodorson

South Africa Yearbook 1998, GCIS

South African Advertising 4th Edition (1, 2, 3), Roger Sinclair

South African Handbook of Public Relations (1, 2), Skinner, Von Essen

South Africa's Most Promising Companies

Speak Up, Robert E Hopkins

Speech and Social Action Strategy of Oral Communication, Ellingsworth, Huber, Clevenger, Theodore

Spraakkommunikasie en Houding, H van Schalkwyk

Spraakopleiding, Cecily Louw, Sann Potgieter

Starting a High-Income Consultancy, James Essigner

Stay Positive! It's all a Matter of Attitude, Elwood N Chapman

Still More Games Trainers Play, John W Newstrom

Strategic Planning: Selected Readings, J William Pfeiffer

Strategic Public Relations (1, 2), Norman Hart

Street Smart Public Relations, John Budd

Taalkommuikasie Afrikaans, H van Schalkwyk, D A Viviers

Technology Connection Strategy and Change, Marc Gerstein

Tekens en Betekenis, J J Roelofse

Television and the PRO (1, 2, 3, 4, 5), Kaimon

Theory and Practice of Training, Buckley, Caple

The House Journal Handbook, Peter C Jackson

The Essence of Leadership, Adwin A Locke

The South African Development Directory, Yzette Terreblanche

Think Tall, Norman Nel

Third World Destiny: Recognising and Seizing the Opportunities Offered by a Changing South Africa, Nick Green, Reg Lascaris

Thirteen Attributes of Success, Dr Brian Jude

This is PR 5th Edition, Doug Newsom, Alan Scott, Judy Vanslyke Turk

Thoughts on Publication Design, Jan V White

Thriving on Chaos, Tom Peters

Throwing the Switches, G Mlokoti

Toegepaste Kommunikasie (1, 2), J Z Eloff, G J van den Heever

Top Consultant (1, 2), Calvert Markham

Top Marketing and Media Companies in the UK, Johan Bloom

Toxic Sludge is Good for You! John C Stauber, Sheldon Rampton

Training for Development, H Swanepoel, F de Beer

Training Managers So That They Can Really Manage, Thomas Quick

Transcultural Management: How to Unlock Global Resources (1, 2), Albert Koopman

Transforming the Crisis-Prone Organization, Panchaut, Mitroff

Truth About Advertising (The), Robert Brandon

Turning Practical Communication into Business Power (1, 2), Bernard Katz

TV Guide for Marketers

Two Ages – the Age of Revolution and the Present Age, Soren Kierkegaard

Understanding and Implementing Performance Management, H Spanenberg

Understanding Financial Statements: A Primer of Useful Statements, James O Gill

Understanding News, John Hartley

Understanding Public Relations (1, 2, 3) R C Krause

Understanding Television, Getruida M du Plooy

Unlimited Power, Anthony Robbins

Use Both Sides of Your Brain, Tony Buzan

Use Your Perfect Memory, Tony Buzan

What Every Manager Needs to Know About Finance (1, 2) Hubert D Vos, William K Fallon

Why Don't People Listen? Hugh Mackay

Winning PR Tactics, Effective Techniques, Peter Sheldon Grecy

Working Woman: Strategies for Survival and Success, Janice LaRouche, Regina Ryan

Workplace Law 4th Edition, John Grogan

World Class! (1, 2), Tom Ferreira, Ingrid Staude

Writer's Digest Handbook of Novel Writing (The), Clark Brohaugh, Woods, Strickland, Bloscksom (editors)

Writing Feature Articles, Hennessy

Writing for the Media (1, 2), Francois Nel

Writing Words That Sell, Suzan Maur, John Butman

Your Own Worst Enemy, Andrew Dubrin

Your Total Image, Philippa Davies

IPRA Gold Papers

Gold Paper 2: General Report on Public Relations Education World Wide, Professor Dr Albert Oeckl

Gold Paper 4: A Model for Public Relations Education for Professional Practice, IPRA Education and Research Committee

Gold Paper 6: Public Relations and Propaganda – Values Compared, Tim Traverse-Healy

Gold Paper 7: Public Relations Education – Recommendations and Standards, Unlisted

Gold Paper 8: Ethical Dilemmas in Public Relations – a Pragmatic Examination, John F Budd Jr

Gold Paper 9: Green Communication in the Age of Sustainable Development, E Bruce Harrison, APR, MIPRA

Gold Paper 10: Quality Customer Satisfaction Public Relations – New Directions for Organisational Communication

Gold Paper 13: Challenges in Communication – State of Art and Future Trends, Anita Weisink

Glossary of public relations terms

ABC: Audit Bureau of Circulations of South Africa. The body responsible for the accurate collection of circulation figures and data relating to all member periodicals and media that sell advertising space.

Accreditation: The professional designation awarded to public relations practitioners. The PRISA Registration System is based on academic qualifications and experience.

Advertising: Paid, non-personal communication through various media by business firms, non-profit organizations, and individuals who are in some way identified in the advertising message and who hope to inform or persuade members of a particular audience.

Advertorial: Advertising on controversial issues, or joint advertising/public relations features to promote a product in a journal.

Annual report: A comprehensive review of an organization's activities and financial standing undertaken annually by a team of internal and external auditors.

APR: Accredited in Public Relations. The highest professional qualification that a member of PRISA can obtain.

Attitude survey: Also known as 'organizational climate', 'environment survey', 'employee relations', and 'human relations' audits or surveys. It can measure feelings about a range of subjects or zoom in on a specific topic, such as benefits.

Audiovisual: Sound and visual device such as synchronized slide presentation with audio cassette, compact disc interactive (CDI), or video cassette. Usually portable.

Awareness survey: Similar to attitude survey and opinion poll, method of researching familiarity with subject, including increased awareness as a result of public relations activity.

Communication audit: A public relations activity focussing exclusively on measuring the communication climate within an organization.

Conference: Defined as a meeting of any organization for consultation. It is intended to stimulate an exchange of ideas between delegates with a similar interest in a particular topic.

Congress: Defined as a formal meeting of delegates for discussion. It would be directed at fairly specific interest groups, such as particular professional or business bodies.

Contact report: Written by account executive after meeting with a client. Should state decisions taken, with right-hand column giving initials of those responsible for next action. Distributed to all relevant parties in consultancy and client sides. Also known as a call report. File of reports called the facts book.

Continuing Professional Development (CPD): An individual programme for members to improve their skill levels.

Convention: Defined as an assembly, especially of representatives or delegates for some common object, or any extraordinary assembly called upon for any special occasion.

Corporate communication: The process by which the identity of an organization is translated into an image. Its exclusive aim is to project the image and identity of the organization.

Corporate culture: An organization's common values, convictions, and behaviour. It provides guidelines for the behaviour of employees within the organization.

Corporate identity: Visible and physical representation of an organization using logo, house colour, typography, clothing, livery, etc.

Corporate image: Mental impression or received image of an organization based on knowledge and experience. Cannot be invented but may be changed. Different people may hold different corporate images, for example, employees, shareholders, distributors, or customers according to their personal knowledge and experience.

Corporate social investment: Funding by the private sector in socio-economic upliftment. Normally divided into internal and external contributions.

CPRCM: Council for Public Relations and Communication Management is a new professional body representing seven communication bodies.

Crisis public relations: Organization of a small crisis management team which has manual of instructions and conducts rehearsals, in readiness to deal with any crisis should one occur, especially in handling the media.

Customer relations: Public relations activity directed at customers such as external house journals, works visits, questionnaires, after-sales services.

Dealer magazine: External house journal addressed to distributors/dealers.

Dealer relations: Public relations activities directed at distributors such as dealer magazines, work visits, window dressing contests, conferences, invitation to exhibition stands, and training schemes for sales assistants.

Desk-top publishing: Use of computer hardware such as Apple Macintosh and software such as PageMaker and Quark Express, which enable editor to set, lay out, and record on disk publications which can be sent or transmitted direct to the printer.

Direct mail: Sometimes referred to as 'junk mail'; is now regarded as one of the most direct and efficient means of reaching individual customers or clients by mail order.

Electronic mail: Delivery of messages, including public relations staff information, via personal computers and hard copy printers.

Electronic media: Newscaster, radio, television, VCR, and via the Internet.

Embargo: Request to editor not to print a story before a stated date and time. Acceptable when international time differences need to be observed. Should be used sparingly.

Employee newspaper: Internal house journal, often tabloid format, but may be A4 magazine.

Employee report: A summary of the annual report in a form that is understandable to employees.

Ethics: Development of professional standards of conduct. PRISA has designed its own Code of Professional Standards.

Eventing: The systematic organization and implementation of a programme of public relations events in order to influence, educate, and inform targeted publics. Includes press conferences, facility visits, dealer seminars, and participation in exhibitions.

Exhibitions: A special occasion when an organization can promote its range of products and services to a selected target market.

External house journals: Those addressed to external readership such as distributors, customers, specifiers, or shareholders.

Fee: Remuneration of a public relations consultant, usually based on an hourly or daily rate which represents time, overheads, and profit, but exclusive of material and expenses. Not to be confused with a retainer which usually only gives exclusivity.

Financial public relations: Specialized field of public relations which deals with financial affairs of a public limited company, or one about to go public. Covers annual report and accounts, financial page news, information for investment analysts, take-over bids, and privatization share flotations. A specialist form of public relations.

Five Ws: Journalist's news story formula. Who is story about, what happened, when did it happen, where did it happen, and why did it happen?

FMCGs: Fast moving consumer goods.

GA: The Global Alliance for Public Relations and Communication Management Associations is a global alliance of some 60 PR associations from around the world.

Hard news: General news about people and events, as distinct from business or product news which may be legitimately used by feature writers. News agencies deal mostly in hard news.

House journal: Also known as house organ or company newspaper. Private journal, either internal for staff or external for outside readers.

House style: Part of corporate identity. Uniform style of design, typography. Usually set out in manual for printing, decorating, and advertising agents to follow.

IBA: Independent Broadcasting Authority. Its primary function is to promote the development of public, private, and community broadcasting services which are responsive to the needs of the public. It is now part of the Independent Communications Authority of South Africa (ICASA).

Image: In public relations, correct impression of organization, its policy, people, products, or services.

Image study: Form of marketing research useful in public relations to determine perceived image of organization, policy, people, products, or services, usually by comparing respondent's view of similar subjects over a range of topics. Semantic differential method of assessment can be used, and results can be demonstrated with sets of graphs which show varying responses, all organizations being compared with one another, the sponsor being one of them.

389

Industrial relations: An interdisciplinary field that encompasses the study of all aspects of people at work.

Institute of Public Relations: British professional body for public relations practitioners. Members elected on basis of experience and CAM Diploma or equivalent. Has Code of Professional Conduct. Publishes journal *Public Relations.* Holds annual Sword of Excellence awards competition.

International Association of Business Communicators: Based in San Francisco but with overseas chapters in many countries including South Africa. Holds accreditation exams and awards ABC. Publishes *Communication World* monthly.

International Public Relations Association: Has senior practitioners members in some 70 countries. Holds World Congress every three years. Publishes Gold papers on topics such as 'A Model for Public Relations Education for Professional Practice' and 'Public Relations Education. Recommendations and Standards'. Publishes members' newsletter and journal *International Public Relations Review.*

Issues advertising: Or advocacy advertising which presents an organization's point of view on current issues such as the environment or government policy.

Lobby correspondents: Journalists accredited to mix with ministers, MPs, and party officials to write about political events and to report 'off the record' statements from 'non-attributable sources' which are usually politicians not wishing to be named.

Lobbyists: Not to be confused with lobby correspondents who are journalists, lobbyists represent pressure groups and will endeavour to inform MPs, Ministers, and civil servants of their causes. Often drawn from the legal profession.

LSM: Living Standards Measurement is an all-races measurement devised to group the population into categories according to standard of living. There are currently eight LSMs identified in the South African market.

Marketing: Marketing is the management process responsible for identifying, anticipating, and satisfying customers' requirements profitably. This goes beyond selling what you have to sell, to selling what you believe people will buy, and to make a profit in so doing. This also goes beyond a mere exchange process.

Marketing communication: All the elements and techniques necessary to communicate with the market ranging from business cards, labels, and packaging to advertising, public relations, and after-sales services.

Marketing mix: All the elements contained in the marketing strategy, but taking in many more elements than the original set, and preferably considered on chronological order of application rather than in the narrow Four Ps concept of product, price, place, and promotion. Public relations is not a separate part of the marketing mix, as advertising is, because there is a public relations aspect to most elements of the mix.

Marketing research: Scientific and statistical study of everything concerned with marketing. Some of its techniques can also be applied to public relations in appreciating and assessing results.

Mass media: Media such as press, radio, television, and cinema which reach large numbers of people as distinct from some private or created public relations media used to reach specific publics.

Media explosion: The development of new media such as cable and satellite television, video, interactive compact discs, teletext, and so on.

Meetings: Defined as an organized assembly for transaction of business. These may be general weekly or monthly meetings, extraordinary meetings or annual general meetings (AGMs).

Mexican Statement: One of the best definitions of public relations resulting from a public relations conference in Mexico City in 1978. Public relations practice is the art and social science of analysing trends, predicting their consequences, counselling organization leaders, and implementing planned programmes of action which will serve both the organization's and the public interest.

Multi-image presentation: Combined audio tape/35 mm slide presentation.

Multiple-screen slide presentation: Theatrical show with large screen made up of multiples of 35 mm slides back-projected by batteries of computerized projectors. Screen can be split into two, four, eight or more smaller pictures simultaneously.

News agencies: Those operating in South Africa include Agence France Presse, Associated Press, Deutsche Presse Agentur, Reuters, and United Press International.

News desk: Part of the newspaper office which receives news from various sources such as reporters, wire services, public relations practitioners, and so on.

News release: News story supplied to the media by a public relations source. Should resemble a news report as printed in the press. Subject should be in first few words. Opening paragraph should summarize whole story and should be capable of telling basic story even if nothing else is printed.

Oramedia: Folk media. Unlike mass media, very personal and addressed to small audiences, being based on local culture and symbolism. Includes rumour, oratory, poetry, music, dance, singing, drums, masks, village theatre, puppets shows, town crier, shadow theatre. Used increasingly in industrial theatre.

Organizational climate: The dominant philosophy that applies within the organization and is responsible for the nature of the relationships within it.

Photo agency: Supplier of news photos to press or other users. Newspapers receive pictures by computer.

Print Media Association: Umbrella body representing different media bodies.

Press conference: An informal media briefing at which journalists are given a statement.

Press kit or pack: Means of assembling press information for use at a press event. Should be convenient to carry and contain only essential material.

Press officer: Member of the public relations team, usually an ex-journalist, who specializes in press relations.

Press relations: Better described as 'media relations', the part of public relations which has to do with supplying news material to the media, including handling press enquiries. A very important part of all public relations practitioners' work.

Press release: See news release.

Press office: At an exhibition, the place where journalists are supplied with media and product information.

PRISA: The Public Relations Institute of Southern Africa. The body representing the interests of public relations practitioners throughout Southern Africa. It publishes *Communika* on a quarterly basis.

Propaganda: Biased information used to gain support for an opinion, cause, or belief. Not to be confused with public relations.

Protocol: The international code of social conduct.

PRSA: The Public Relations Society of America, the body responsible for serving the needs of the public relations profession in North America. It publishes the *Public Relations Journal* monthly.

Public affairs: Mainly an American idea, those aspects of public relations which deal with corporate rather than product matters. Considered by some to be an artificial division.

Public information: Term used primarily by government agencies, social service organizations and universities to describe their public relations activities.

Public relations: As defined by PRISA, 'public relations practice is the management, through communication, of perceptions and strategic relationships between an organization and its internal and external stakeholders'.

Publicity: Good or bad result of something being made public.

Publics: Groups of people with which an organization communicates, for example neighbours, potential employees, suppliers, consumers, opinion leaders, shareholders, and others. Many more categories than the target audiences in advertising.

Readership survey: Carried out normally every two years to ascertain employees' opinions about the content, style, and level of interest in a company's house journal or newsletter.

Retainer: Term often used wrongly to mean fee but should refer to an exclusivity fee should professional services be required from time to time.

Reputation management: It is how companies in a variety of industries compete for prestige and achieve celebrity status. It revolves around building and sustaining a good name for a company.

Sales promotion: Marketing activity whereby a product is given extrinsic value such as a gift or price reduction. Not to be confused with public relations.

SARAD: South African Rates and Data. A directory providing information on circulation and readership of leading media operations.

Seminar: Defined as a conference of specialists. It attracts people with a highly technical interest in a particular subject and has limited interest value to outsiders. It is run on the same lines as a conference.

Seven-point formula: The SOLAADS for news releases: 1. Subject 2. Organization 3. Location 4. Advantages 5. Application 6. Details 7. Source.

Symposium: Defined as a set of contributions from various authors and points of view. Opposing and even conflicting views are presented. The main difference between a symposium and a conference is that delegates can only question speakers from the floor, and not put opposing viewpoints. There is one chairperson throughout, as opposed to congresses where there might be a different chairperson for different sessions.

Upward communication: Communication from staff to management as seen with speak-up schemes, quality circles, open-door policies, works councils, co-partnerships, and house journals with candid reader comments.

Videocassette: Largely replaced 16 mm and 35 mm film, important public relations medium as house journal, documentary, or for induction and training purposes, and for use at press receptions and on exhibition stands. Advantage of compactness compared with cans of film.

Video conference: Arrangement by which interested parties can be linked together either by phone or television in order to conduct business.

Video news release: Usually offered to television companies rather than distributed like printed news release. Means of providing topical background information for news and other television programmes.

Workshop: A combination of a seminar and practical discussion involving the speaker and delegates.

World wide web: Portion of the Internet devoted to the transfer of information via text, illustrations and sound. Public relations firms, media, advertisers and others maintain websites on the web for this purpose.

Suggested websites

Media related websites

- Media Institute of Southern Africa: www.misa.org
- Media Tenor: www.mediatenor.co.za
- BizCommunity (Daily media, marketing and community news): www.bizcommunity.co.za

Public Relations websites

- Public Relations Institute of Southern Africa: www.prisa.co.za
- International Public Relations Association: www.ipra.org
- Institute for Public Relations Research: http://www.instituteforpr.org/research/
- Public Relations Society of America (PRSA): http://www.prsa.org/
- Public Relations student society of America (PRSSA): www.prssa.org

Communication websites

- South African Communications Association (SACOMM): www.ukzn.ac.za/sacomm
- International Association of Business Communicators: http://www.iabc.co.za/

Marketing websites

- Marketing Web: www.marketingweb.co.za
- Brands South Africa: www.brandsouth-africa.com/
- Institute of Marketing Management: www.imm.co.za
- Business Marketing Association: http://www.marketing.org/
- Marketing Resources for Marketing Professionals: http://www.marketing-profs.com/
- The chartered Institute of Marketing: http://www.cim.co.uk/cim/index.cfm
- American Marketing Association: http://www.marketingpower.com/
- Word of Mouth Marketing Association: http://www.womma.org/index.htm

Index